This is the back!

This manga collection is translated into English but oriented in right-to-left reading format at the creator's request, maintaining the artwork's visual orientation as originally published in Japan. If you've never read manga in this way before, take a look at the diagram below to give yourself an idea of how to go about it. Basically, you'll be starting in the upper right corner and will read each balloon and panel moving right to left. It may take some getting used to, but you should get the hang of it very quickly. Have fun!

publisher Mike Richardson • executive vice president Neil Hankerson • chief financial officer Tom Weddle • vice president of publishing Randy Stradley • vice president of business development Michael Martens • vice president of business affairs Anita Nelson • vice president of marketing Micha Hershman • vice president of product development David Scroggy • vice president of information technology Dale LaFountain • director of purchasing Darlene Vogel • general counsel Ken Lizzi • editorial director Davey Estrada • senior managing editor Scott Allie • senior books editor Chris Warner • executive editor Diana Schutz • director of design and production Cary Grazzini • art director Lia Ribacchi • director of scheduling Cara Niece

VAMPIRE HUNTER D

HIDEYUKI KIKUCHI | ILLUSTRATIONS BY YOSHITAKA AMANO

From creator Hideyuki Kikuchi, one of Japan's leading horror authors, with illustrations by renowned Japanese artist Yoshitaka Amano, this series is here printed in an English translation for the first time anywhere!

AVAILABLE AT YOUR LOCAL COMICS SHOP OR BOOKSTORE

To find a comics shop near you, visit comicshoplocator.com • For more information or to order direct: On the web: DarkHorse.com • E-mail: mailorder@DarkHorse.com • Phone: 1-800-862-0052 Mon.–Fri. 9 AM to 5 PM Pacific Time.

Vampire Hunter D © Hideyuki Kikuchi. Originally Published in Japan by ASAHI SONORAMA CO., LTD. Dark Horse Books® and the Dark Horse logo are registered trademarks of Dark Horse Comics, Inc. (BL 7061)

YASUHIRO NIGHTOW 内藤泰弘

TRIGUN

On the forbidding desert planet of Gunsmoke, a sixty-billion-double-dollar bounty hangs over the head of Vash the Stampede, a pistol-packing pacifist with a weapon capable of punching holes in a planet. Every trigger-happy psycho in creation is aiming to claim Vash dead or alive—preferably dead!—and although Vash is an avowed pacifist, he won't go down without a fight. And when Vash fights, destruction is sure to follow!

ヘルシング HELLSING

DELUXE EDITIONS

BY
KOHTA HIRANO
1998–2022

AN ENGINEERED ARMY OF VAMPIRES emerges from
the darkness under the blood-red banner of the swastika,
and the war for the future begins in London. Two groups,
the shadowy Hellsing Organization and the Iscariot Agency
of the Catholic Church, stand between the undead and the
extermination of humanity. But can the forces of the Holy
Church ever ally with a group that uses unholy creatures
itself, including Alucard, the mightiest vampire of all?
Kohta Hirano's manga sensation is now presented in
elegant hardcover editions, each collecting over 650 pages
of wild action, grisly horror, and savage imagination.

VOLUME 1
ISBN 978-1-50671-553-7 • $49.99

VOLUME 2
ISBN 978-1-50672-001-2 • $49.99

VOLUME 3
ISBN 978-1-50672-002-9 • $49.99

DARK
HORSE
MANGA

AVAILABLE AT YOUR LOCAL COMICS
SHOP OR BOOKSTORE

TO FIND A COMICS SHOP IN YOUR AREA,
VISIT COMICSHOPLOCATOR.COM

For more information or to order direct, visit darkhorse.com

HELLSING DELUXE EDITION
© KOHTA HIRANO
Originally published in Japan by SHONEN GAHOSHA Co., Ltd., TOKYO.
English translation rights arranged with SHONEN GAHOSHA Co., Ltd., TOKYO
through TOHAN CORPORATION, TOKYO.
Dark Horse Manga is a trademark of Dark Horse Comics LLC.
All rights reserved. (BL7043)

NO GUTS, NO GLORY!

BERSERK

DELUXE EDITIONS
BY KENTARO MIURA

Berserk has outraged, horrified, and delighted manga and anime fanatics since 1989, inspiring a plethora of wildly popular TV series, feature films, and video games. Now, the champion of adult fantasy manga is presented in oversized deluxe hardcover editions, each collecting three volumes of this mindblowing series!

VOLUME ONE
ISBN 978-1-50671-198-0
VOLUME TWO
ISBN 978-1-50671-199-7
VOLUME THREE
ISBN 978-1-50671-200-0
VOLUME FOUR
ISBN 978-1-50671-521-6
VOLUME FIVE
ISBN 978-1-50671-522-3
VOLUME SIX
ISBN 978-1-50671-523-0
VOLUME SEVEN
ISBN 978-1-50671-790-6
VOLUME EIGHT
ISBN 978-1-50671-791-3
VOLUME NINE
ISBN 978-1-50671-792-0
VOLUME TEN
ISBN 978-1-50672-754-7
VOLUME ELEVEN
ISBN 978-1-50672-755-4

$49.99 EACH

AVAILABLE AT YOUR LOCAL COMICS SHOP OR BOOKSTORE
To find a comics shop in your area, visit comicshoplocator.com | For more information or to order direct, visit darkhorse.com

DARKHORSE.COM

BERSERK

Created by Kentaro Miura, *Berserk* is manga mayhem to the extreme—violent, horrifying, and mercilessly funny—and the wellspring for the internationally popular anime series. Not for the squeamish or the easily offended, *Berserk* asks for no quarter—and offers none!

Presented uncensored in the original Japanese format!

VOLUME 1
ISBN 978-1-59307-020-5

VOLUME 2
ISBN 978-1-59307-021-2

VOLUME 3
ISBN 978-1-59307-022-9

VOLUME 4
ISBN 978-1-59307-203-2

VOLUME 5
ISBN 978-1-59307-251-3

VOLUME 6
ISBN 978-1-59307-252-0

VOLUME 7
ISBN 978-1-59307-328-2

VOLUME 8
ISBN 978-1-59307-329-9

VOLUME 9
ISBN 978-1-59307-330-5

VOLUME 10
ISBN 978-1-59307-331-2

VOLUME 11
ISBN 978-1-59307-470-8

VOLUME 12
ISBN 978-1-59307-484-5

VOLUME 13
ISBN 978-1-59307-500-2

VOLUME 14
ISBN 978-1-59307-501-9

VOLUME 15
ISBN 978-1-59307-577-4

VOLUME 16
ISBN 978-1-59307-706-8

VOLUME 17
ISBN 978-1-59307-742-6

VOLUME 18
ISBN 978-1-59307-743-3

VOLUME 19
ISBN 978-1-59307-744-0

VOLUME 20
ISBN 978-1-59307-745-7

VOLUME 21
ISBN 978-1-59307-746-4

VOLUME 22
ISBN 978-1-59307-863-8

VOLUME 23
ISBN 978-1-59307-864-5

VOLUME 24
ISBN 978-1-59307-865-2

VOLUME 25
ISBN 978-1-59307-921-5

VOLUME 26
ISBN 978-1-59307-922-2

VOLUME 27
ISBN 978-1-59307-923-9

VOLUME 28
ISBN 978-1-59582-209-3

VOLUME 29
ISBN 978-1-59582-210-9

VOLUME 30
ISBN 978-1-59582-211-6

VOLUME 31
ISBN 978-1-59582-366-3

VOLUME 32
ISBN 978-1-59582-367-0

VOLUME 33
ISBN 978-1-59582-372-4

VOLUME 34
ISBN 978-1-59582-532-2

VOLUME 35
ISBN 978-1-59582-695-4

VOLUME 36
ISBN 978-1-59582-942-9

VOLUME 37
ISBN 978-1-61655-205-3

VOLUME 38
ISBN 978-1-50670-398-5

VOLUME 39
ISBN 978-1-50670-708-2

VOLUME 40
ISBN 978-1-50671-498-1

BERSERK OFFICIAL GUIDEBOOK
ISBN 978-1-50670-706-8

BERSERK: THE FLAME DRAGON KNIGHT
Written by Matoko Fukami and Kentaro Miura
ISBN 978-1-50670-939-0

$14.99 EACH!

AVAILABLE AT YOUR LOCAL COMICS SHOP OR BOOKSTORE
To find a comics shop near your area, visit comicshoplocator.com. For more information or to order direct: On the web: darkhorse.com | E-mail: mailorder@darkhorse.com | Phone: 1-800-862-0052 Mon.–Fri. 9 a.m. to 5 p.m. Pacific Time.

DARK HORSE MANGA

DARKHORSE.COM

ベルセルク

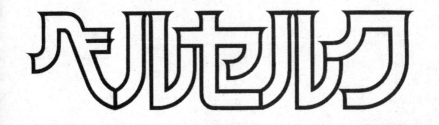

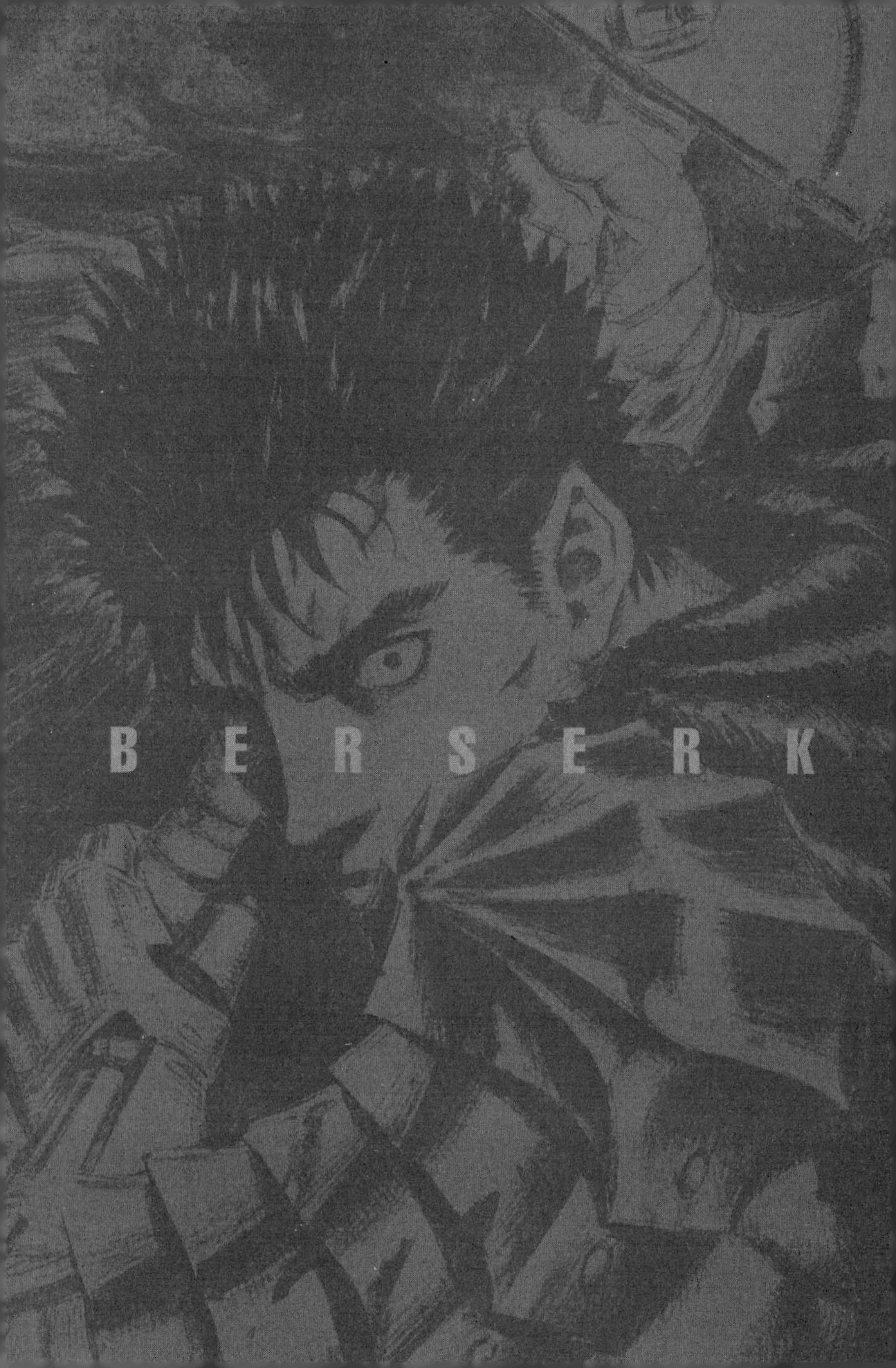
BERSERK

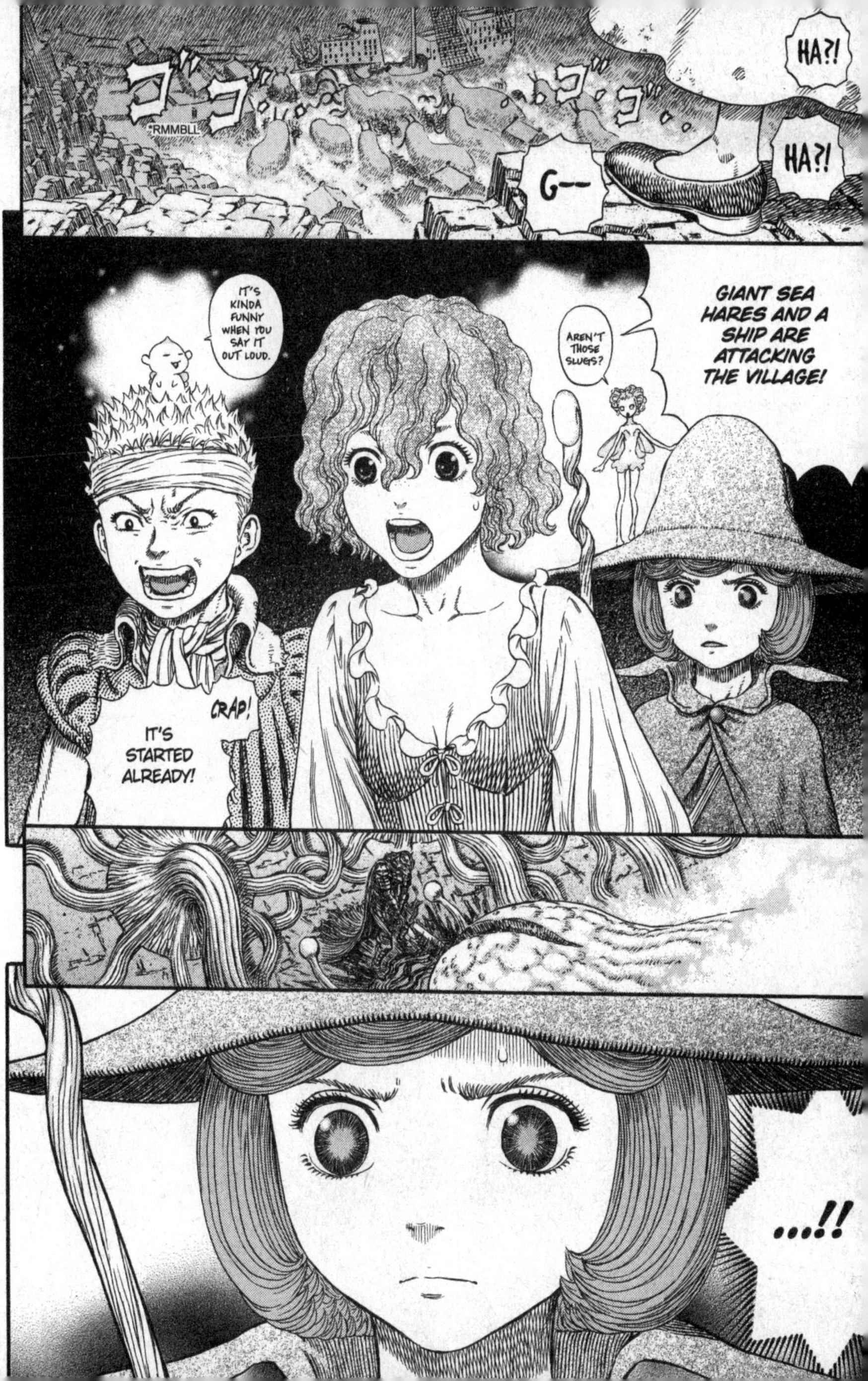

HA?!
HA?!
G--
*RMMBLL
GIANT SEA HARES AND A SHIP ARE ATTACKING THE VILLAGE!
AREN'T THOSE SLUGS?
IT'S KINDA FUNNY WHEN YOU SAY IT OUT LOUD.
CRAP!
IT'S STARTED ALREADY!
...?!!

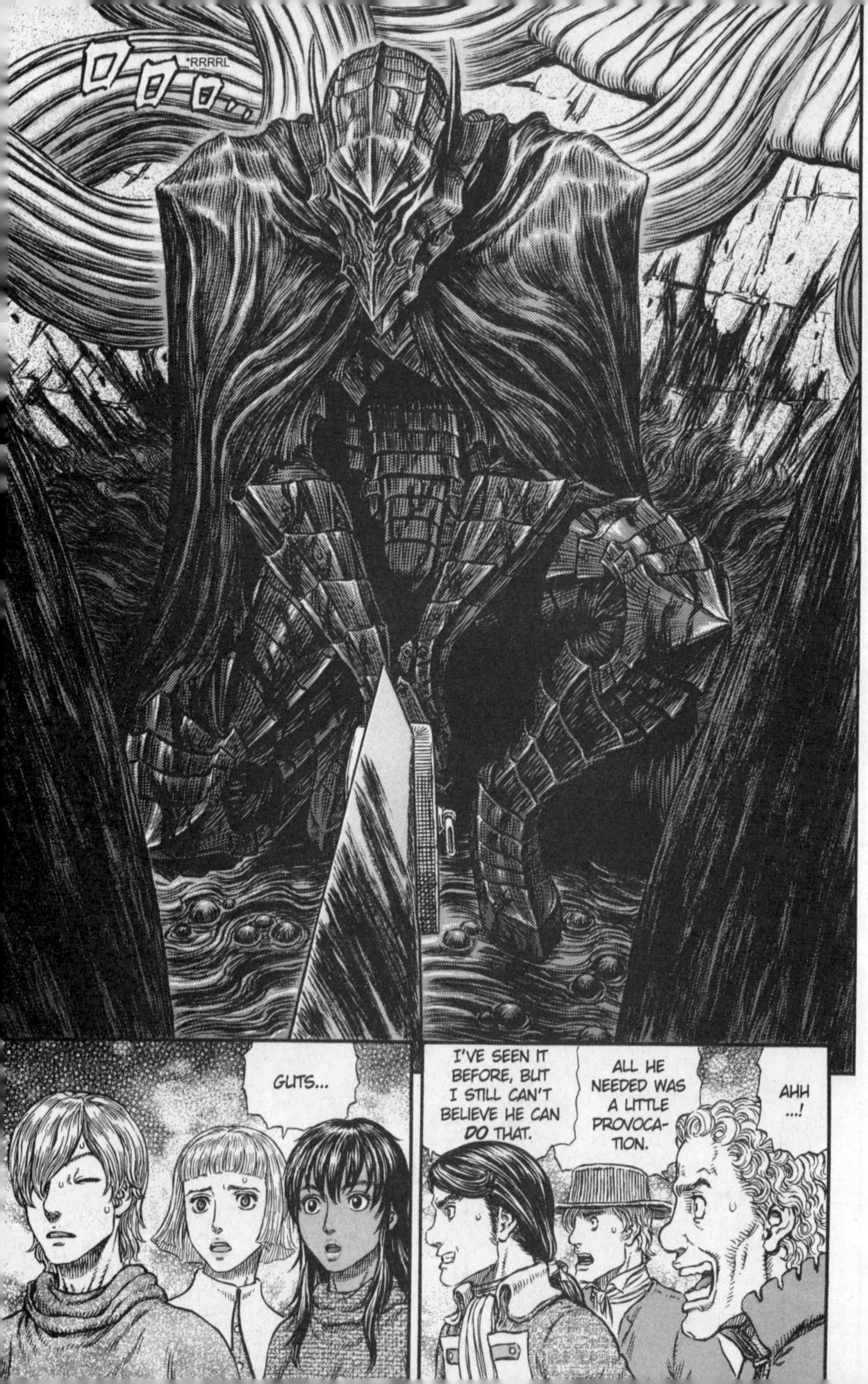
ロロロ...
*RRRRL
AHH ...!
ALL HE NEEDED WAS A LITTLE PROVOCATION.
I'VE SEEN IT BEFORE, BUT I STILL CAN'T BELIEVE HE CAN *DO* THAT.
GUTS...

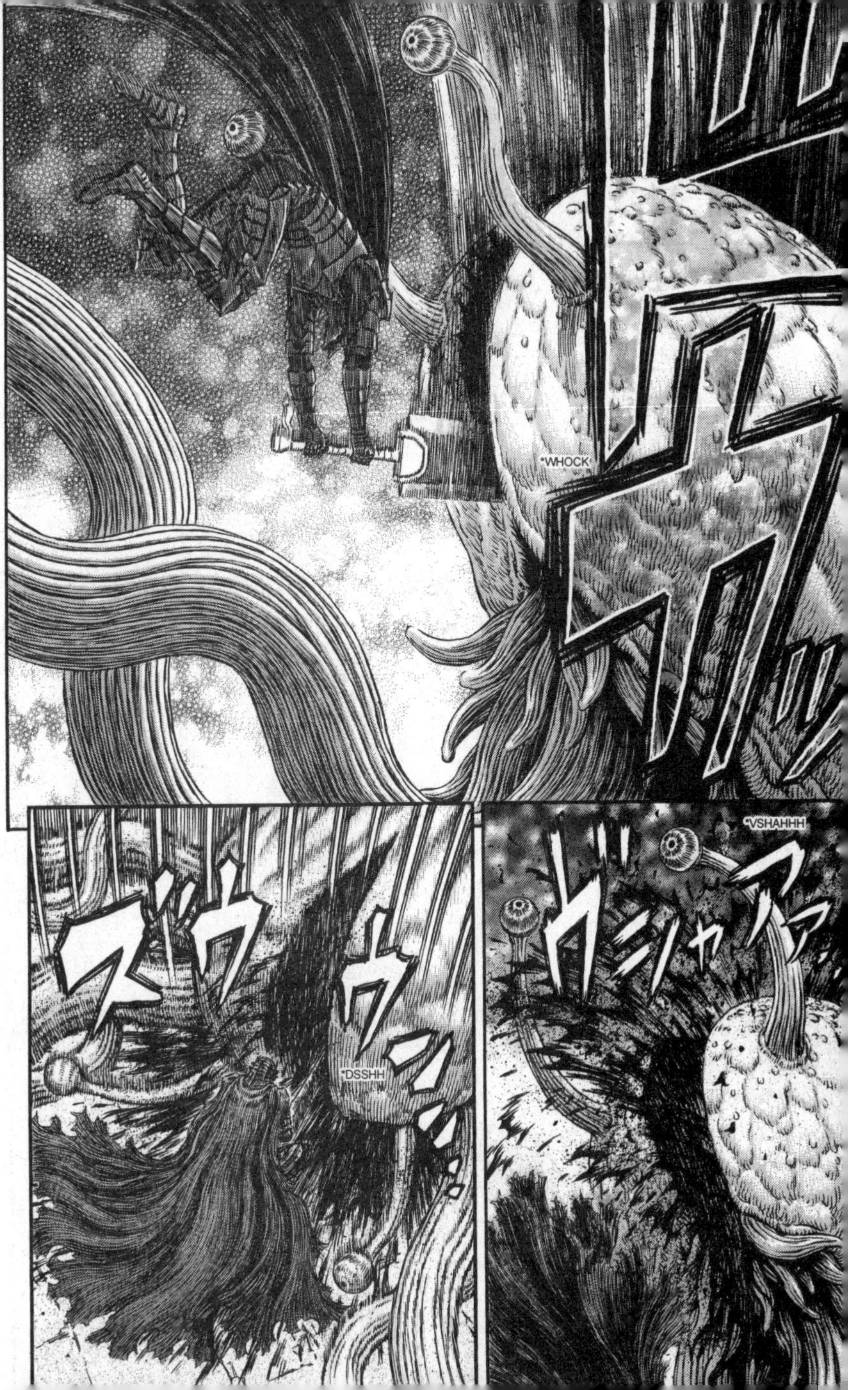
*WHOCK
*VSHAHHH
*DSSHH

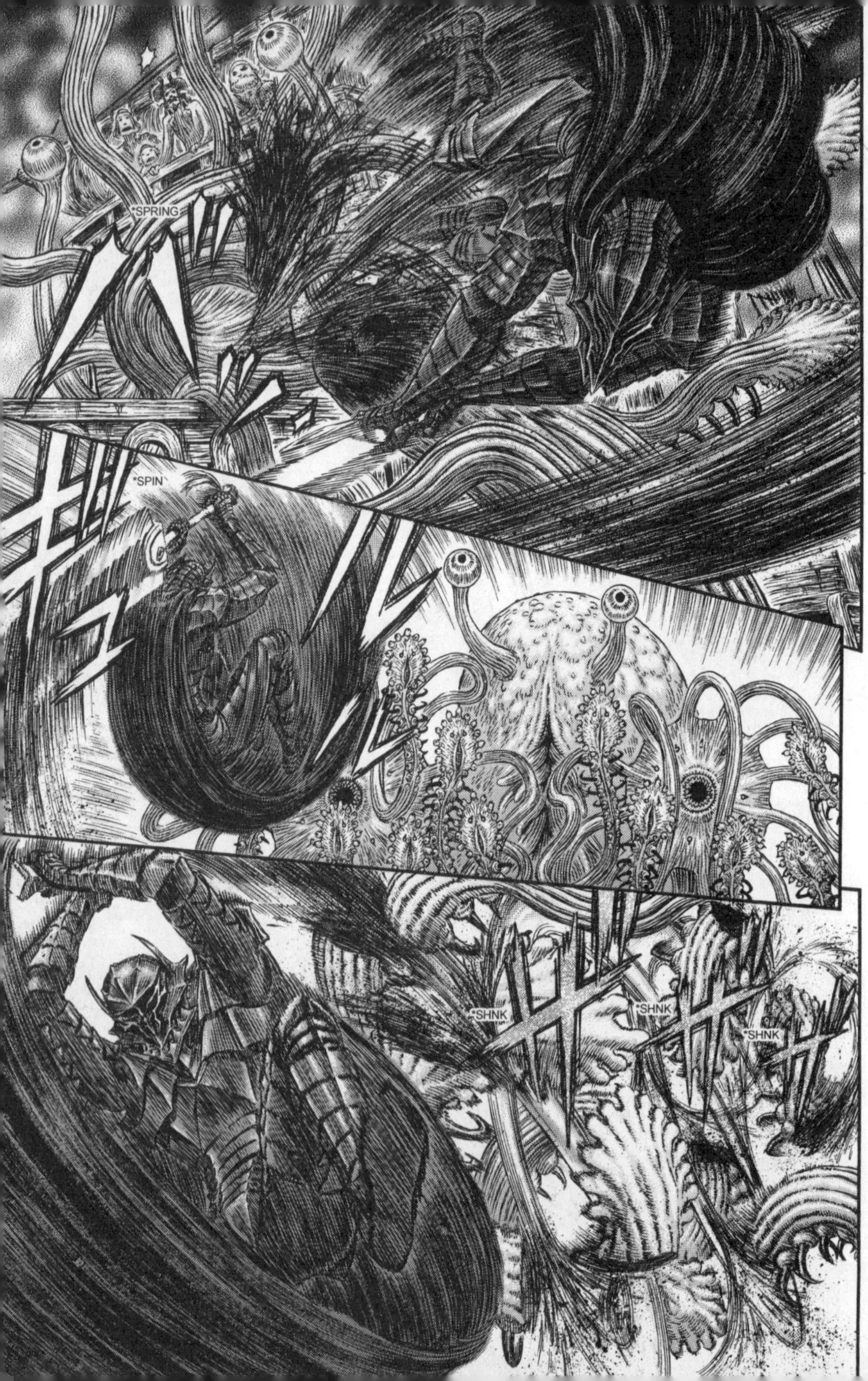
*SPRING
*SPIN
*SHNK
*SHNK
*SHNK

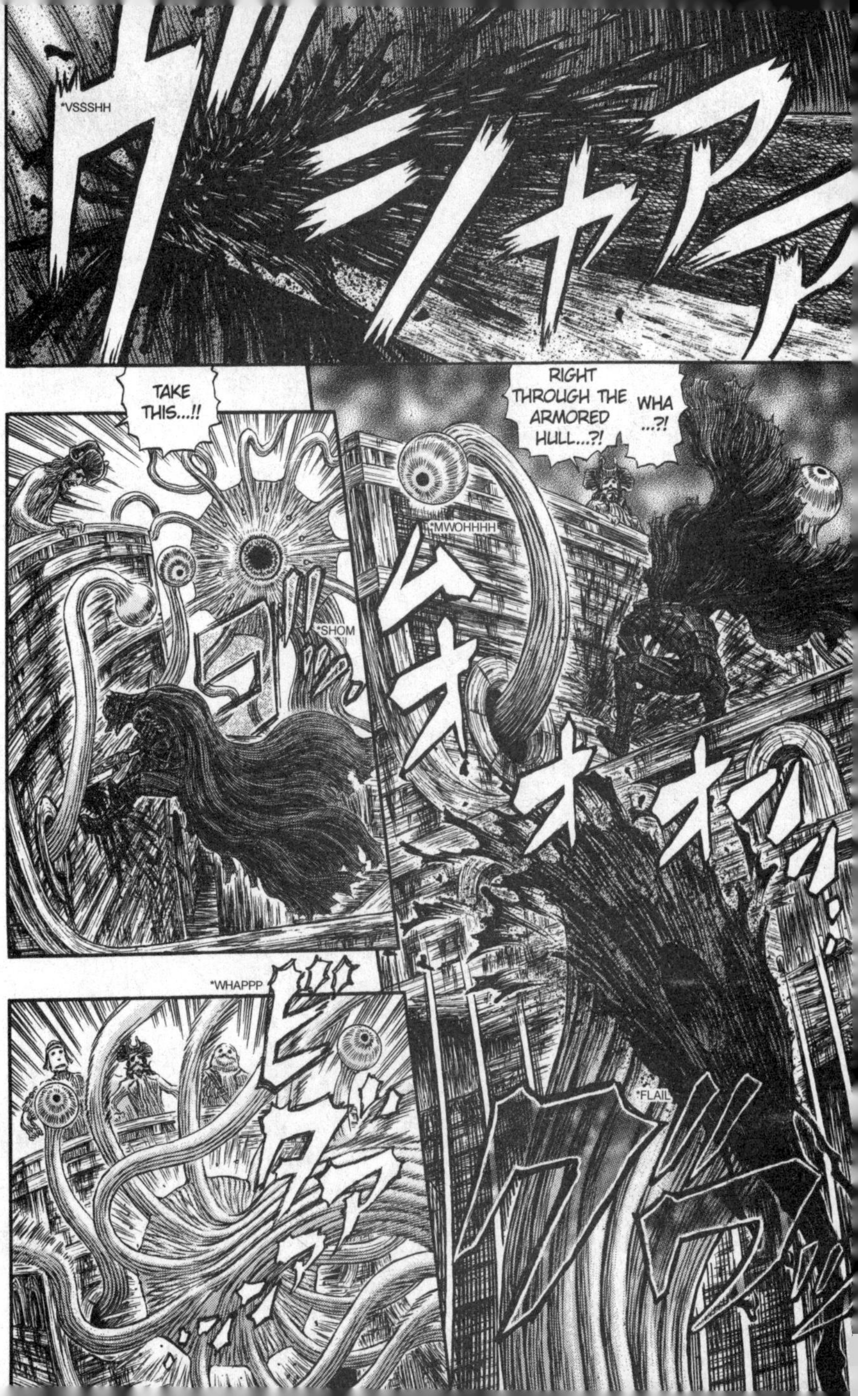
*VSSSHH
WHA ...?!
RIGHT THROUGH THE ARMORED HULL...?!
*MWOHHHH
*FLAIL
TAKE THIS...!!
*SHOM
*WHAPPP

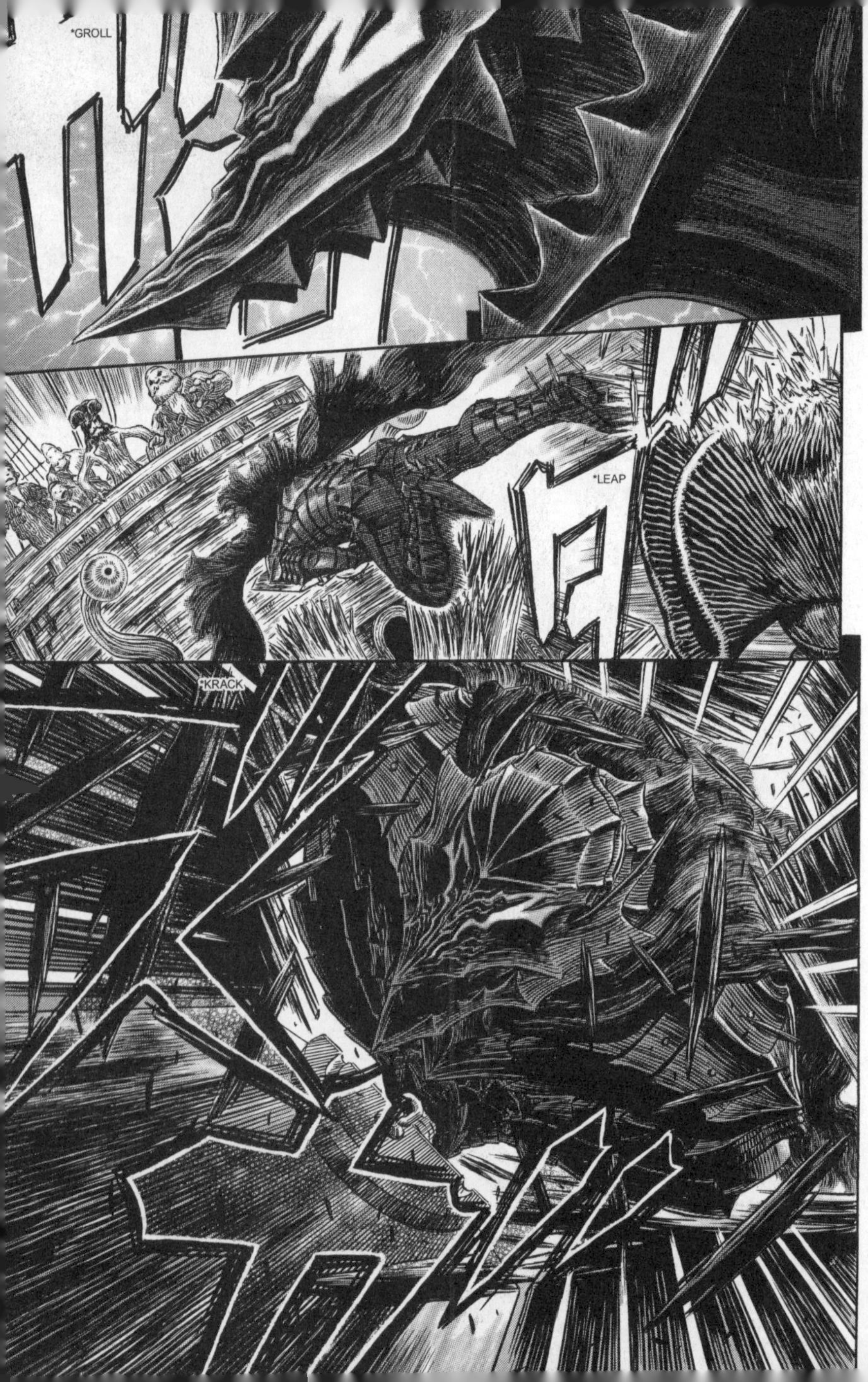
*GROLL
*LEAP
*KRACK

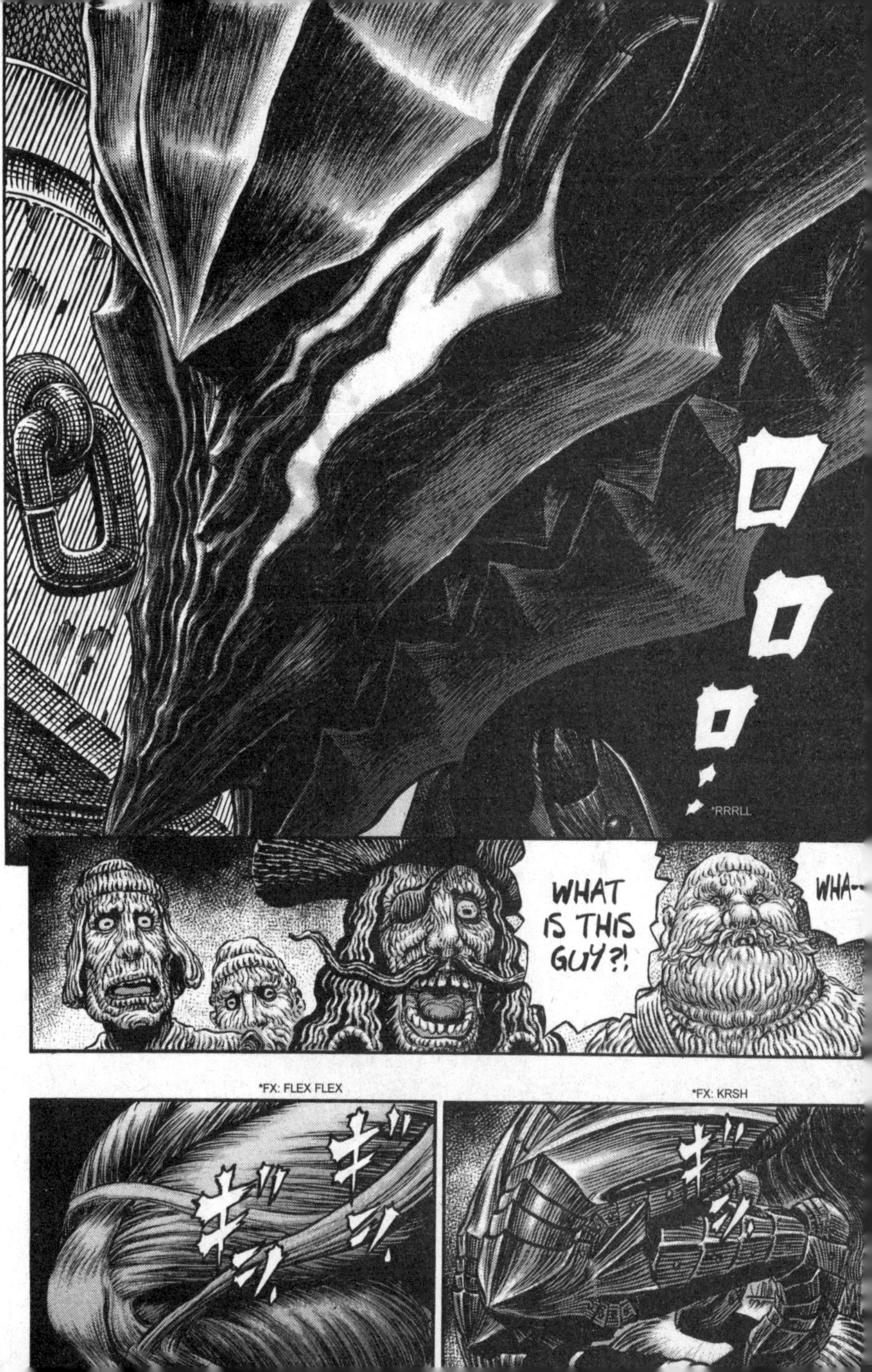
*RRRLL
WHA--
WHAT IS THIS GUY?!
*FX: KRSH
*FX: FLEX FLEX

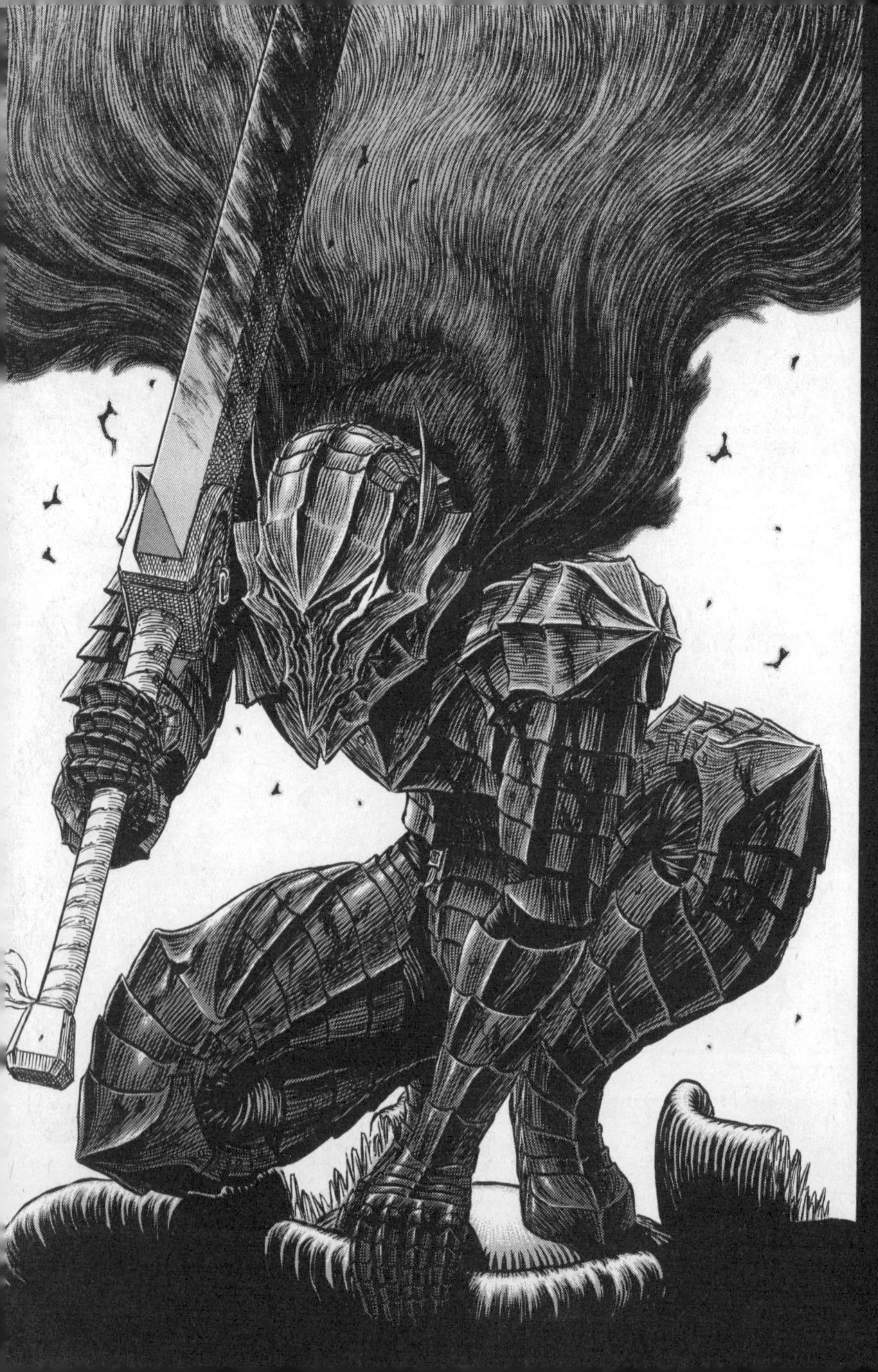

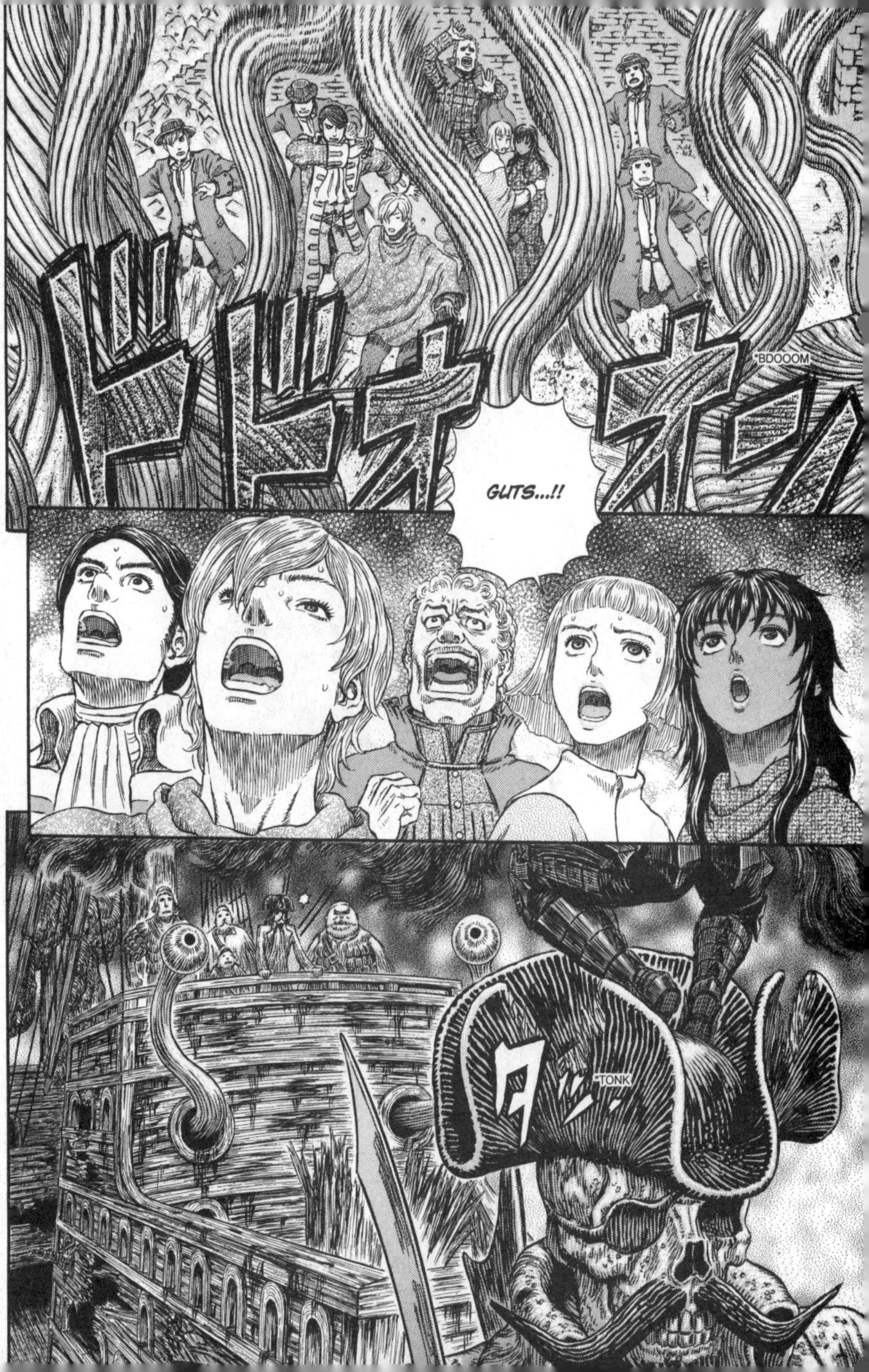
*BDOOOM
GUTS...!!
*TONK

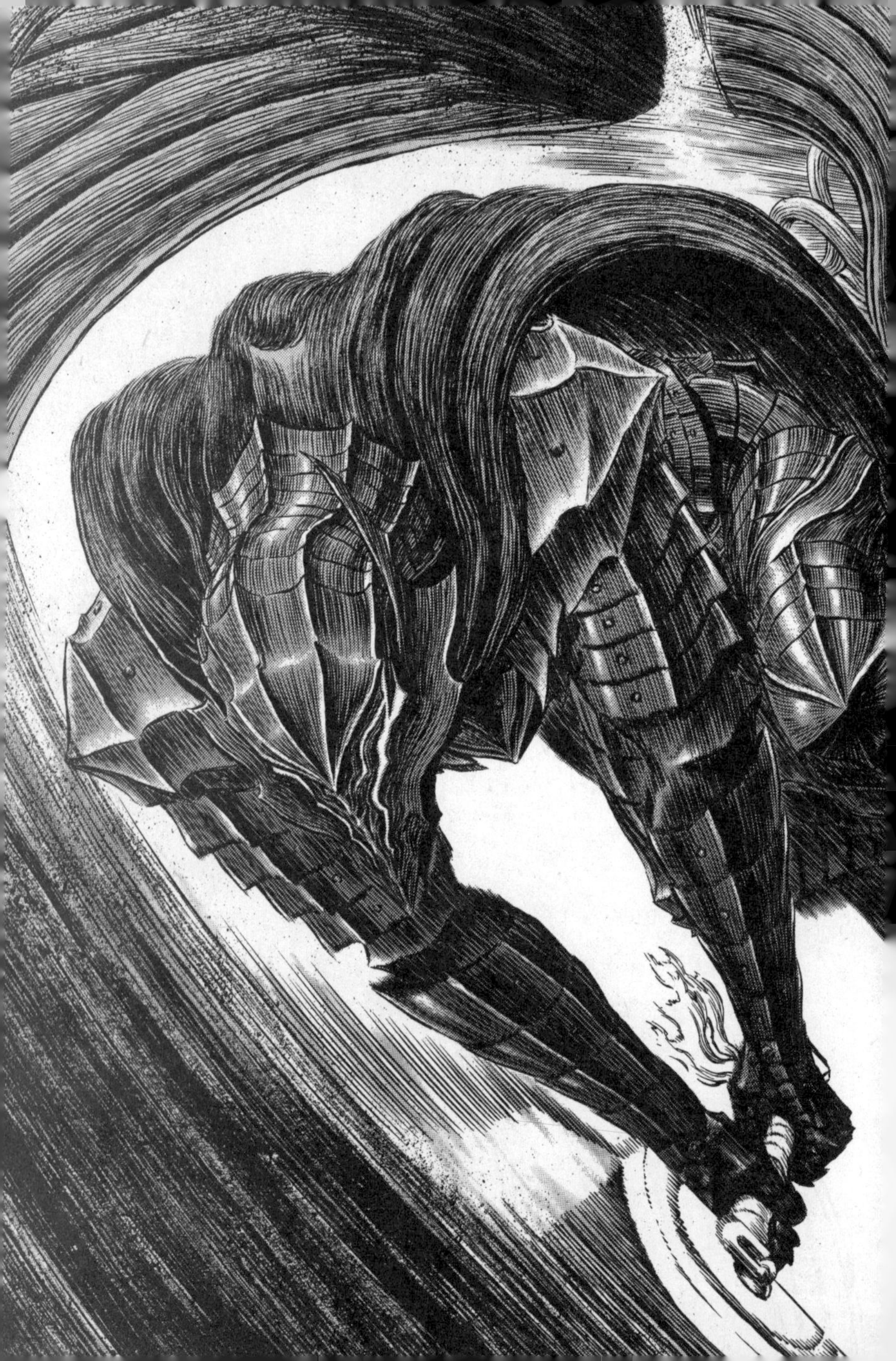

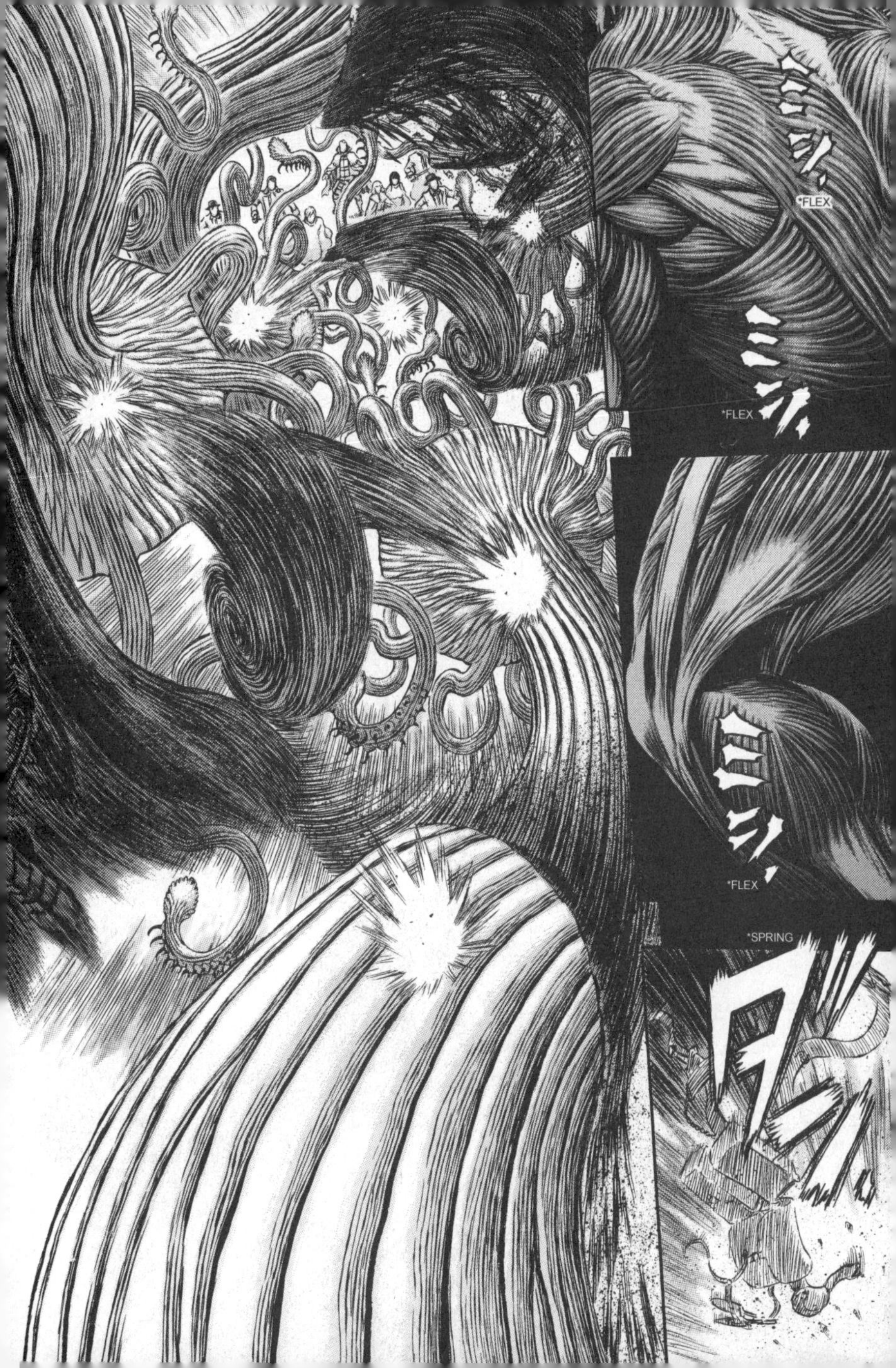
*FLEX
*FLEX
*FLEX
*SPRING

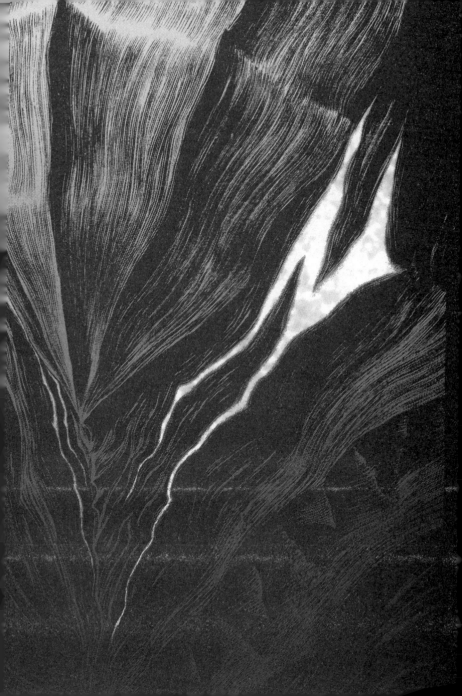

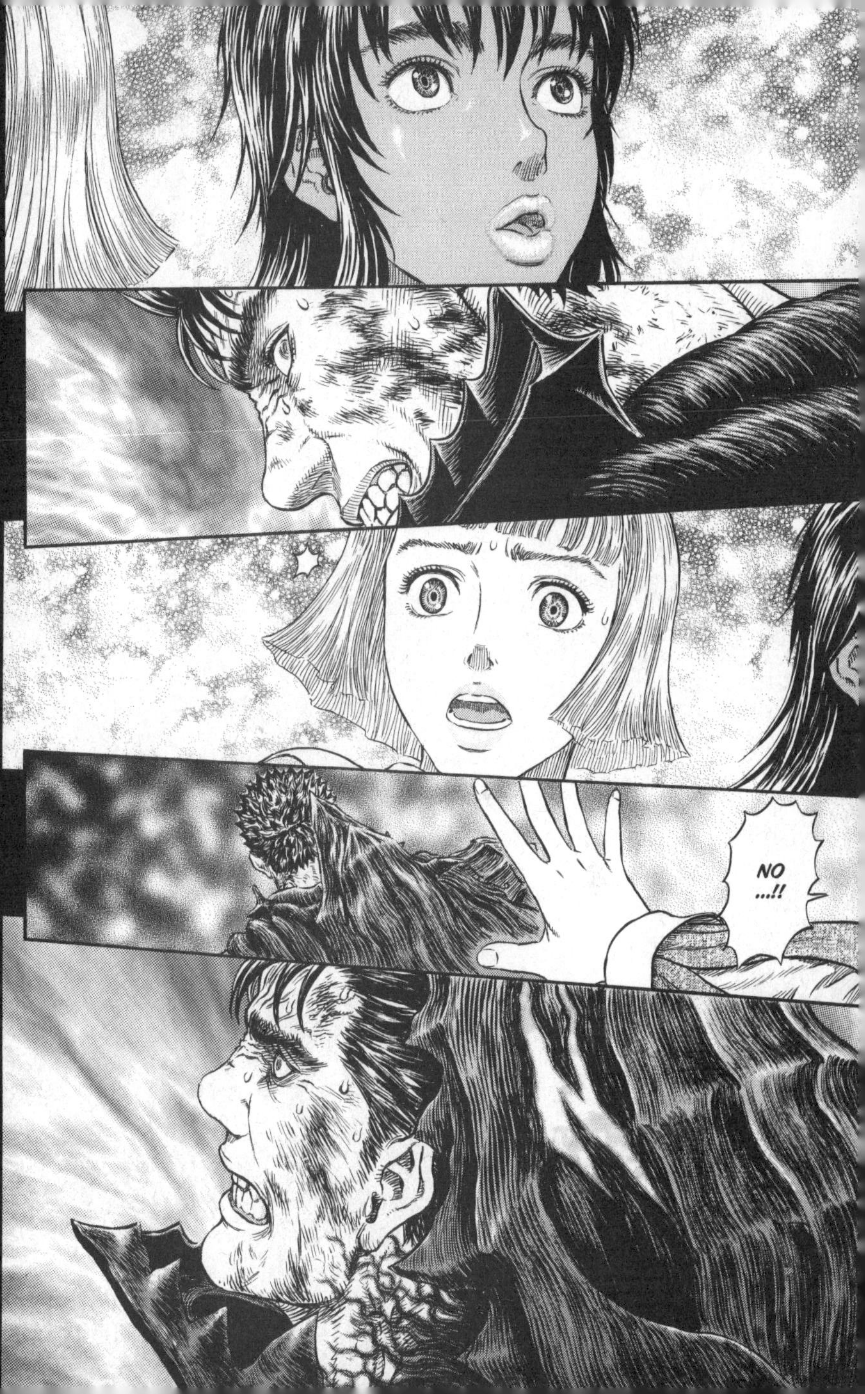
NO
...!!

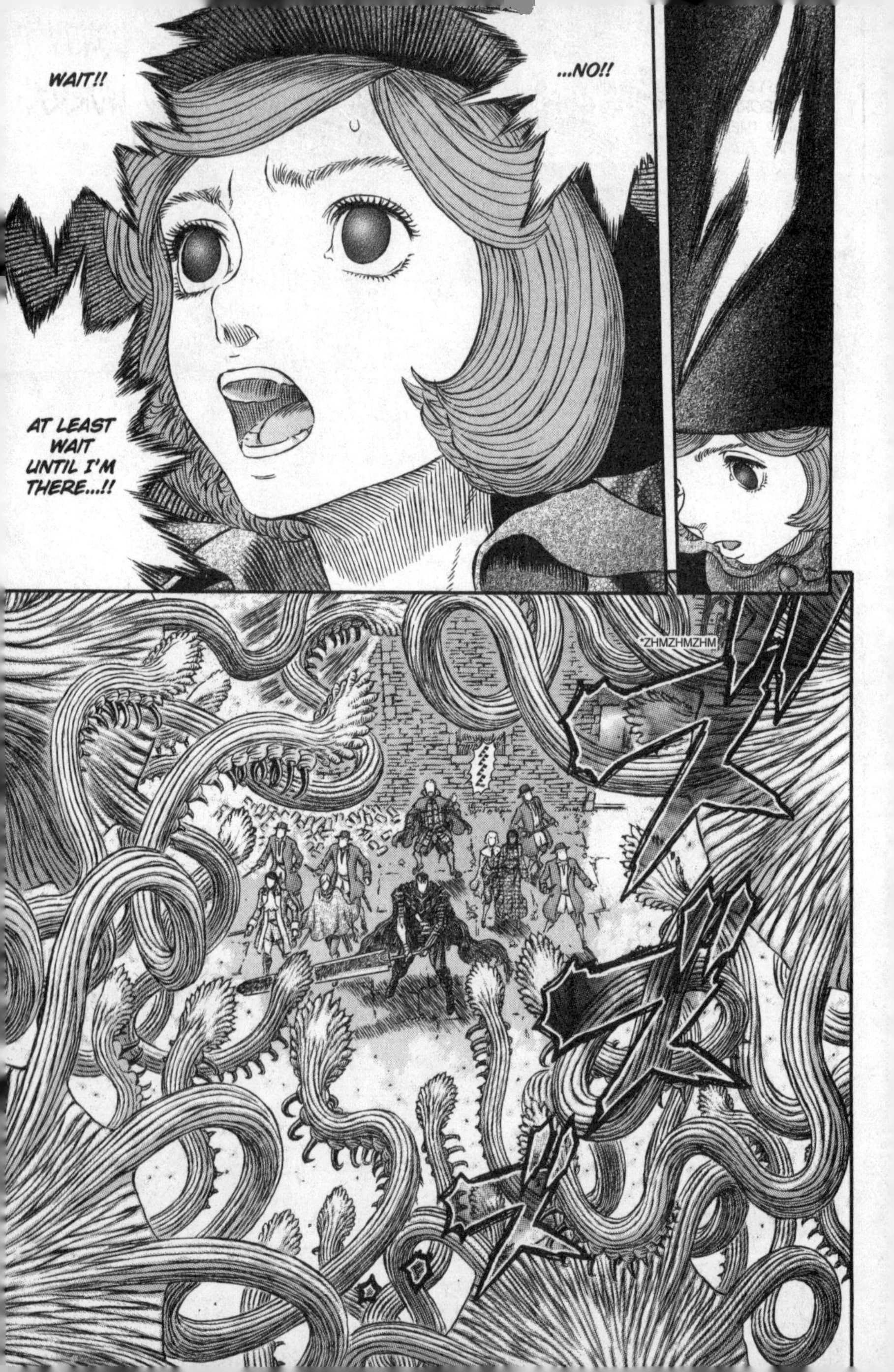
...NO!!
WAIT!!
AT LEAST WAIT UNTIL I'M THERE...!!
*ZHMZHMZHM

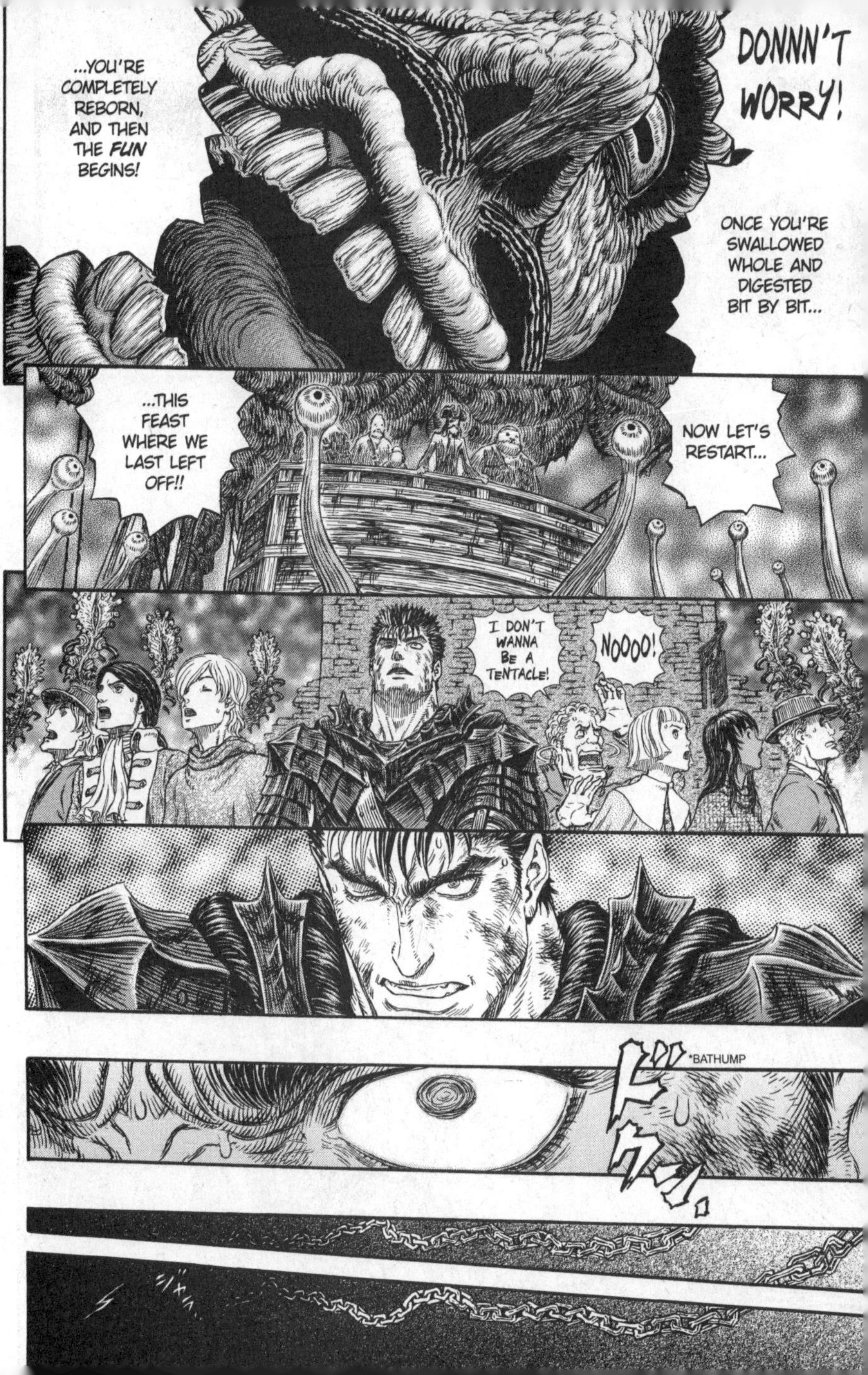
DONNN'T WORRY!
ONCE YOU'RE SWALLOWED WHOLE AND DIGESTED BIT BY BIT...
...YOU'RE COMPLETELY REBORN, AND THEN THE FUN BEGINS!
NOW LET'S RESTART...
...THIS FEAST WHERE WE LAST LEFT OFF!!
NOOOO!
I DON'T WANNA BE A TENTACLE!
*BATHUMP

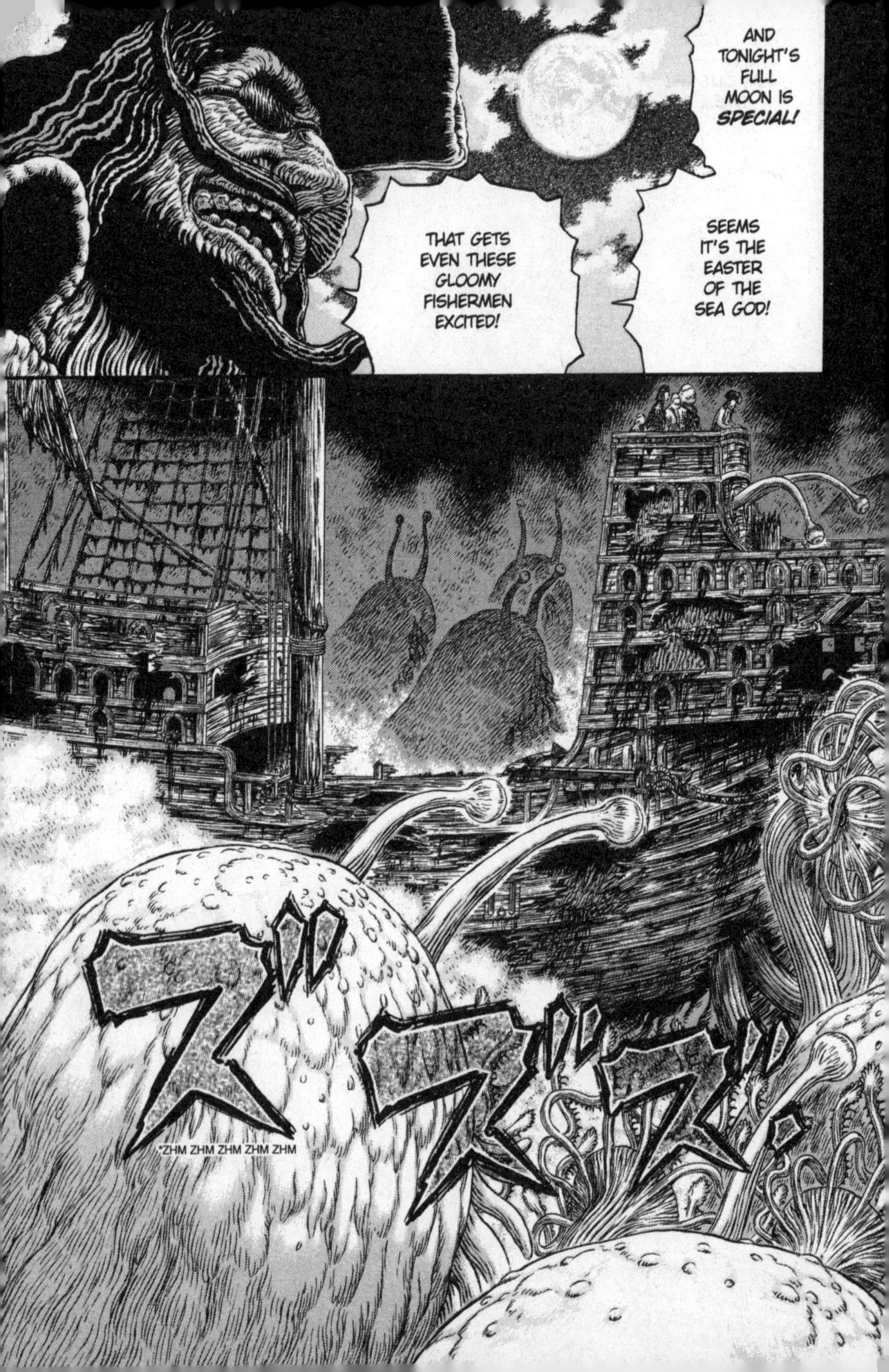
AND TONIGHT'S FULL MOON IS **SPECIAL!**
SEEMS IT'S THE EASTER OF THE SEA GOD!
THAT GETS EVEN THESE GLOOMY FISHERMEN EXCITED!
ズズズズ
*ZHM ZHM ZHM ZHM ZHM

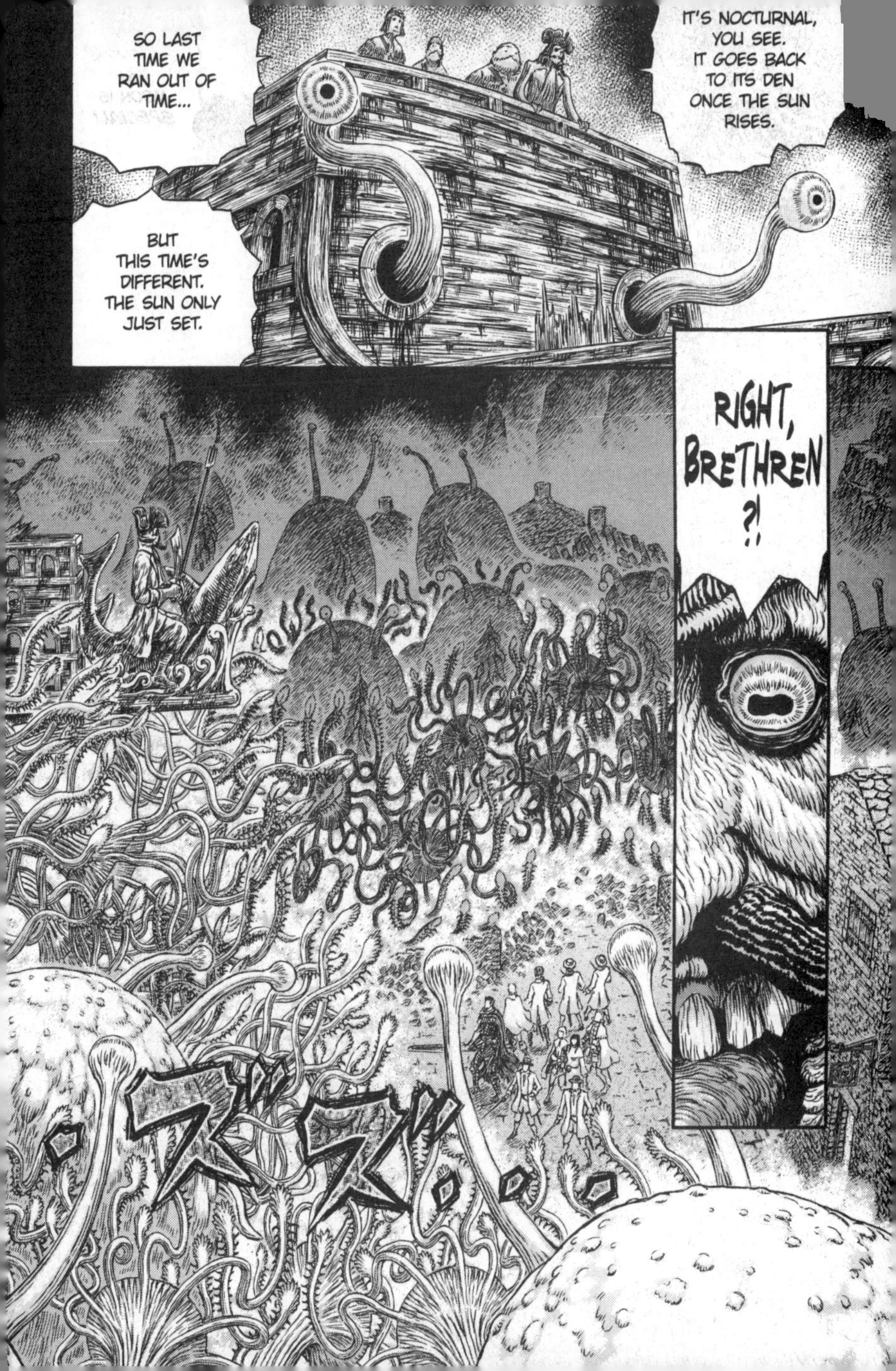
IT'S NOCTURNAL, YOU SEE. IT GOES BACK TO ITS DEN ONCE THE SUN RISES.
SO LAST TIME WE RAN OUT OF TIME...
BUT THIS TIME'S DIFFERENT. THE SUN ONLY JUST SET.
RIGHT, BRETHREN?!

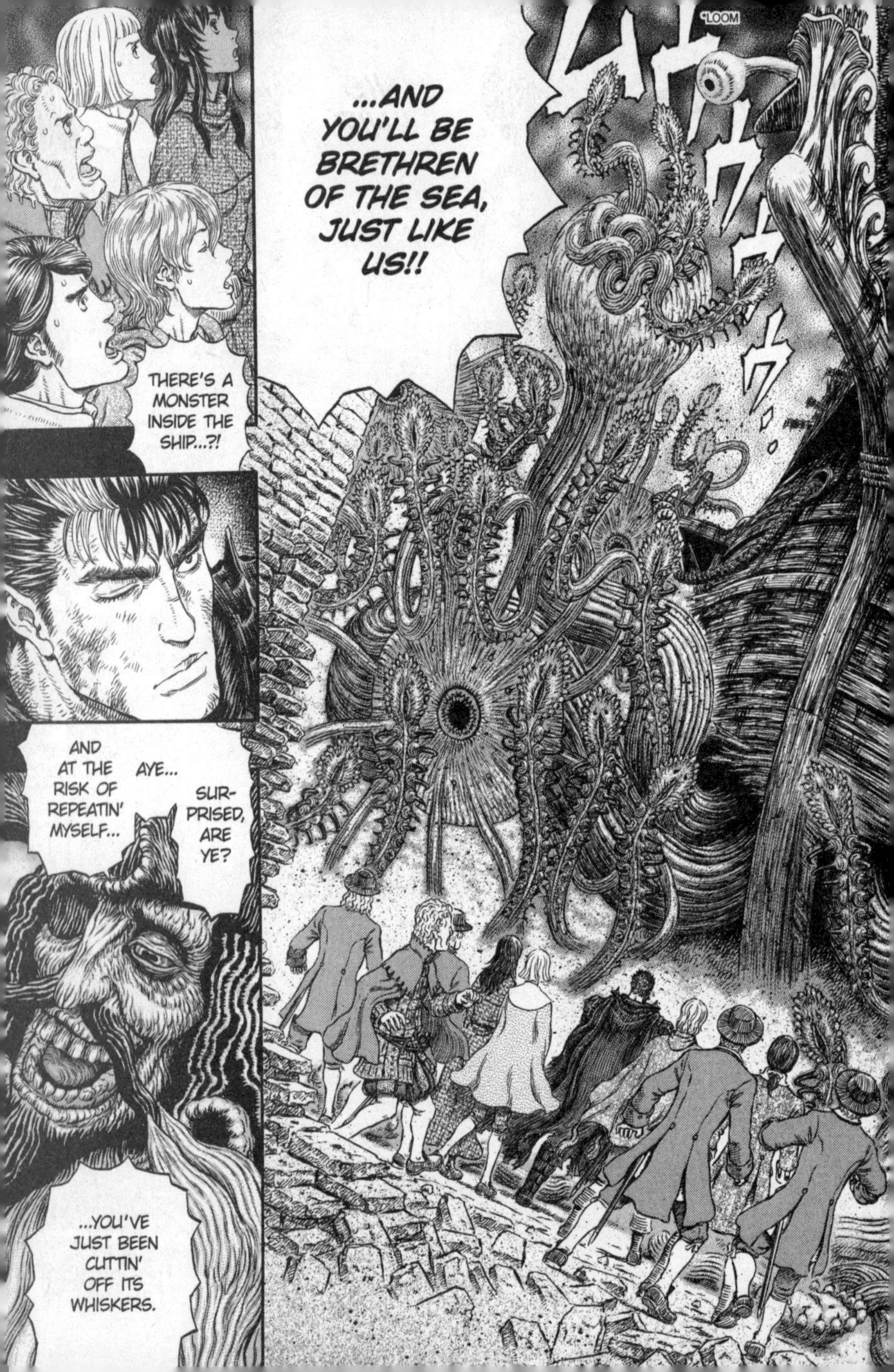
*LOOM
...AND YOU'LL BE BRETHREN OF THE SEA, JUST LIKE US!!
THERE'S A MONSTER INSIDE THE SHIP...?!
AYE...
SUR- PRISED, ARE YE?
AND AT THE RISK OF REPEATIN' MYSELF...
...YOU'VE JUST BEEN CUTTIN' OFF ITS WHISKERS.

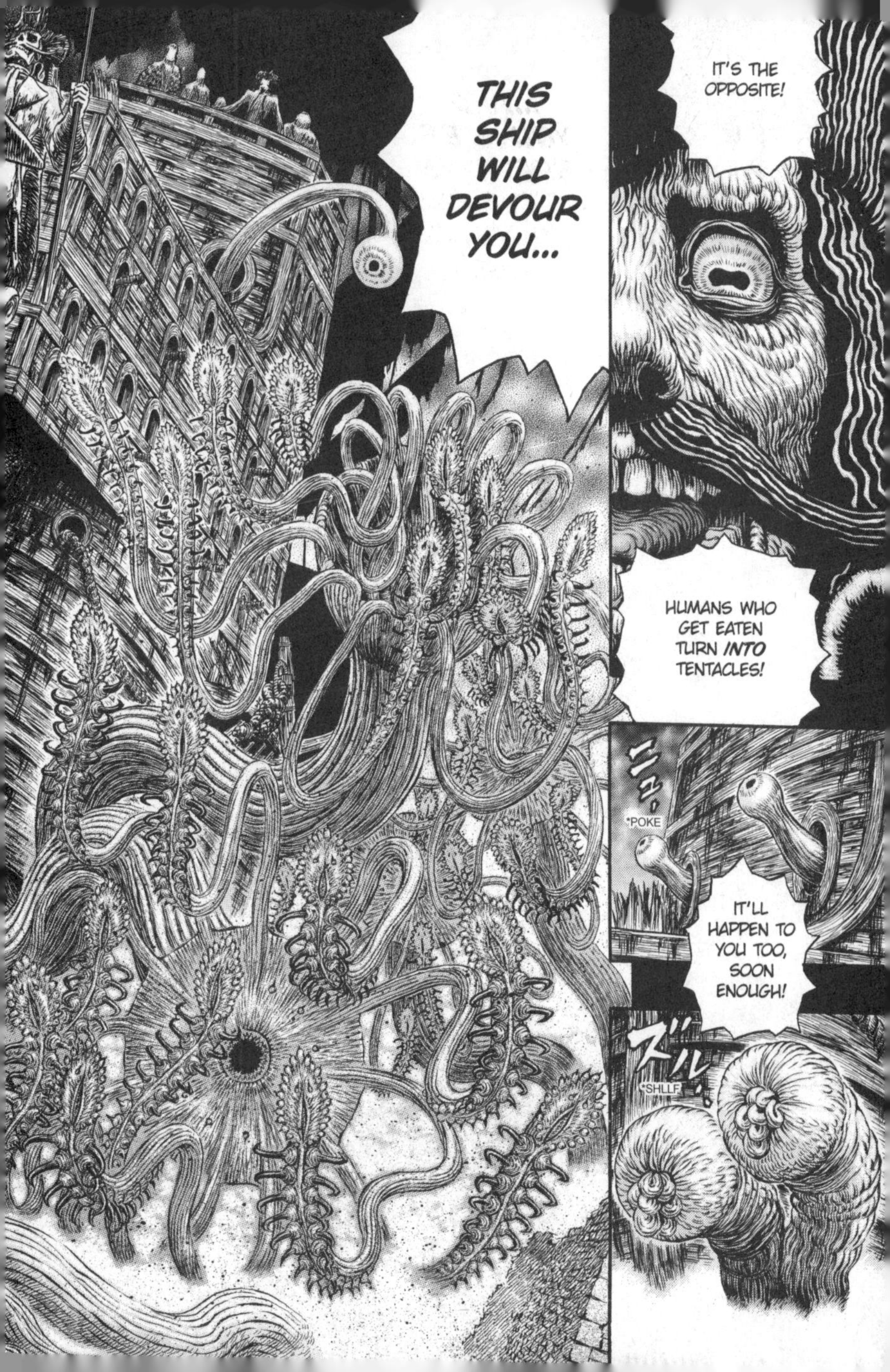

IT'S THE OPPOSITE!
HUMANS WHO GET EATEN TURN *INTO* TENTACLES!
ニュ
*POKE
IT'LL HAPPEN TO YOU TOO, SOON ENOUGH!
ズル
*SHLLF
THIS SHIP WILL DEVOUR YOU...

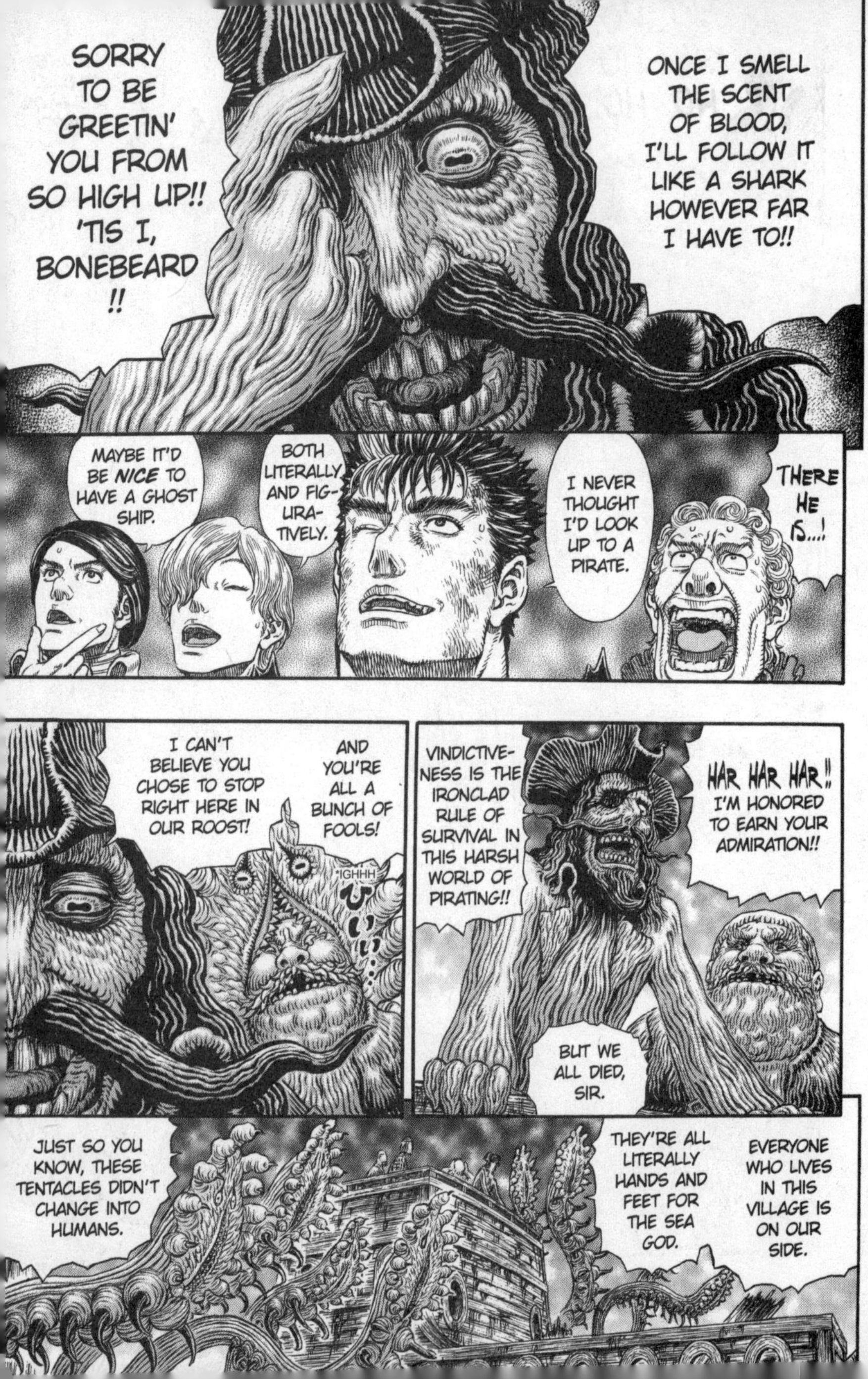
ONCE I SMELL THE SCENT OF BLOOD, I'LL FOLLOW IT LIKE A SHARK HOWEVER FAR I HAVE TO!!
SORRY TO BE GREETIN' YOU FROM SO HIGH UP!! 'TIS I, BONEBEARD!!
THERE HE IS...!
I NEVER THOUGHT I'D LOOK UP TO A PIRATE.
BOTH LITERALLY AND FIGURATIVELY.
MAYBE IT'D BE *NICE* TO HAVE A GHOST SHIP.
HAR HAR HAR!! I'M HONORED TO EARN YOUR ADMIRATION!!
VINDICTIVENESS IS THE IRONCLAD RULE OF SURVIVAL IN THIS HARSH WORLD OF PIRATING!!
BUT WE ALL DIED, SIR.
AND YOU'RE ALL A BUNCH OF FOOLS!
I CAN'T BELIEVE YOU CHOSE TO STOP RIGHT HERE IN OUR ROOST!
*IGHHH
EVERYONE WHO LIVES IN THIS VILLAGE IS ON OUR SIDE.
THEY'RE ALL LITERALLY HANDS AND FEET FOR THE SEA GOD.
JUST SO YOU KNOW, THESE TENTACLES DIDN'T CHANGE INTO HUMANS.

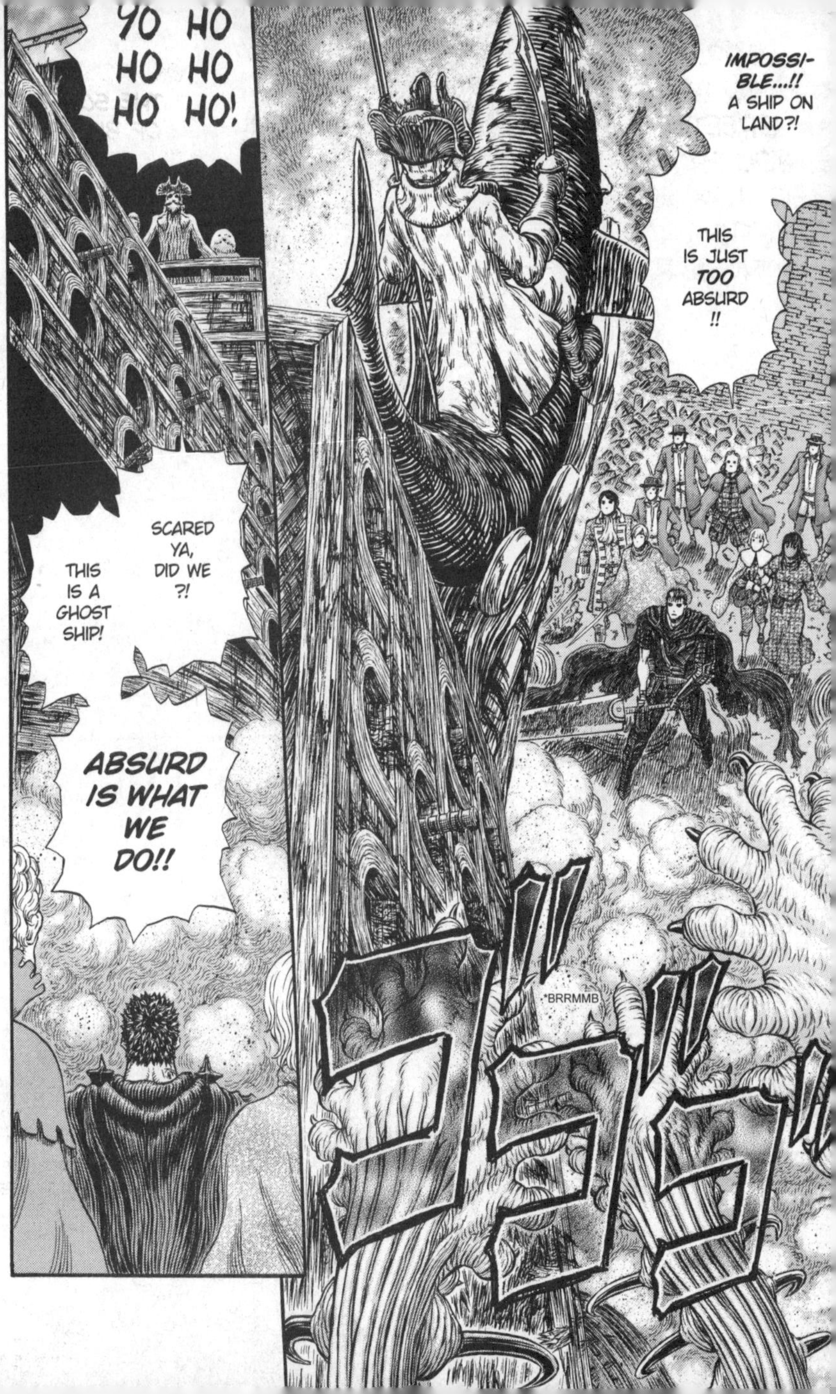
IMPOSSI-
BLE...!!
A SHIP ON
LAND?!
THIS
IS JUST
TOO
ABSURD
!!
*BRRMMB
YO HO
HO HO
HO HO!
SCARED
YA,
DID WE
?!
THIS
IS A
GHOST
SHIP!
ABSURD
IS WHAT
WE
DO!!

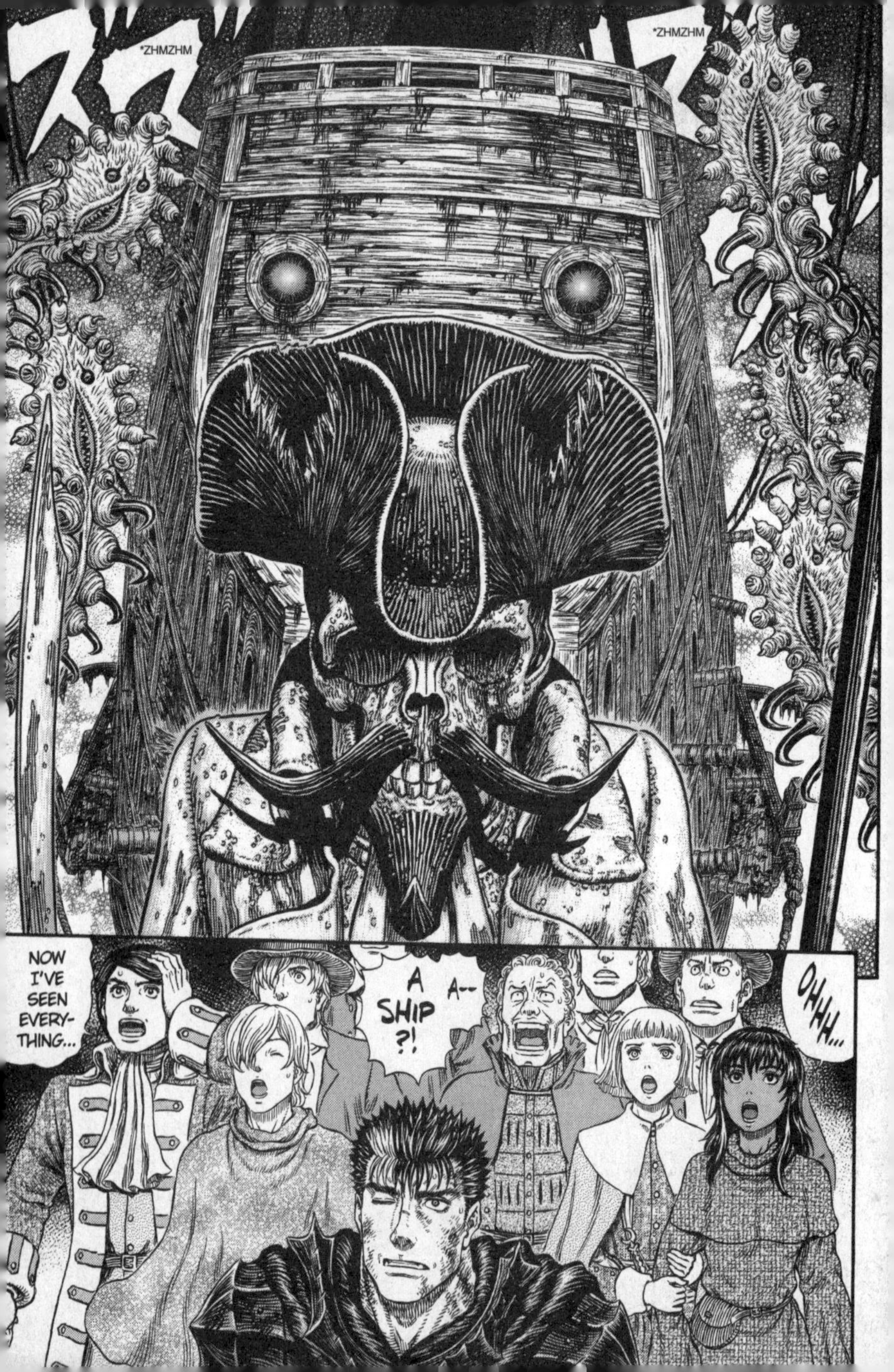
*ZHMZHM
*ZHMZHM
OHHH...
A--
A SHIP ?!
NOW I'VE SEEN EVERY-THING...

幻造世界（ファンタジア）篇／妖精島の章

触手船

THE TENTACLED SHIP

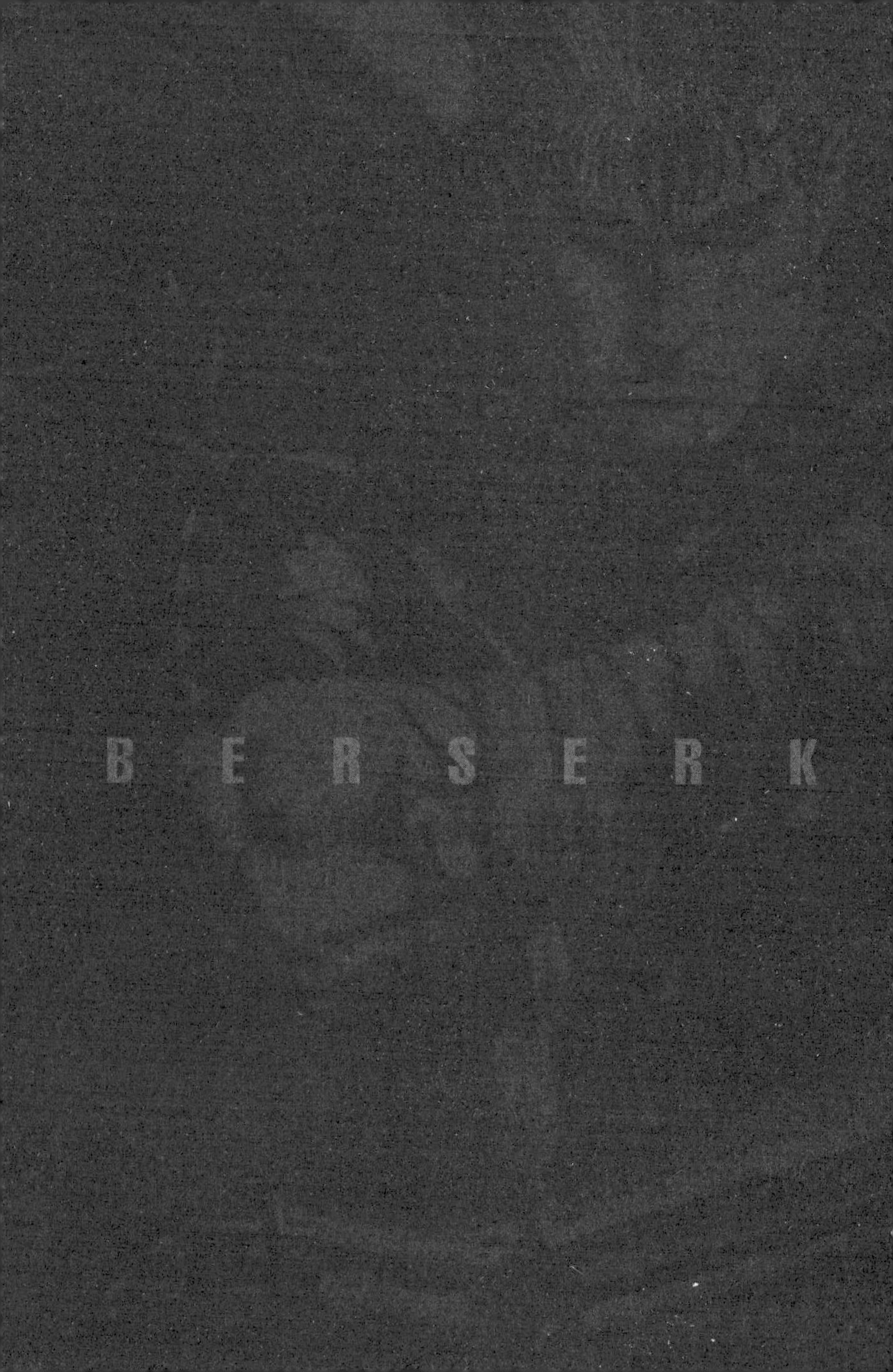
BERSERK

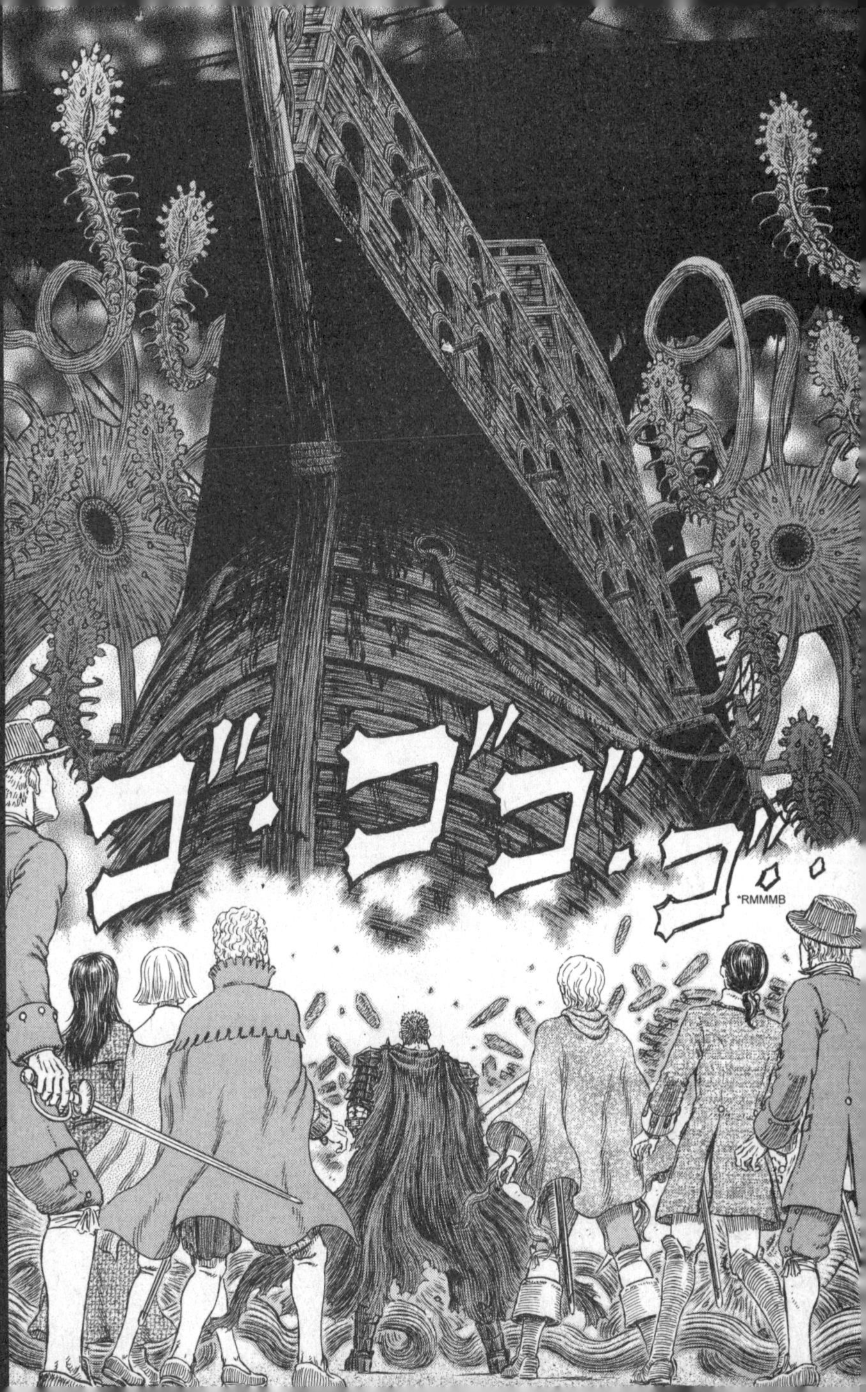
ゴゴゴゴゴ
*RMMMB

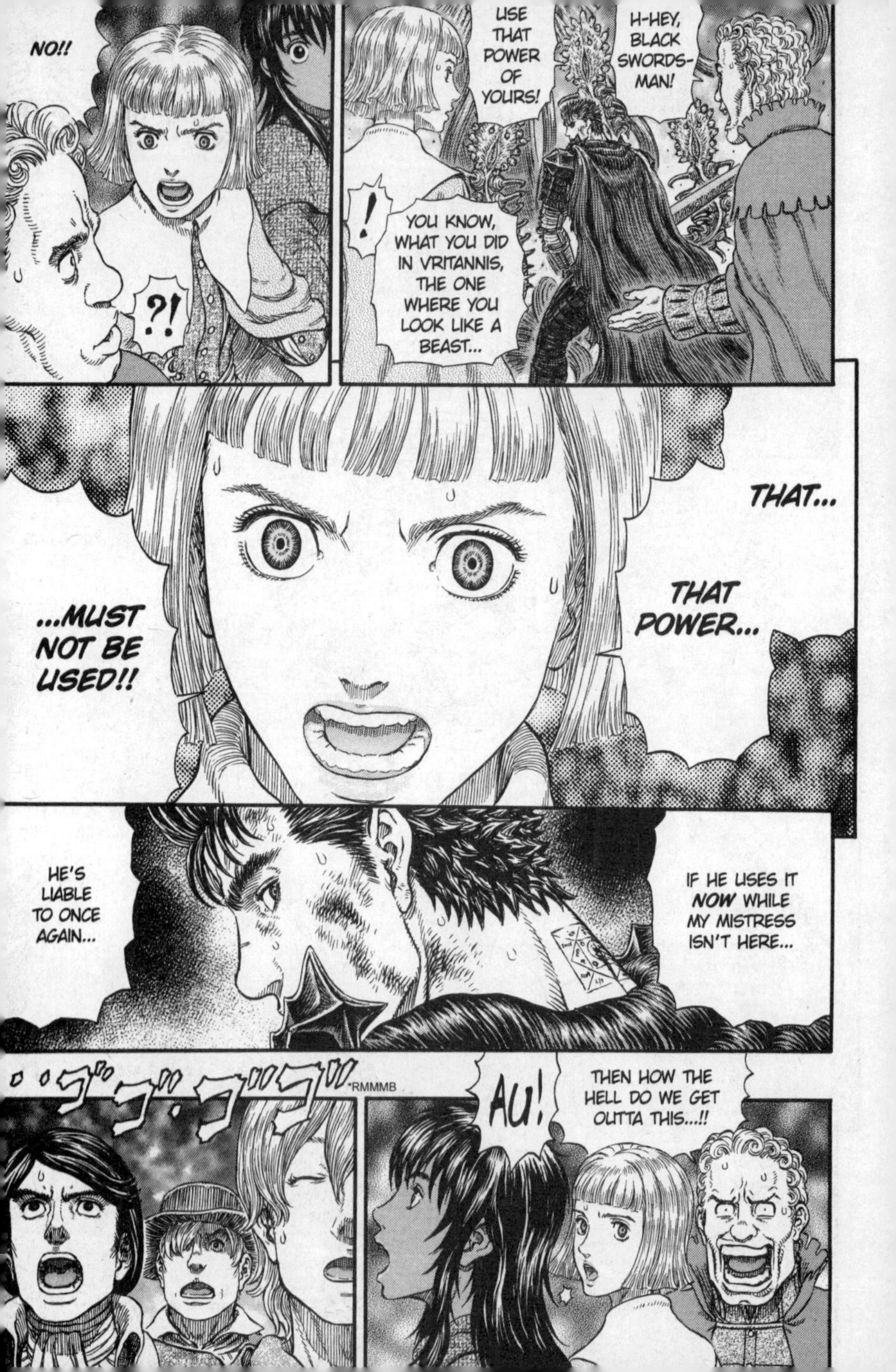
H-HEY, BLACK SWORDS-MAN!
USE THAT POWER OF YOURS!
!
YOU KNOW, WHAT YOU DID IN VRITANNIS, THE ONE WHERE YOU LOOK LIKE A BEAST...
NO!!
?!
THAT...
THAT POWER...
...MUST NOT BE USED!!
IF HE USES IT *NOW* WHILE MY MISTRESS ISN'T HERE...
HE'S LIABLE TO ONCE AGAIN...
THEN HOW THE HELL DO WE GET OUTTA THIS...!!
AU!
*RMMMB

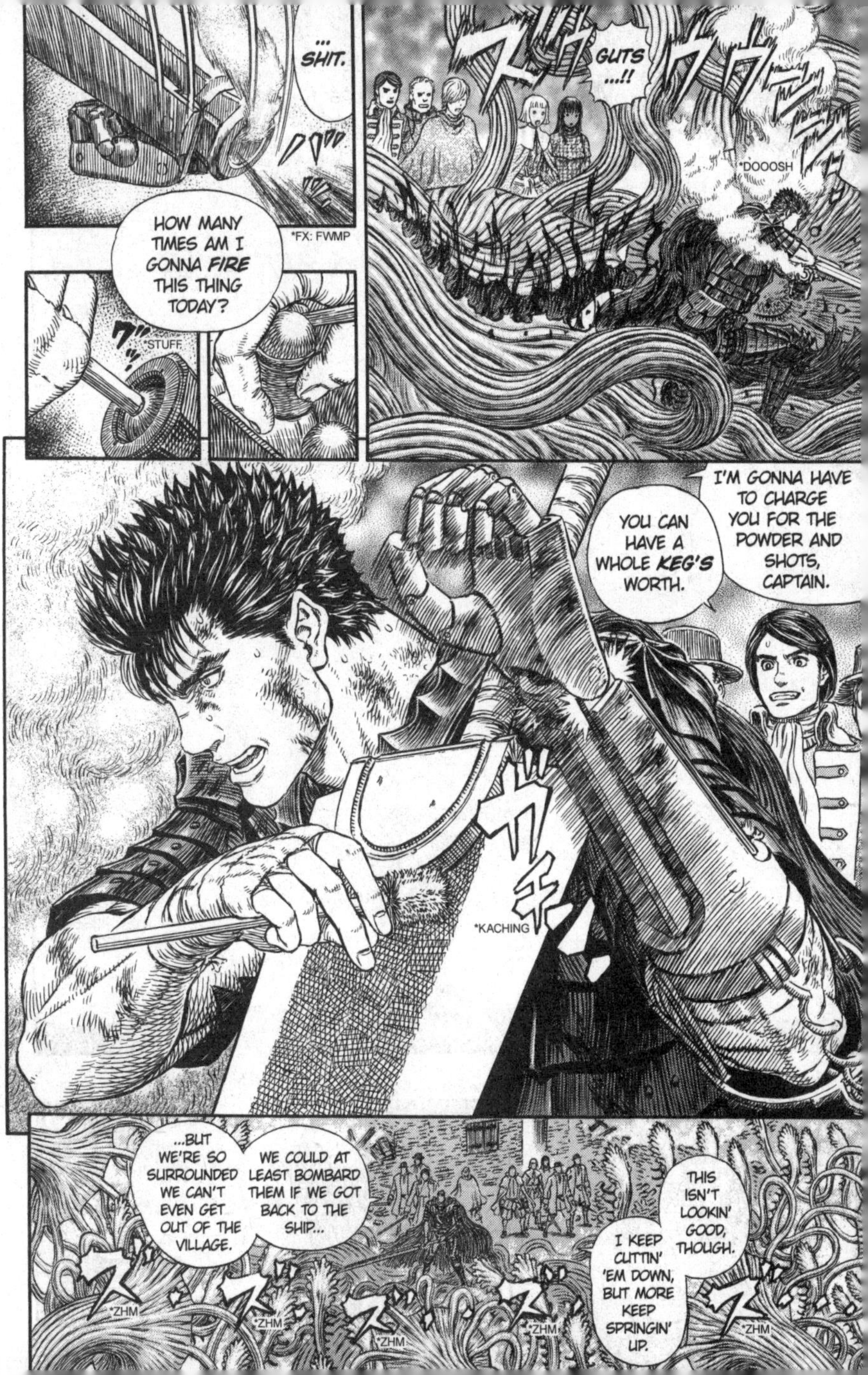

GUTS ...!!
*DOOOSH
... SHIT.
*FX: FWMP
HOW MANY TIMES AM I GONNA **FIRE** THIS THING TODAY?
*STUFF
I'M GONNA HAVE TO CHARGE YOU FOR THE POWDER AND SHOTS, CAPTAIN.
YOU CAN HAVE A WHOLE **KEG'S** WORTH.
*KACHING
THIS ISN'T LOOKIN' GOOD, THOUGH.
I KEEP CUTTIN' 'EM DOWN, BUT MORE KEEP SPRINGIN' UP.
WE COULD AT LEAST BOMBARD THEM IF WE GOT BACK TO THE SHIP...
...BUT WE'RE SO SURROUNDED WE CAN'T EVEN GET OUT OF THE VILLAGE.
*ZHM
*ZHM
*ZHM
*ZHM
*ZHM

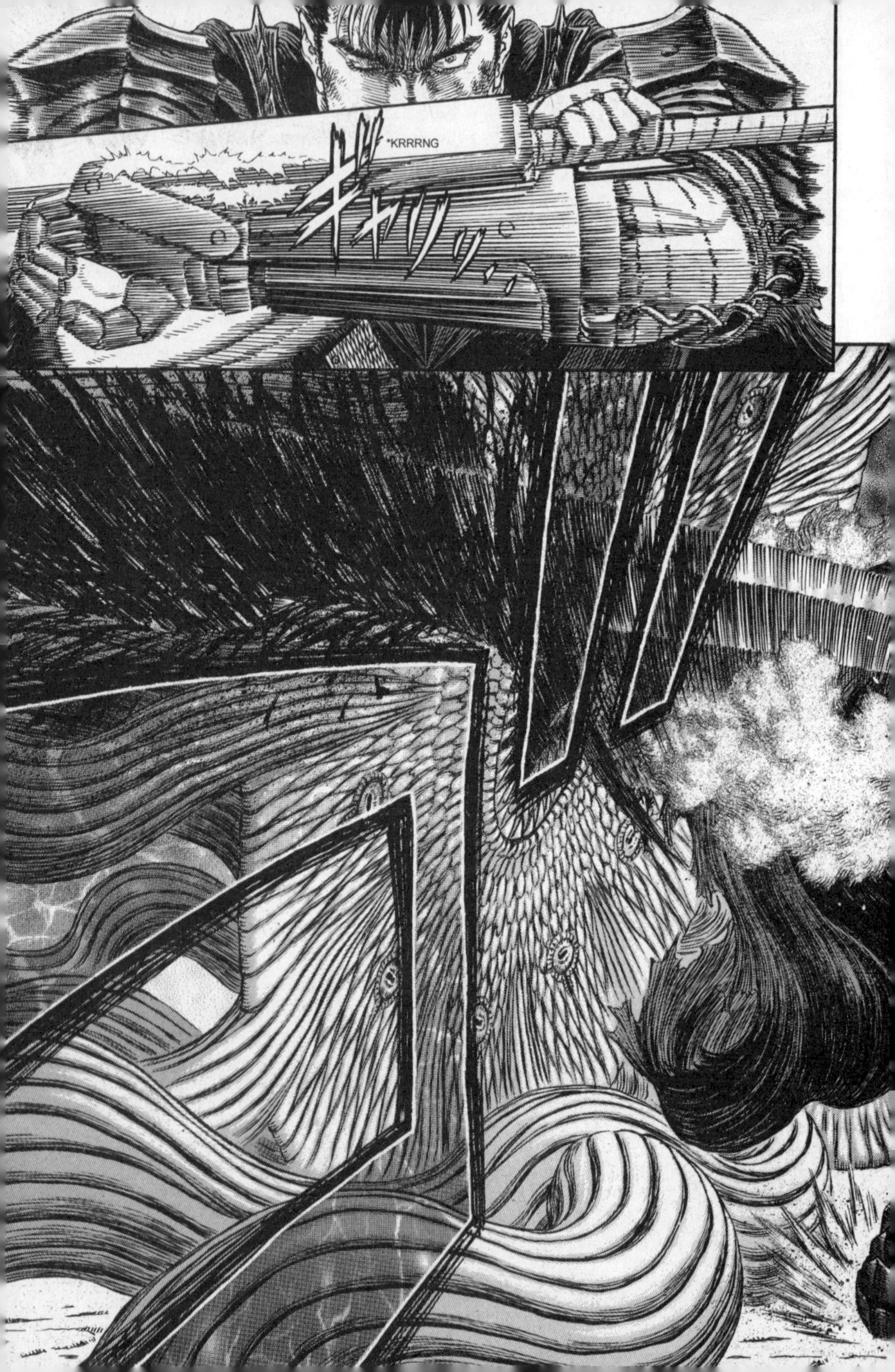
*KRRRNG

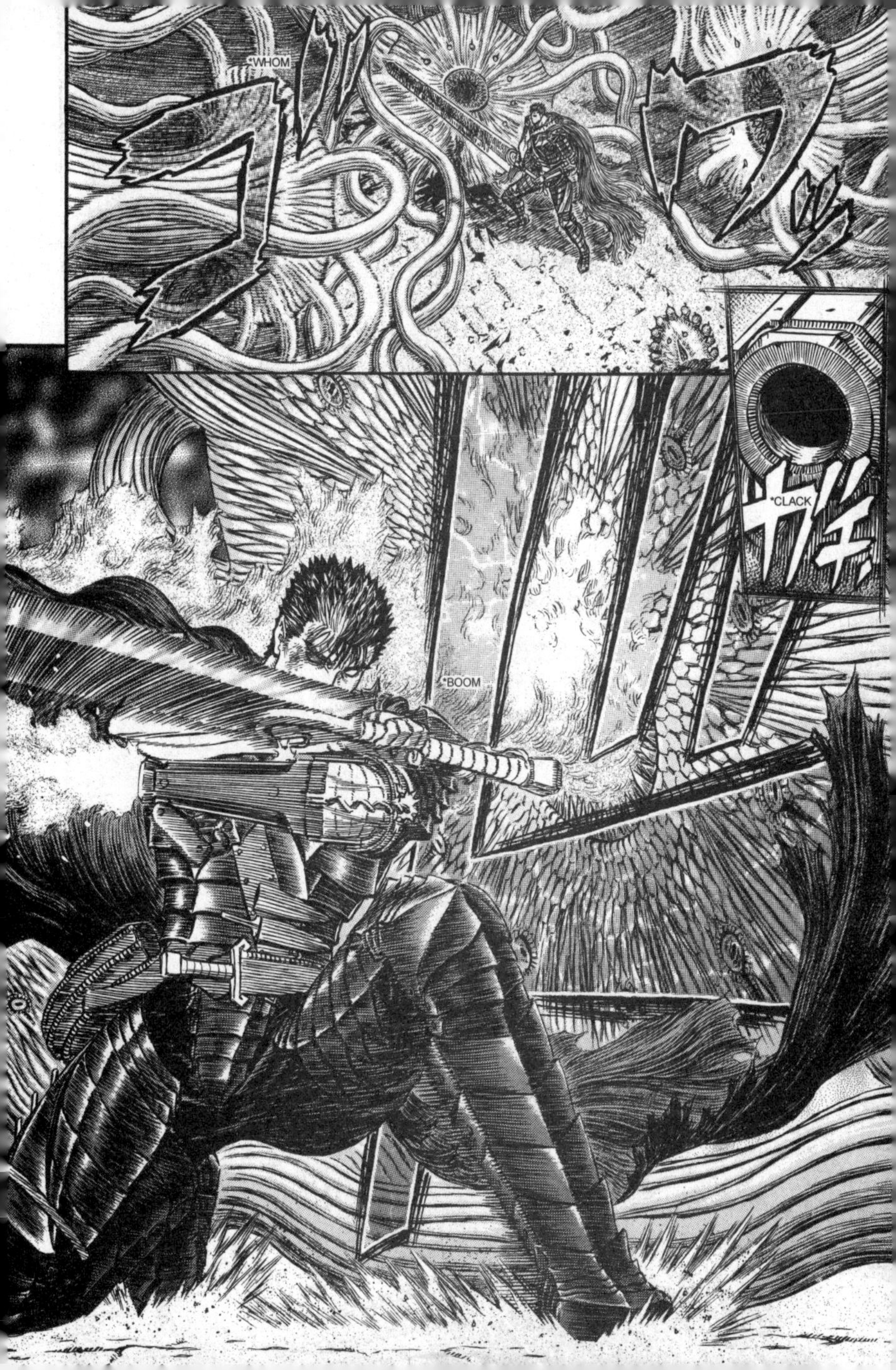
*WHOM
*CLACK
*BOOM

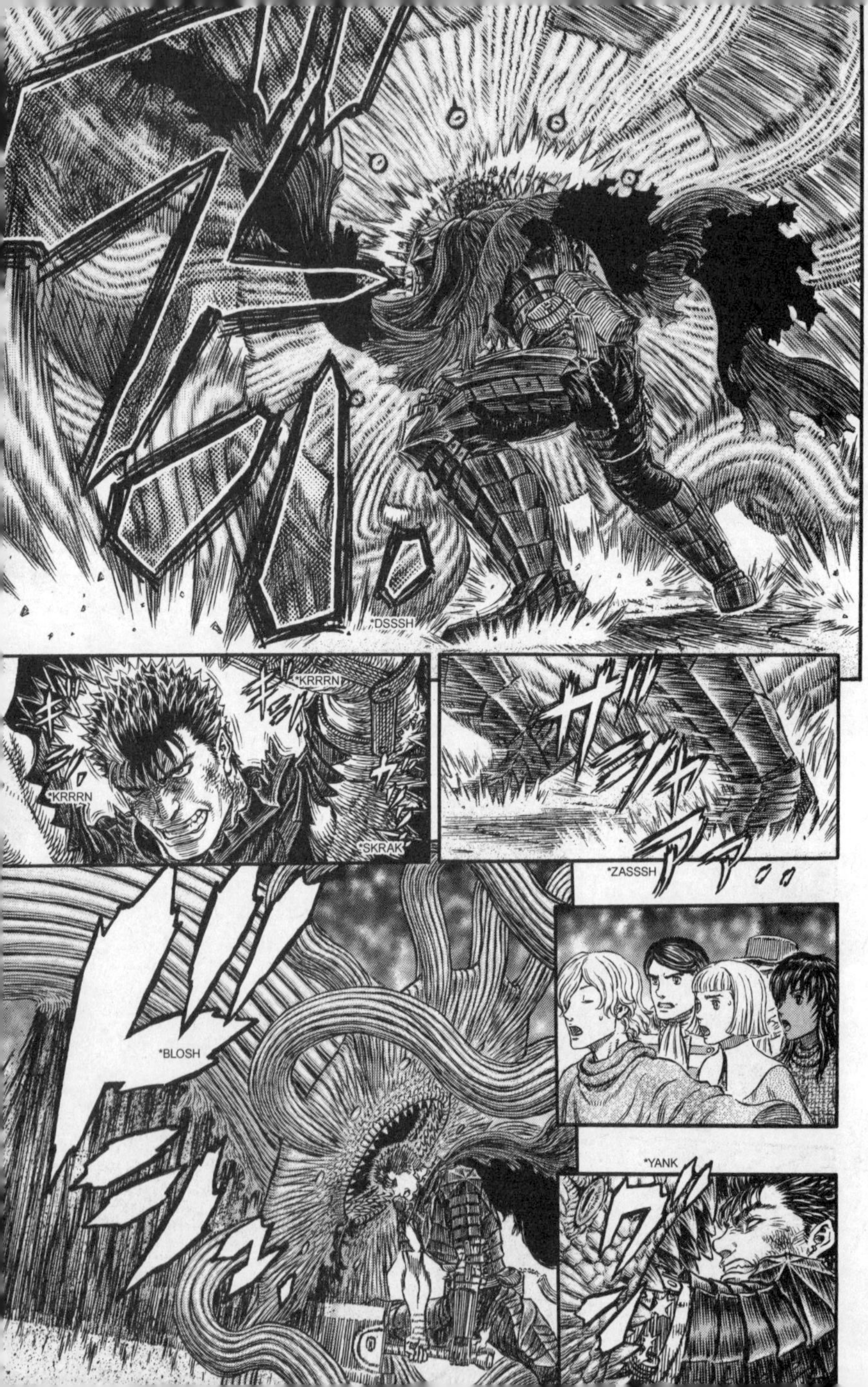
*DSSSH
*ZASSSH
*KRRRN
*KRRRN
*SKRAK
*YANK
*BLOSH

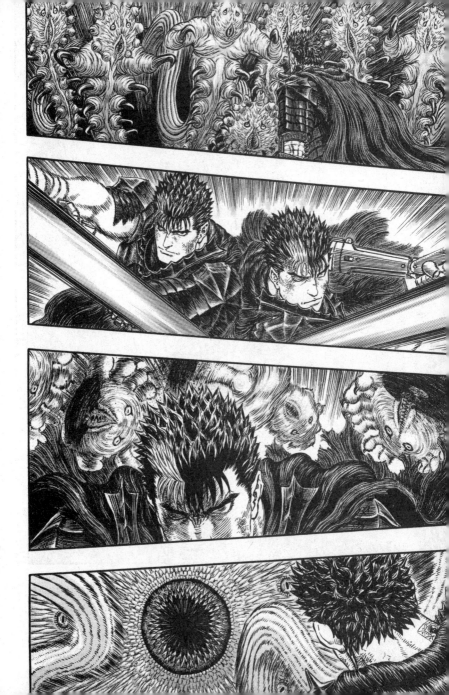

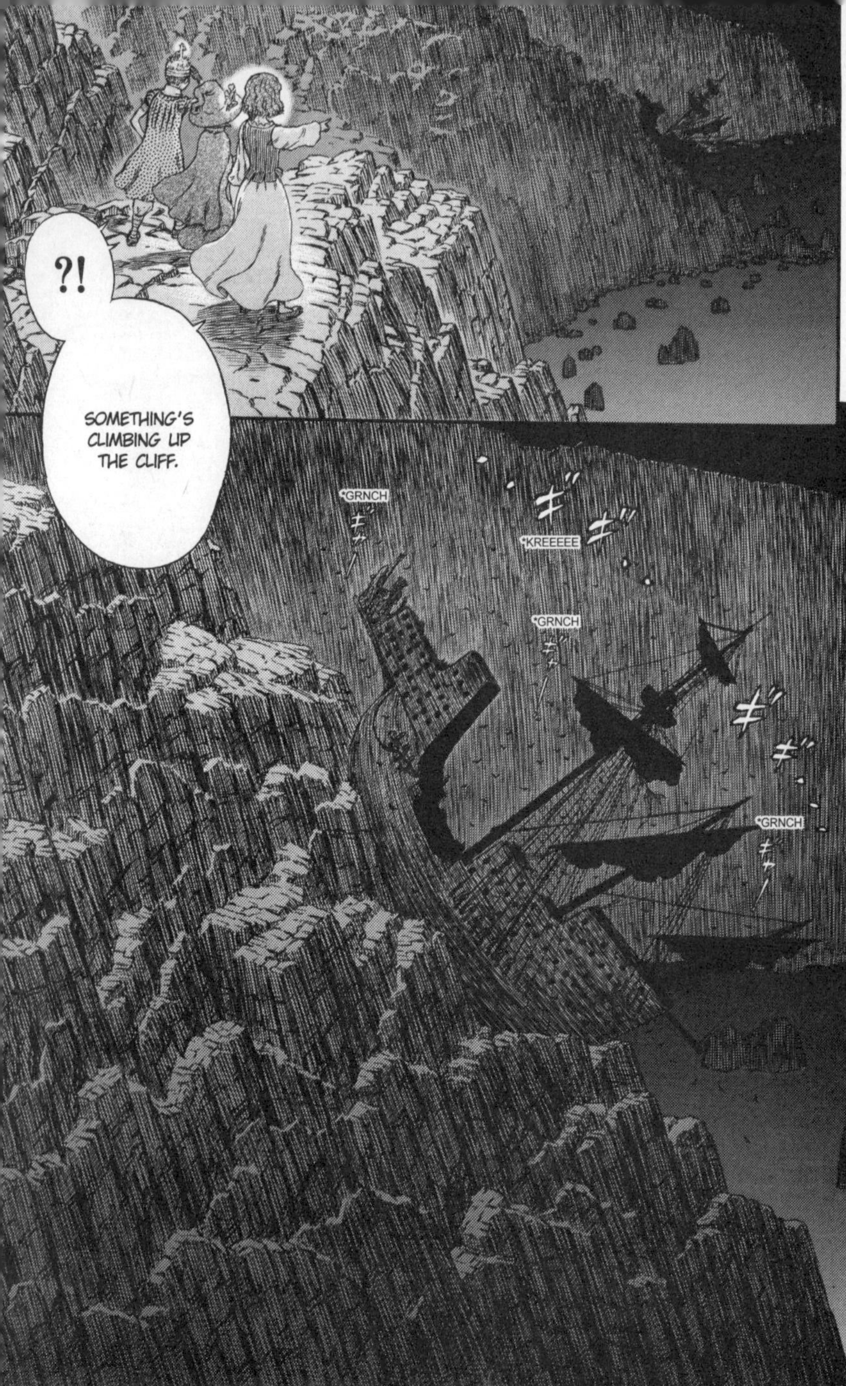
?!
SOMETHING'S CLIMBING UP THE CLIFF.
*GRNCH
*KREEEEE
*GRNCH
*GRNCH

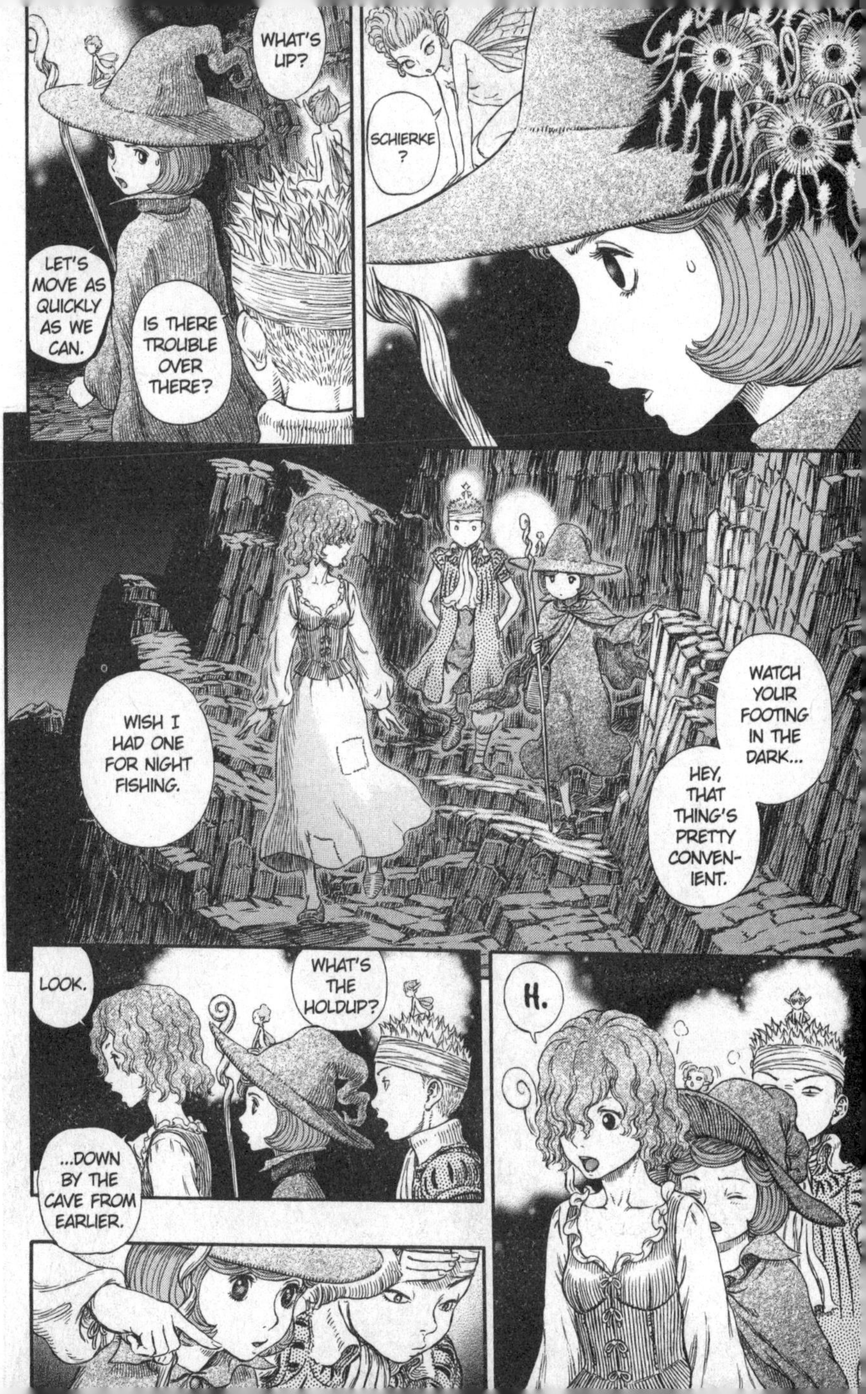
SCHIERKE ?
WHAT'S UP?
IS THERE TROUBLE OVER THERE?
LET'S MOVE AS QUICKLY AS WE CAN.
WATCH YOUR FOOTING IN THE DARK...
HEY, THAT THING'S PRETTY CONVEN-IENT.
WISH I HAD ONE FOR NIGHT FISHING.
H.
WHAT'S THE HOLDUP?
LOOK.
...DOWN BY THE CAVE FROM EARLIER.

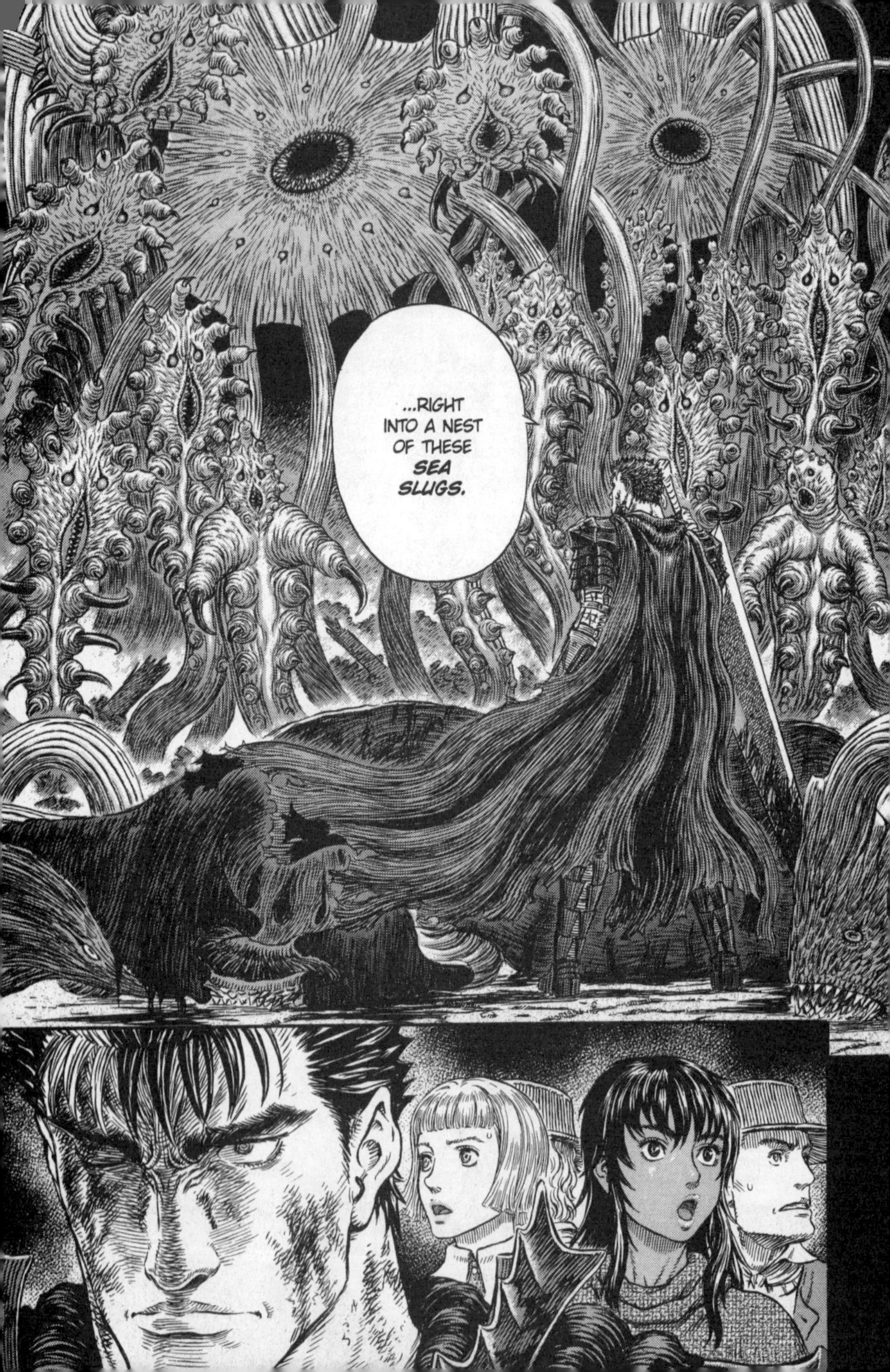
...RIGHT INTO A NEST OF THESE SEA SLUGS.

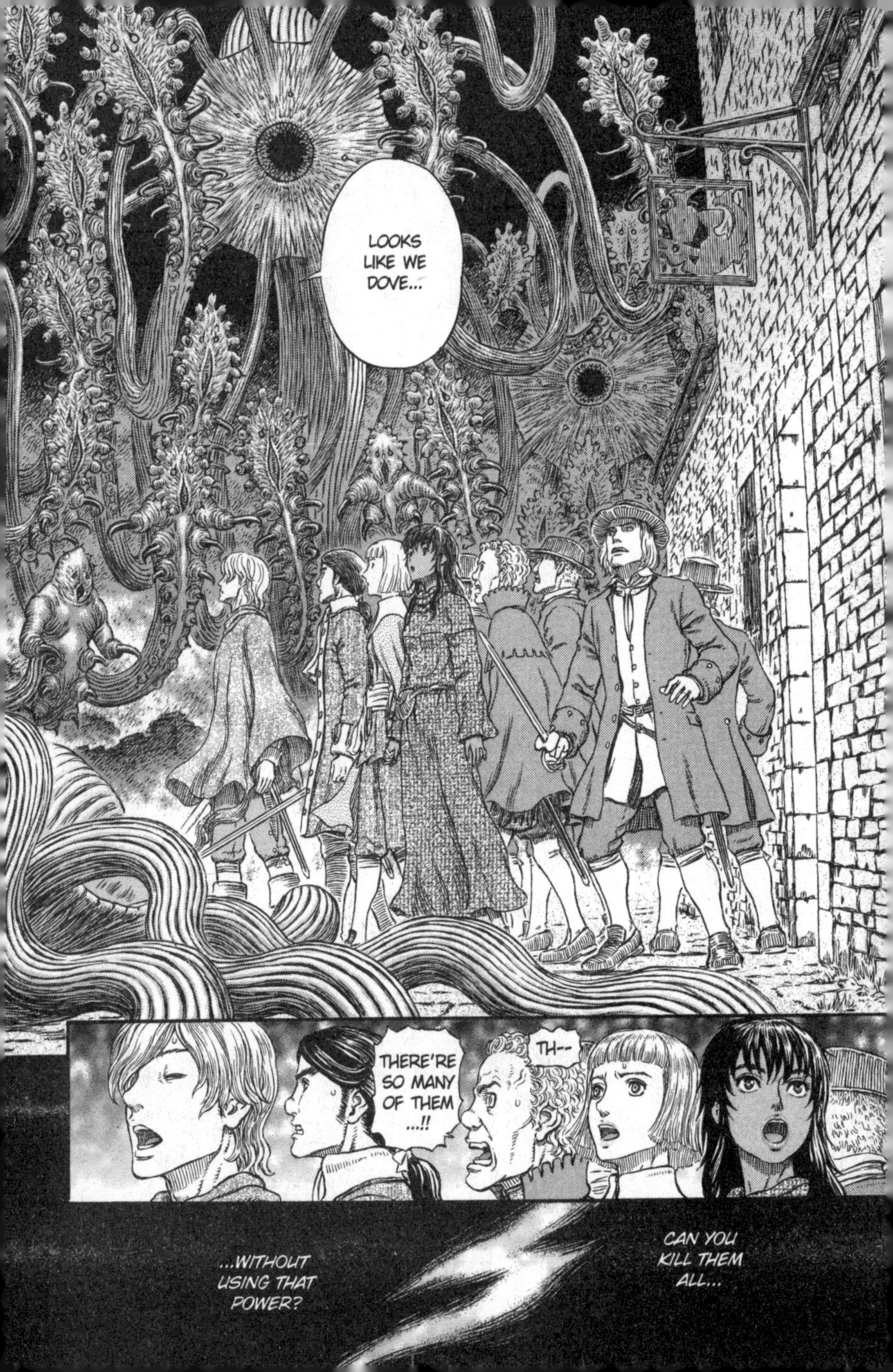
LOOKS LIKE WE DOVE...
TH--
THERE'RE SO MANY OF THEM ...!!
CAN YOU KILL THEM ALL...
...WITHOUT USING THAT POWER?

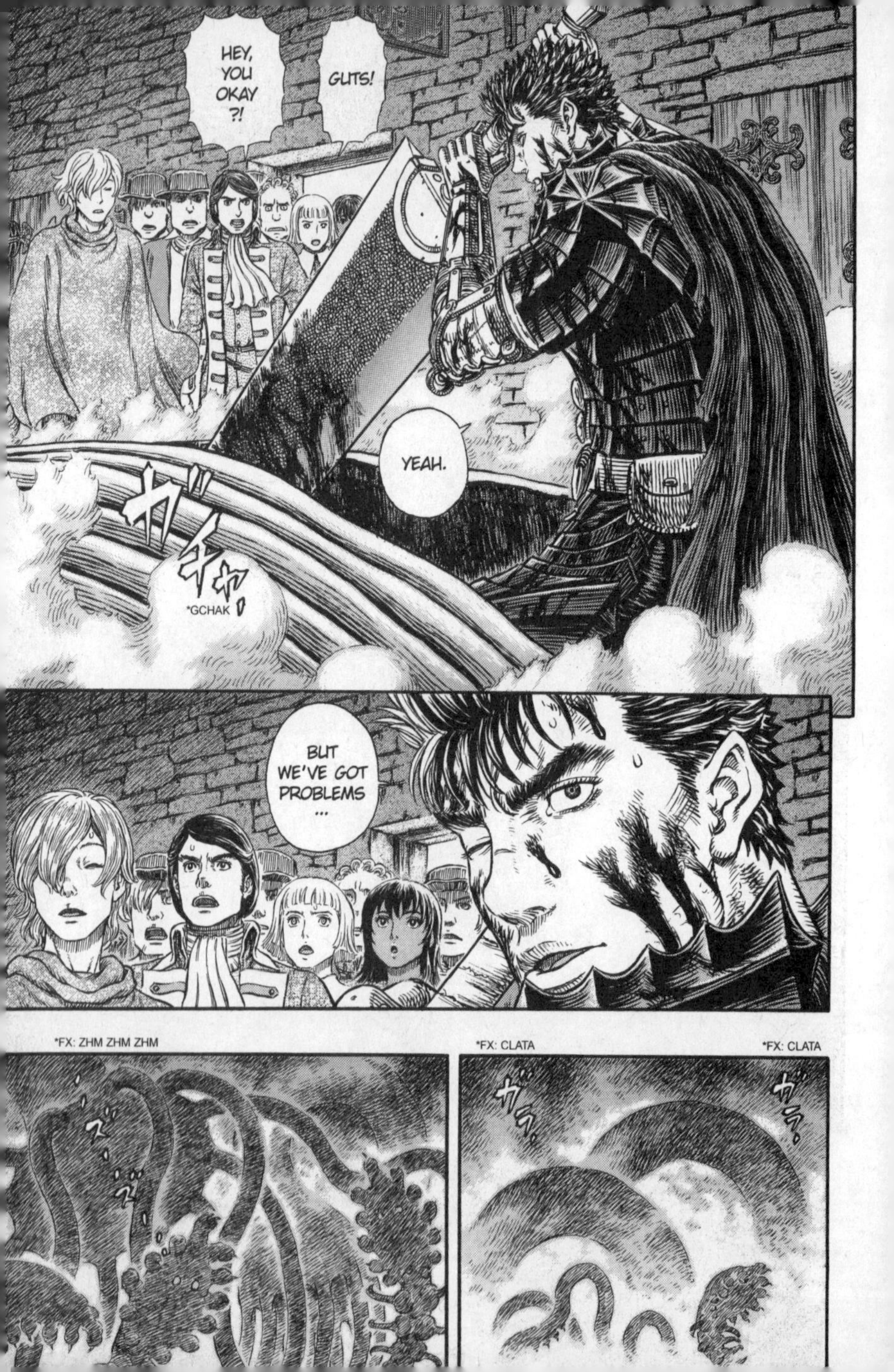
GUTS!
HEY, YOU OKAY ?!
YEAH.
*GCHAK
BUT WE'VE GOT PROBLEMS ...
*FX: CLATA
*FX: CLATA
*FX: ZHM ZHM ZHM

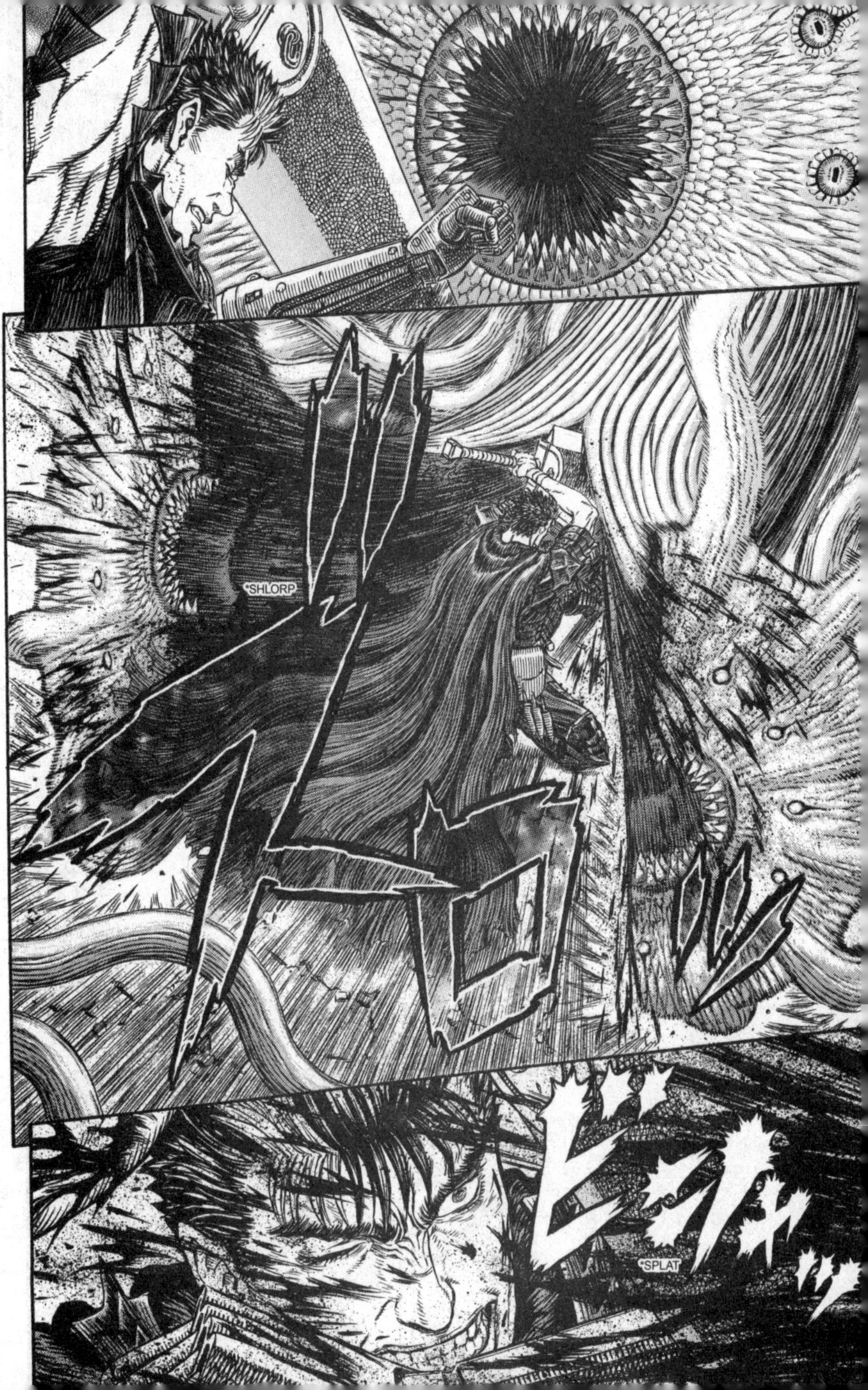
*SHLORP
*SPLAT

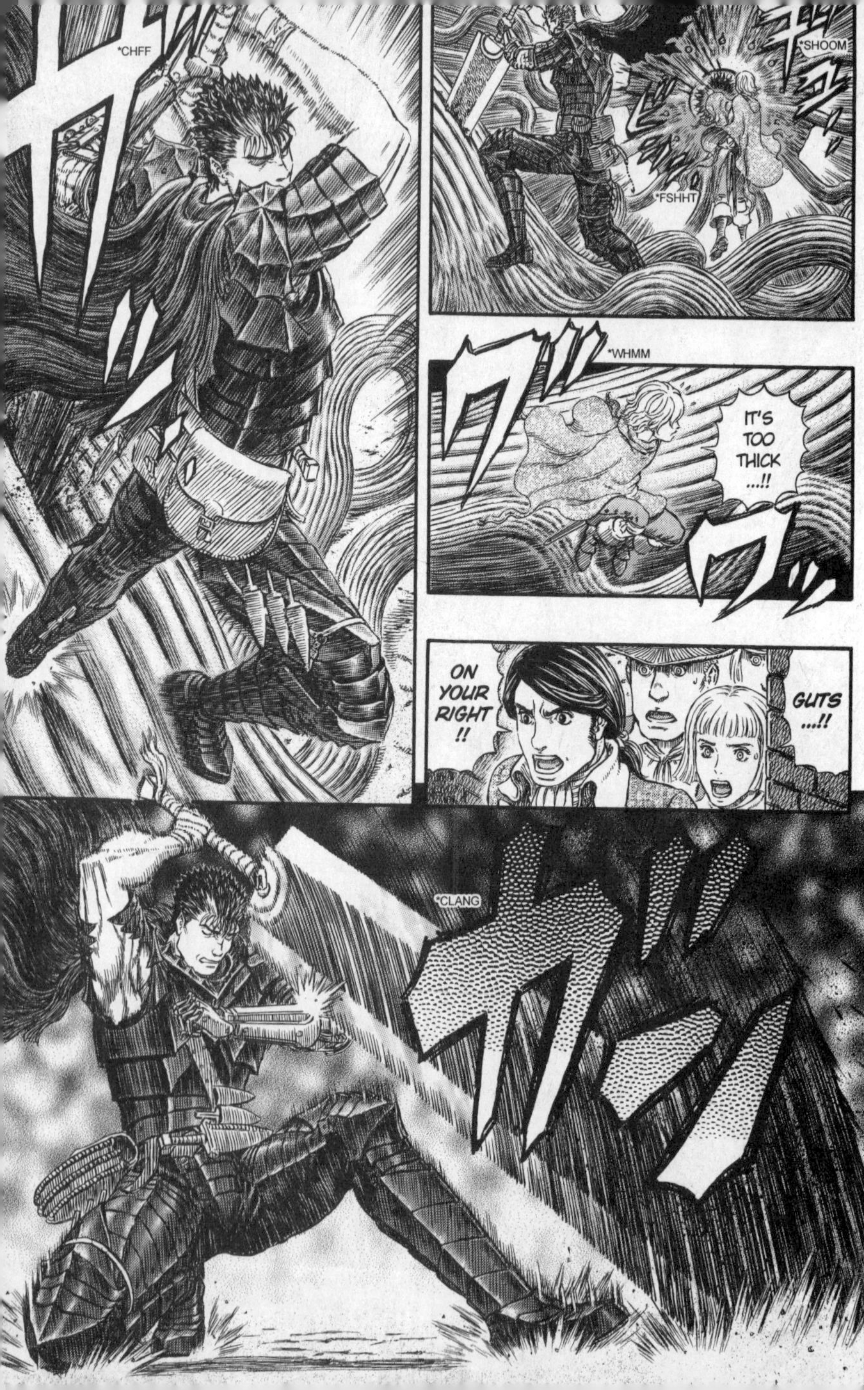
*SHOOM
*FSHHT
*WHMM
IT'S TOO THICK ...!!
GUTS ...!!
ON YOUR RIGHT !!
*CHFF
*CLANG

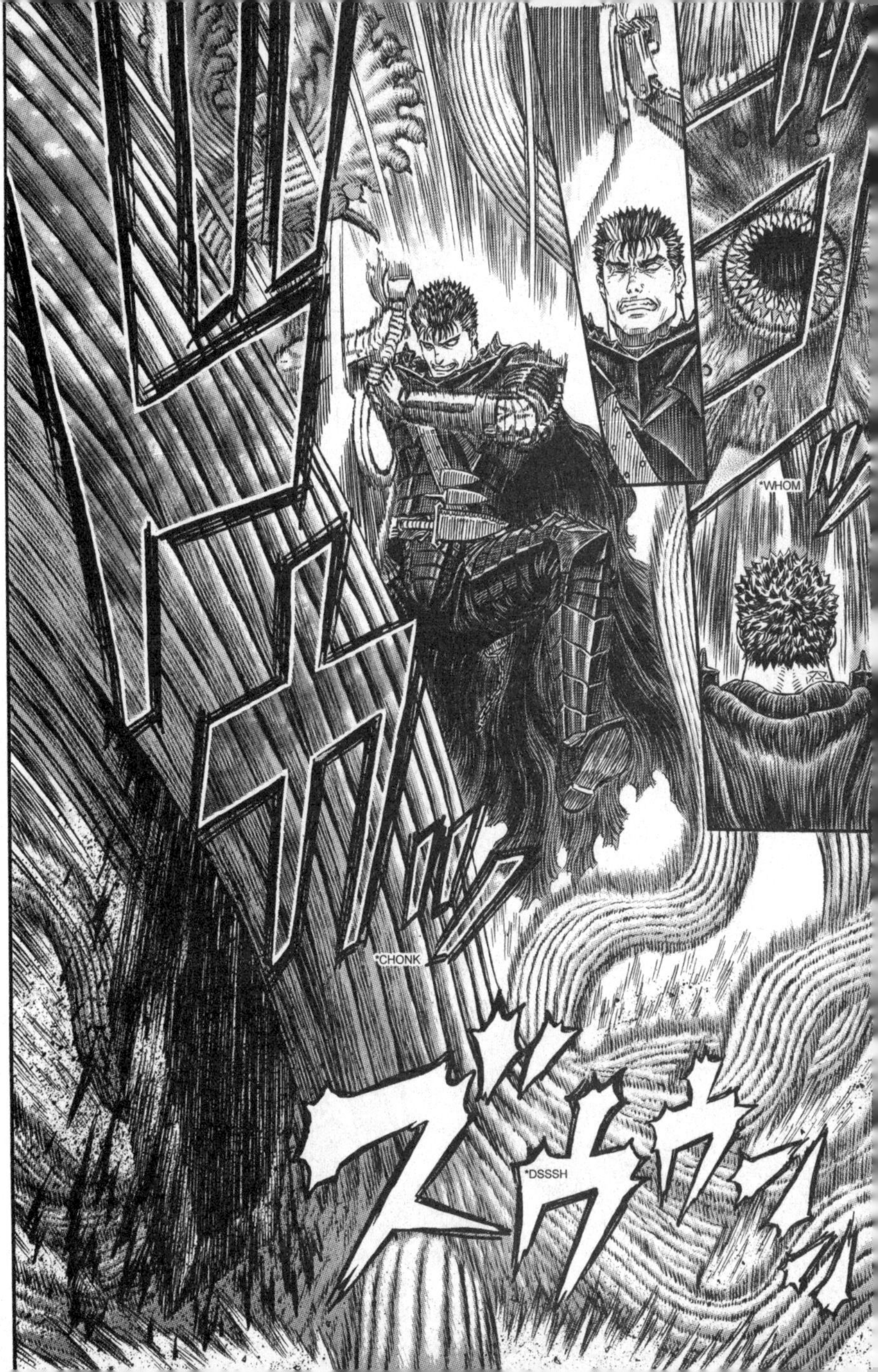
*WHOM
*CHONK
*DSSSH

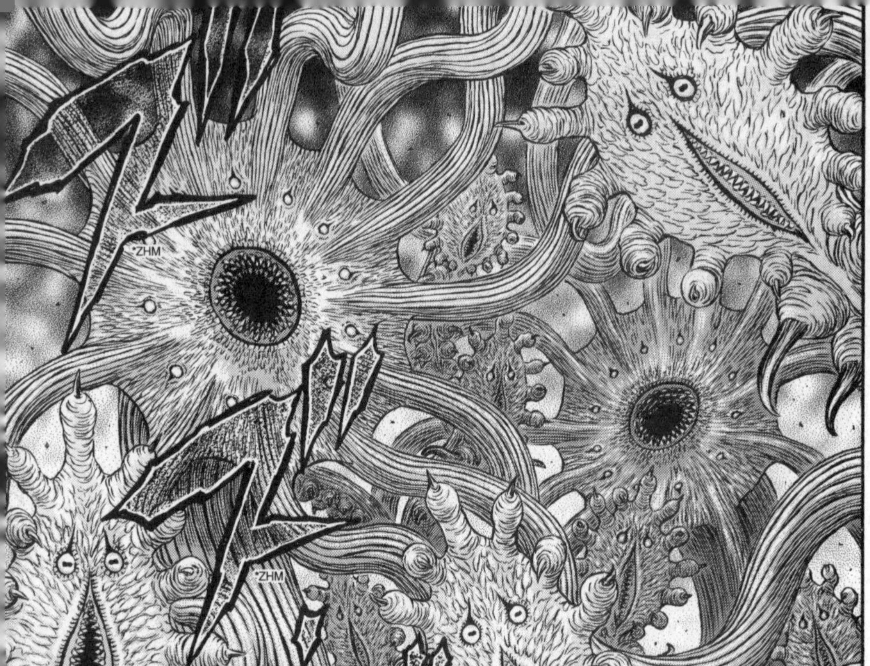
ZHM
ZHM
ZHM
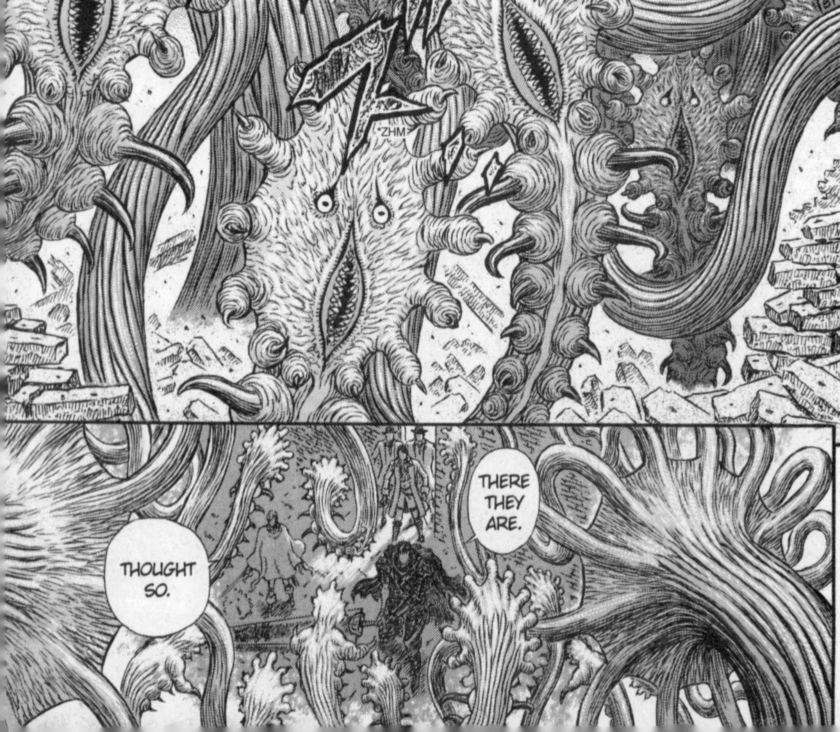
THERE THEY ARE.
THOUGHT SO.

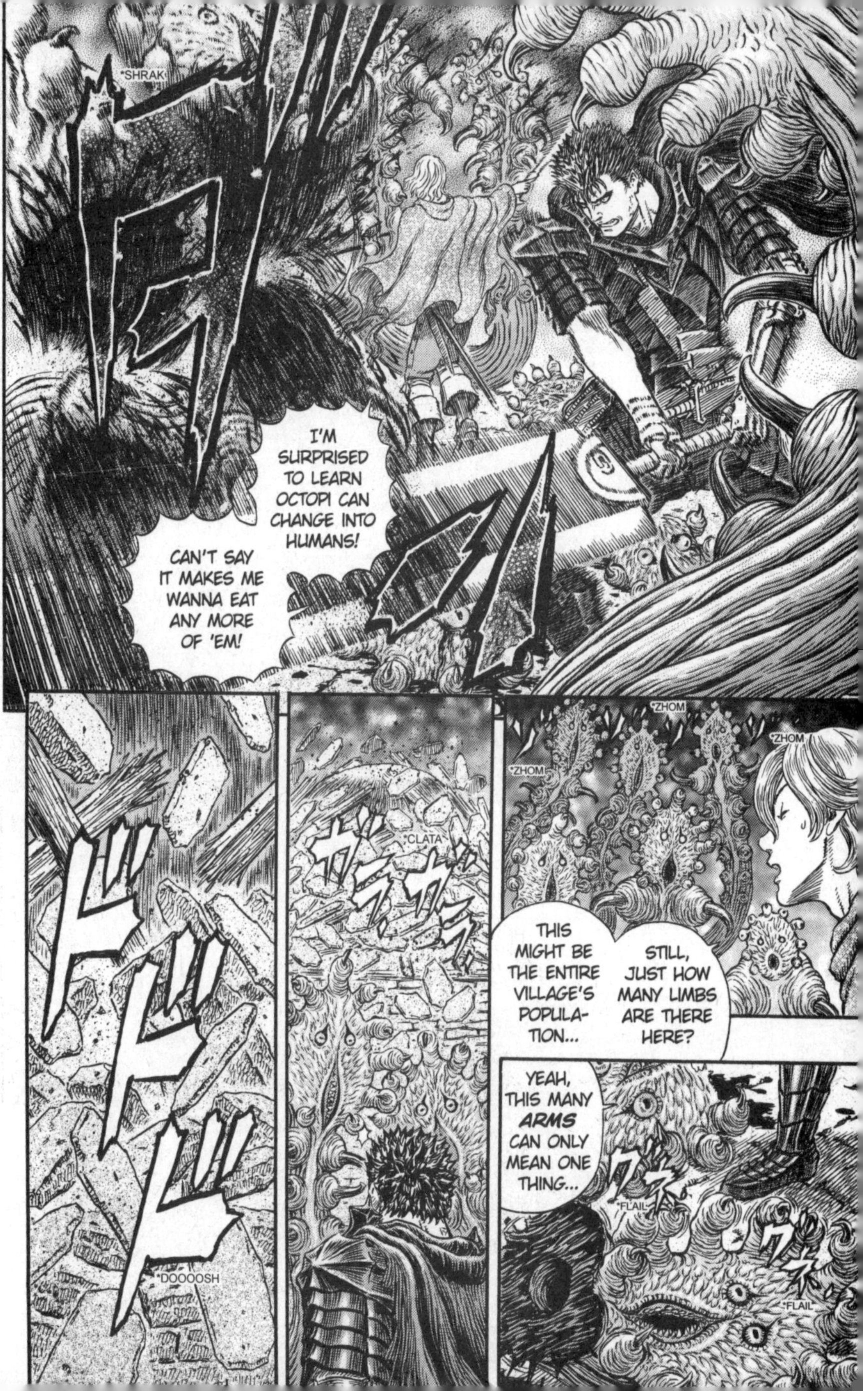
*SHRAK
I'M SURPRISED TO LEARN OCTOPI CAN CHANGE INTO HUMANS!
CAN'T SAY IT MAKES ME WANNA EAT ANY MORE OF 'EM!
*ZHOM
*ZHOM
*ZHOM
STILL, JUST HOW MANY LIMBS ARE THERE HERE?
THIS MIGHT BE THE ENTIRE VILLAGE'S POPULA-TION...
YEAH, THIS MANY **ARMS** CAN ONLY MEAN ONE THING...
*FLAIL
*FLAIL
*CLATA
*DOOOOSH

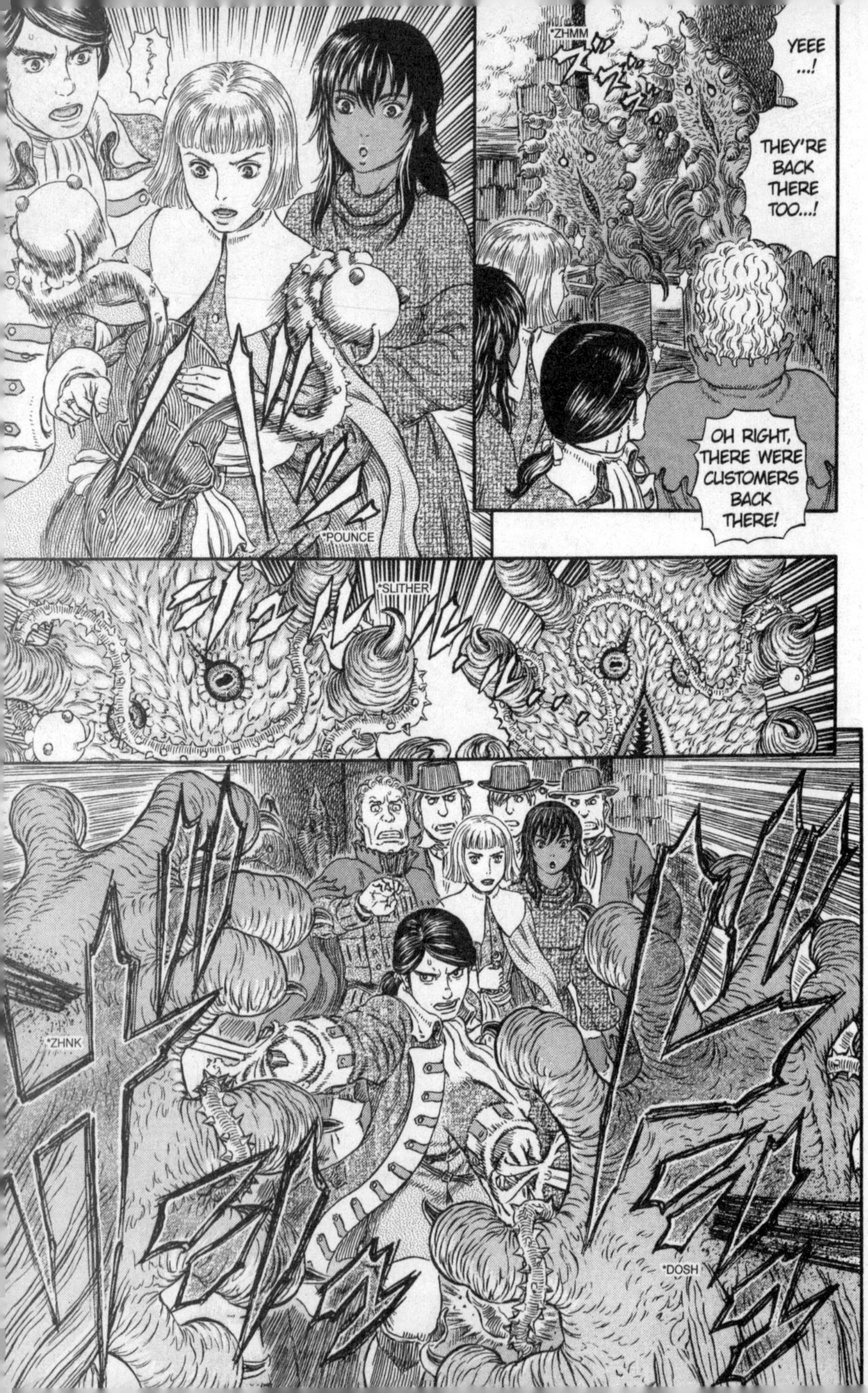

YEEE ...!
THEY'RE BACK THERE TOO...!
*ZHMM
OH RIGHT, THERE WERE CUSTOMERS BACK THERE!
*POUNCE
*SLITHER
*ZHNK
*DOSH

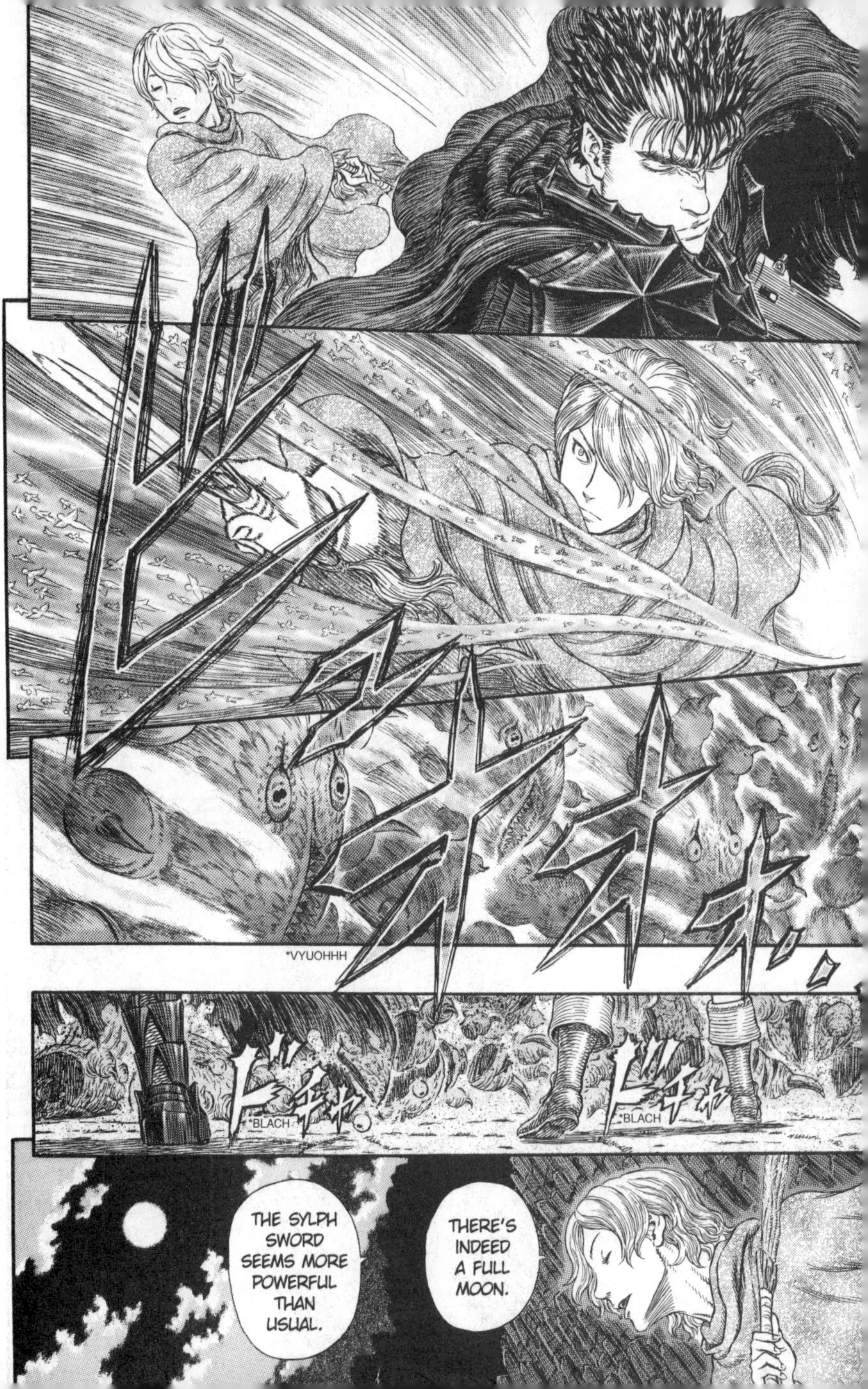
*VYUOHHH
*BLACH
*BLACH
THERE'S INDEED A FULL MOON.
THE SYLPH SWORD SEEMS MORE POWERFUL THAN USUAL.

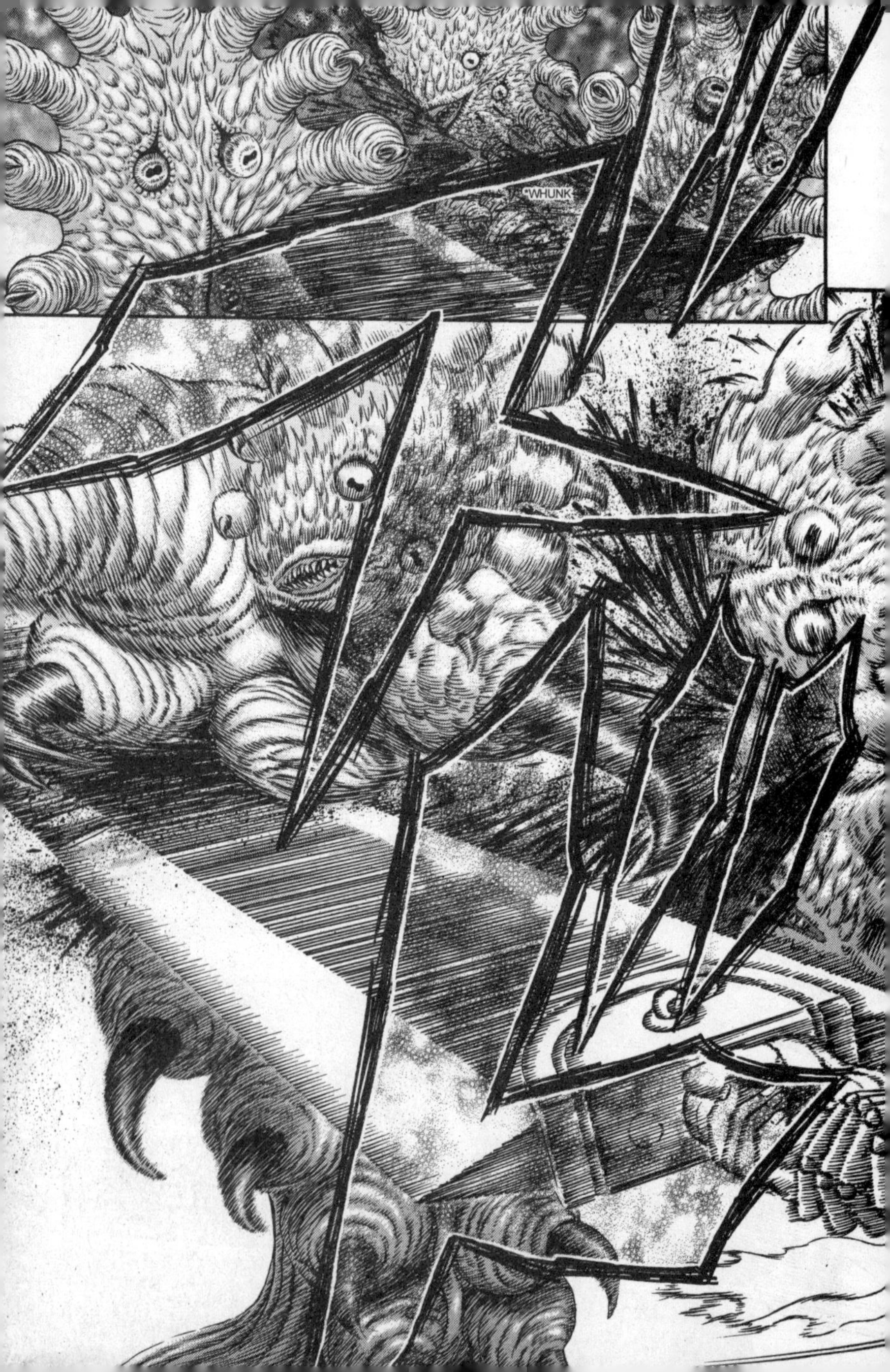
WHUNK

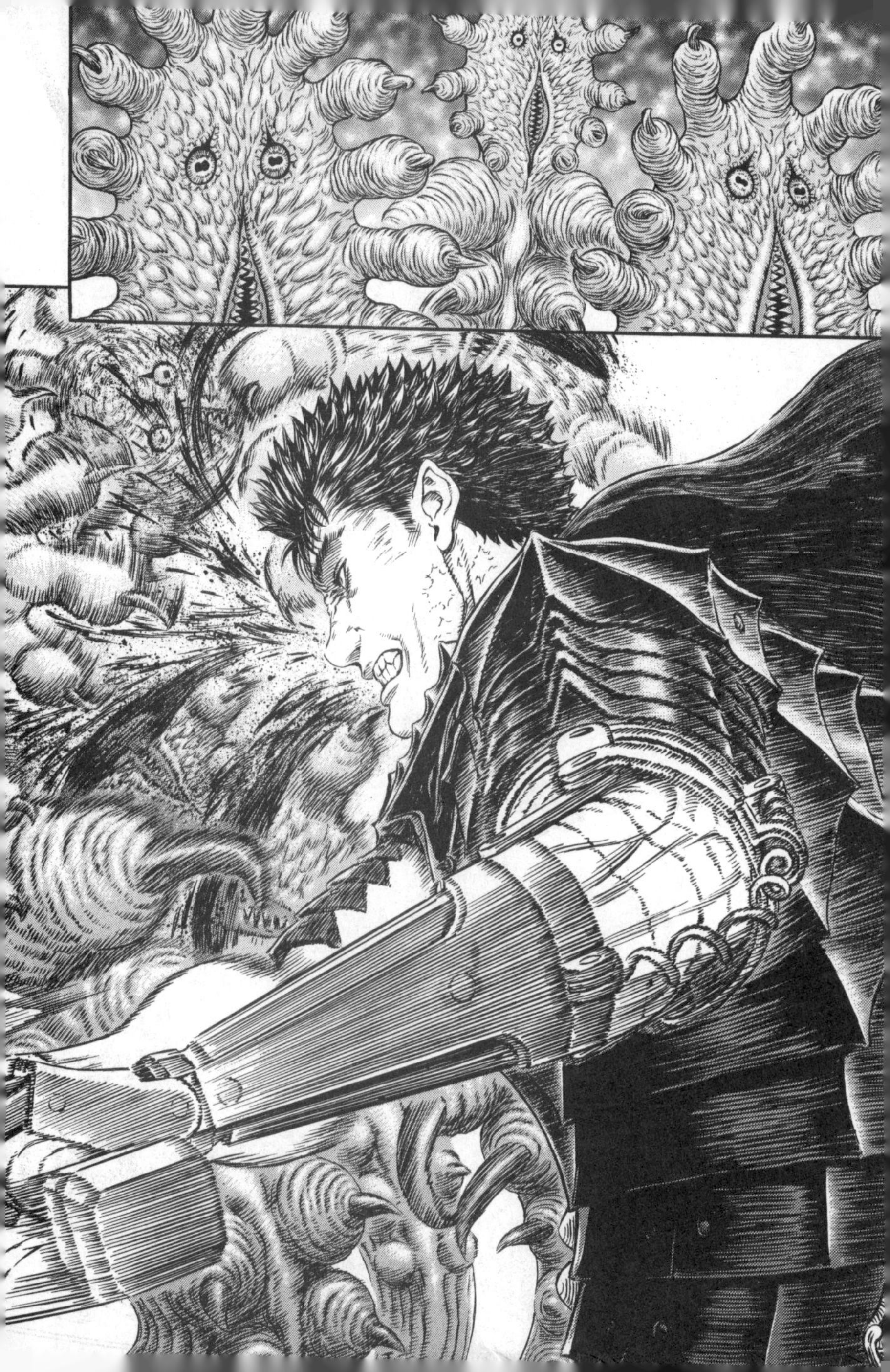

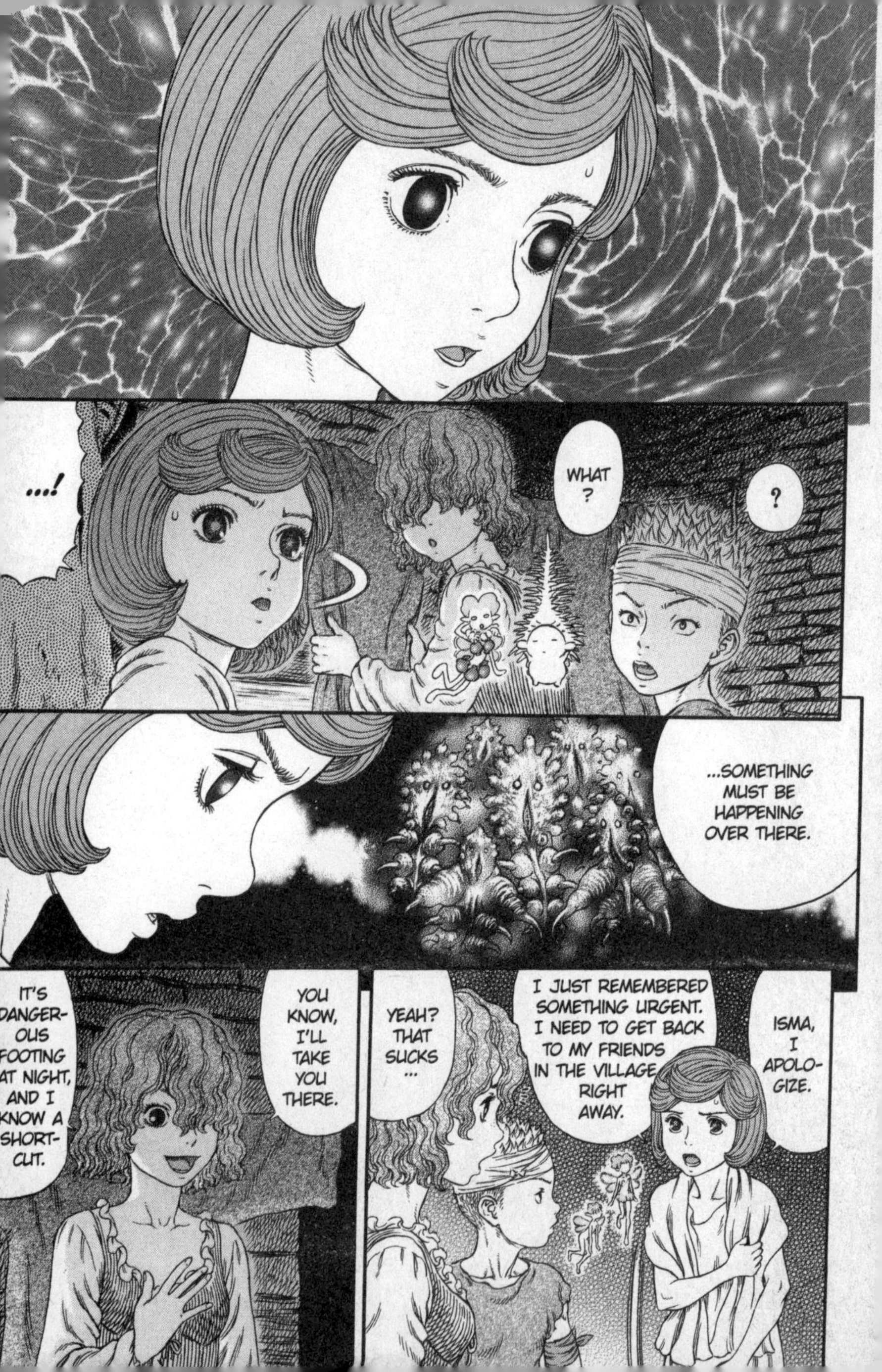
?
WHAT ?
...!
...SOMETHING MUST BE HAPPENING OVER THERE.
ISMA, I APOLOGIZE.
I JUST REMEMBERED SOMETHING URGENT. I NEED TO GET BACK TO MY FRIENDS IN THE VILLAGE RIGHT AWAY.
YEAH? THAT SUCKS...
YOU KNOW, I'LL TAKE YOU THERE.
IT'S DANGEROUS FOOTING AT NIGHT, AND I KNOW A SHORTCUT.

幻造世界〈ファンタジア〉篇／妖精島の章

人触手

HUMAN TENTACLES

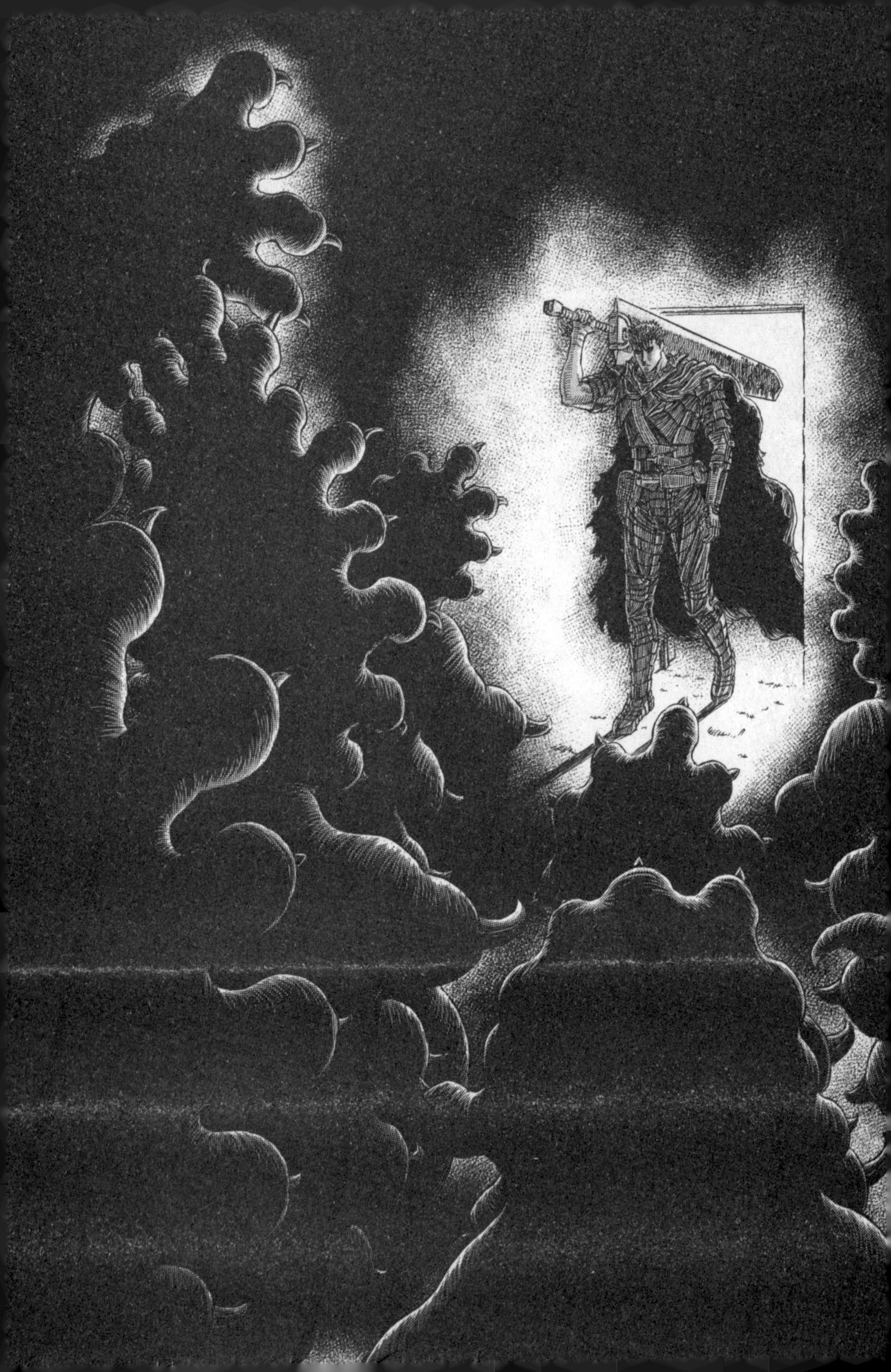

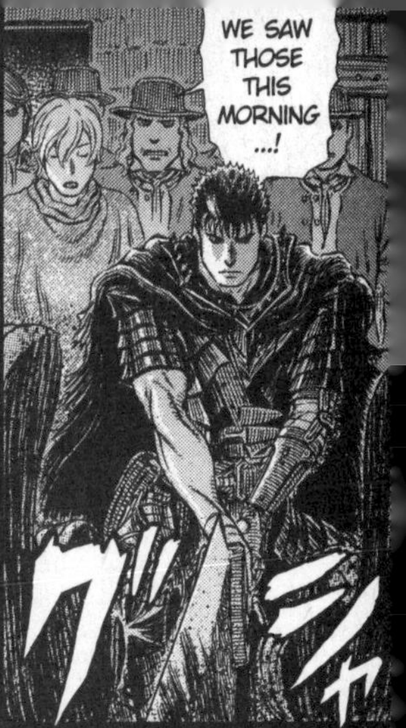
WE SAW THOSE THIS MORNING ...!

*FX: GLCH

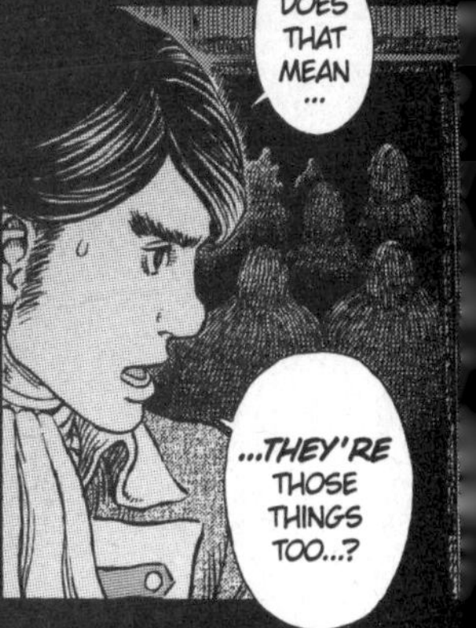
DOES THAT MEAN ...
...THEY'RE THOSE THINGS TOO...?

*FX: GCHAK

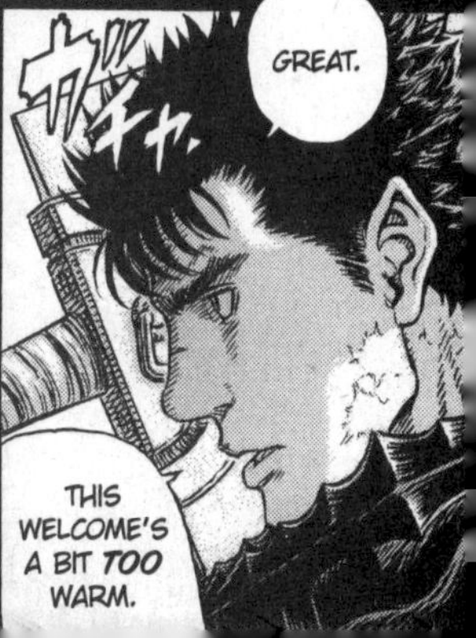
GREAT.
THIS WELCOME'S A BIT TOO WARM.

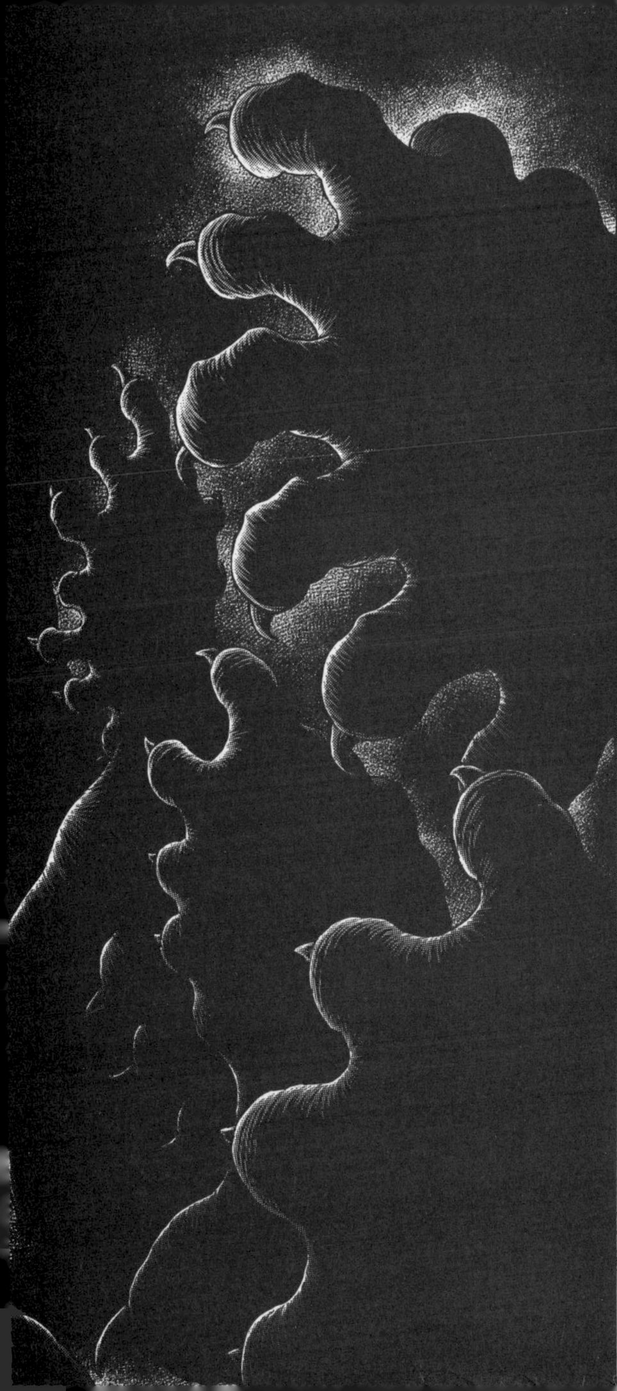

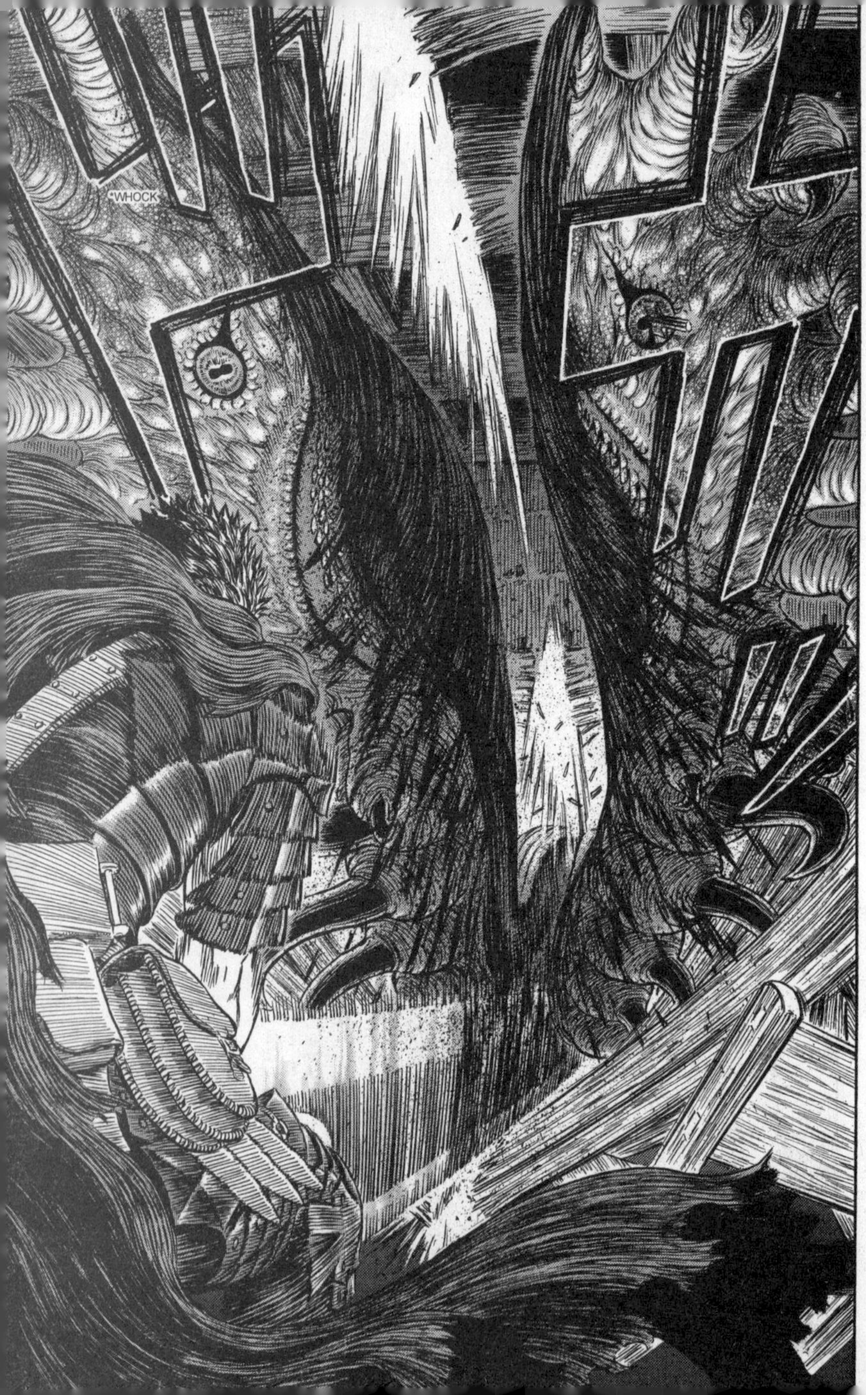
*WHOCK

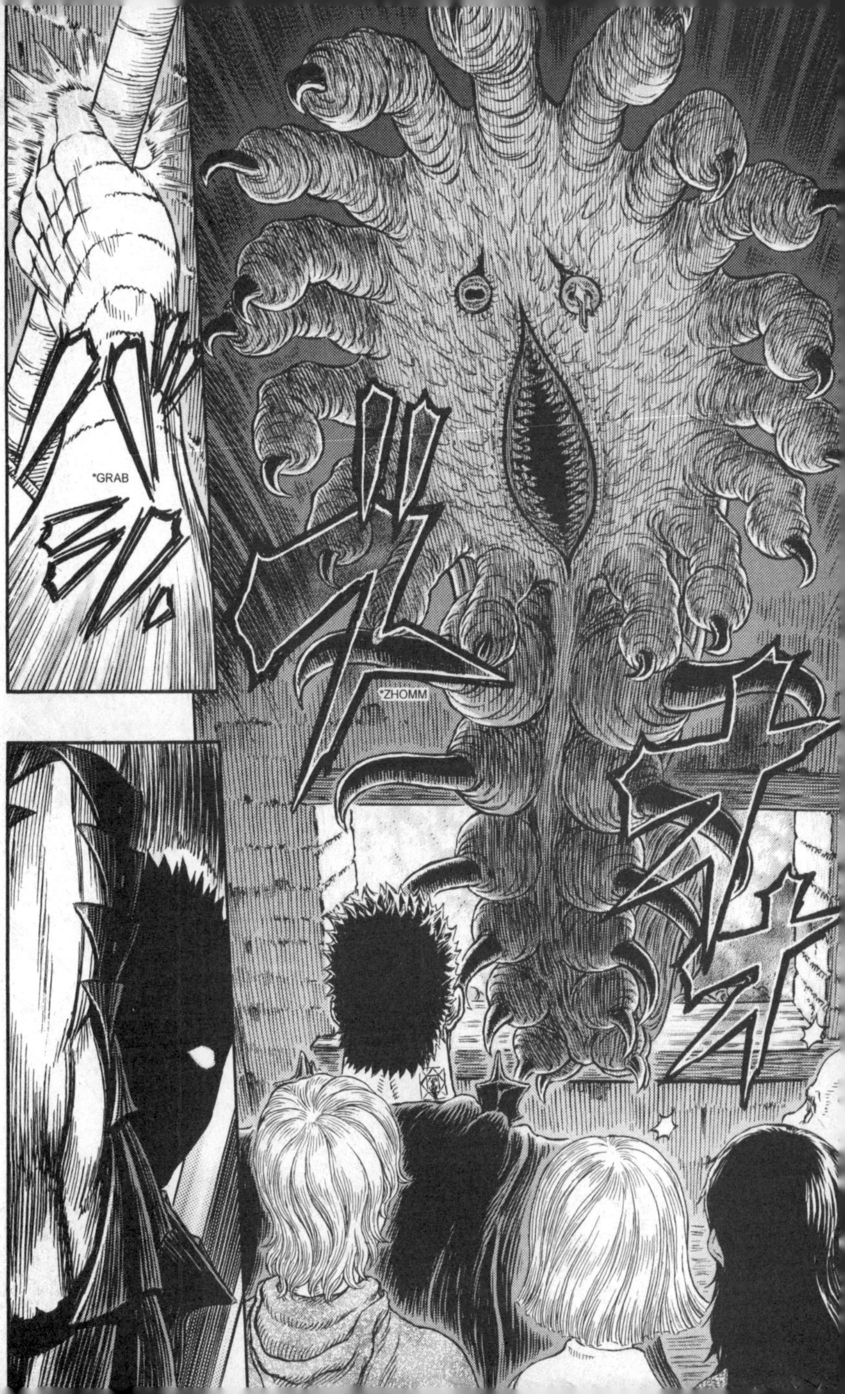
*ZHOMM
*GRAB

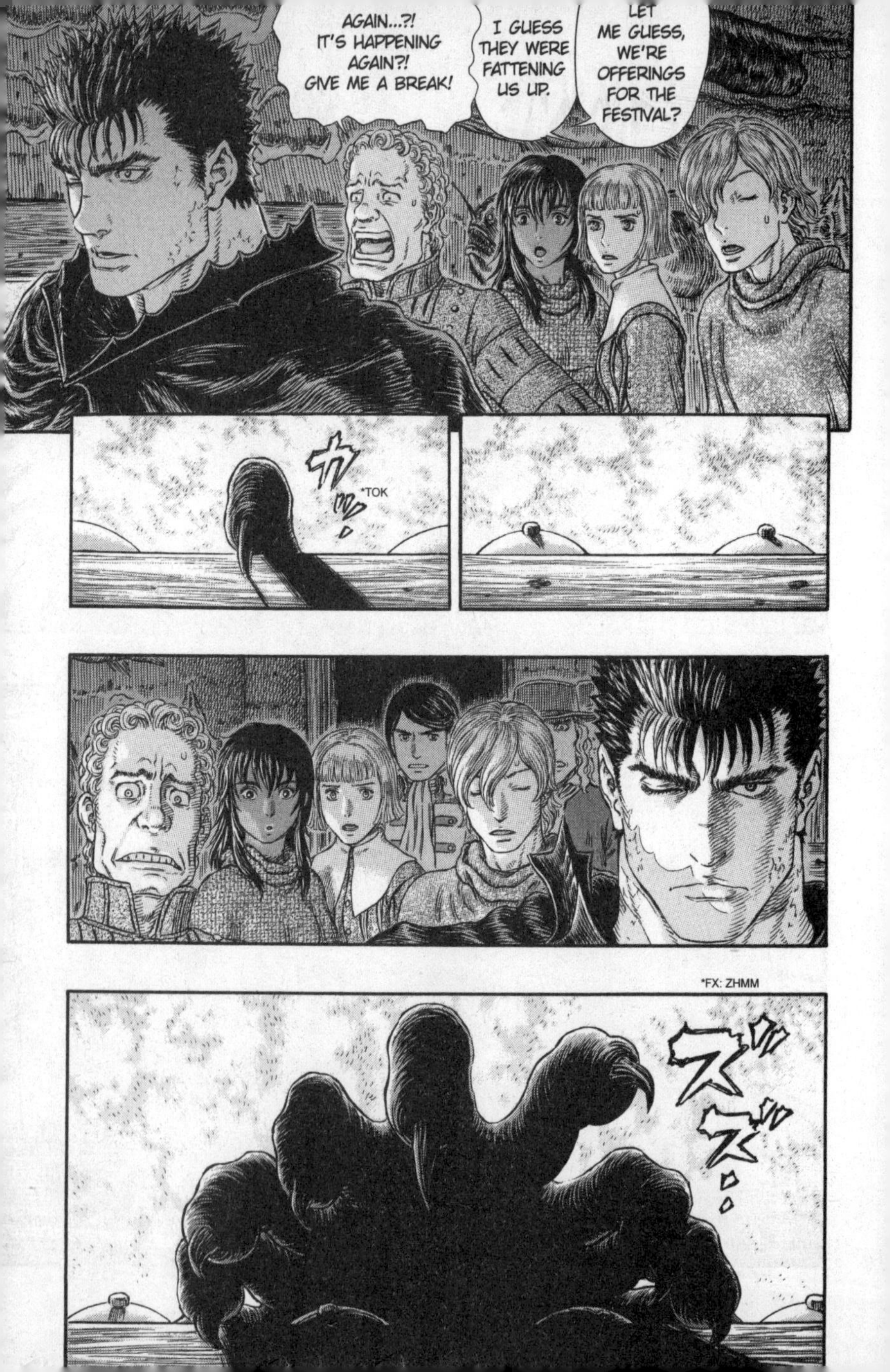
LET ME GUESS, WE'RE OFFERINGS FOR THE FESTIVAL?
I GUESS THEY WERE FATTENING US UP.
AGAIN...?! IT'S HAPPENING AGAIN?! GIVE ME A BREAK!
*TOK
*FX: ZHMM

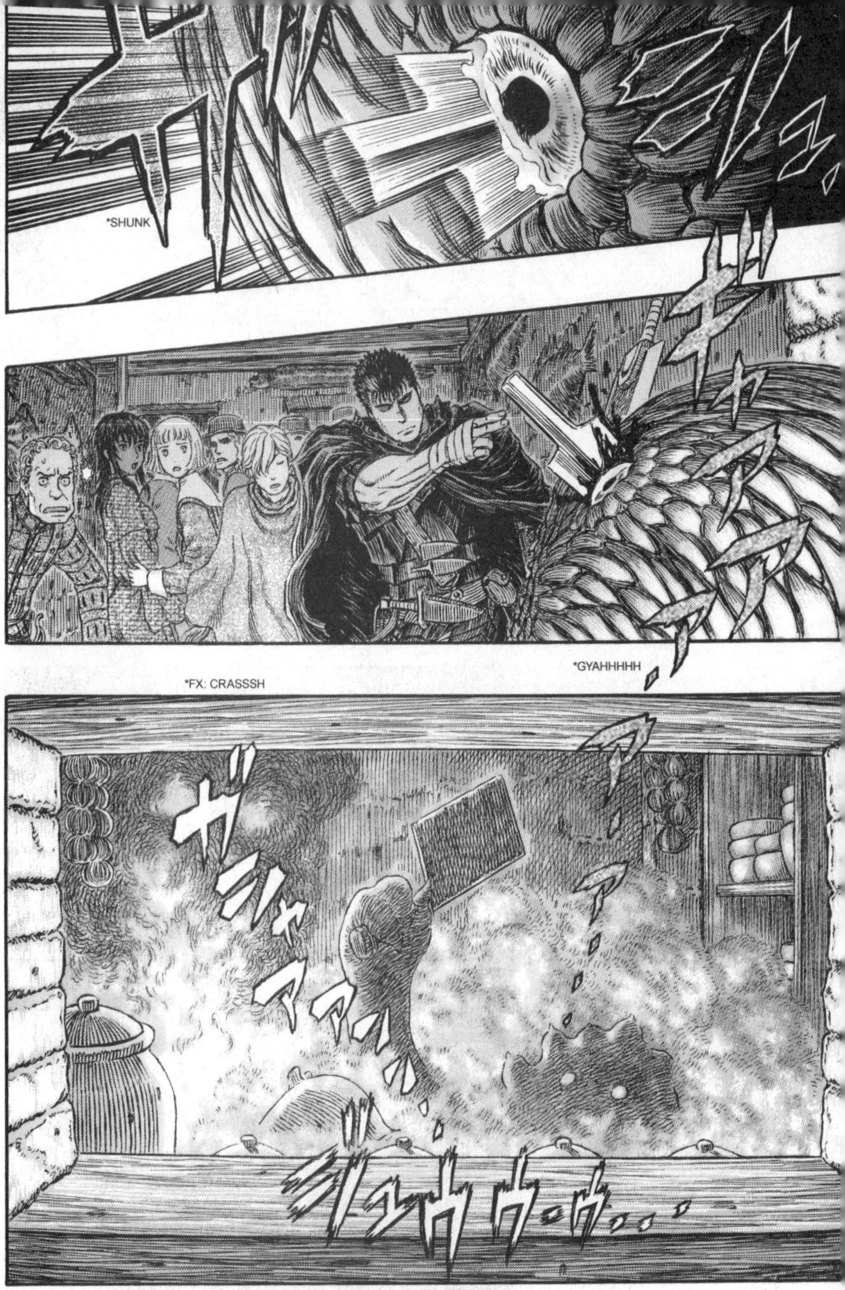
*SHUNK
*GYAHHHHH
*FX: CRASSSH
*FX: JSSHHHH

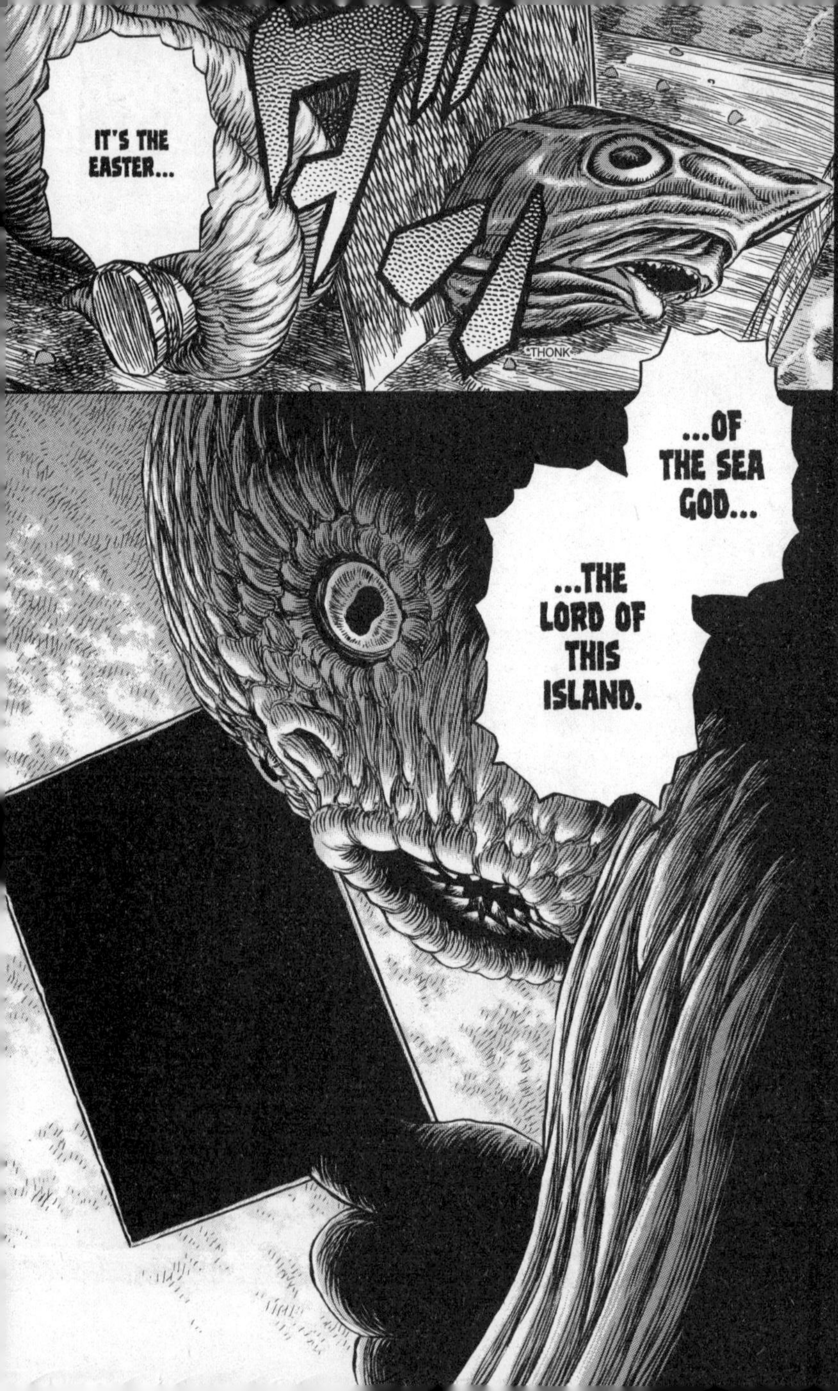
IT'S THE EASTER...
THONK
...OF THE SEA GOD...
...THE LORD OF THIS ISLAND.

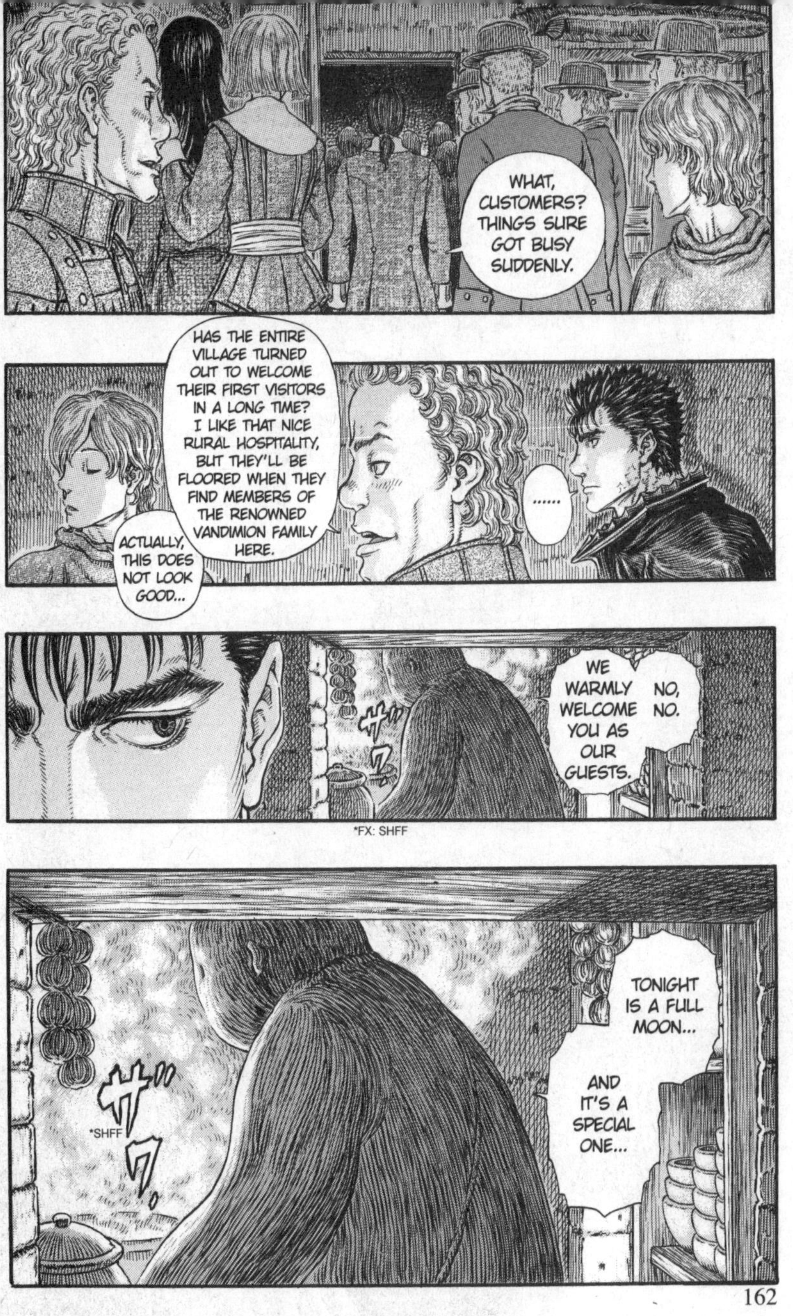
WHAT, CUSTOMERS? THINGS SURE GOT BUSY SUDDENLY.
......
HAS THE ENTIRE VILLAGE TURNED OUT TO WELCOME THEIR FIRST VISITORS IN A LONG TIME? I LIKE THAT NICE RURAL HOSPITALITY, BUT THEY'LL BE FLOORED WHEN THEY FIND MEMBERS OF THE RENOWNED VANDIMION FAMILY HERE.
ACTUALLY, THIS DOES NOT LOOK GOOD...
NO, NO.
WE WARMLY WELCOME YOU AS OUR GUESTS.
*FX: SHFF
TONIGHT IS A FULL MOON...
AND IT'S A SPECIAL ONE...
*SHFF

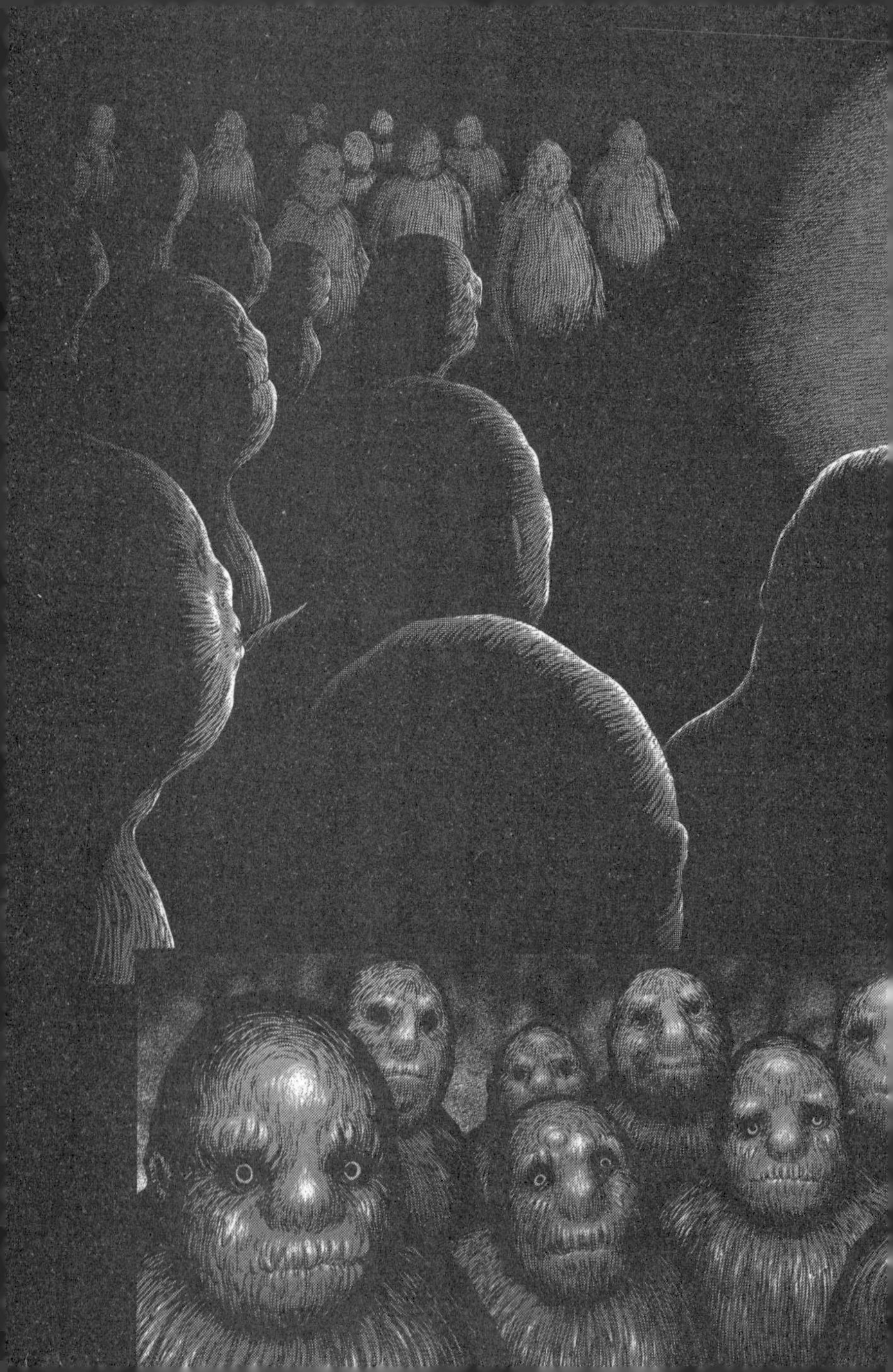

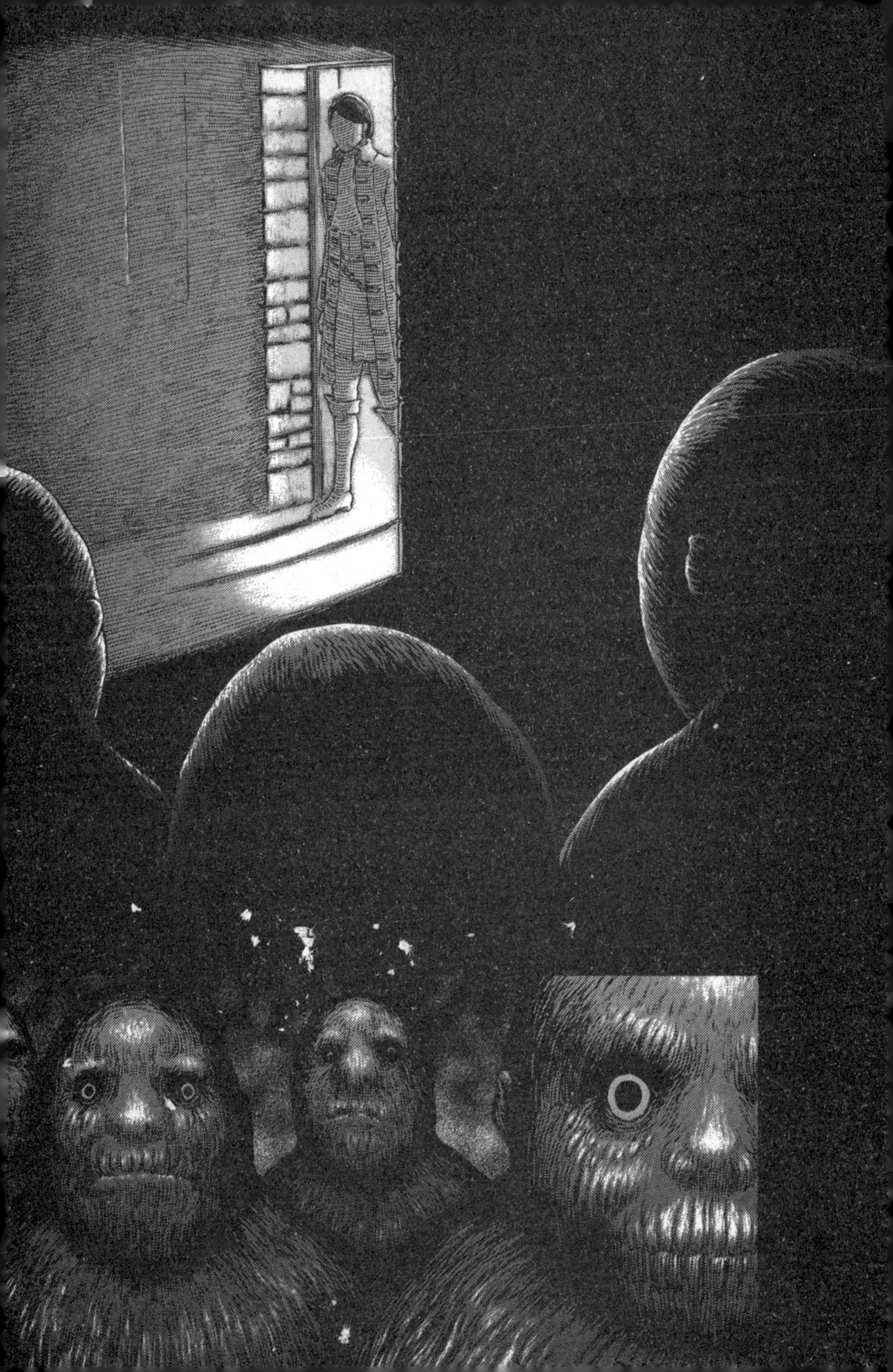

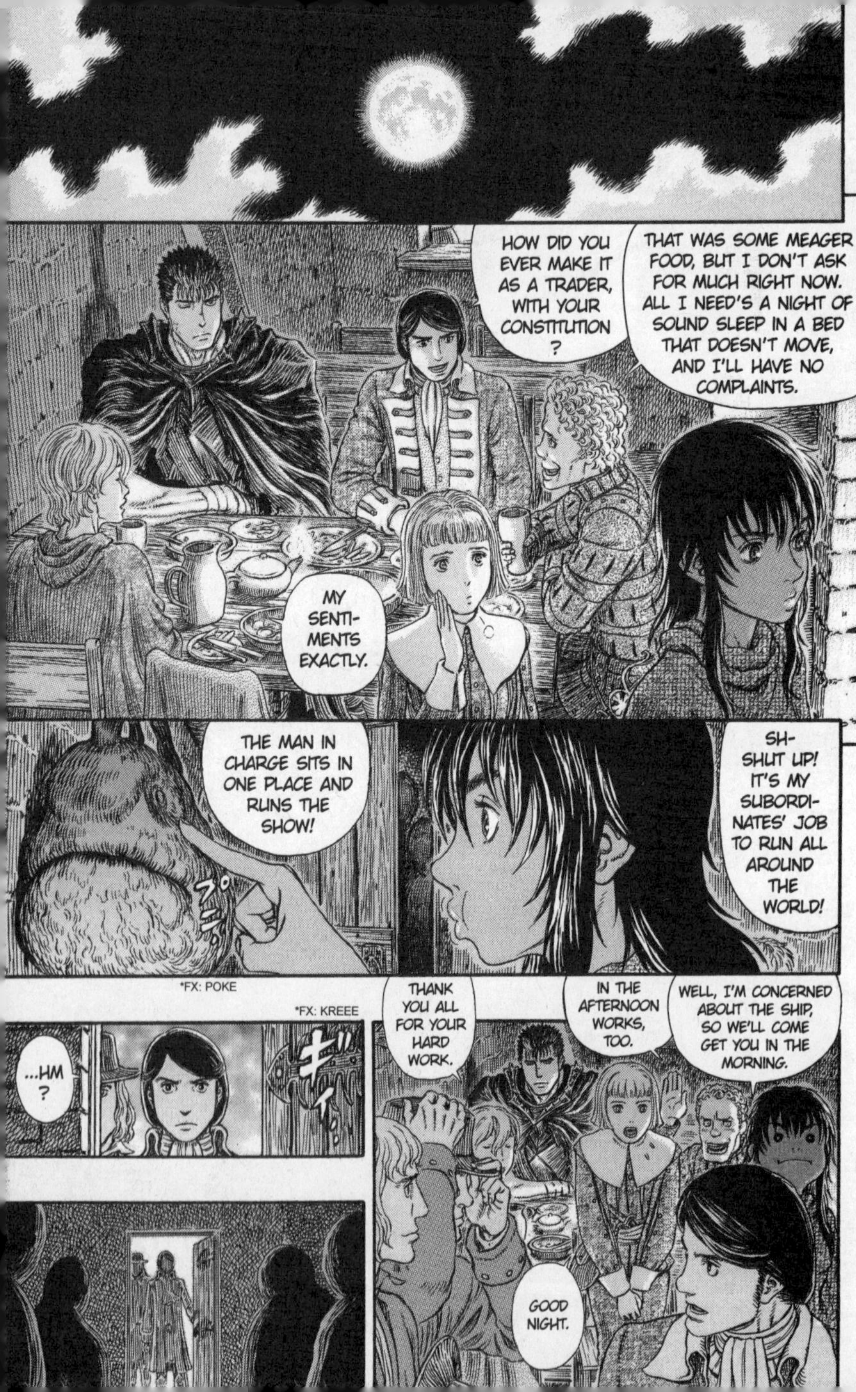
THAT WAS SOME MEAGER FOOD, BUT I DON'T ASK FOR MUCH RIGHT NOW. ALL I NEED'S A NIGHT OF SOUND SLEEP IN A BED THAT DOESN'T MOVE, AND I'LL HAVE NO COMPLAINTS.
HOW DID YOU EVER MAKE IT AS A TRADER, WITH YOUR CONSTITUTION?
MY SENTI-MENTS EXACTLY.
SH-SHUT UP! IT'S MY SUBORDI-NATES' JOB TO RUN ALL AROUND THE WORLD!
THE MAN IN CHARGE SITS IN ONE PLACE AND RUNS THE SHOW!
*FX: POKE
WELL, I'M CONCERNED ABOUT THE SHIP, SO WE'LL COME GET YOU IN THE MORNING.
IN THE AFTERNOON WORKS, TOO.
THANK YOU ALL FOR YOUR HARD WORK.
GOOD NIGHT.
*FX: KREEE
...HM?

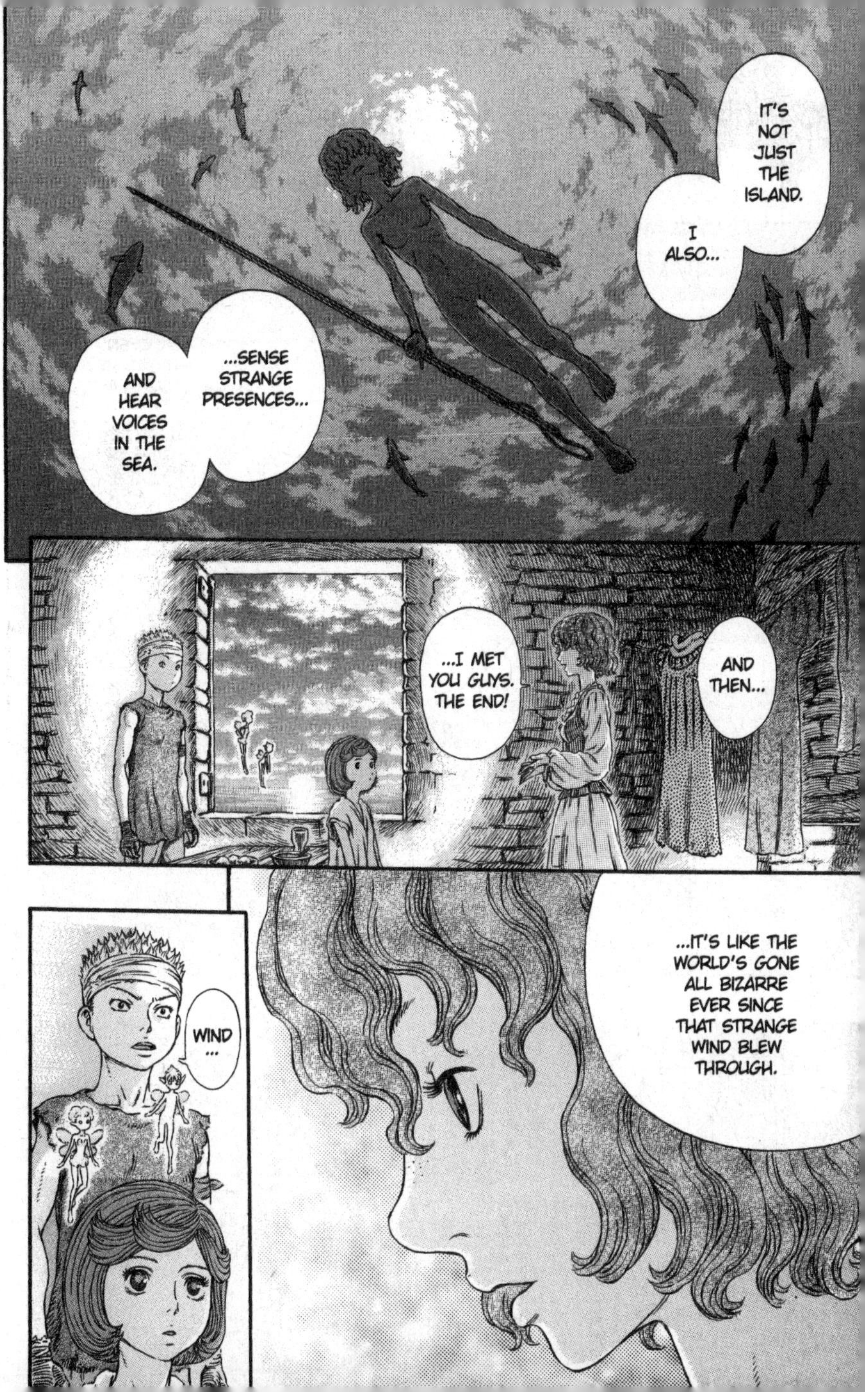
IT'S NOT JUST THE ISLAND.
I ALSO...
...SENSE STRANGE PRESENCES...
AND HEAR VOICES IN THE SEA.
AND THEN...
...I MET YOU GUYS. THE END!
...IT'S LIKE THE WORLD'S GONE ALL BIZARRE EVER SINCE THAT STRANGE WIND BLEW THROUGH.
WIND ...

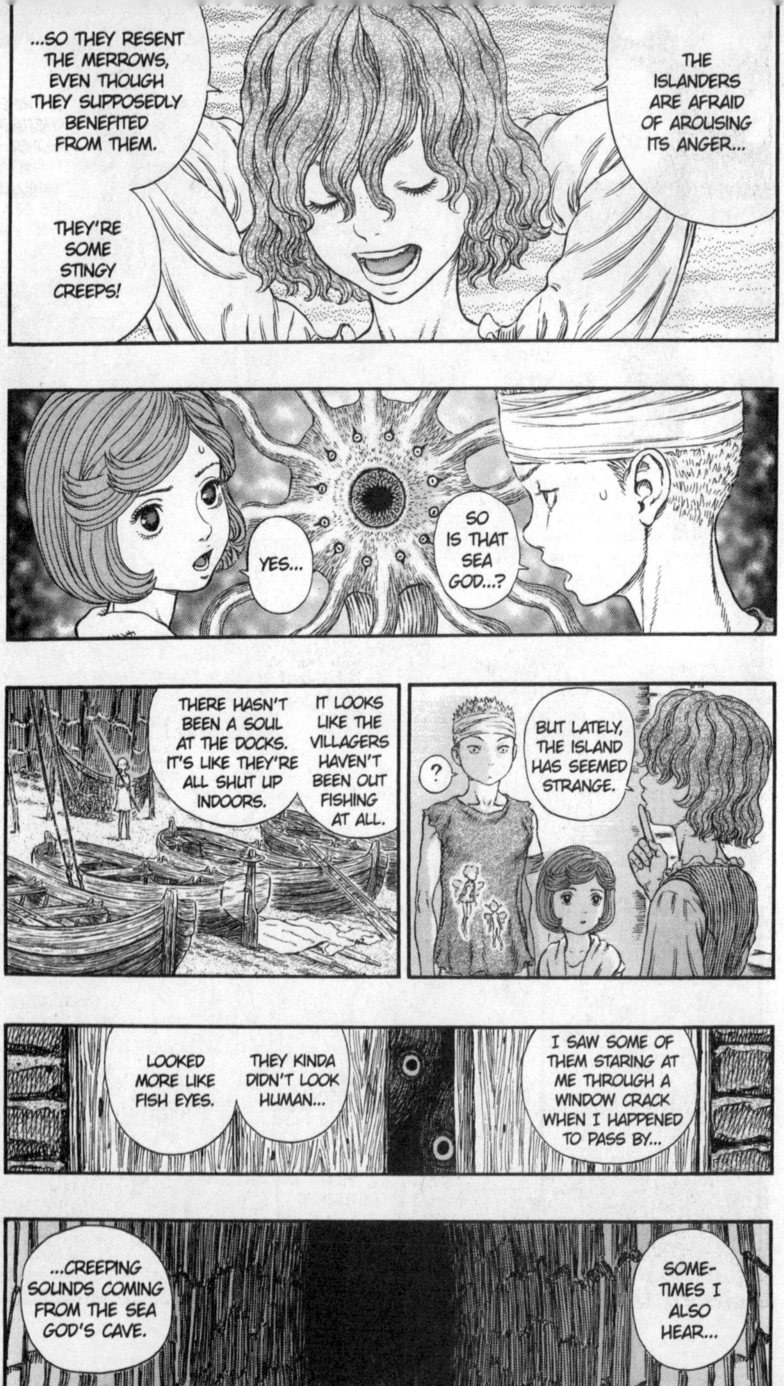
THE ISLANDERS ARE AFRAID OF AROUSING ITS ANGER...
...SO THEY RESENT THE MERROWS, EVEN THOUGH THEY SUPPOSEDLY BENEFITED FROM THEM.
THEY'RE SOME STINGY CREEPS!
SO IS THAT SEA GOD...?
YES...
BUT LATELY, THE ISLAND HAS SEEMED STRANGE.
?
IT LOOKS LIKE THE VILLAGERS HAVEN'T BEEN OUT FISHING AT ALL.
THERE HASN'T BEEN A SOUL AT THE DOCKS. IT'S LIKE THEY'RE ALL SHUT UP INDOORS.
I SAW SOME OF THEM STARING AT ME THROUGH A WINDOW CRACK WHEN I HAPPENED TO PASS BY...
THEY KINDA DIDN'T LOOK HUMAN...
LOOKED MORE LIKE FISH EYES.
SOME-TIMES I ALSO HEAR...
...CREEPING SOUNDS COMING FROM THE SEA GOD'S CAVE.

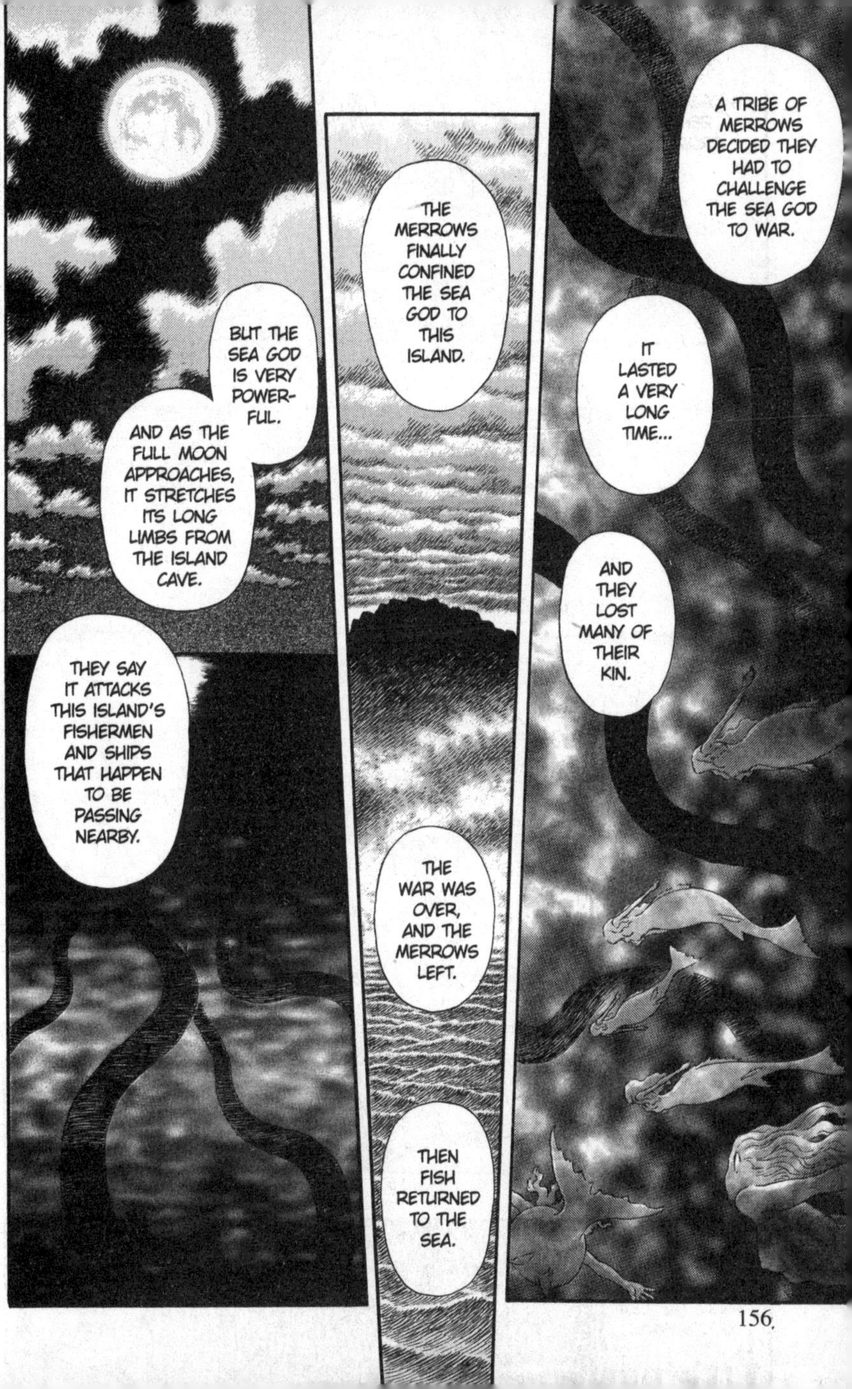
A TRIBE OF MERROWS DECIDED THEY HAD TO CHALLENGE THE SEA GOD TO WAR.
IT LASTED A VERY LONG TIME...
AND THEY LOST MANY OF THEIR KIN.
THE MERROWS FINALLY CONFINED THE SEA GOD TO THIS ISLAND.
THE WAR WAS OVER, AND THE MERROWS LEFT.
THEN FISH RETURNED TO THE SEA.
BUT THE SEA GOD IS VERY POWER-FUL.
AND AS THE FULL MOON APPROACHES, IT STRETCHES ITS LONG LIMBS FROM THE ISLAND CAVE.
THEY SAY IT ATTACKS THIS ISLAND'S FISHERMEN AND SHIPS THAT HAPPEN TO BE PASSING NEARBY.

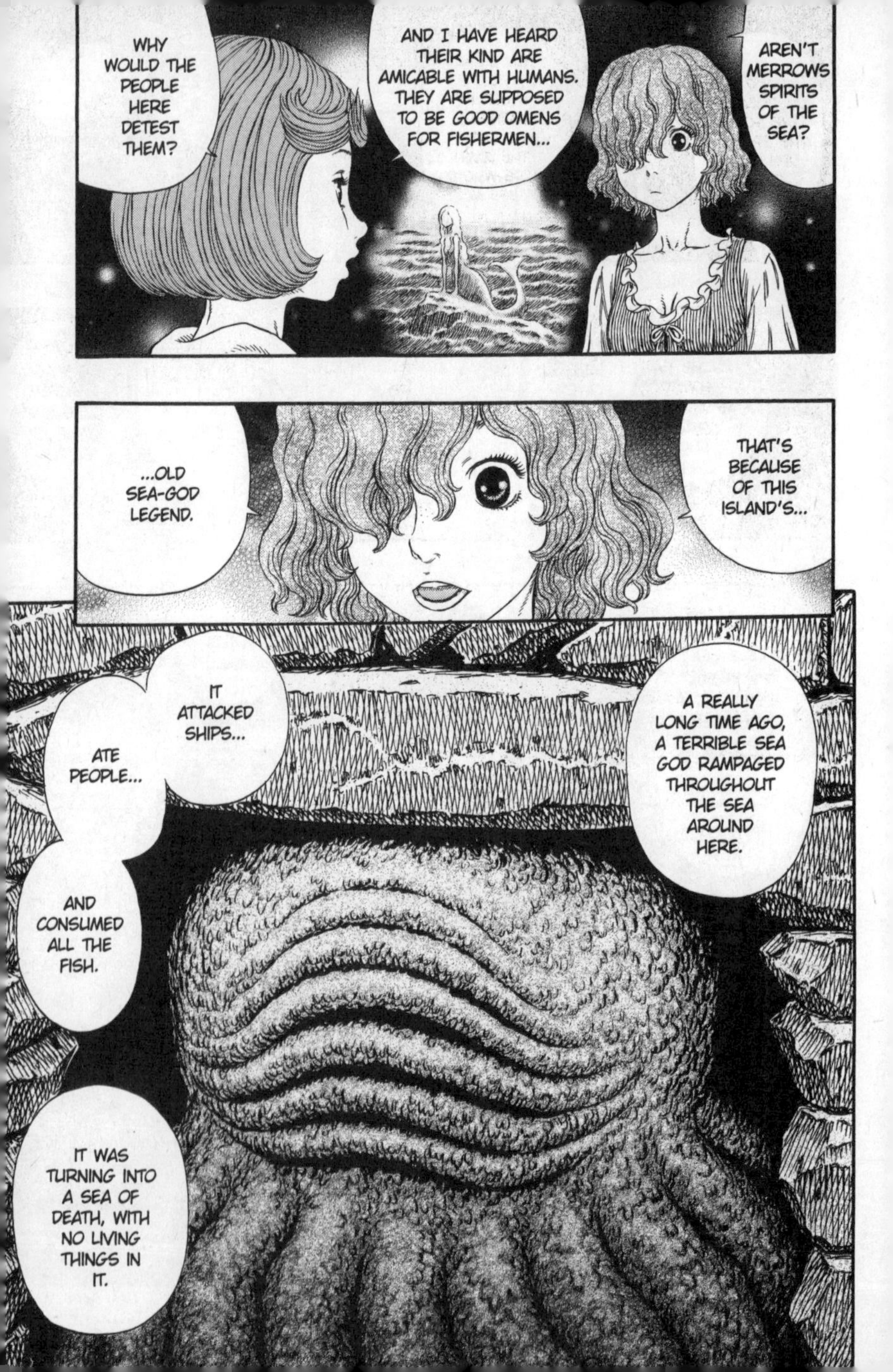
AREN'T MERROWS SPIRITS OF THE SEA?
AND I HAVE HEARD THEIR KIND ARE AMICABLE WITH HUMANS. THEY ARE SUPPOSED TO BE GOOD OMENS FOR FISHERMEN...
WHY WOULD THE PEOPLE HERE DETEST THEM?
THAT'S BECAUSE OF THIS ISLAND'S...
...OLD SEA-GOD LEGEND.
A REALLY LONG TIME AGO, A TERRIBLE SEA GOD RAMPAGED THROUGHOUT THE SEA AROUND HERE.
IT ATTACKED SHIPS...
ATE PEOPLE...
AND CONSUMED ALL THE FISH.
IT WAS TURNING INTO A SEA OF DEATH, WITH NO LIVING THINGS IN IT.

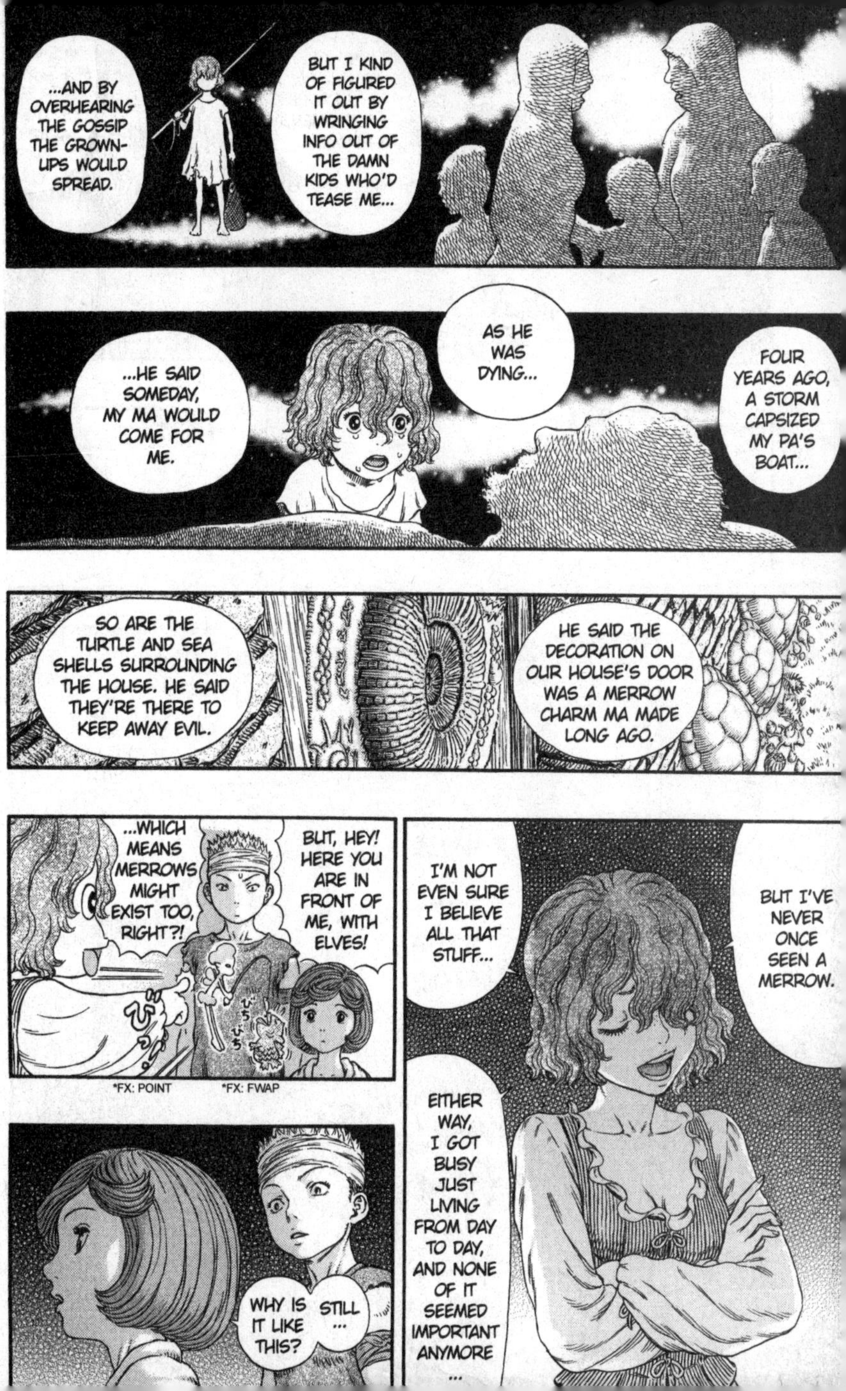
BUT I KIND OF FIGURED IT OUT BY WRINGING INFO OUT OF THE DAMN KIDS WHO'D TEASE ME...
...AND BY OVERHEARING THE GOSSIP THE GROWN-UPS WOULD SPREAD.
FOUR YEARS AGO, A STORM CAPSIZED MY PA'S BOAT...
AS HE WAS DYING...
...HE SAID SOMEDAY, MY MA WOULD COME FOR ME.
HE SAID THE DECORATION ON OUR HOUSE'S DOOR WAS A MERROW CHARM MA MADE LONG AGO.
SO ARE THE TURTLE AND SEA SHELLS SURROUNDING THE HOUSE. HE SAID THEY'RE THERE TO KEEP AWAY EVIL.
BUT I'VE NEVER ONCE SEEN A MERROW.
I'M NOT EVEN SURE I BELIEVE ALL THAT STUFF...
EITHER WAY, I GOT BUSY JUST LIVING FROM DAY TO DAY, AND NONE OF IT SEEMED IMPORTANT ANYMORE ...
BUT, HEY! HERE YOU ARE IN FRONT OF ME, WITH ELVES!
...WHICH MEANS MERROWS MIGHT EXIST TOO, RIGHT?!
*FX: POINT
*FX: FWAP
STILL ...
WHY IS IT LIKE THIS?

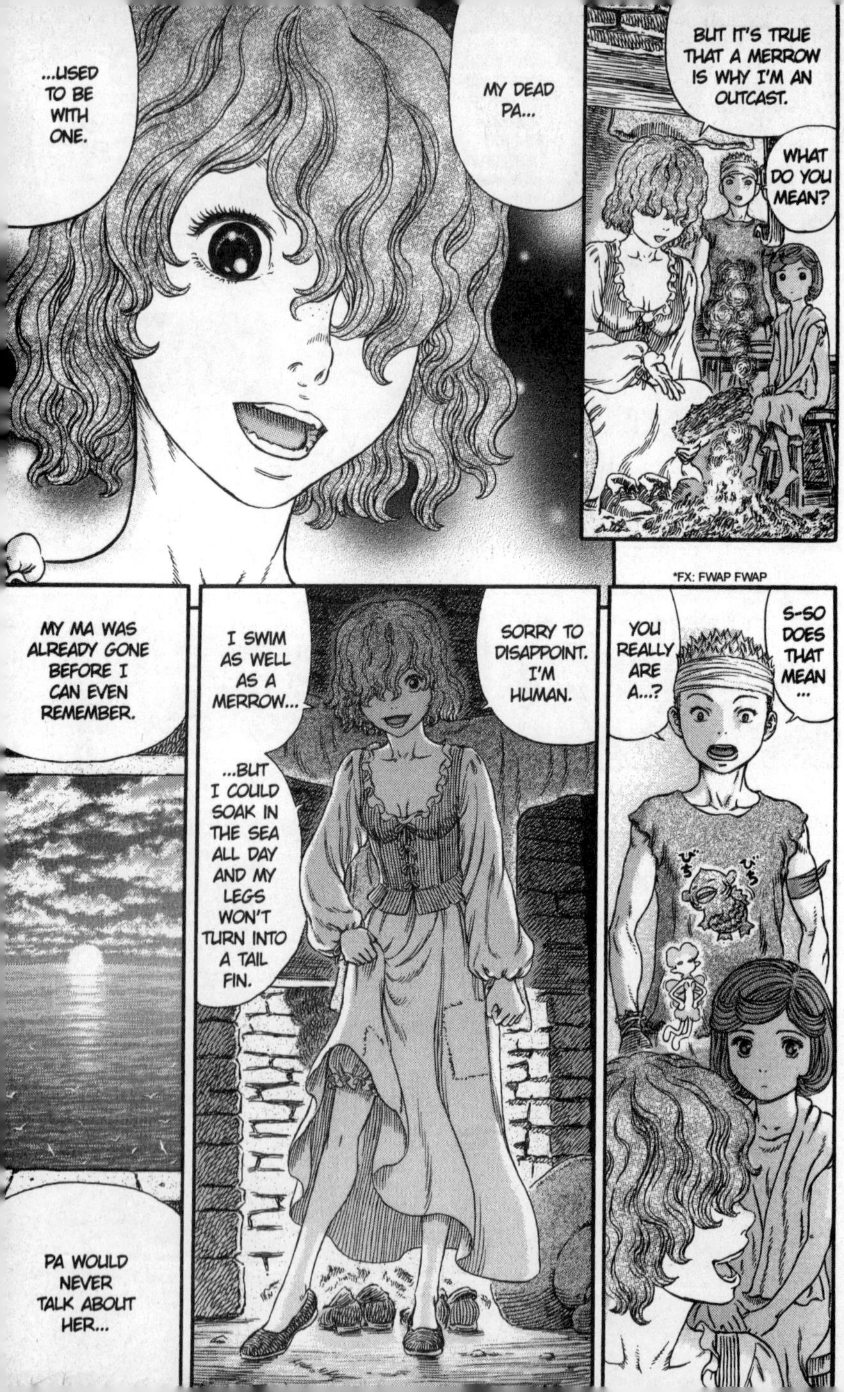
BUT IT'S TRUE THAT A MERROW IS WHY I'M AN OUTCAST.
WHAT DO YOU MEAN?
*FX: FWAP FWAP
MY DEAD PA...
...USED TO BE WITH ONE.
S-SO DOES THAT MEAN ...
YOU REALLY ARE A...?
SORRY TO DISAPPOINT. I'M HUMAN.
I SWIM AS WELL AS A MERROW...
...BUT I COULD SOAK IN THE SEA ALL DAY AND MY LEGS WON'T TURN INTO A TAIL FIN.
MY MA WAS ALREADY GONE BEFORE I CAN EVEN REMEMBER.
PA WOULD NEVER TALK ABOUT HER...

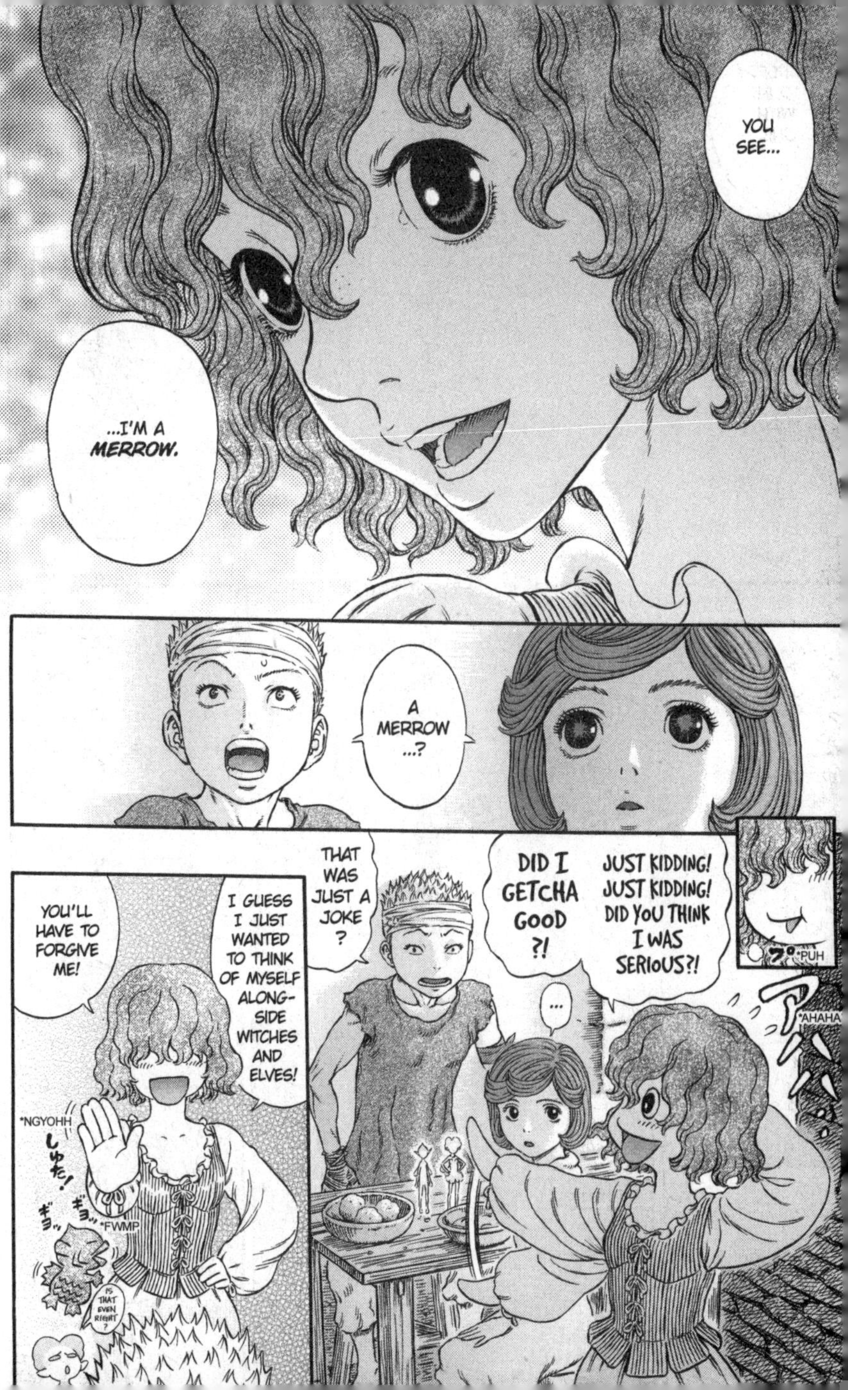
YOU SEE...
...I'M A MERROW.
A MERROW ...?
*PUH
JUST KIDDING! JUST KIDDING! DID YOU THINK I WAS SERIOUS?!
DID I GETCHA GOOD ?!
THAT WAS JUST A JOKE ?
...
*AHAHA
I GUESS I JUST WANTED TO THINK OF MYSELF ALONG-SIDE WITCHES AND ELVES!
YOU'LL HAVE TO FORGIVE ME!
*NGYOHH
*FWMP
IS THAT EVEN RIGHT ?

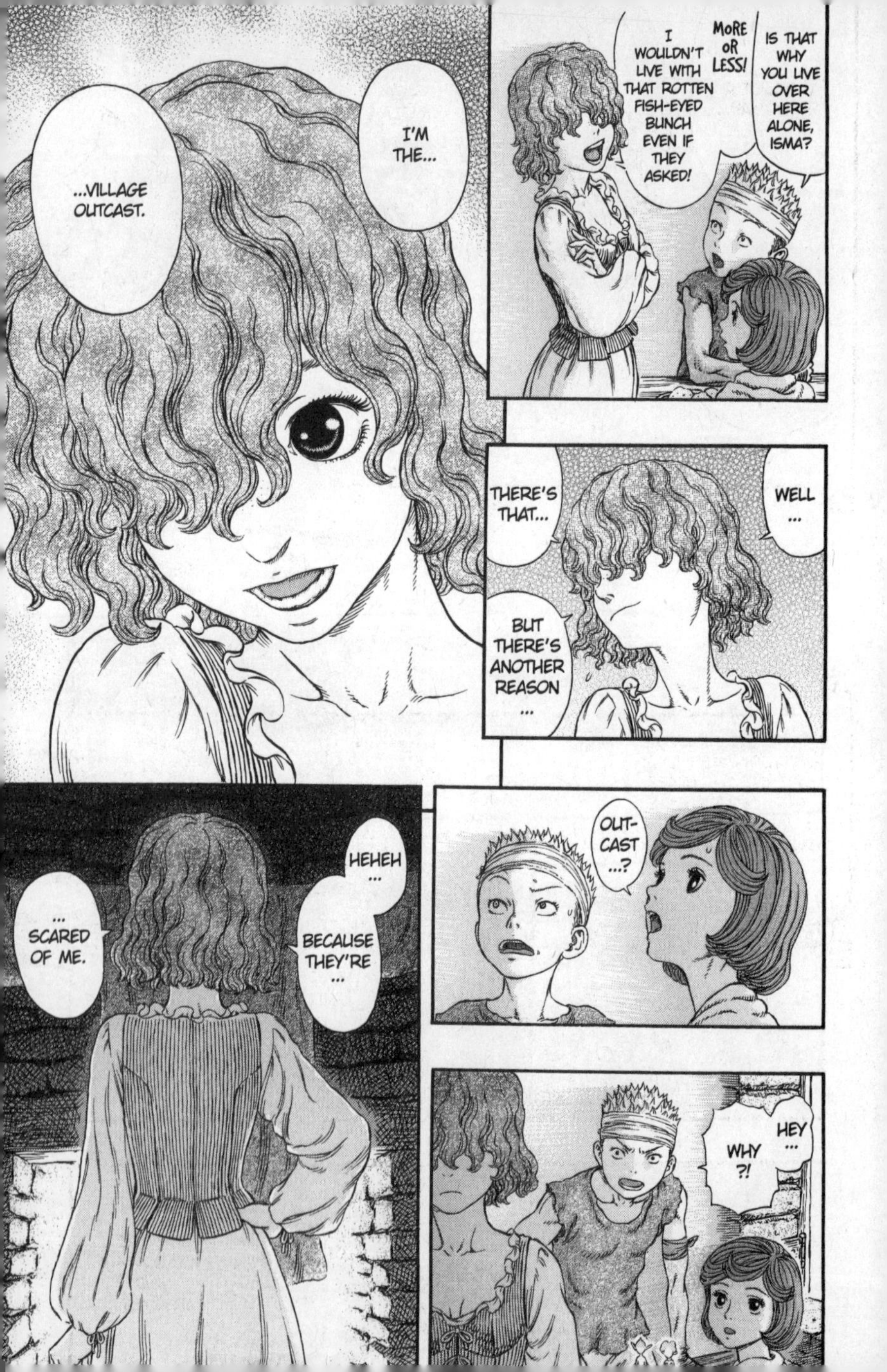
IS THAT WHY YOU LIVE OVER HERE ALONE, ISMA?
MORE OR LESS!
I WOULDN'T LIVE WITH THAT ROTTEN FISH-EYED BUNCH EVEN IF THEY ASKED!
WELL ...
THERE'S THAT...
BUT THERE'S ANOTHER REASON ...
I'M THE...
...VILLAGE OUTCAST.
OUT-CAST ...?
HEY ...
WHY ?!
HEHEH ...
BECAUSE THEY'RE ...
... SCARED OF ME.

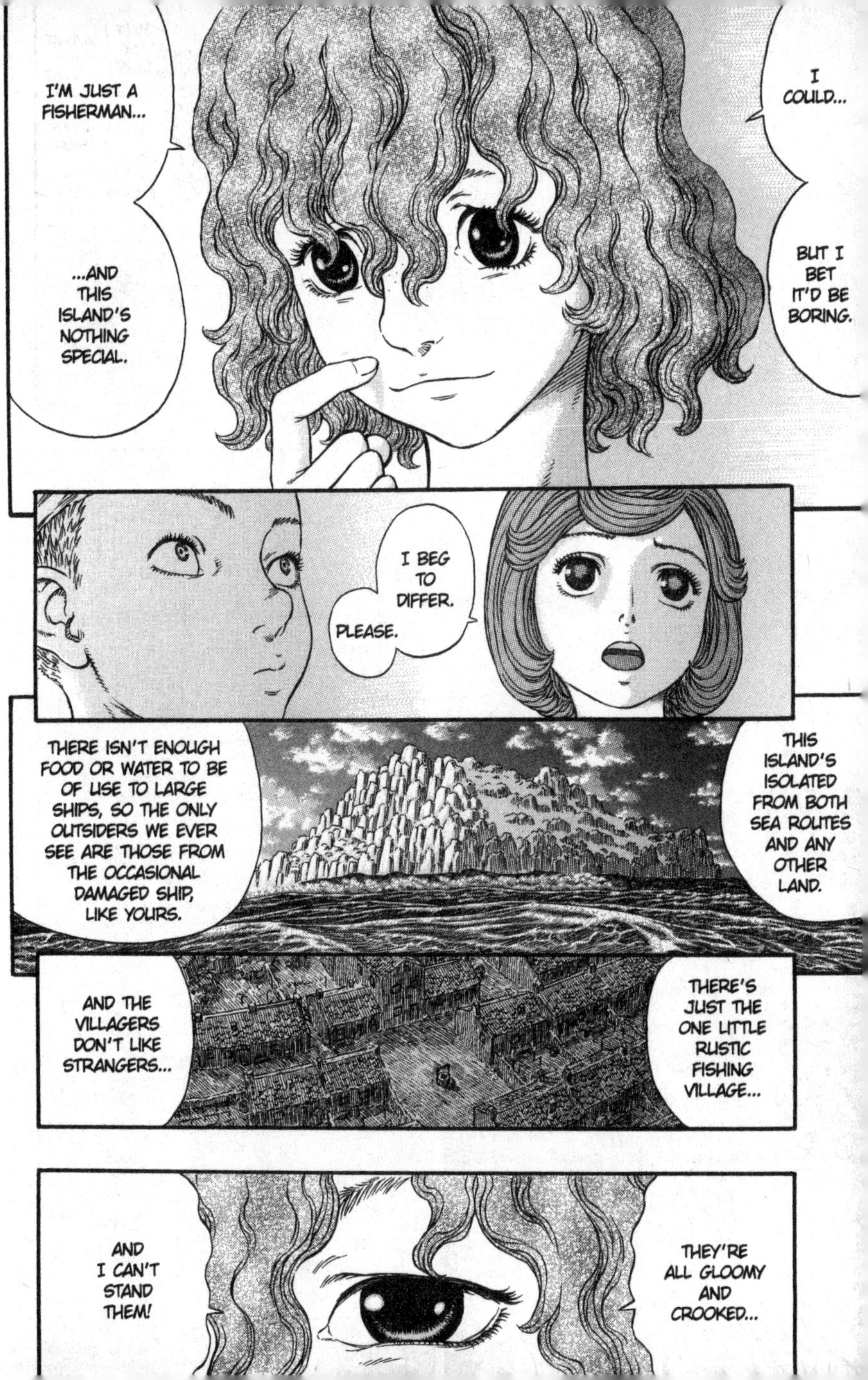
I COULD...
I'M JUST A FISHERMAN...
BUT I BET IT'D BE BORING.
...AND THIS ISLAND'S NOTHING SPECIAL.
I BEG TO DIFFER. PLEASE.
THIS ISLAND'S ISOLATED FROM BOTH SEA ROUTES AND ANY OTHER LAND.
THERE ISN'T ENOUGH FOOD OR WATER TO BE OF USE TO LARGE SHIPS, SO THE ONLY OUTSIDERS WE EVER SEE ARE THOSE FROM THE OCCASIONAL DAMAGED SHIP, LIKE YOURS.
THERE'S JUST THE ONE LITTLE RUSTIC FISHING VILLAGE...
AND THE VILLAGERS DON'T LIKE STRANGERS...
THEY'RE ALL GLOOMY AND CROOKED...
AND I CAN'T STAND THEM!

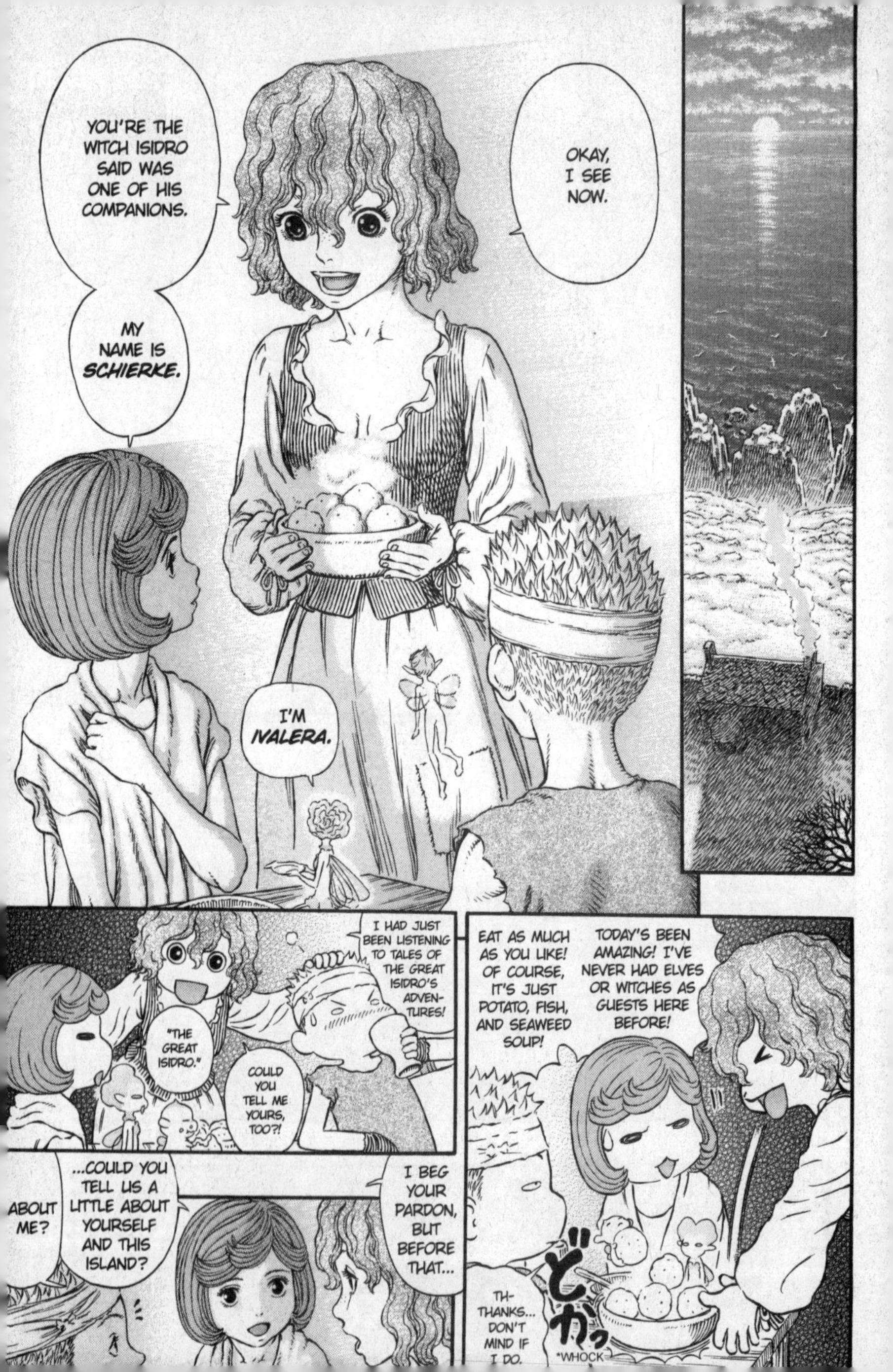
OKAY, I SEE NOW.
YOU'RE THE WITCH ISIDRO SAID WAS ONE OF HIS COMPANIONS.
MY NAME IS **SCHIERKE.**
I'M ***IVALERA.***
TODAY'S BEEN AMAZING! I'VE NEVER HAD ELVES OR WITCHES AS GUESTS HERE BEFORE!
EAT AS MUCH AS YOU LIKE! OF COURSE, IT'S JUST POTATO, FISH, AND SEAWEED SOUP!
どがっ
*WHOCK
TH-THANKS... DON'T MIND IF I DO.
I HAD JUST BEEN LISTENING TO TALES OF THE GREAT ISIDRO'S ADVENTURES!
COULD YOU TELL ME YOURS, TOO?!
"THE GREAT ISIDRO."
I BEG YOUR PARDON, BUT BEFORE THAT...
...COULD YOU TELL US A LITTLE ABOUT YOURSELF AND THIS ISLAND?
ABOUT ME?

幻造世界〈ファンタジア〉篇 妖精島の章

禍海の者共

DENIZENS OF THE SINISTER SEA

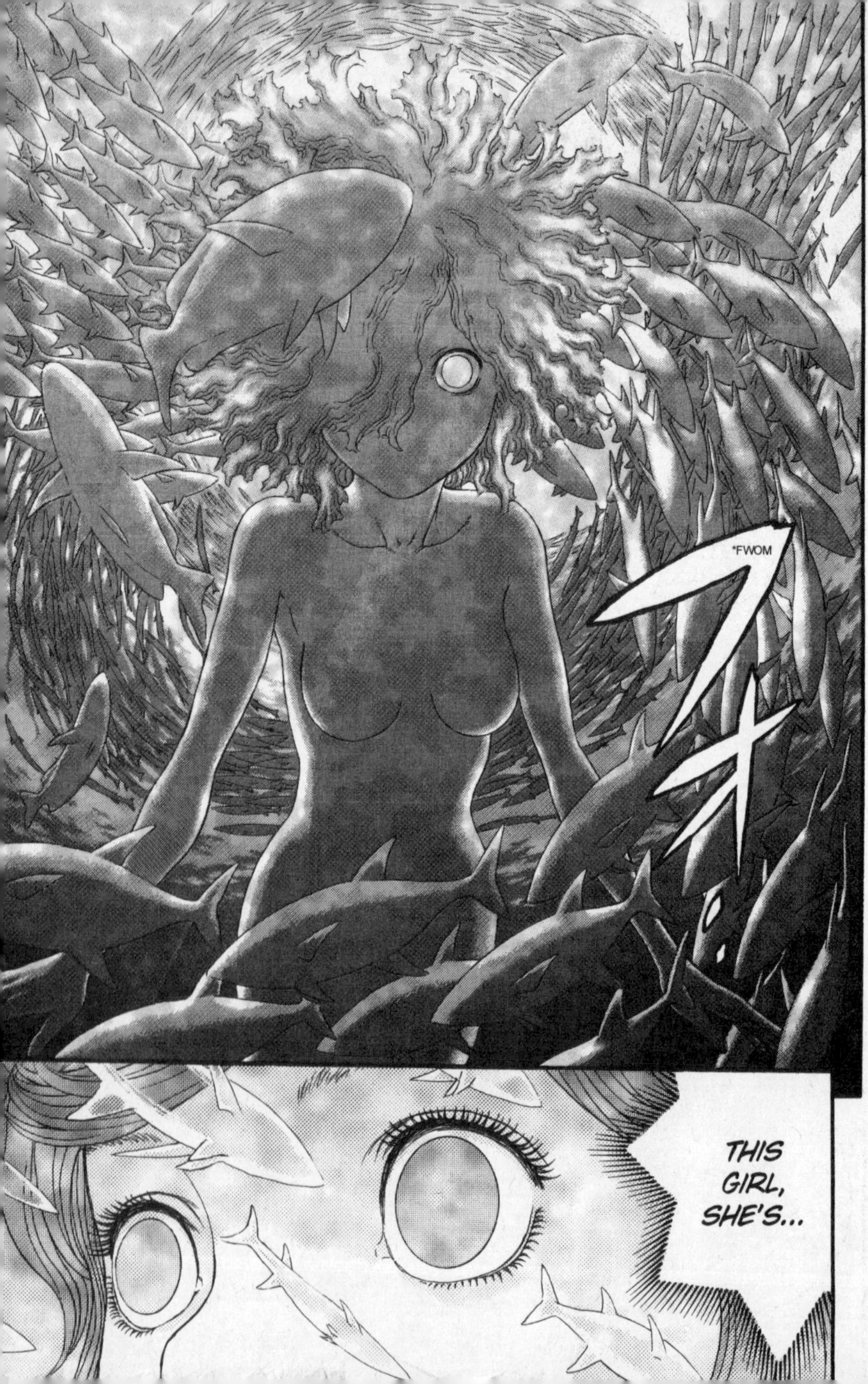
*FWOM
THIS GIRL, SHE'S...

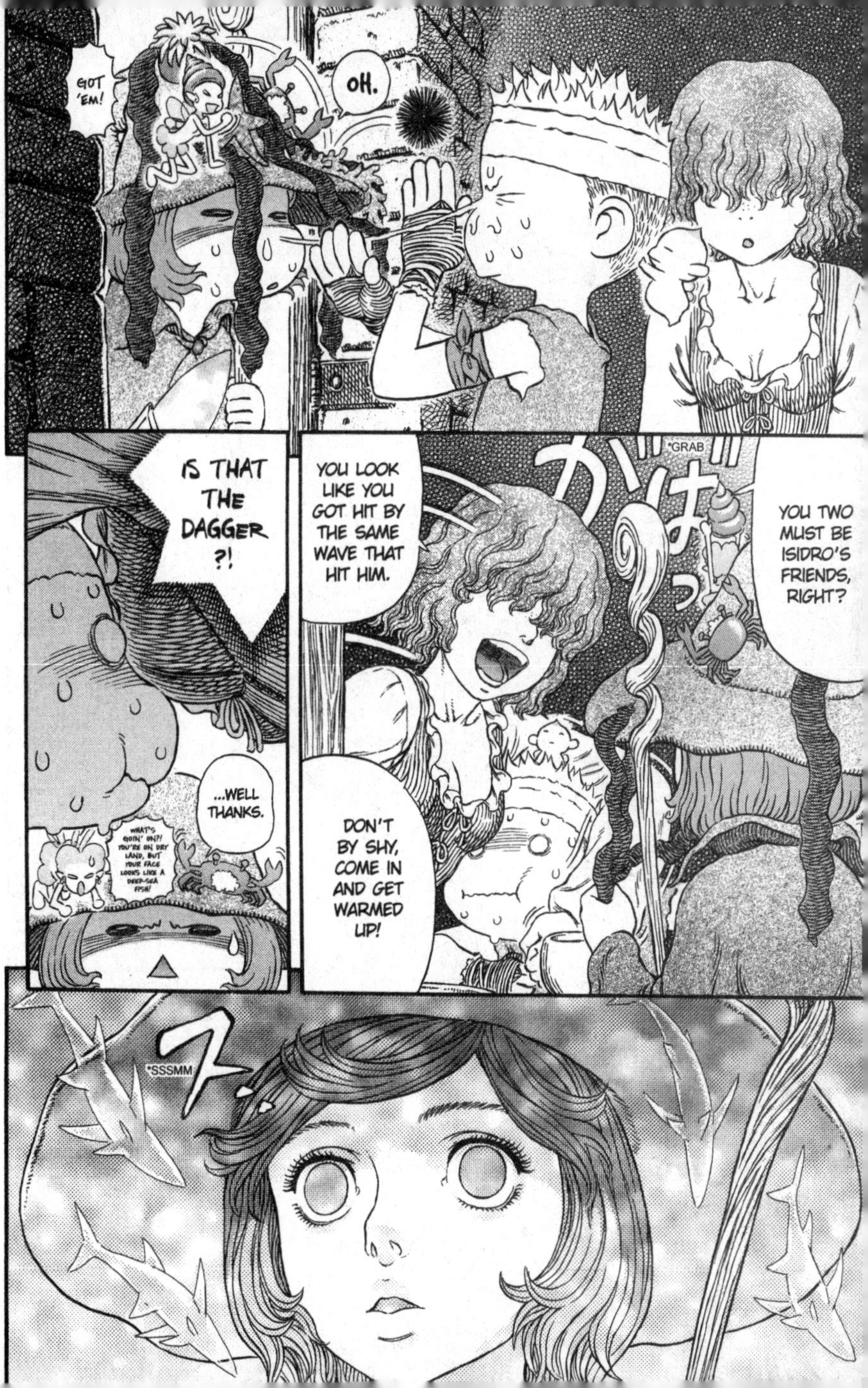
OH.
GOT 'EM!
*GRAB
YOU TWO MUST BE ISIDRO'S FRIENDS, RIGHT?
YOU LOOK LIKE YOU GOT HIT BY THE SAME WAVE THAT HIT HIM.
DON'T BY SHY, COME IN AND GET WARMED UP!
IS THAT THE DAGGER ?!
...WELL THANKS.
WHAT'S GOIN' ON?! YOU'RE ON DRY LAND, BUT YOUR FACE LOOKS LIKE A DEEP-SEA FISH!
*SSSMM

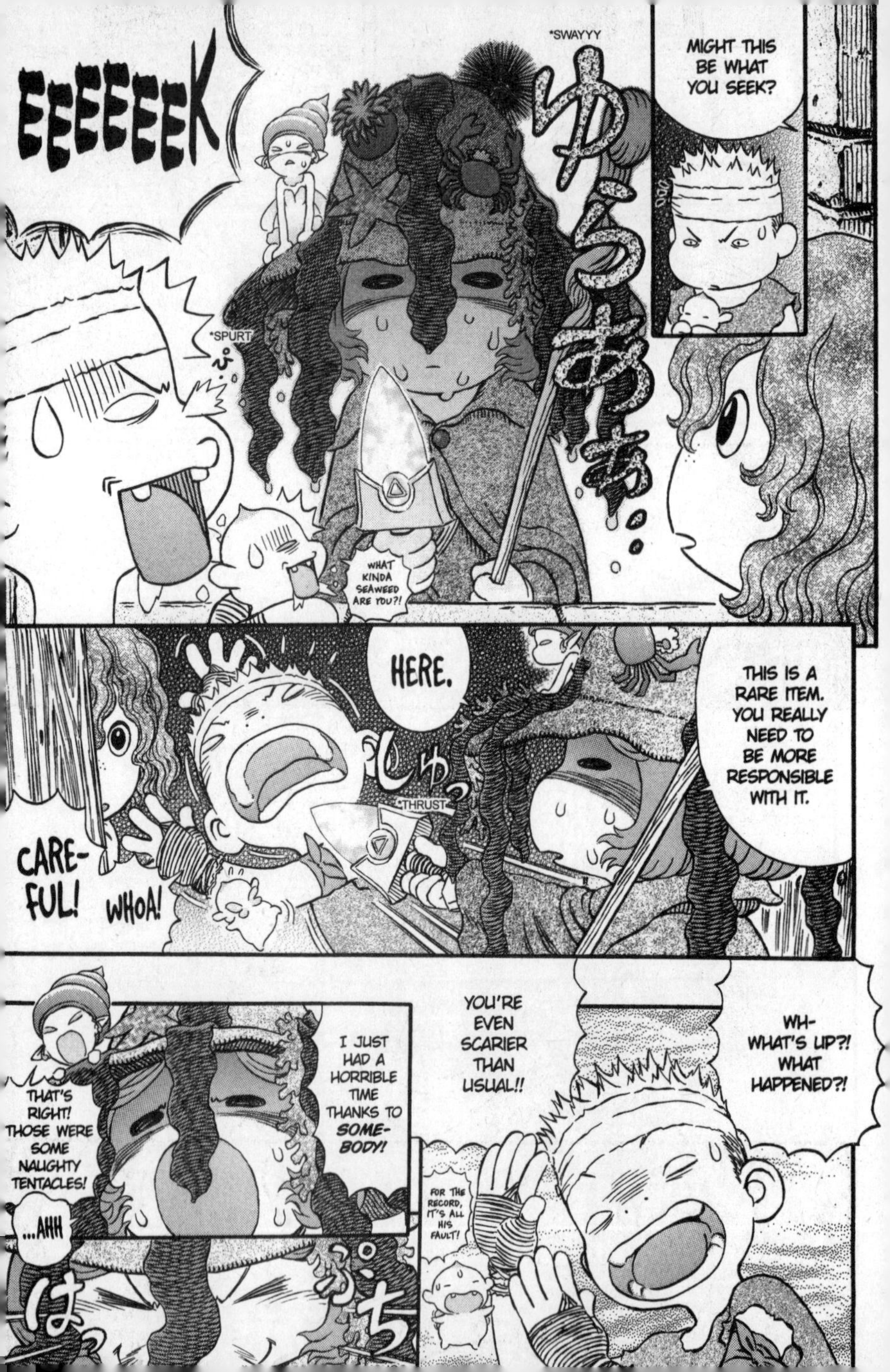
MIGHT THIS BE WHAT YOU SEEK?
ゆらあぁ
*SWAYYY
EEEEEEK
*SPURT
ぷ
WHAT KINDA SEAWEED ARE YOU?!
THIS IS A RARE ITEM. YOU REALLY NEED TO BE MORE RESPONSIBLE WITH IT.
HERE.
しゅっ
*THRUST
WHOA!
CARE-FUL!
WH-WHAT'S UP?! WHAT HAPPENED?!
YOU'RE EVEN SCARIER THAN USUAL!!
FOR THE RECORD, IT'S ALL HIS FAULT!
I JUST HAD A HORRIBLE TIME THANKS TO SOME-BODY!
THAT'S RIGHT! THOSE WERE SOME NAUGHTY TENTACLES!
...AHH
ぷち
はっ

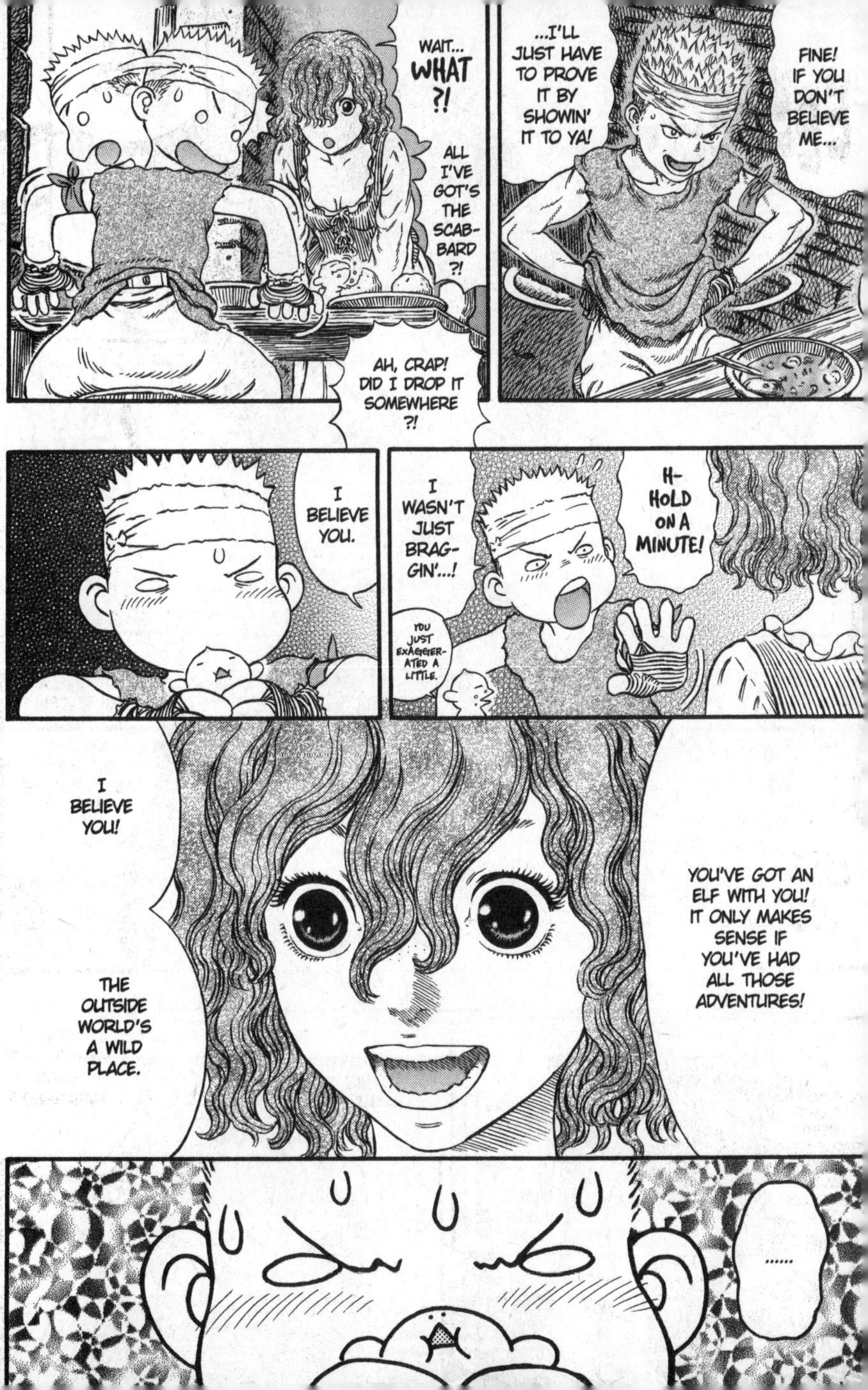
FINE! IF YOU DON'T BELIEVE ME...
...I'LL JUST HAVE TO PROVE IT BY SHOWIN' IT TO YA!
WAIT... WHAT ?!
ALL I'VE GOT'S THE SCABBARD ?!
AH, CRAP! DID I DROP IT SOMEWHERE ?!
H-HOLD ON A MINUTE!
I WASN'T JUST BRAGGIN'...!
YOU JUST EXAGGERATED A LITTLE.
I BELIEVE YOU.
YOU'VE GOT AN ELF WITH YOU! IT ONLY MAKES SENSE IF YOU'VE HAD ALL THOSE ADVENTURES!
I BELIEVE YOU!
THE OUTSIDE WORLD'S A WILD PLACE.
......

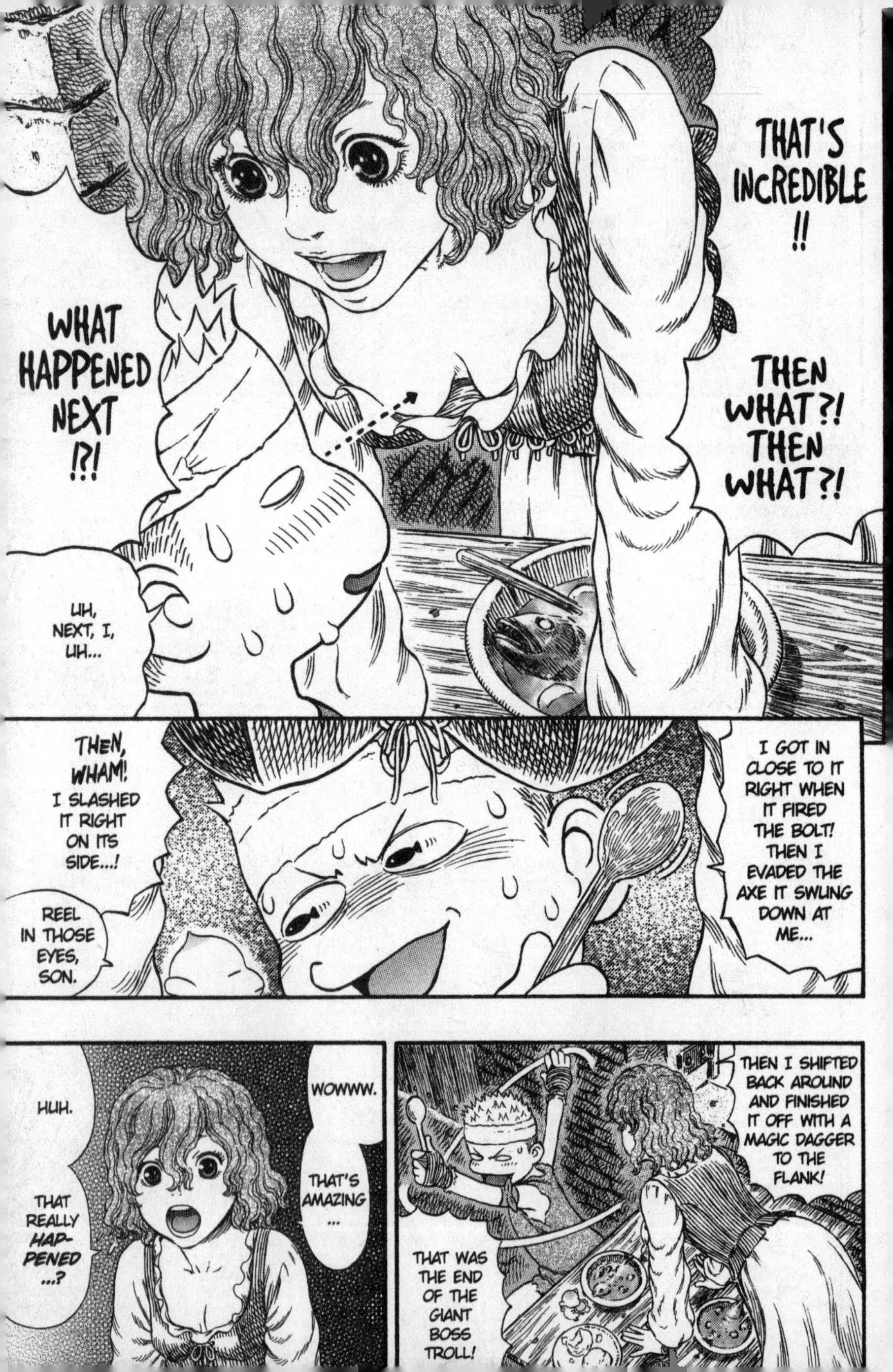

THAT'S INCREDIBLE !!
THEN WHAT?! THEN WHAT?!
WHAT HAPPENED NEXT !?!
UH, NEXT, I, UH...
I GOT IN CLOSE TO IT RIGHT WHEN IT FIRED THE BOLT! THEN I EVADED THE AXE IT SWUNG DOWN AT ME...
THEN, WHAM! I SLASHED IT RIGHT ON ITS SIDE...!
REEL IN THOSE EYES, SON.
THEN I SHIFTED BACK AROUND AND FINISHED IT OFF WITH A MAGIC DAGGER TO THE FLANK!
THAT WAS THE END OF THE GIANT BOSS TROLL!
WOWWW.
THAT'S AMAZING ...
HUH.
THAT REALLY HAPPENED ...?

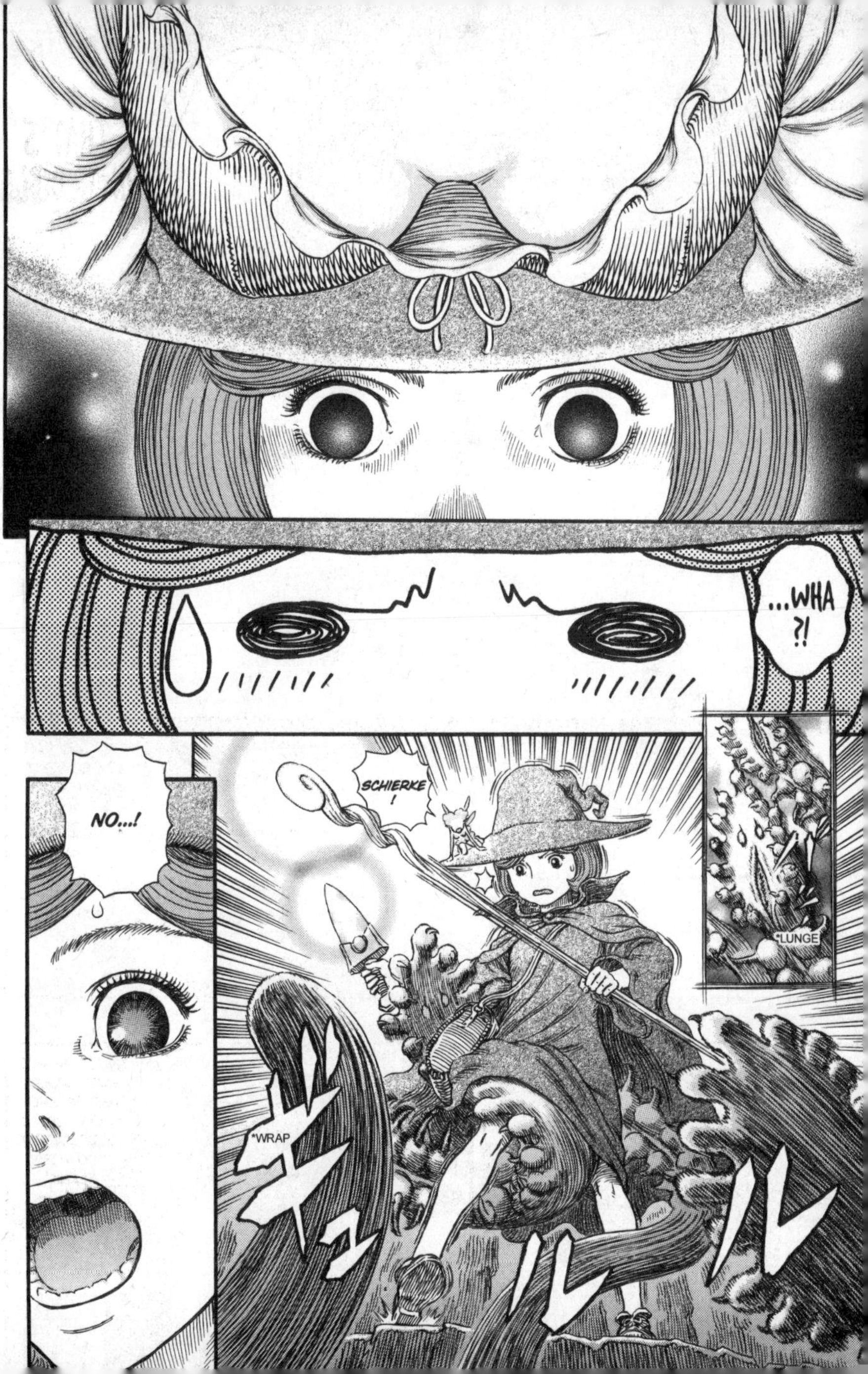
...WHA ?!
*LUNGE
SCHIERKE !
*WRAP
NO...!

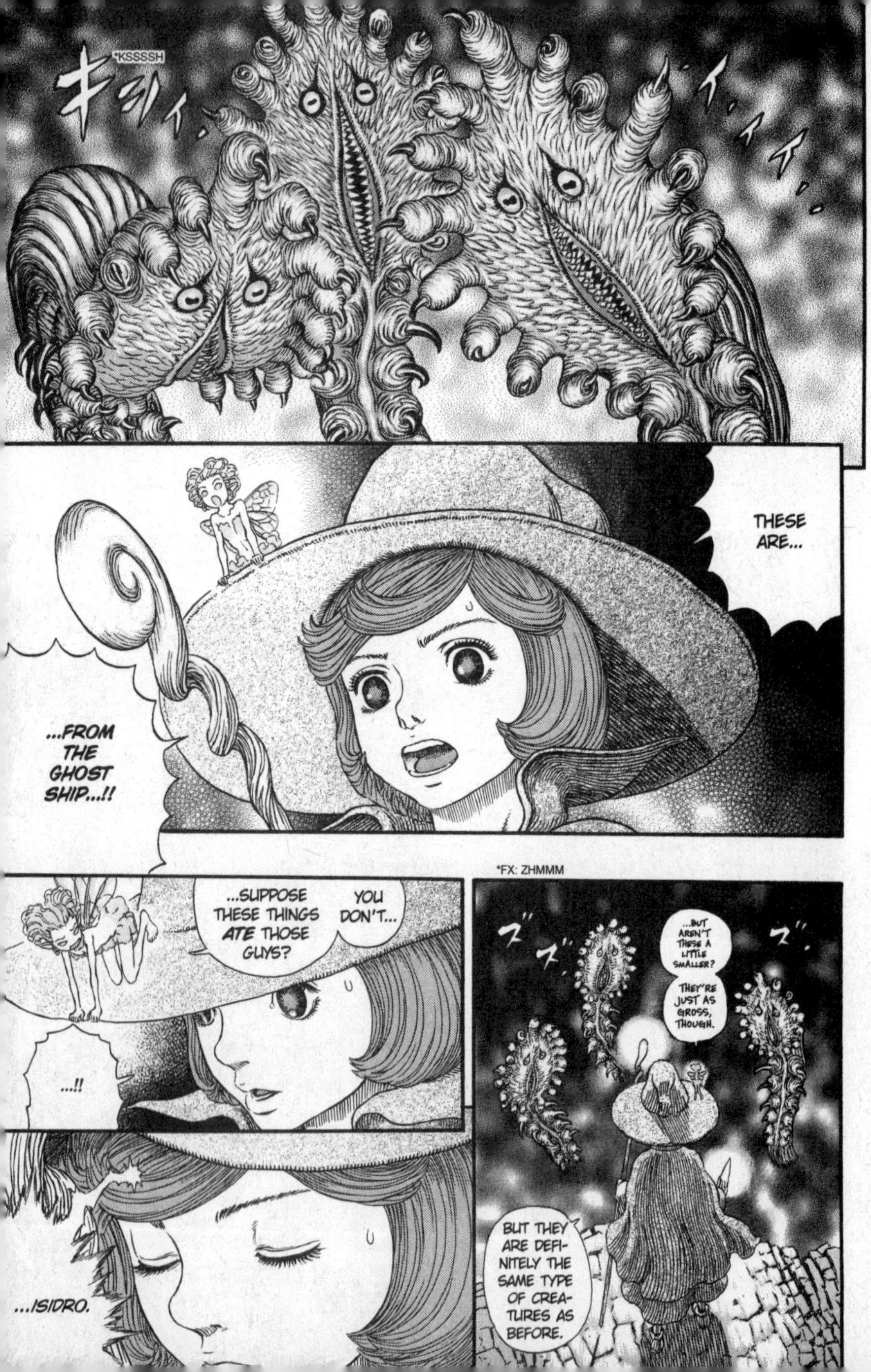
*KSSSSH
THESE ARE...
...FROM THE GHOST SHIP...!!
*FX: ZHMMM
...BUT AREN'T THESE A LITTLE SMALLER?
THEY'RE JUST AS GROSS, THOUGH.
BUT THEY ARE DEFINITELY THE SAME TYPE OF CREATURES AS BEFORE.
YOU DON'T...
...SUPPOSE THESE THINGS *ATE* THOSE GUYS?
...!!
...ISIDRO.

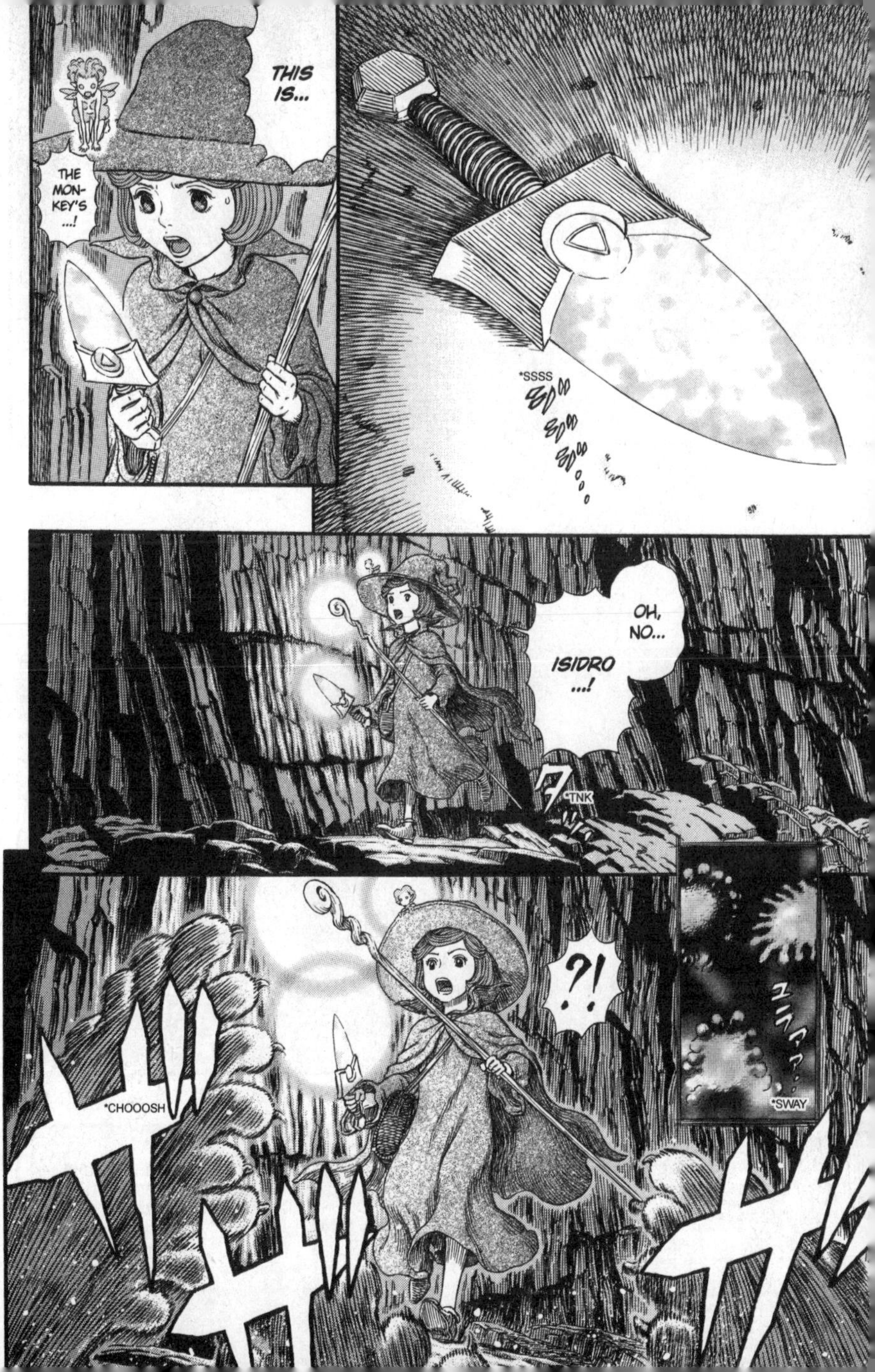
*SSSS
THIS IS...
THE MON-KEY'S ...!
OH, NO...
ISIDRO ...!
*TNK
*SWAY
?!
*CHOOOSH

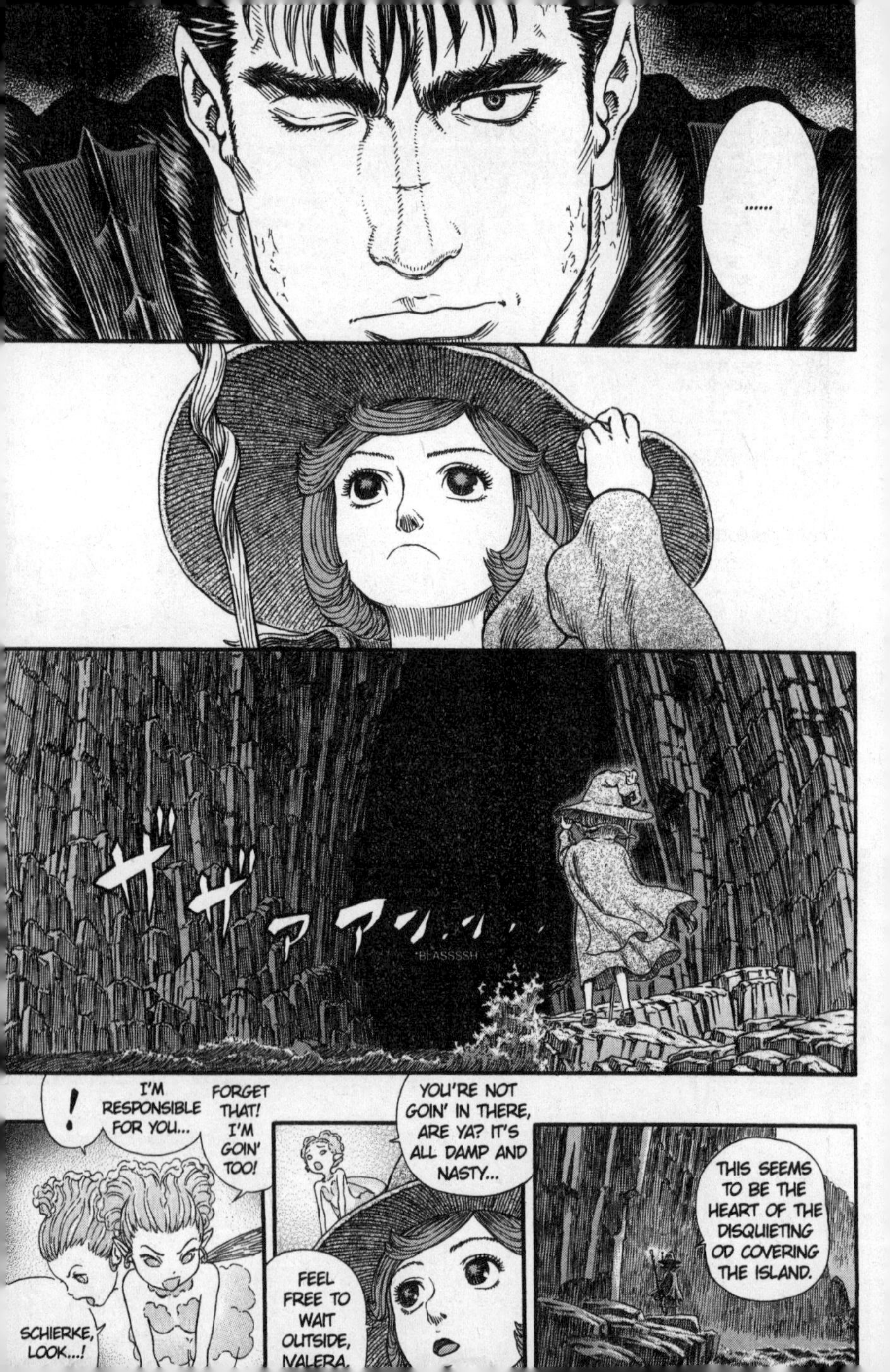
......
ザザァアン…
*BLASSSSH
THIS SEEMS TO BE THE HEART OF THE DISQUIETING OD COVERING THE ISLAND.
YOU'RE NOT GOIN' IN THERE, ARE YA? IT'S ALL DAMP AND NASTY...
FEEL FREE TO WAIT OUTSIDE, IVALERA.
FORGET THAT! I'M GOIN' TOO!
I'M RESPONSIBLE FOR YOU...
!
SCHIERKE, LOOK...!

SORRY, SIRS. BUT PLEASE SERVE YOURSELVES. I NEED TO GET SOME INGREDIENTS FROM THE BACK ROOM.

IT'S OKAY, I'LL GET IT.

HELL! WE WERE GOING TO STAY THE NIGHT HERE, TOO! TALK ABOUT POOR SERVICE.

*FX: SHFF

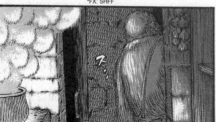

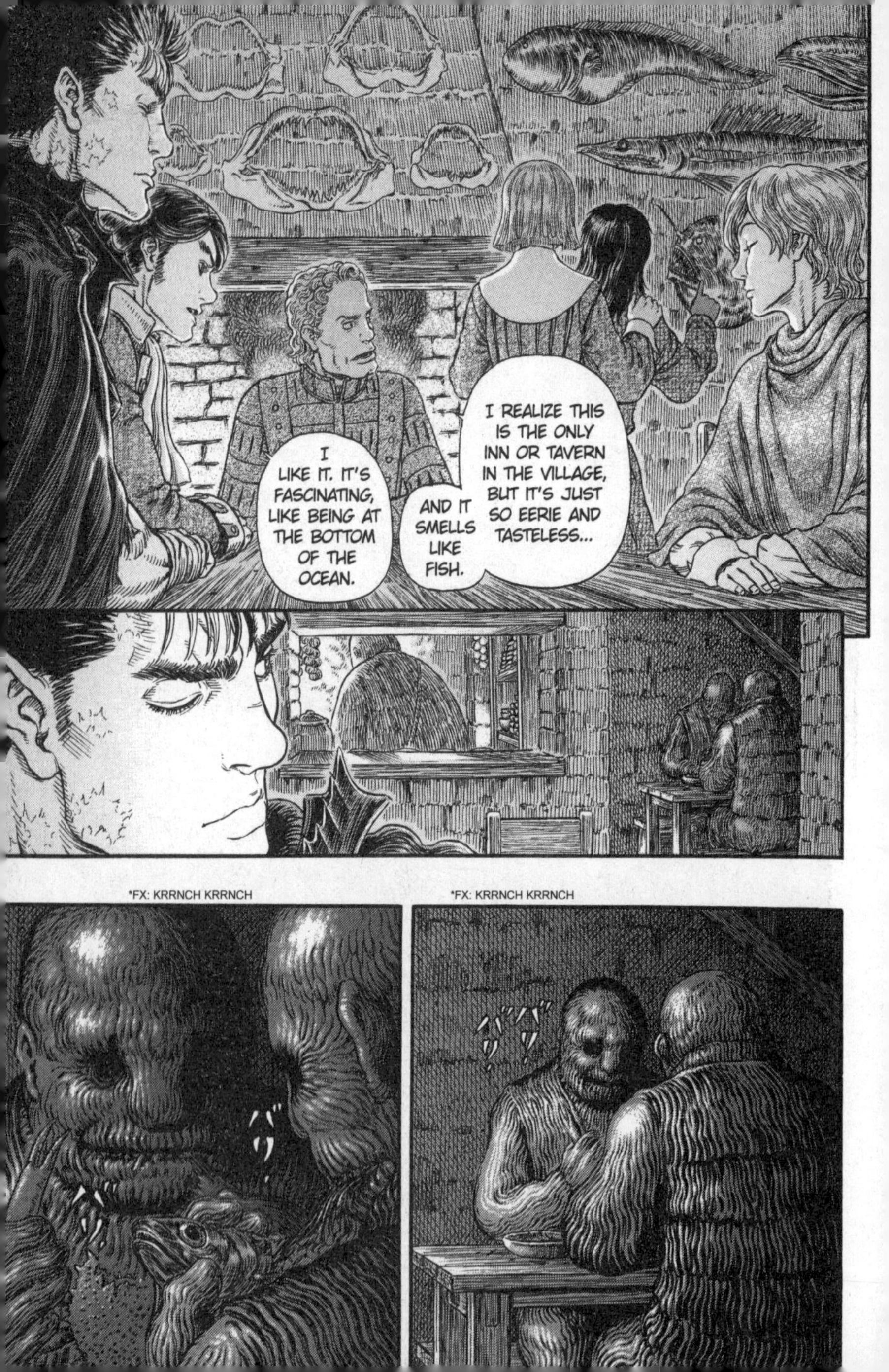
I REALIZE THIS IS THE ONLY INN OR TAVERN IN THE VILLAGE, BUT IT'S JUST SO EERIE AND TASTELESS...
AND IT SMELLS LIKE FISH.
I LIKE IT. IT'S FASCINATING, LIKE BEING AT THE BOTTOM OF THE OCEAN.
*FX: KRRNCH KRRNCH
*FX: KRRNCH KRRNCH

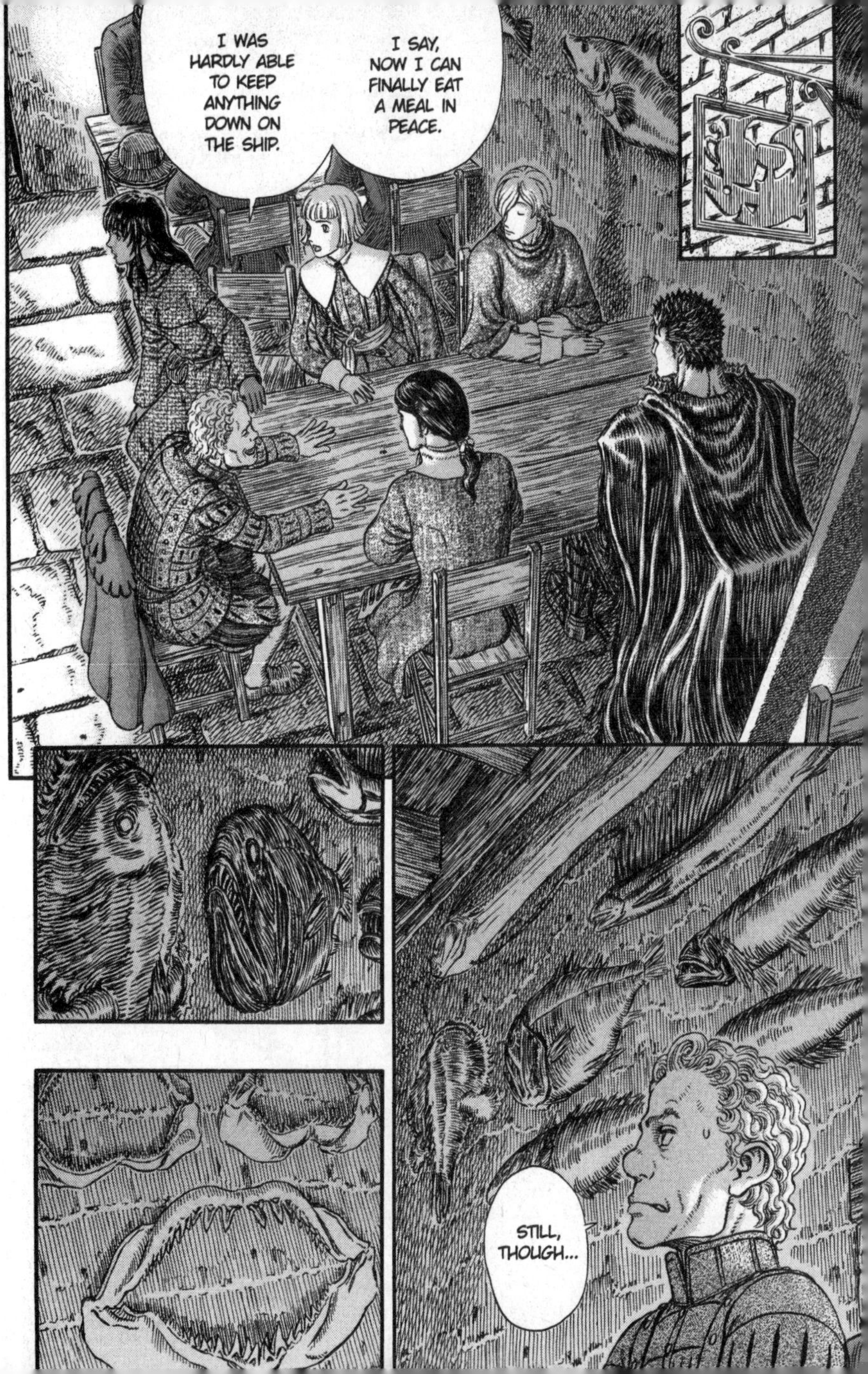
I SAY, NOW I CAN FINALLY EAT A MEAL IN PEACE.
I WAS HARDLY ABLE TO KEEP ANYTHING DOWN ON THE SHIP.
STILL, THOUGH...

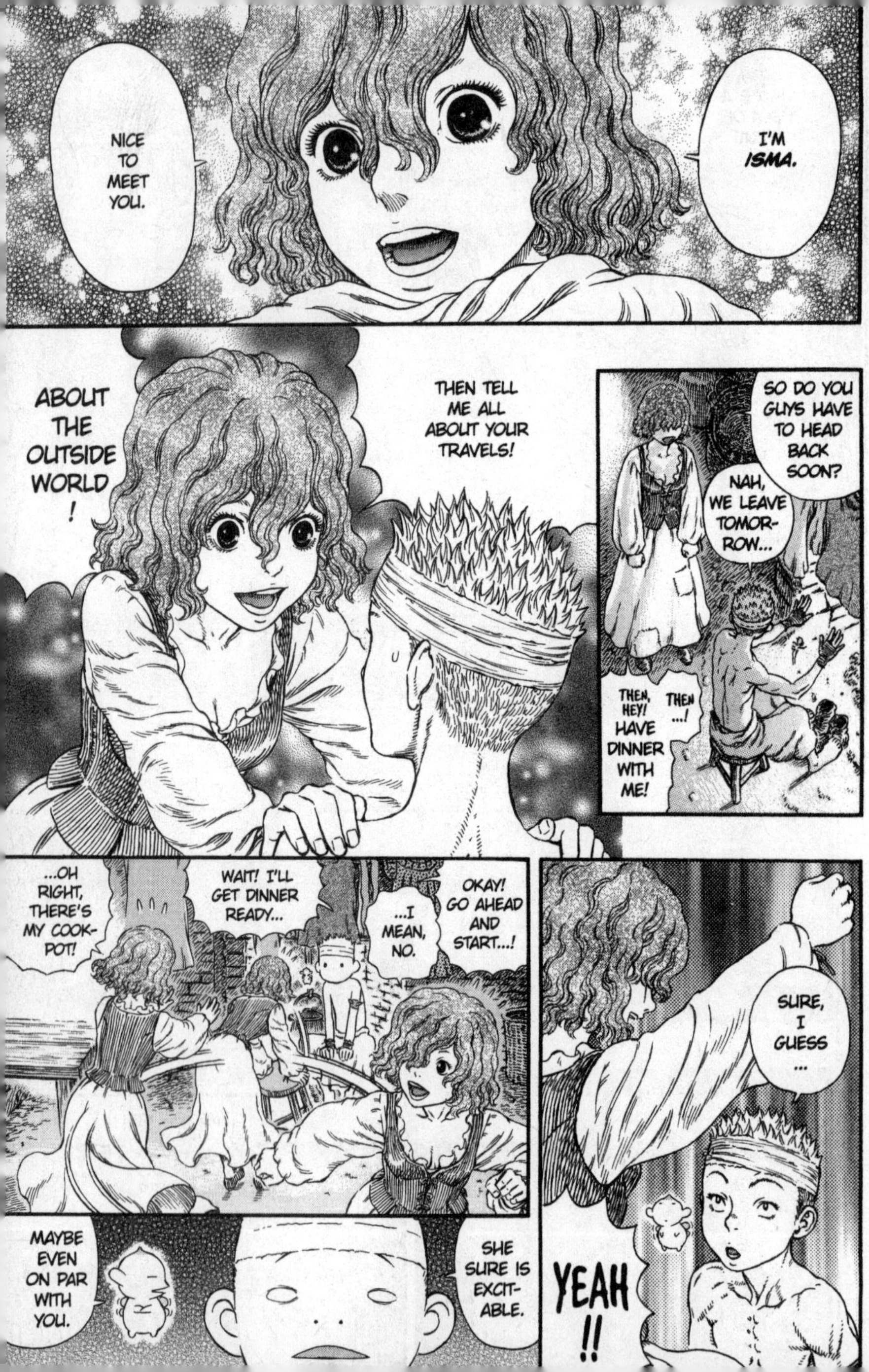
I'M *ISMA.*
NICE TO MEET YOU.
SO DO YOU GUYS HAVE TO HEAD BACK SOON?
NAH, WE LEAVE TOMOR-ROW...
THEN ...!
THEN, HEY! HAVE DINNER WITH ME!
THEN TELL ME ALL ABOUT YOUR TRAVELS!
ABOUT THE OUTSIDE WORLD !
SURE, I GUESS ...
YEAH !!
OKAY! GO AHEAD AND START...!
...I MEAN, NO.
WAIT! I'LL GET DINNER READY...
...OH RIGHT, THERE'S MY COOK-POT!
SHE SURE IS EXCIT-ABLE.
MAYBE EVEN ON PAR WITH YOU.

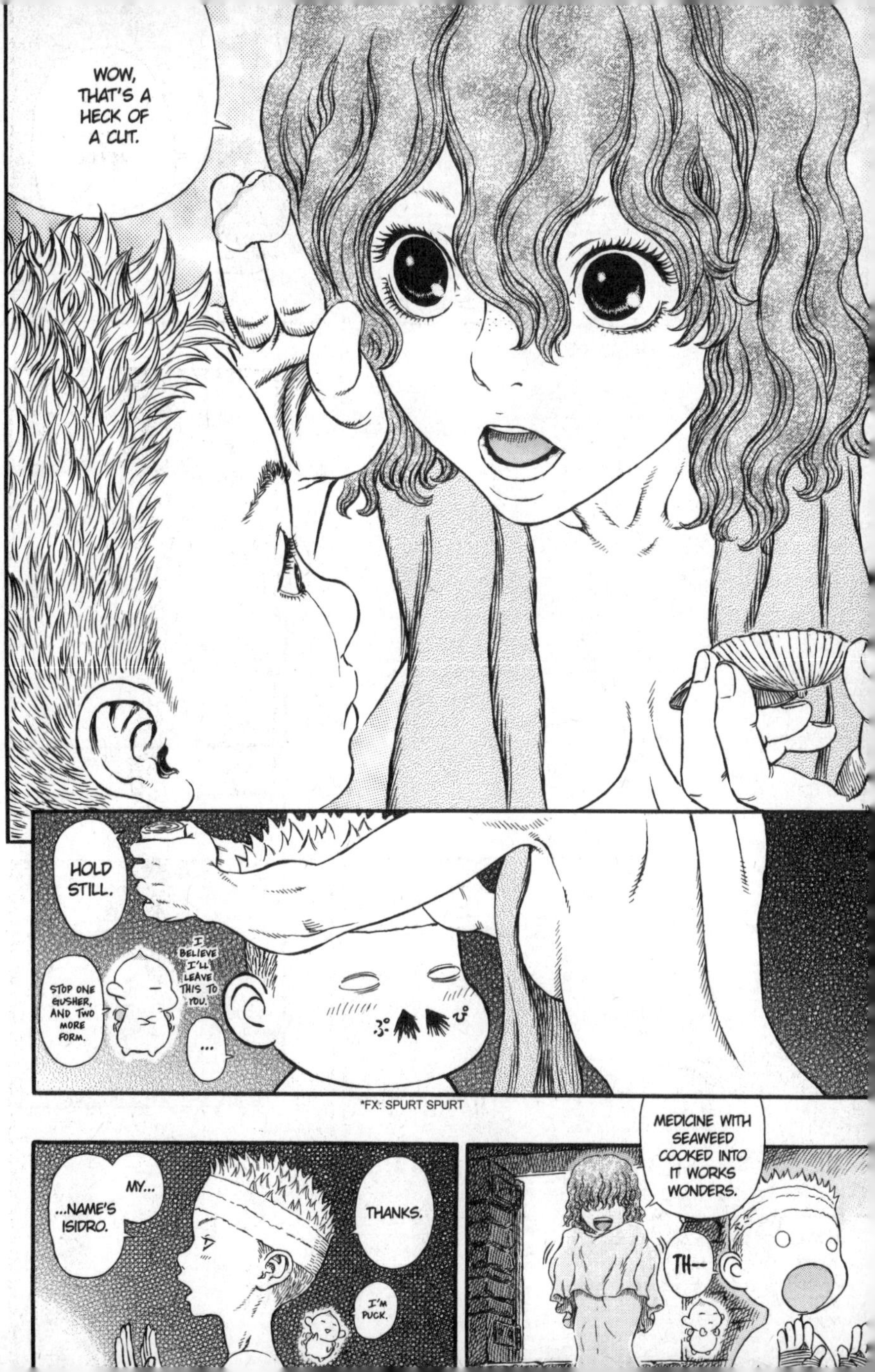
WOW, THAT'S A HECK OF A CUT.
HOLD STILL.
I BELIEVE I'LL LEAVE THIS TO YOU.
STOP ONE GUSHER, AND TWO MORE FORM.
...
MEDICINE WITH SEAWEED COOKED INTO IT WORKS WONDERS.
TH--
THANKS.
MY...
...NAME'S ISIDRO.
I'M PUCK.

*FX: SPURT SPURT

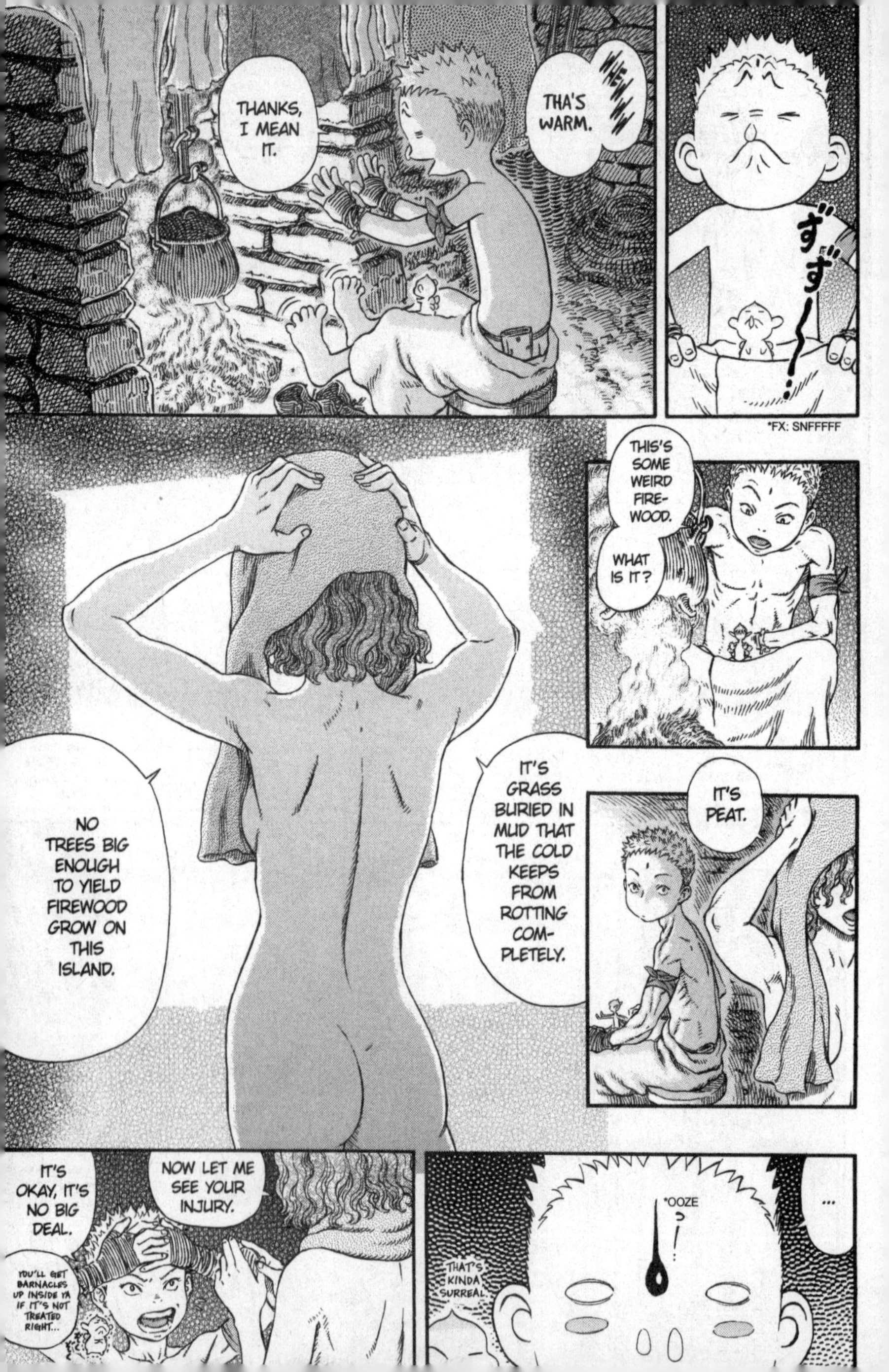
ずずー
*FX: SNFFFFF
WHEW
THA'S WARM.
THANKS, I MEAN IT.
THIS'S SOME WEIRD FIRE-WOOD.
WHAT IS IT?
IT'S PEAT.
IT'S GRASS BURIED IN MUD THAT THE COLD KEEPS FROM ROTTING COM-PLETELY.
NO TREES BIG ENOUGH TO YIELD FIREWOOD GROW ON THIS ISLAND.
...
*OOZE
THAT'S KINDA SURREAL.
NOW LET ME SEE YOUR INJURY.
IT'S OKAY, IT'S NO BIG DEAL.
YOU'LL GET BARNACLES UP INSIDE YA IF IT'S NOT TREATED RIGHT...

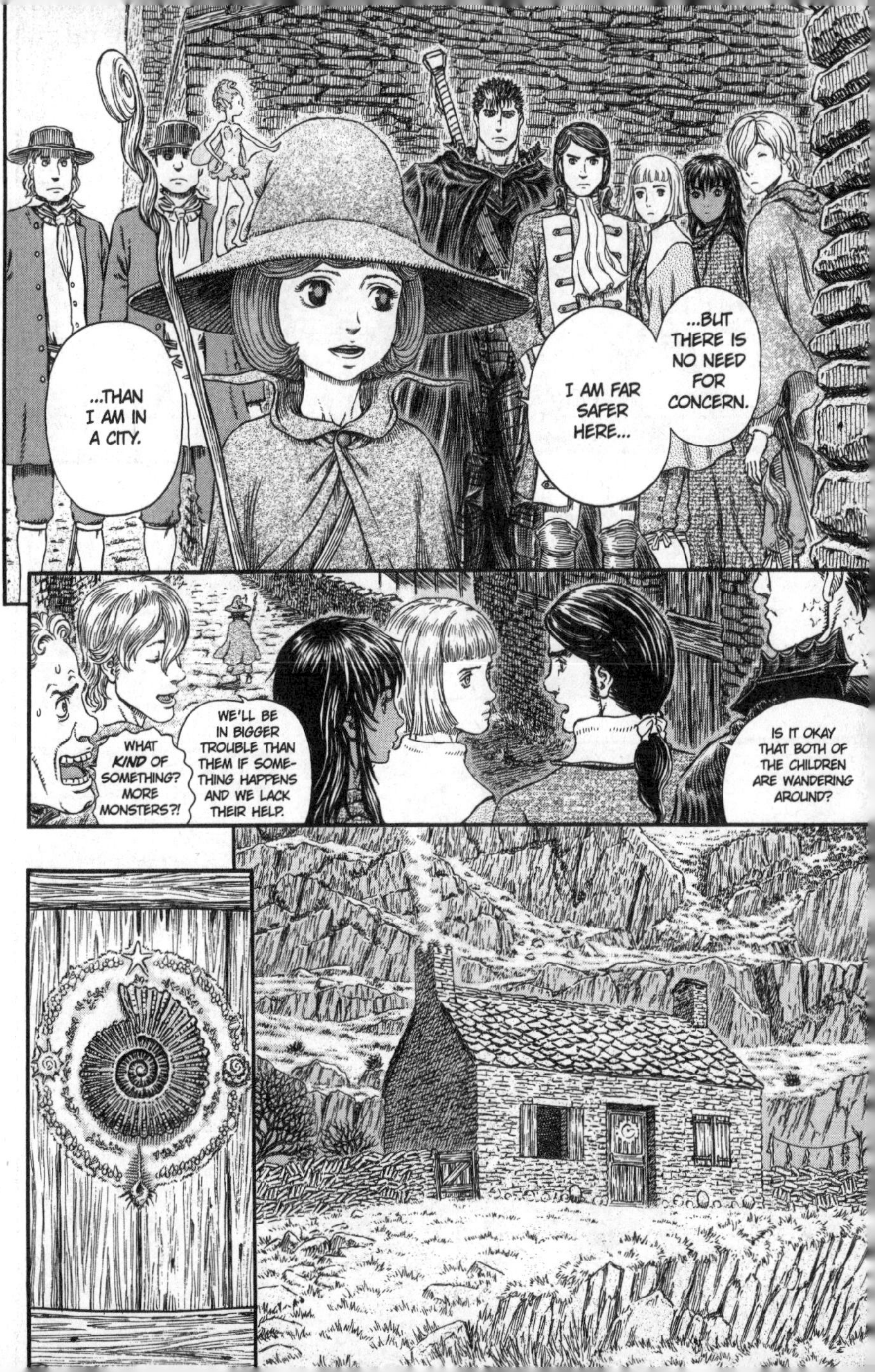
...BUT THERE IS NO NEED FOR CONCERN.
I AM FAR SAFER HERE...
...THAN I AM IN A CITY.
IS IT OKAY THAT BOTH OF THE CHILDREN ARE WANDERING AROUND?
WE'LL BE IN BIGGER TROUBLE THAN THEM IF SOME-THING HAPPENS AND WE LACK THEIR HELP.
WHAT *KIND* OF SOMETHING? MORE MONSTERS?!

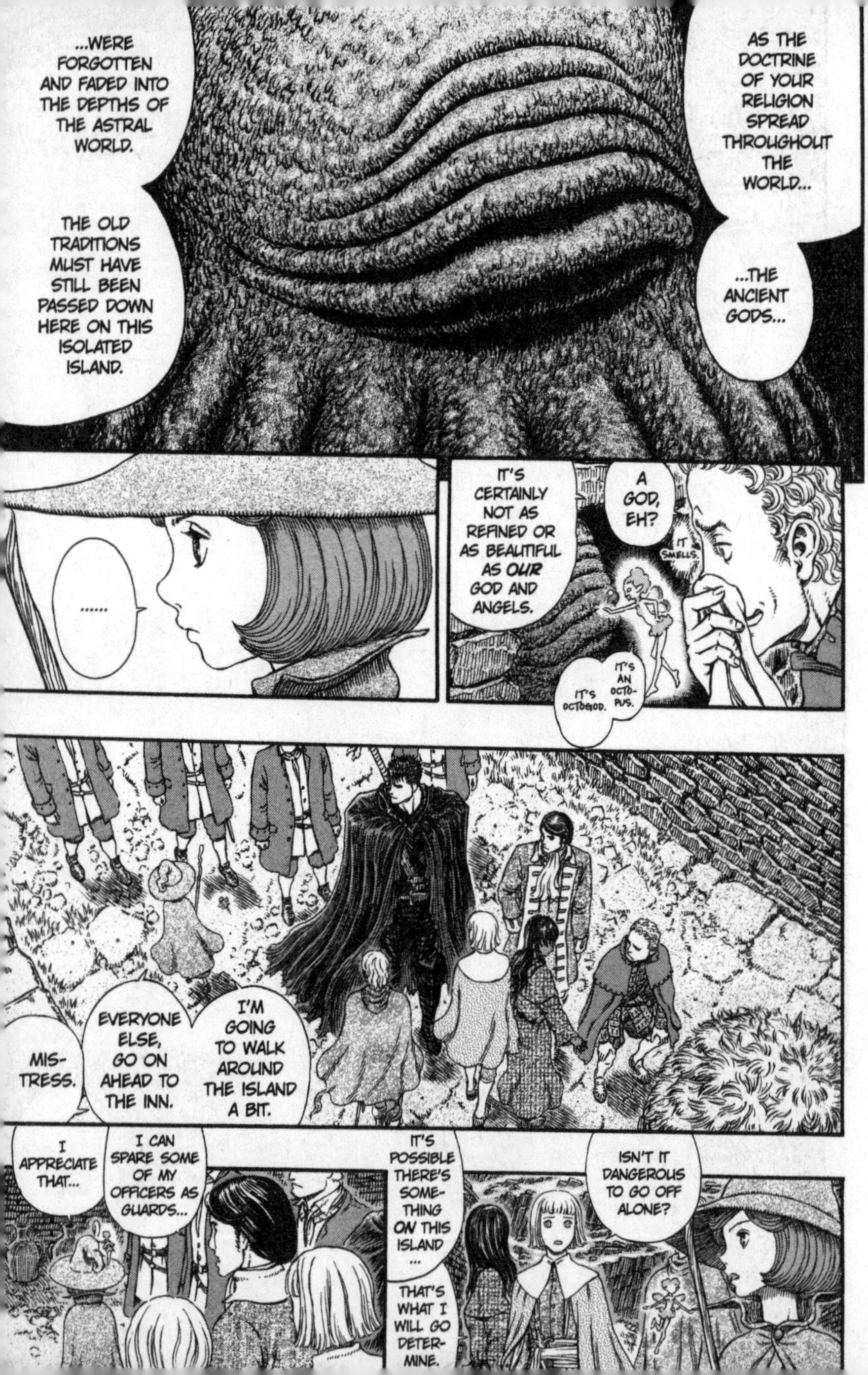

AS THE DOCTRINE OF YOUR RELIGION SPREAD THROUGHOUT THE WORLD...
...THE ANCIENT GODS...
...WERE FORGOTTEN AND FADED INTO THE DEPTHS OF THE ASTRAL WORLD.
THE OLD TRADITIONS MUST HAVE STILL BEEN PASSED DOWN HERE ON THIS ISOLATED ISLAND.
A GOD, EH?
IT SMELLS.
IT'S CERTAINLY NOT AS REFINED OR AS BEAUTIFUL AS OUR GOD AND ANGELS.
IT'S AN OCTO-PUS.
IT'S OCTOGOD.
......
I'M GOING TO WALK AROUND THE ISLAND A BIT.
EVERYONE ELSE, GO ON AHEAD TO THE INN.
MIS-TRESS.
ISN'T IT DANGEROUS TO GO OFF ALONE?
IT'S POSSIBLE THERE'S SOME-THING ON THIS ISLAND ...
THAT'S WHAT I WILL GO DETER-MINE.
I CAN SPARE SOME OF MY OFFICERS AS GUARDS...
I APPRECIATE THAT...

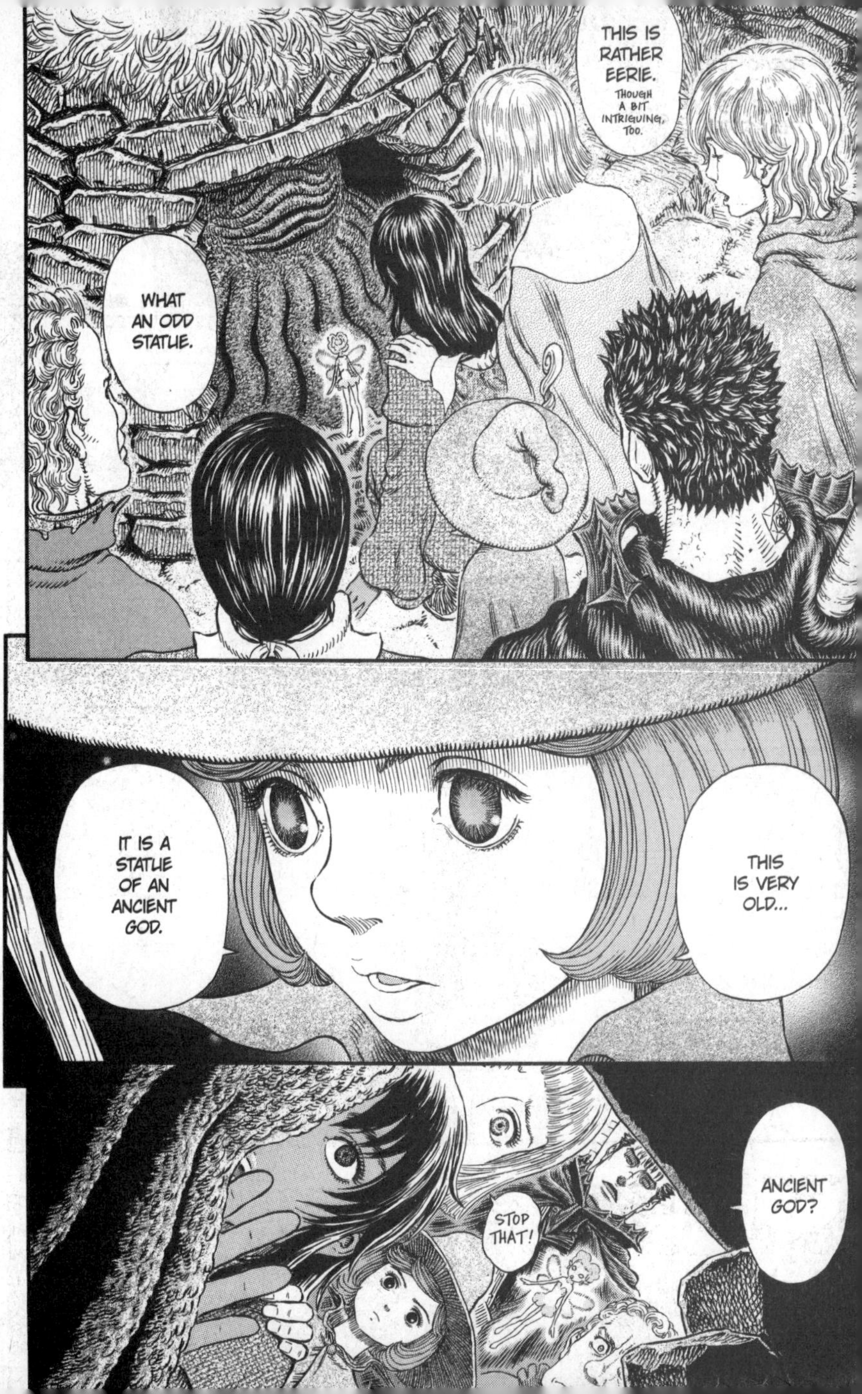
THIS IS RATHER EERIE.
THOUGH A BIT INTRIGUING, TOO.
WHAT AN ODD STATUE.
THIS IS VERY OLD...
IT IS A STATUE OF AN ANCIENT GOD.
ANCIENT GOD?
STOP THAT!

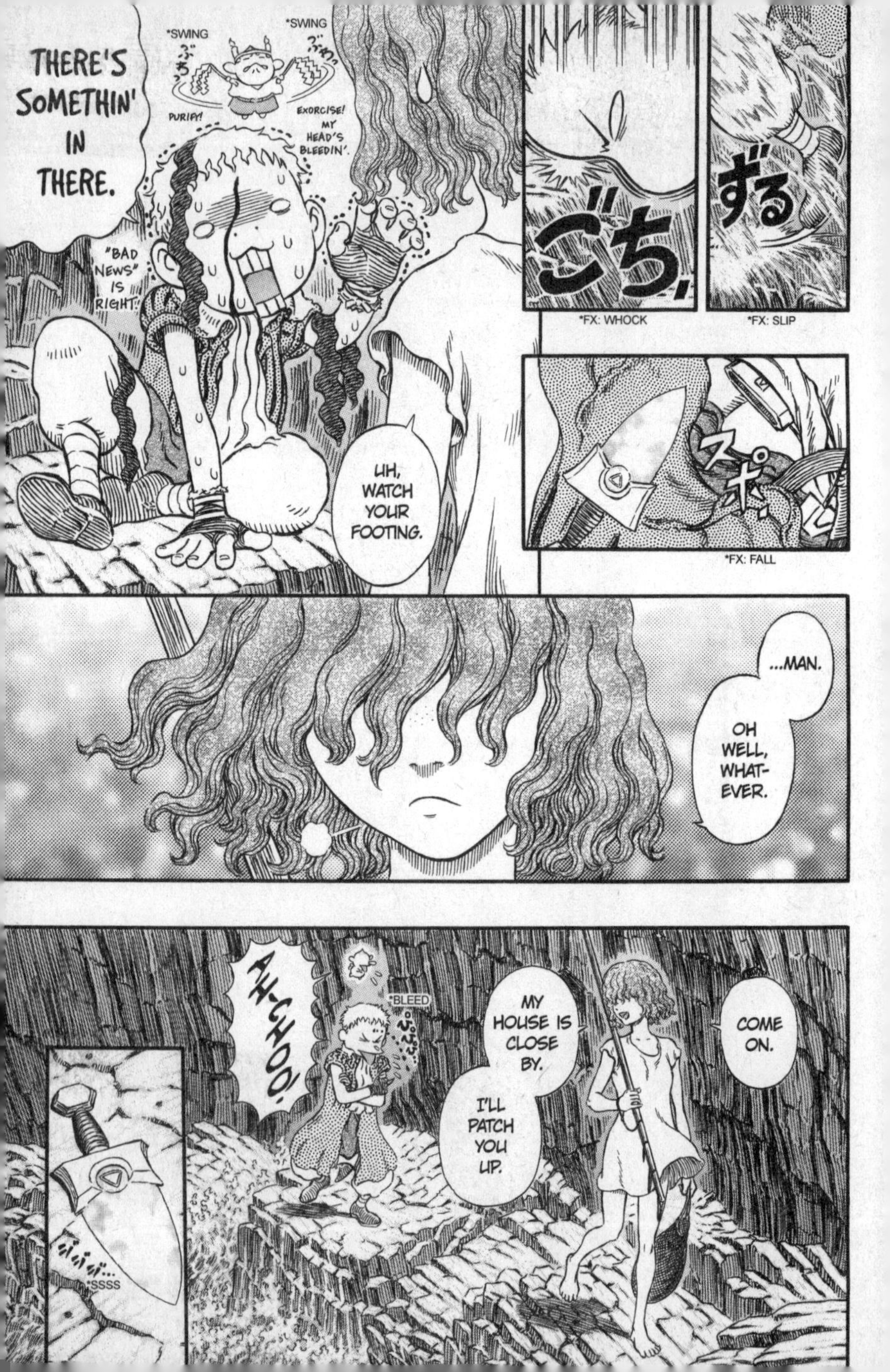

ずる
*FX: SLIP
ごち,
*FX: WHOCK
スポ
*FX: FALL
*SWING
EXORCISE! MY HEAD'S BLEEDIN'.
*SWING
PURIFY!
THERE'S SOMETHIN' IN THERE.
UH, WATCH YOUR FOOTING.
"BAD NEWS" IS RIGHT!
...MAN.
OH WELL, WHATEVER.
COME ON.
MY HOUSE IS CLOSE BY.
I'LL PATCH YOU UP.
*BLEED
AH-CHOO!
*SSSS

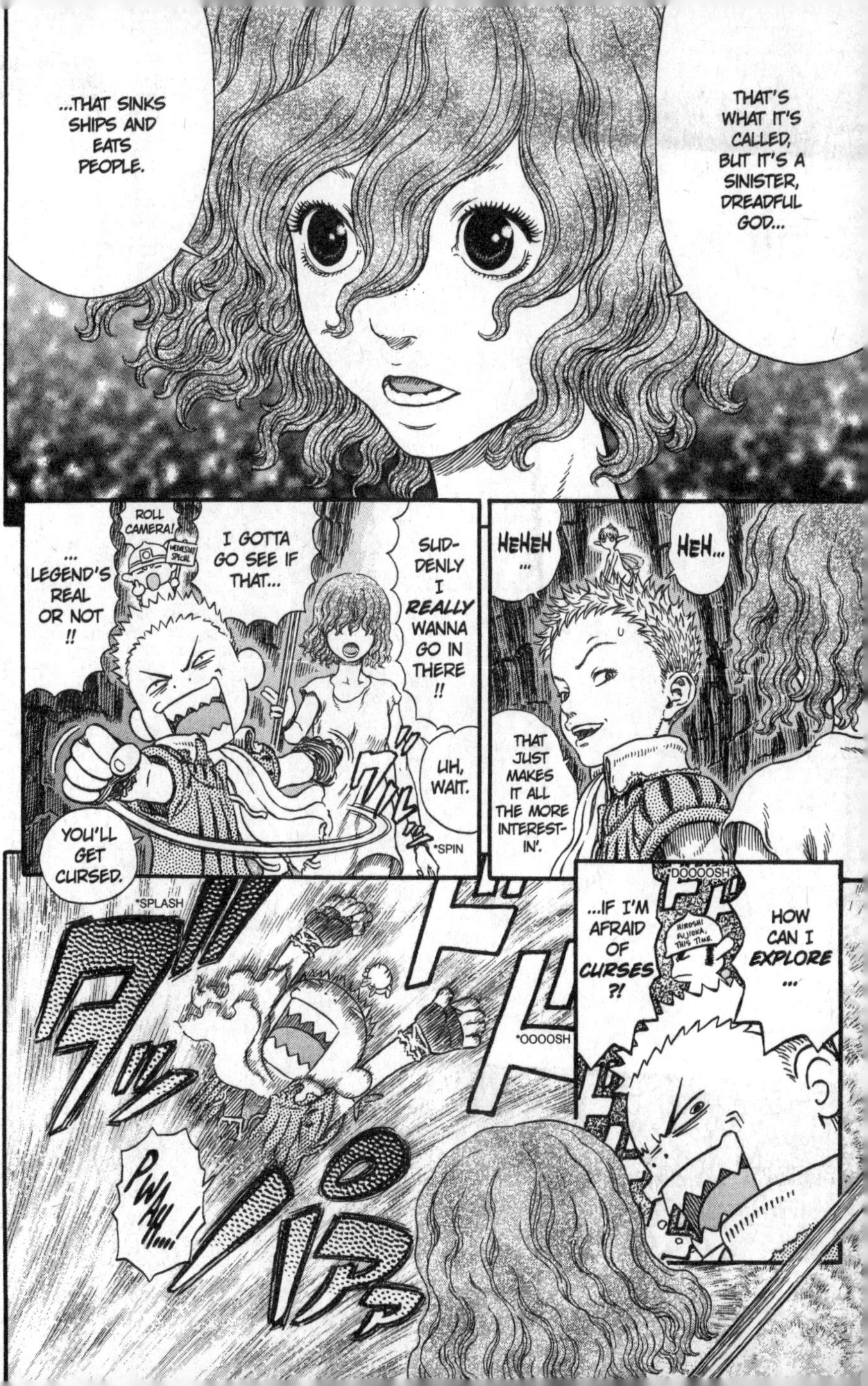
THAT'S WHAT IT'S CALLED, BUT IT'S A SINISTER, DREADFUL GOD...
...THAT SINKS SHIPS AND EATS PEOPLE.
HEH...
HEHEH ...
THAT JUST MAKES IT ALL THE MORE INTEREST-IN'.
SUD-DENLY I *REALLY* WANNA GO IN THERE !!
I GOTTA GO SEE IF THAT...
ROLL CAMERA!
WEDNESDAY SPECIAL
... LEGEND'S REAL OR NOT !!
UH, WAIT.
*SPIN
YOU'LL GET CURSED.
*DOOOOSH
HOW CAN I *EXPLORE* ...
...IF I'M AFRAID OF *CURSES* ?!
HIROSHI FUJIOKA, THIS TIME.
*OOOOSH
*SPLASH
PWAH...!

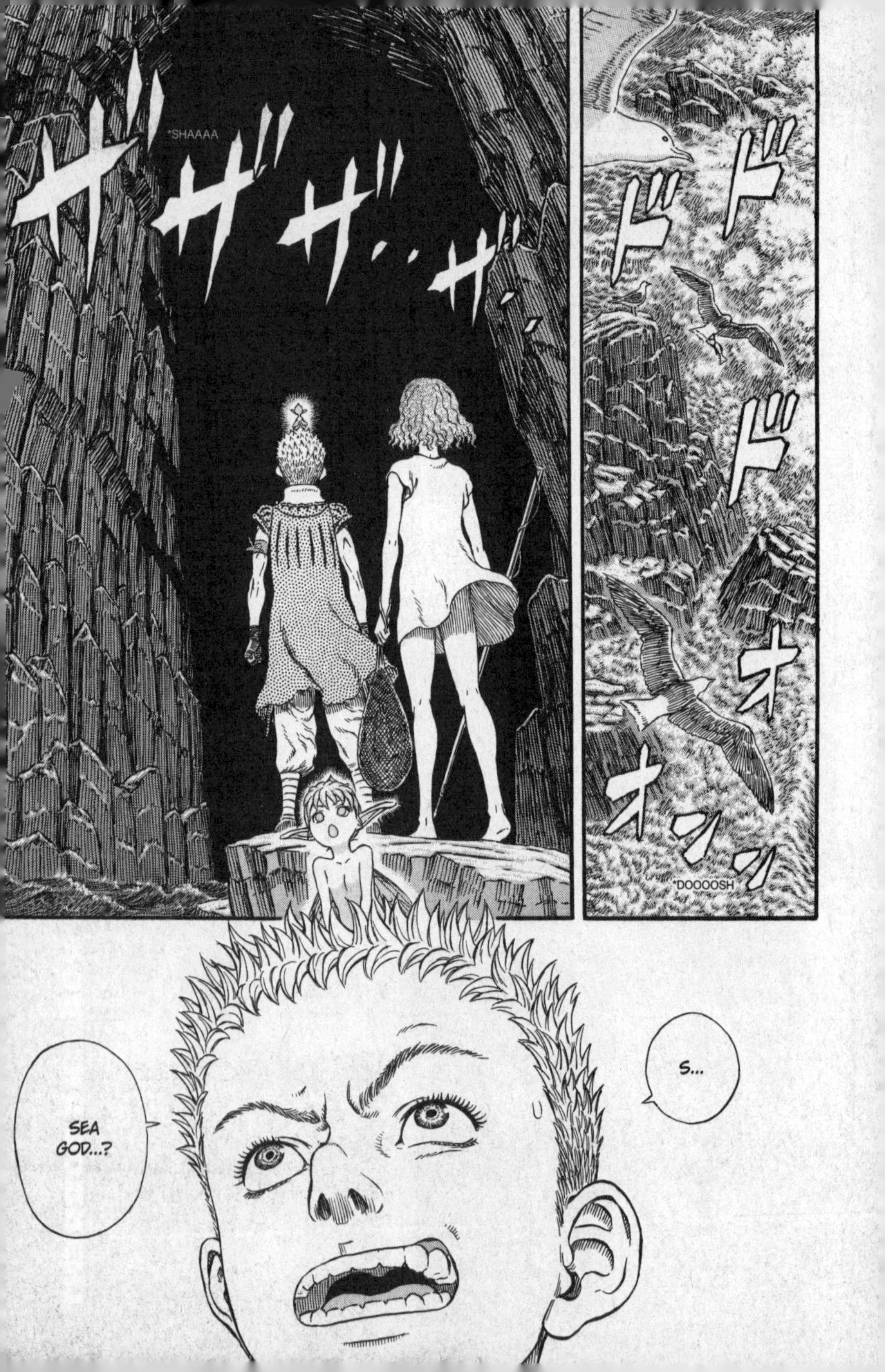
*DOOOOSH
*SHAAAA
S...
SEA GOD...?

鳴る瀬ろの娘

GIRL OF THE ROARING TORRENT

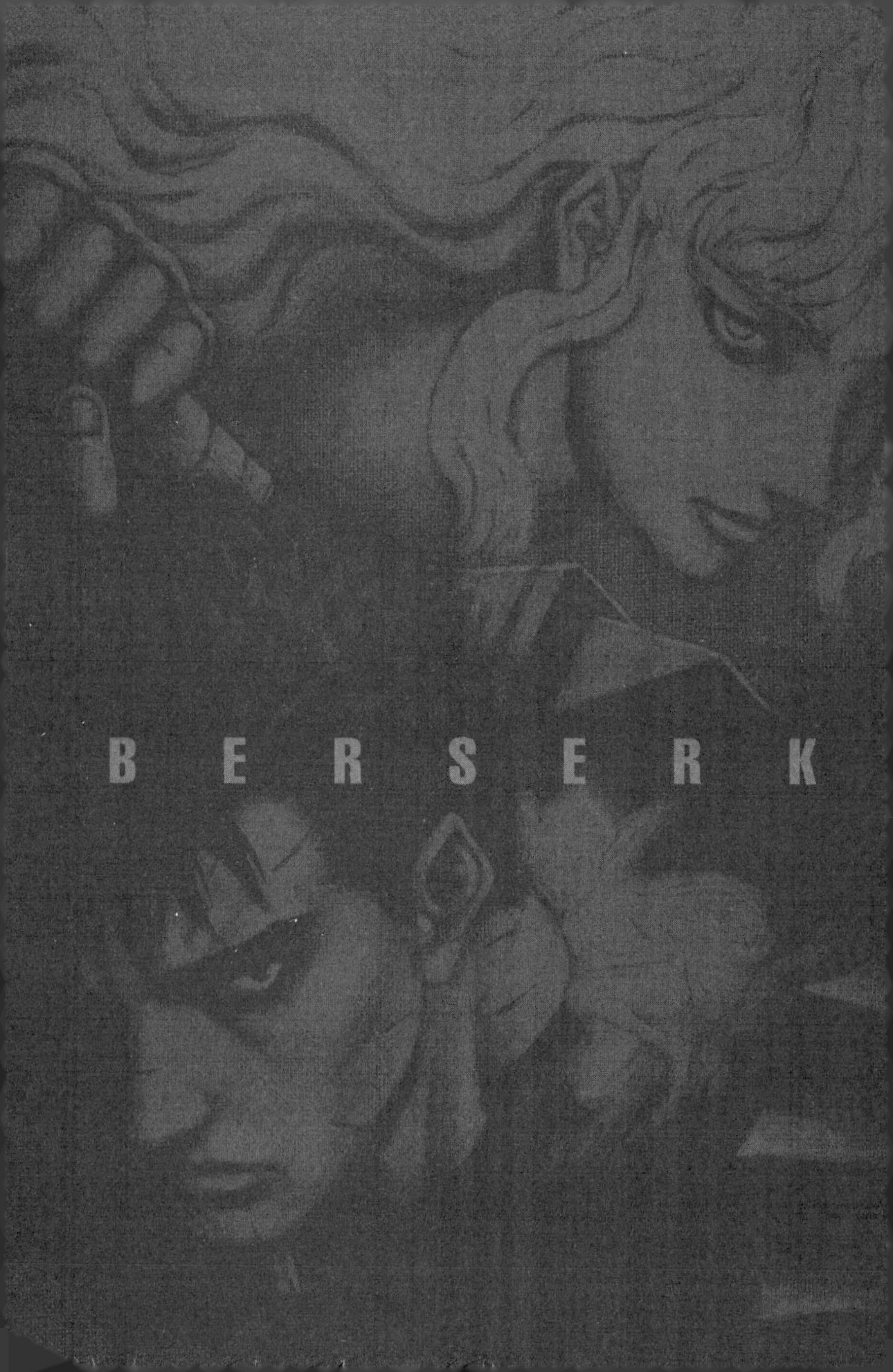
BERSERK

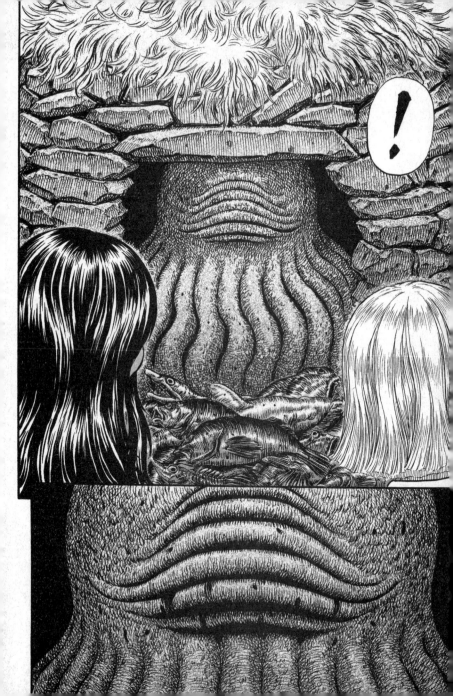

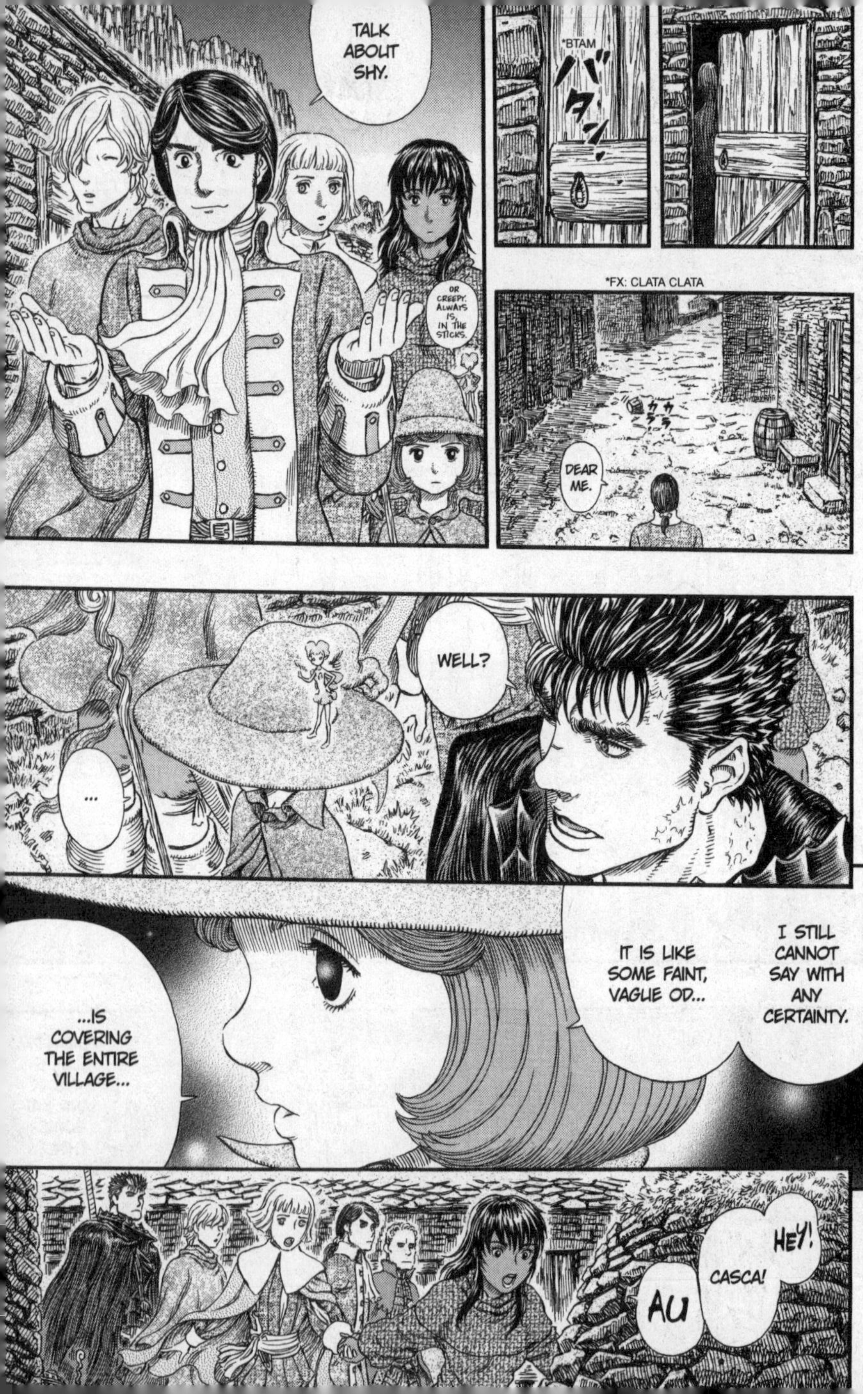
*BTAM
*FX: CLATA CLATA
DEAR ME.
TALK ABOUT SHY.
OR CREEPY. ALWAYS IS, IN THE STICKS.
WELL?
...
I STILL CANNOT SAY WITH ANY CERTAINTY.
IT IS LIKE SOME FAINT, VAGUE OD...
...IS COVERING THE ENTIRE VILLAGE...
HEY!
CASCA!
AU

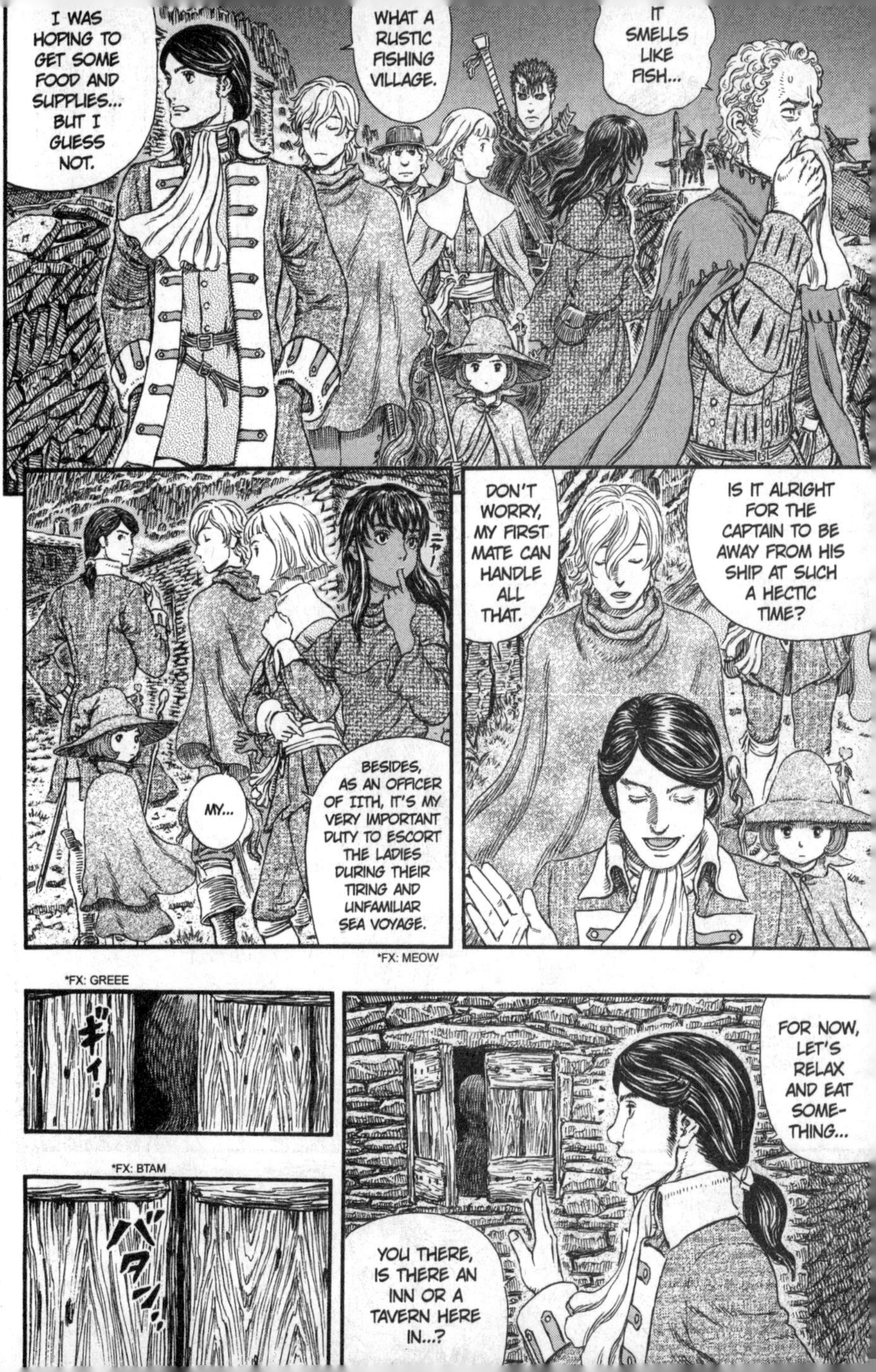
IT SMELLS LIKE FISH...
WHAT A RUSTIC FISHING VILLAGE.
I WAS HOPING TO GET SOME FOOD AND SUPPLIES... BUT I GUESS NOT.
IS IT ALRIGHT FOR THE CAPTAIN TO BE AWAY FROM HIS SHIP AT SUCH A HECTIC TIME?
DON'T WORRY, MY FIRST MATE CAN HANDLE ALL THAT.
BESIDES, AS AN OFFICER OF IITH, IT'S MY VERY IMPORTANT DUTY TO ESCORT THE LADIES DURING THEIR TIRING AND UNFAMILIAR SEA VOYAGE.
MY...
*FX: MEOW
FOR NOW, LET'S RELAX AND EAT SOME-THING...
YOU THERE, IS THERE AN INN OR A TAVERN HERE IN...?
*FX: GREEE
*FX: BTAM

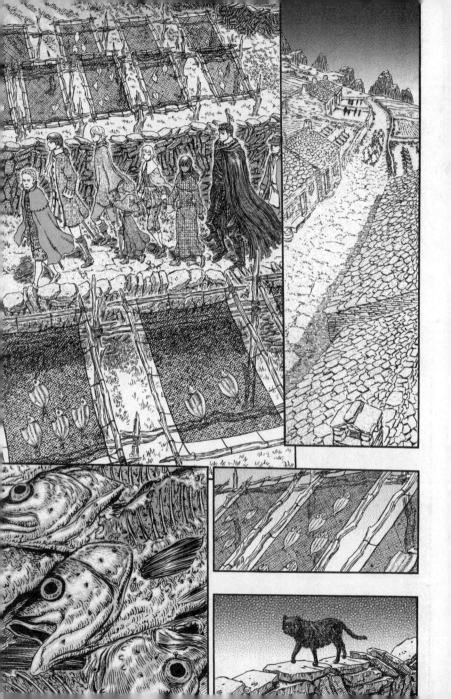

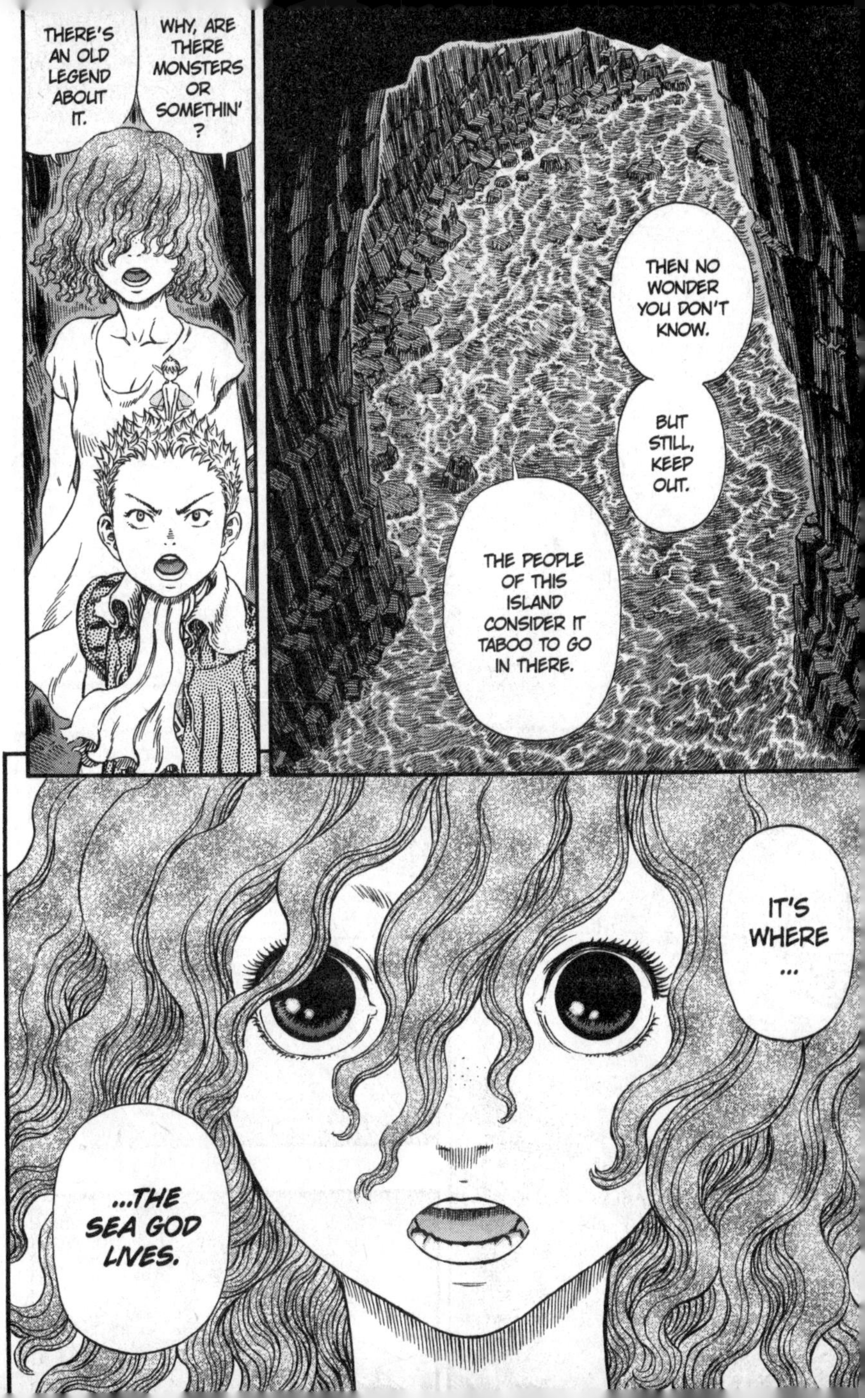
THEN NO WONDER YOU DON'T KNOW.
BUT STILL, KEEP OUT.
THE PEOPLE OF THIS ISLAND CONSIDER IT TABOO TO GO IN THERE.
WHY, ARE THERE MONSTERS OR SOMETHIN'?
THERE'S AN OLD LEGEND ABOUT IT.
IT'S WHERE ...
...THE SEA GOD LIVES.

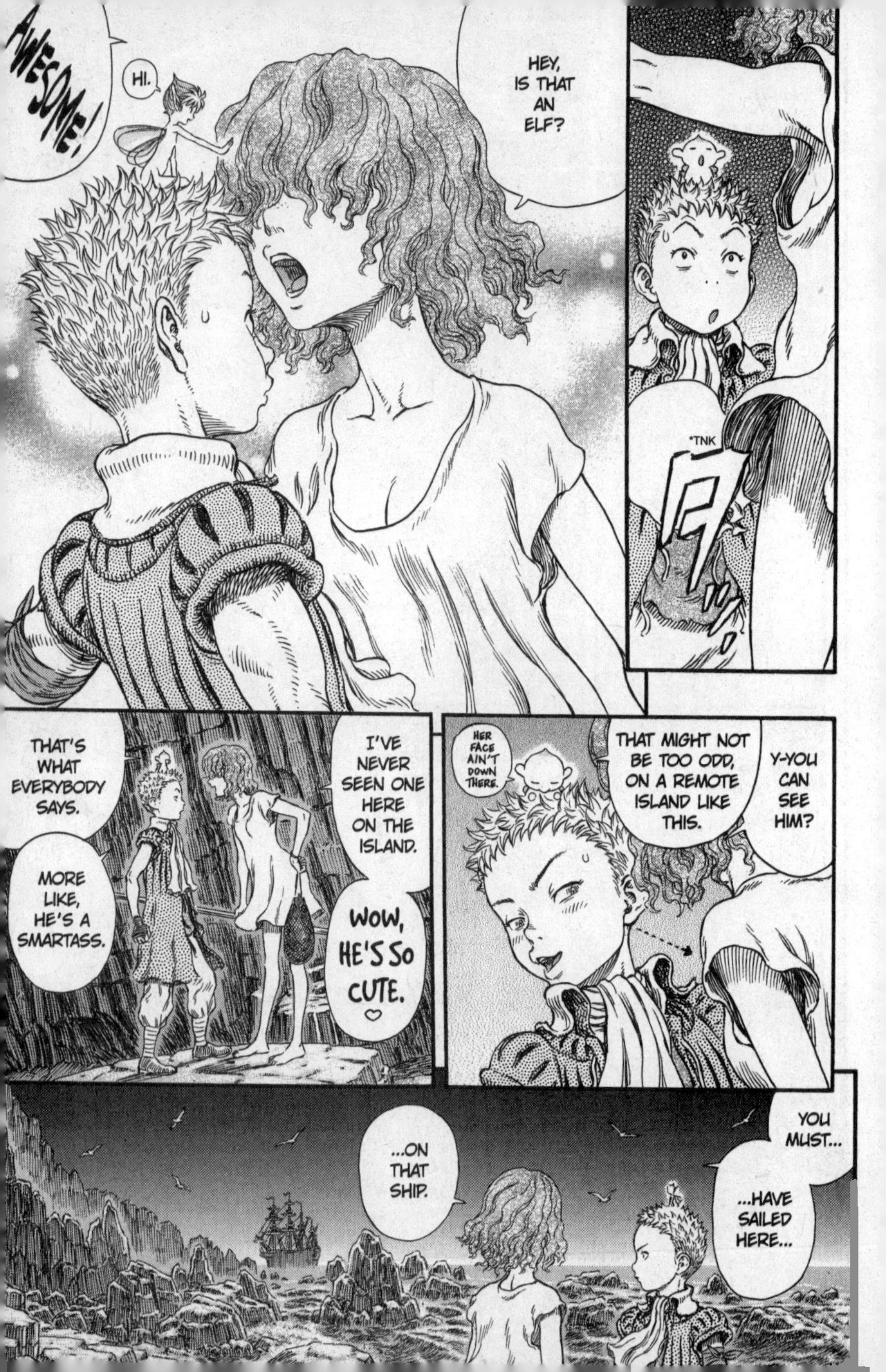
*TNK
HEY, IS THAT AN ELF?
HI.
AWESOME!
Y-YOU CAN SEE HIM?
THAT MIGHT NOT BE TOO ODD, ON A REMOTE ISLAND LIKE THIS.
HER FACE AIN'T DOWN THERE.
I'VE NEVER SEEN ONE HERE ON THE ISLAND.
THAT'S WHAT EVERYBODY SAYS.
WOW, HE'S SO CUTE.
MORE LIKE, HE'S A SMARTASS.
YOU MUST...
...HAVE SAILED HERE...
...ON THAT SHIP.

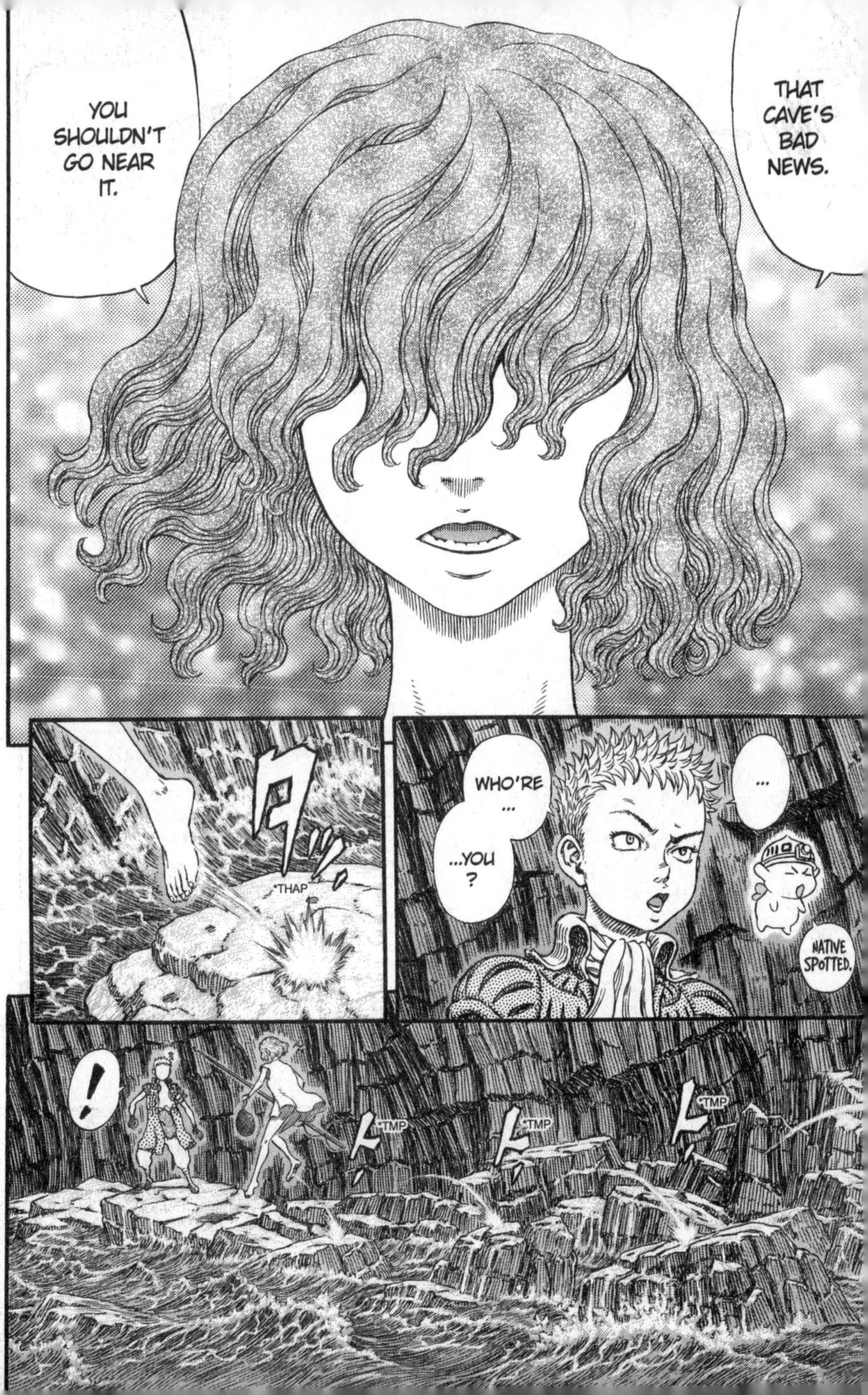
THAT CAVE'S BAD NEWS.
YOU SHOULDN'T GO NEAR IT.
WHO'RE ...
...YOU ?
...
NATIVE SPOTTED.
*THAP
!
*TMP
*TMP
*TMP

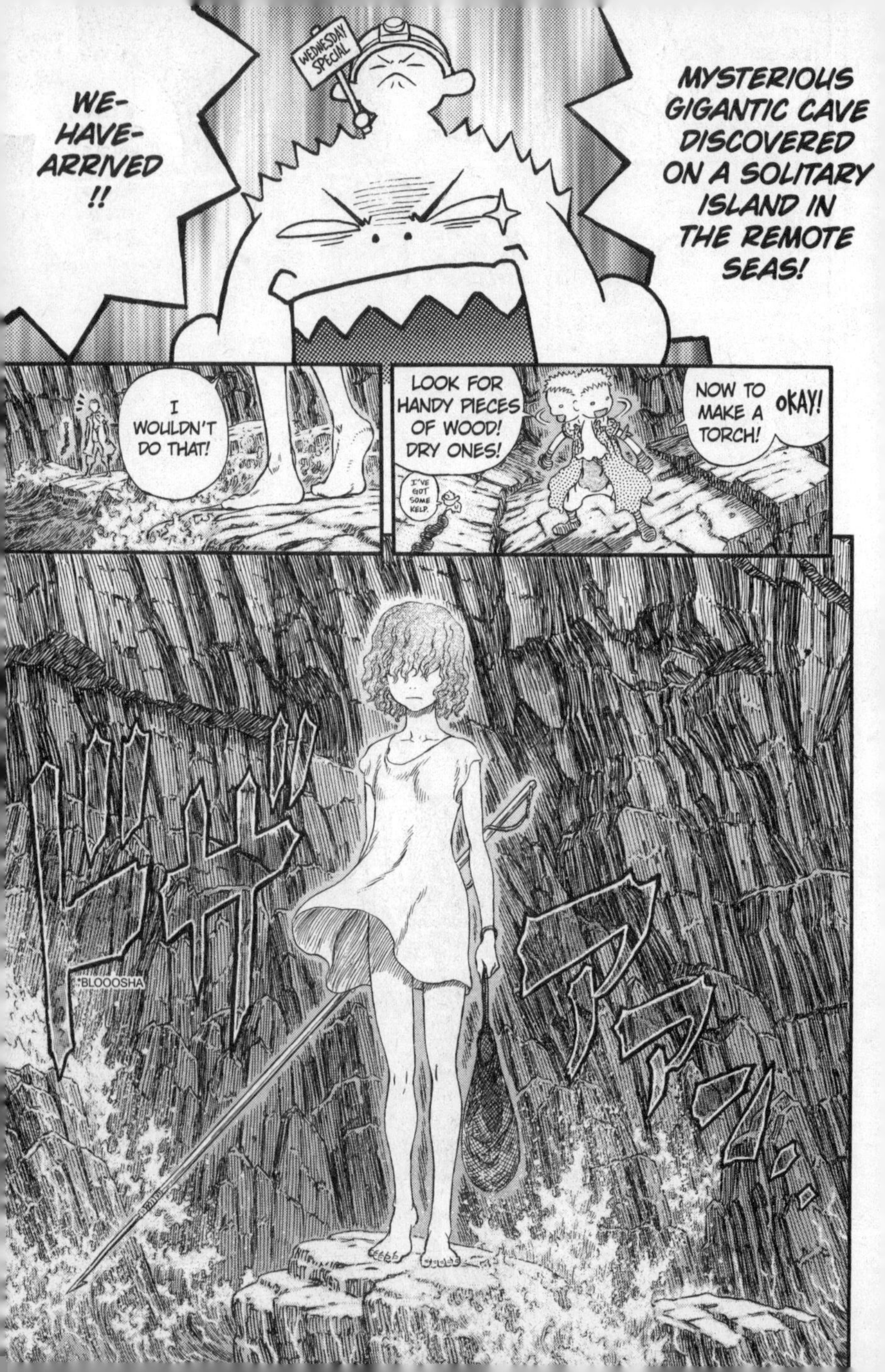
MYSTERIOUS GIGANTIC CAVE DISCOVERED ON A SOLITARY ISLAND IN THE REMOTE SEAS!
WEDNESDAY SPECIAL
WE- HAVE- ARRIVED !!
OKAY!
NOW TO MAKE A TORCH!
LOOK FOR HANDY PIECES OF WOOD! DRY ONES!
I'VE GOT SOME KELP.
I WOULDN'T DO THAT!
BLOOOSHA

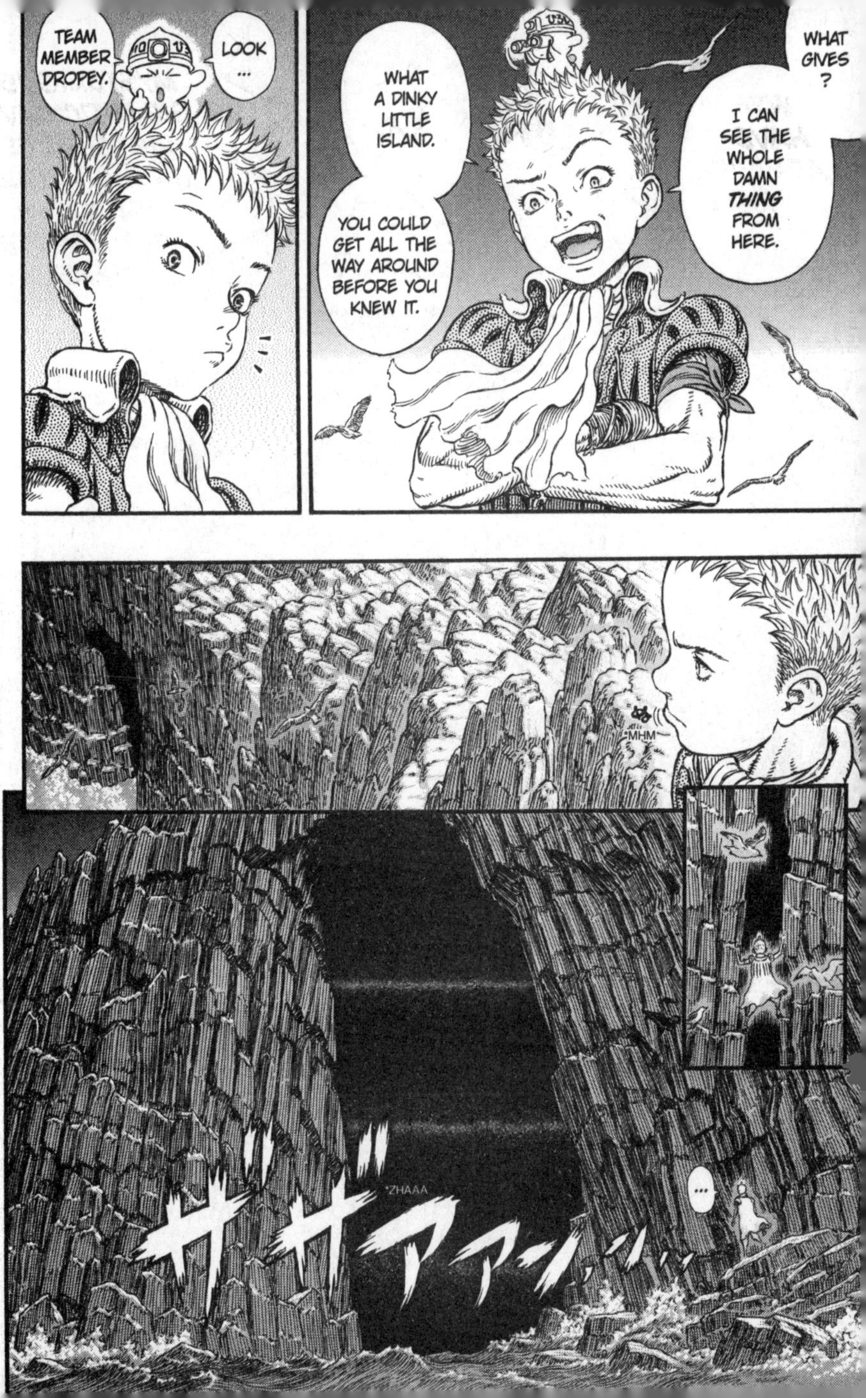
WHAT GIVES?
I CAN SEE THE WHOLE DAMN THING FROM HERE.
WHAT A DINKY LITTLE ISLAND.
YOU COULD GET ALL THE WAY AROUND BEFORE YOU KNEW IT.
LOOK ...
TEAM MEMBER DROPEY.
*MHM
...
*ZHAAA

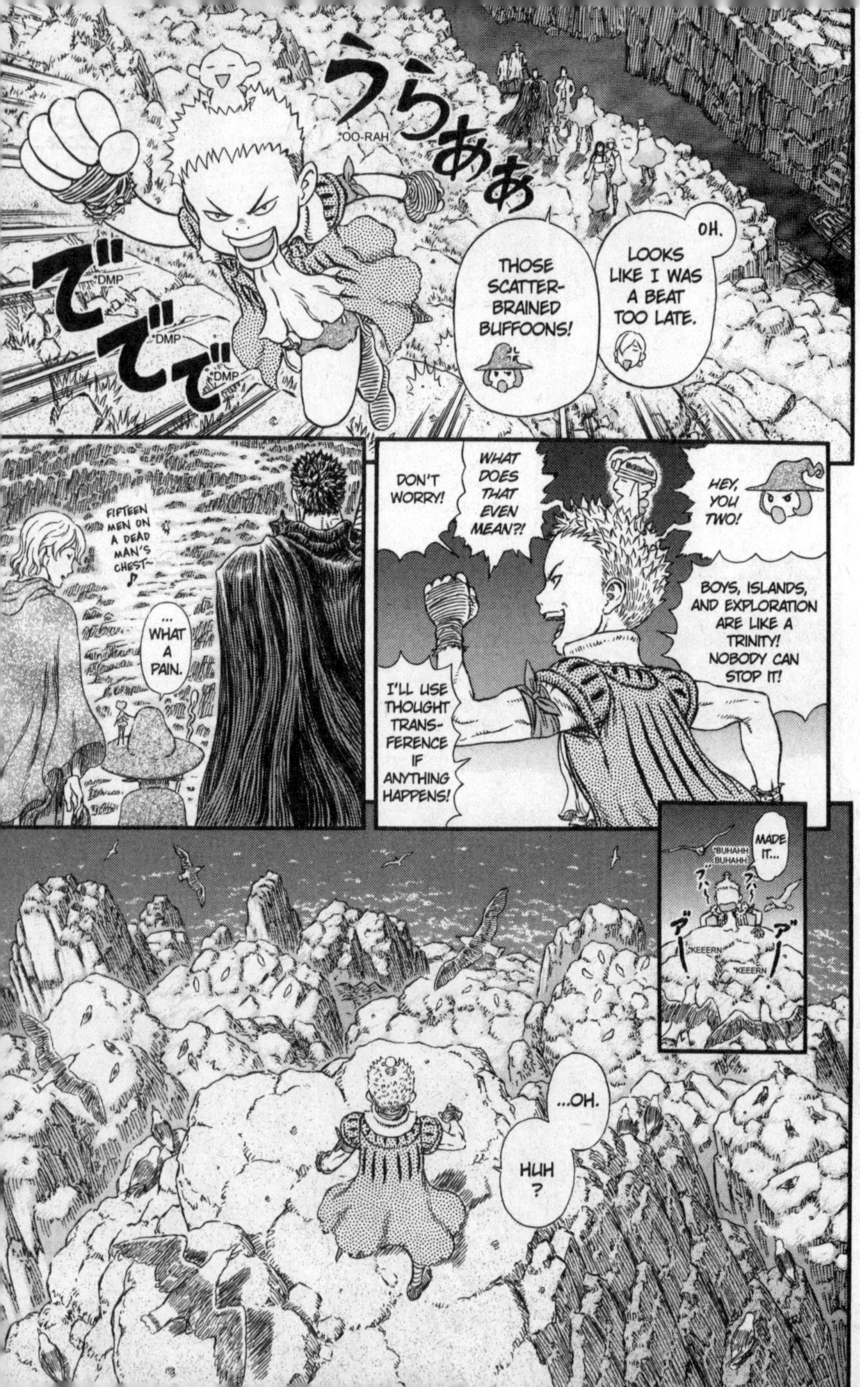
うらあぁ
*OO-RAH
でででで
*DMP
*DMP
*DMP
OH.
LOOKS LIKE I WAS A BEAT TOO LATE.
THOSE SCATTER-BRAINED BUFFOONS!
HEY, YOU TWO!
BOYS, ISLANDS, AND EXPLORATION ARE LIKE A TRINITY! NOBODY CAN STOP IT!
WHAT DOES THAT EVEN MEAN?!
DON'T WORRY!
I'LL USE THOUGHT TRANS-FERENCE IF ANYTHING HAPPENS!
FIFTEEN MEN ON A DEAD MAN'S CHEST~♪
...WHAT A PAIN.
MADE IT...
*BUHAHH BUHAHH
ア゛ー
ア゛ー
*KEEERN
*KEEERN
...OH.
HUH?

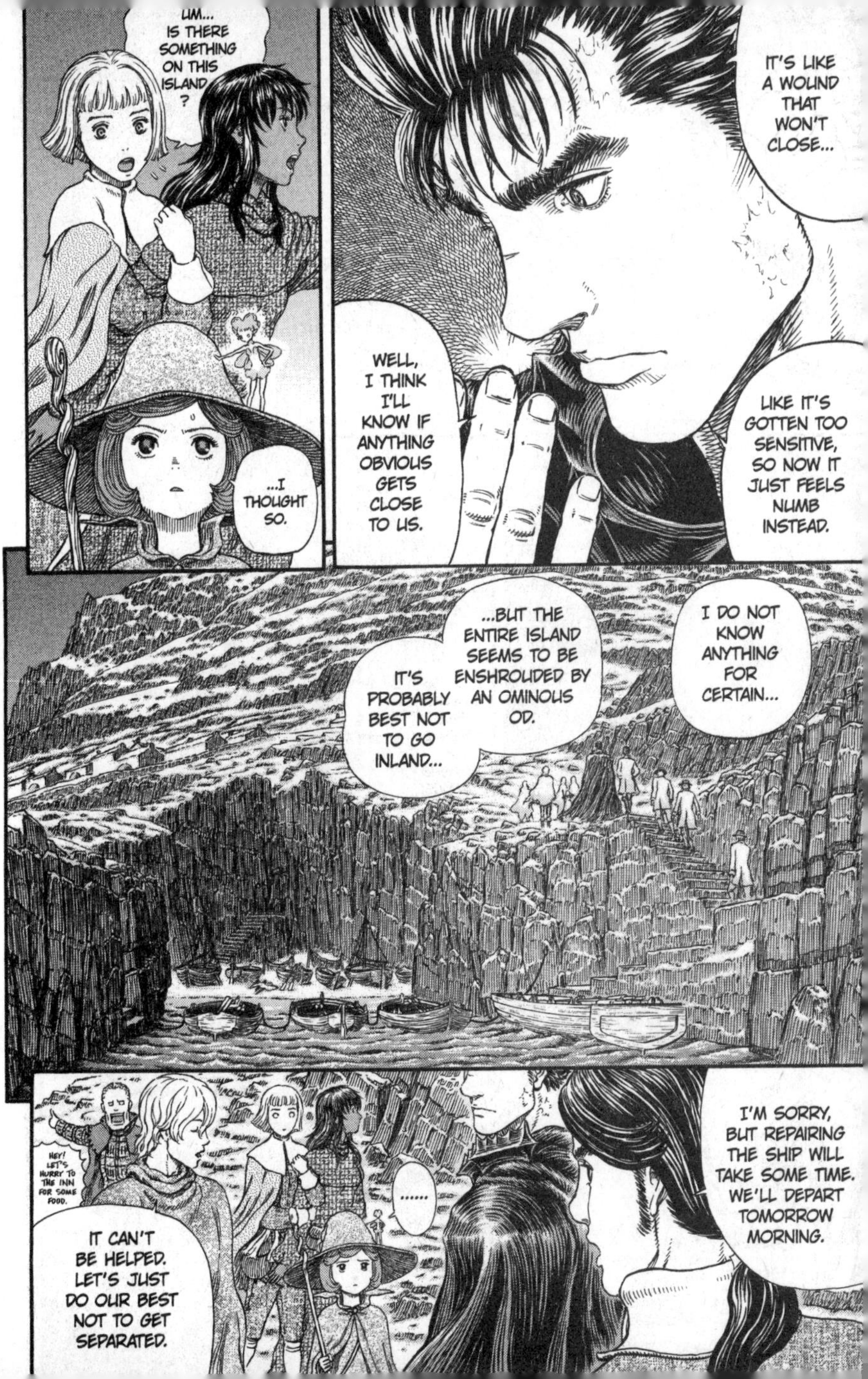
IT'S LIKE A WOUND THAT WON'T CLOSE...
LIKE IT'S GOTTEN TOO SENSITIVE, SO NOW IT JUST FEELS NUMB INSTEAD.
WELL, I THINK I'LL KNOW IF ANYTHING OBVIOUS GETS CLOSE TO US.
UM... IS THERE SOMETHING ON THIS ISLAND?
...I THOUGHT SO.
I DO NOT KNOW ANYTHING FOR CERTAIN...
...BUT THE ENTIRE ISLAND SEEMS TO BE ENSHROUDED BY AN OMINOUS OD.
IT'S PROBABLY BEST NOT TO GO INLAND...
I'M SORRY, BUT REPAIRING THE SHIP WILL TAKE SOME TIME. WE'LL DEPART TOMORROW MORNING.
......
HEY! LET'S HURRY TO THE INN FOR SOME FOOD.
IT CAN'T BE HELPED. LET'S JUST DO OUR BEST NOT TO GET SEPARATED.

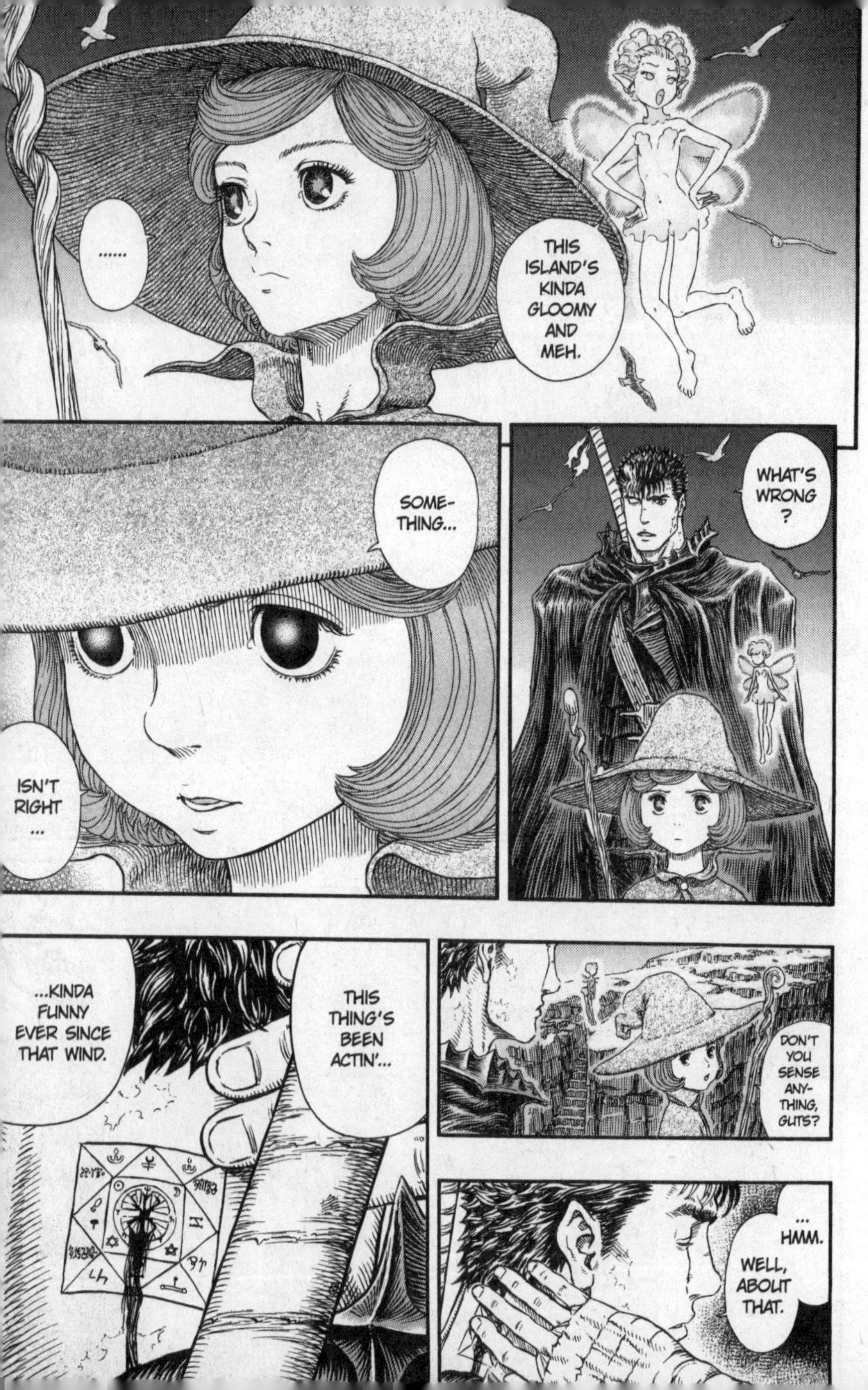
THIS ISLAND'S KINDA GLOOMY AND MEH.
......
WHAT'S WRONG ?
SOME-THING...
ISN'T RIGHT ...
DON'T YOU SENSE ANY-THING, GUTS?
... HMM.
WELL, ABOUT THAT.
THIS THING'S BEEN ACTIN'...
...KINDA FUNNY EVER SINCE THAT WIND.

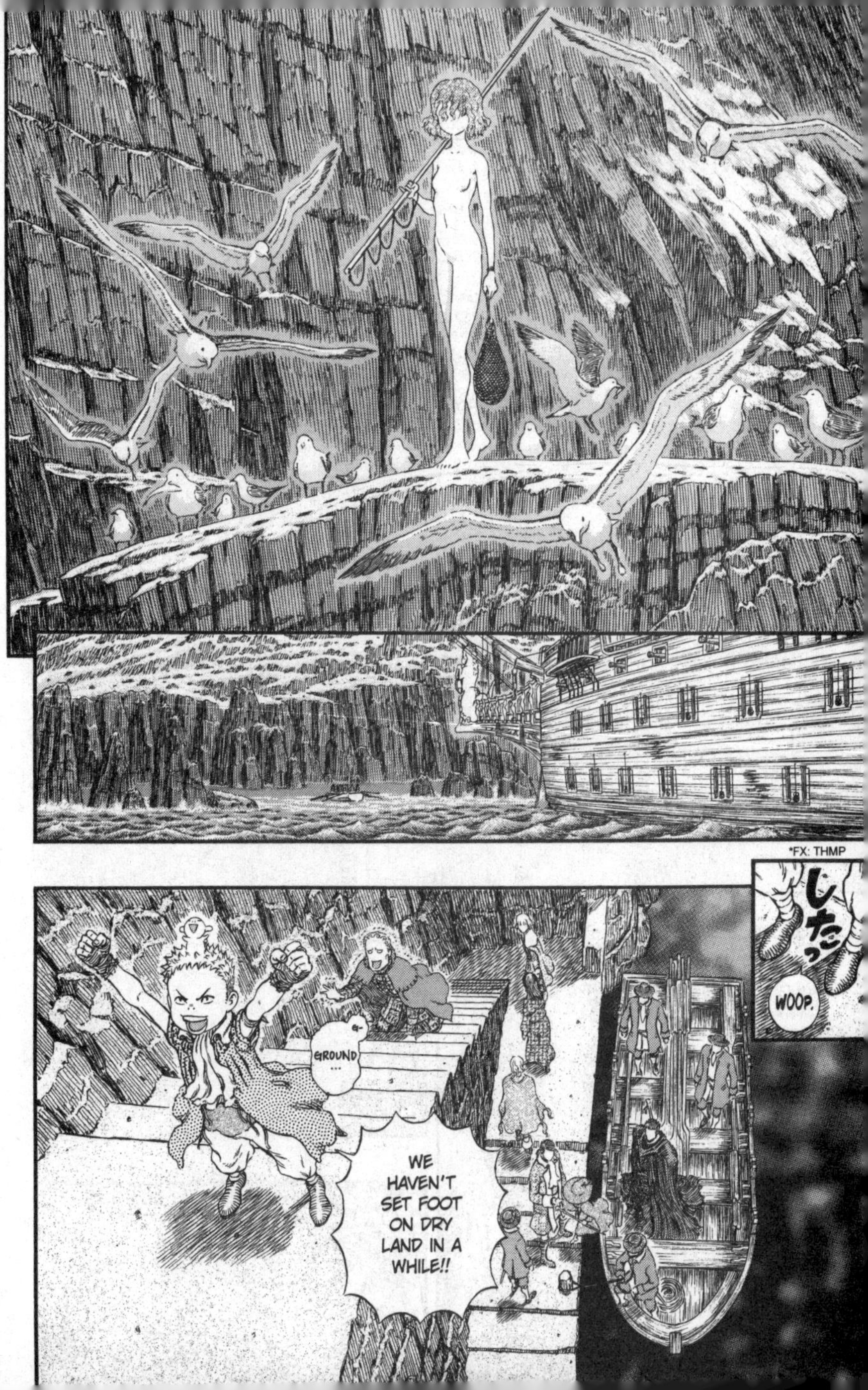
*FX: THMP
したっ
WOOP.
G-GROUND...
WE HAVEN'T SET FOOT ON DRY LAND IN A WHILE!!

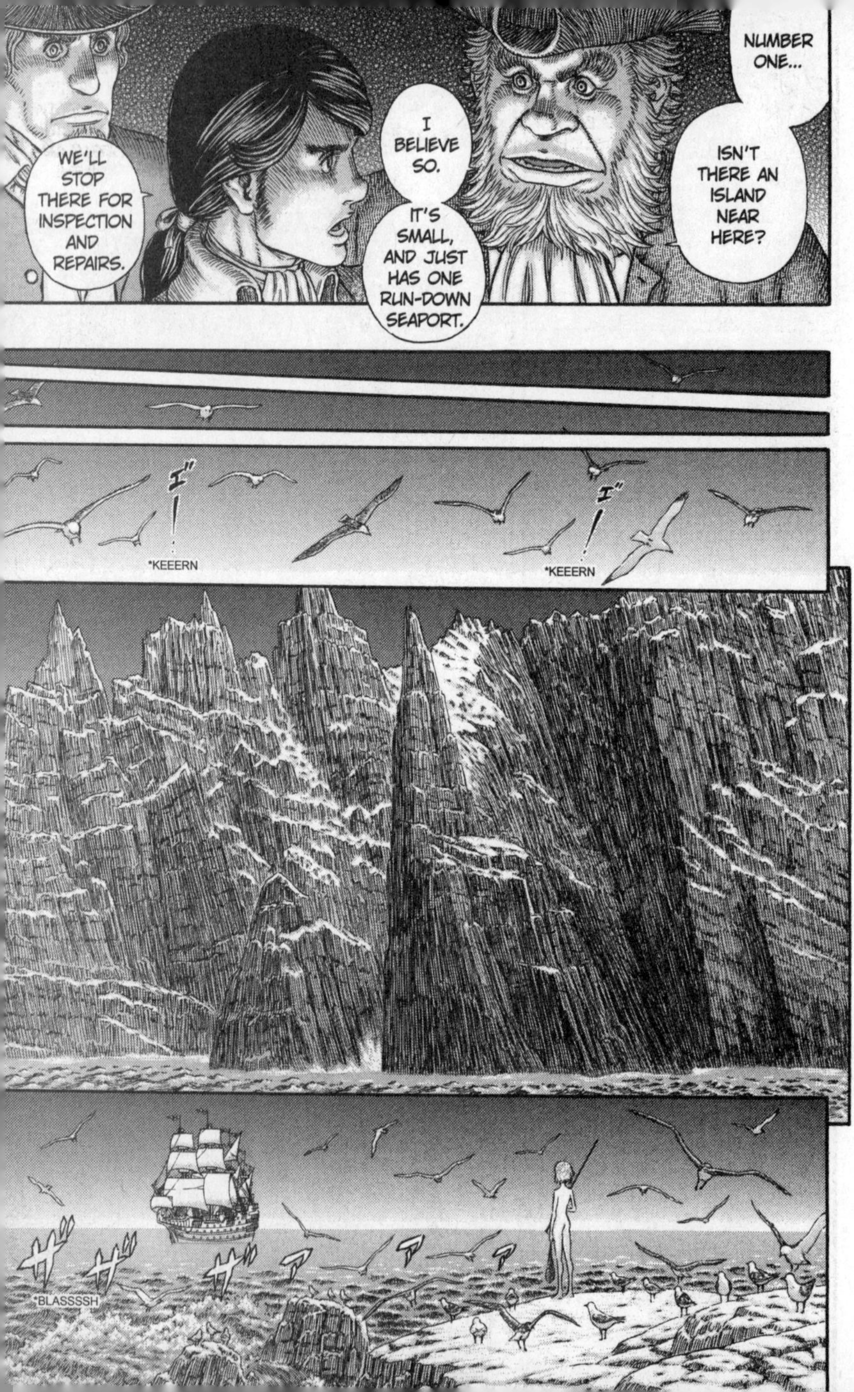
NUMBER ONE...
ISN'T THERE AN ISLAND NEAR HERE?
I BELIEVE SO.
IT'S SMALL, AND JUST HAS ONE RUN-DOWN SEAPORT.
WE'LL STOP THERE FOR INSPECTION AND REPAIRS.
*KEEERN
*KEEERN
*BLASSSSH

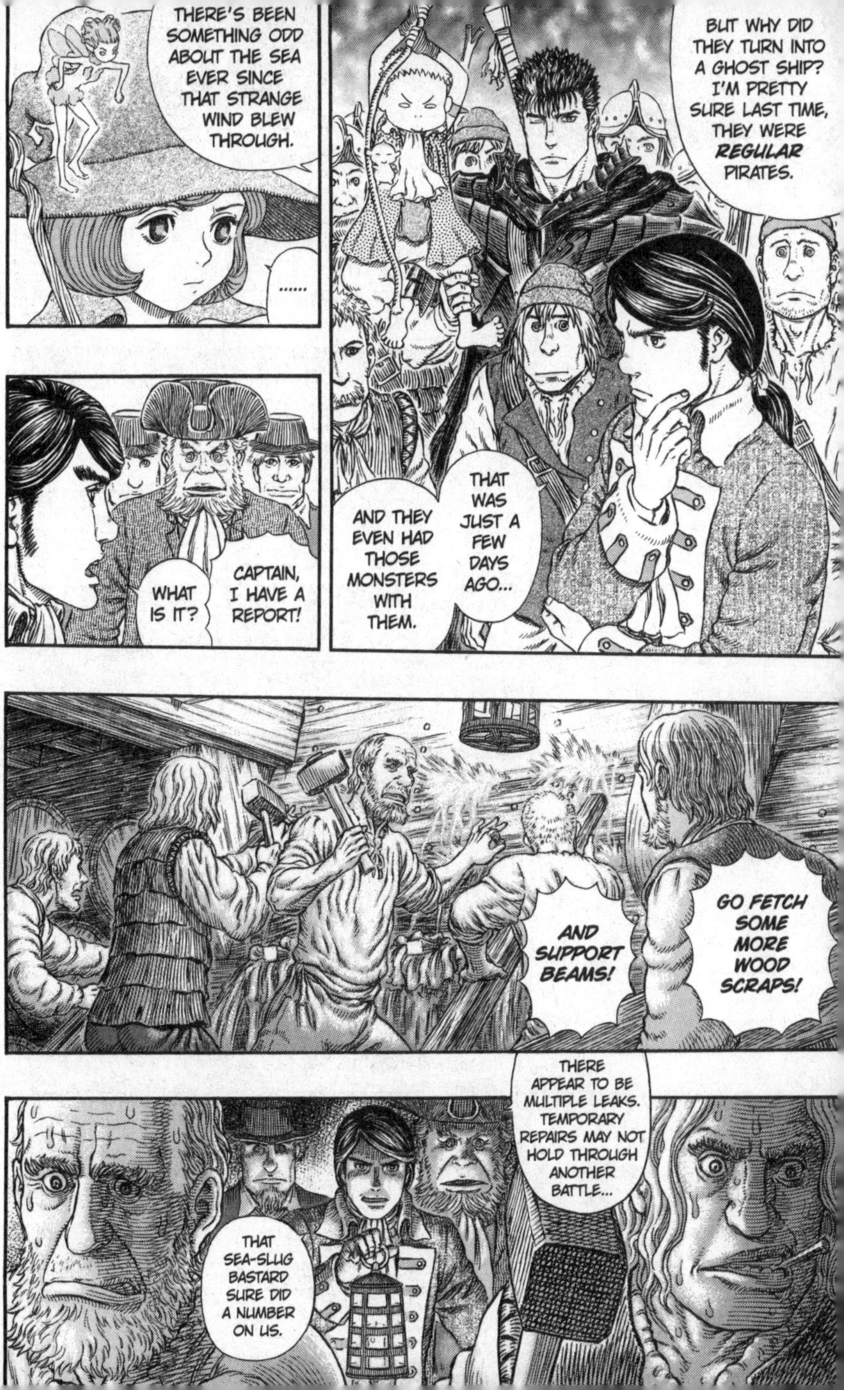
BUT WHY DID THEY TURN INTO A GHOST SHIP? I'M PRETTY SURE LAST TIME, THEY WERE REGULAR PIRATES.
THAT WAS JUST A FEW DAYS AGO...
AND THEY EVEN HAD THOSE MONSTERS WITH THEM.
THERE'S BEEN SOMETHING ODD ABOUT THE SEA EVER SINCE THAT STRANGE WIND BLEW THROUGH.
......
CAPTAIN, I HAVE A REPORT!
WHAT IS IT?
GO FETCH SOME MORE WOOD SCRAPS!
AND SUPPORT BEAMS!
THERE APPEAR TO BE MULTIPLE LEAKS. TEMPORARY REPAIRS MAY NOT HOLD THROUGH ANOTHER BATTLE...
THAT SEA-SLUG BASTARD SURE DID A NUMBER ON US.

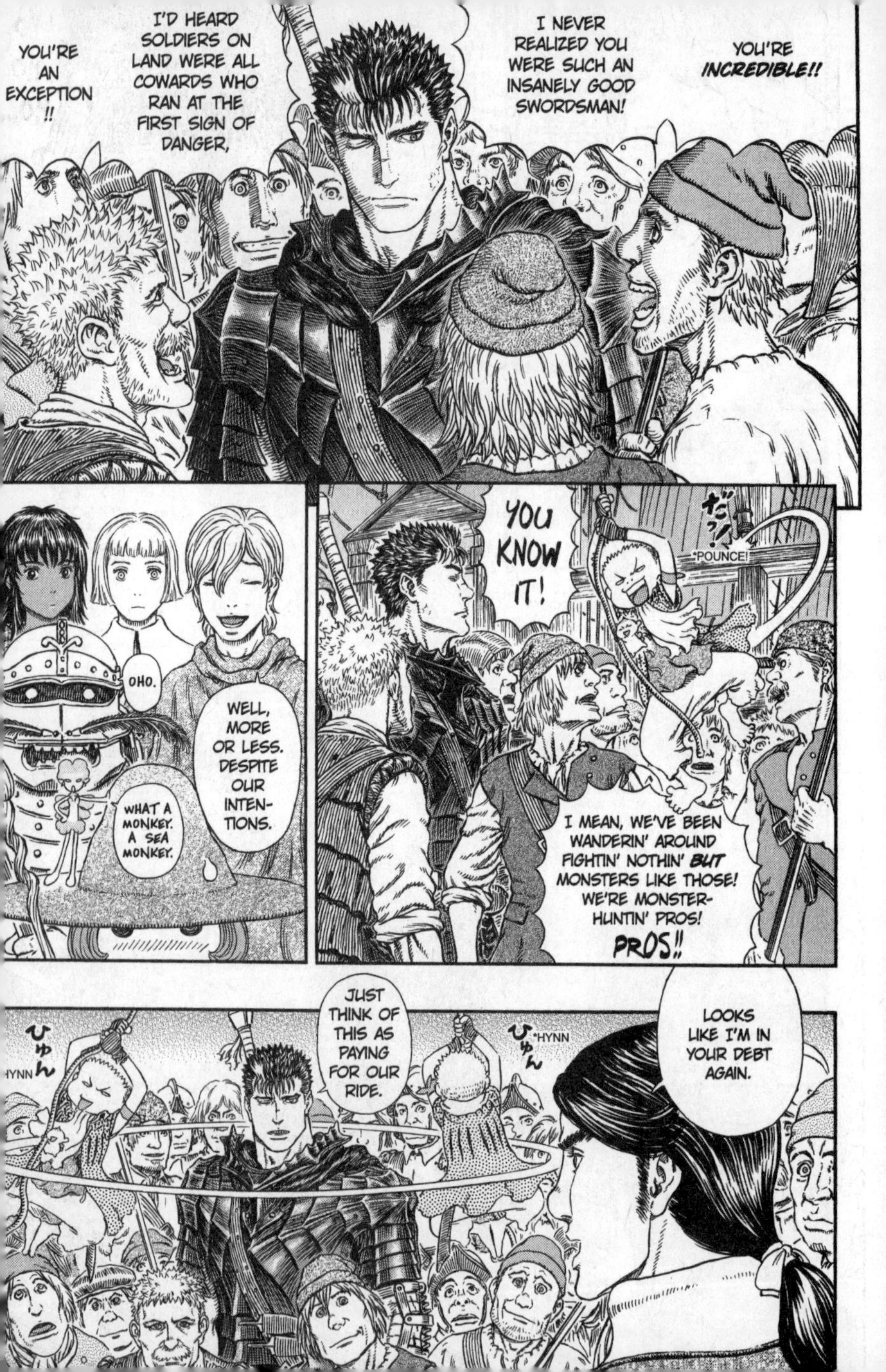
YOU'RE INCREDIBLE!!
I NEVER REALIZED YOU WERE SUCH AN INSANELY GOOD SWORDSMAN!
I'D HEARD SOLDIERS ON LAND WERE ALL COWARDS WHO RAN AT THE FIRST SIGN OF DANGER,
YOU'RE AN EXCEPTION!!
*POUNCE!
YOU KNOW IT!
I MEAN, WE'VE BEEN WANDERIN' AROUND FIGHTIN' NOTHIN' BUT MONSTERS LIKE THOSE! WE'RE MONSTER-HUNTIN' PROS! PROS!!
WELL, MORE OR LESS. DESPITE OUR INTENTIONS.
OHO.
WHAT A MONKEY. A SEA MONKEY.
LOOKS LIKE I'M IN YOUR DEBT AGAIN.
ひゅん *HYNN
JUST THINK OF THIS AS PAYING FOR OUR RIDE.
ひゅん HYNN

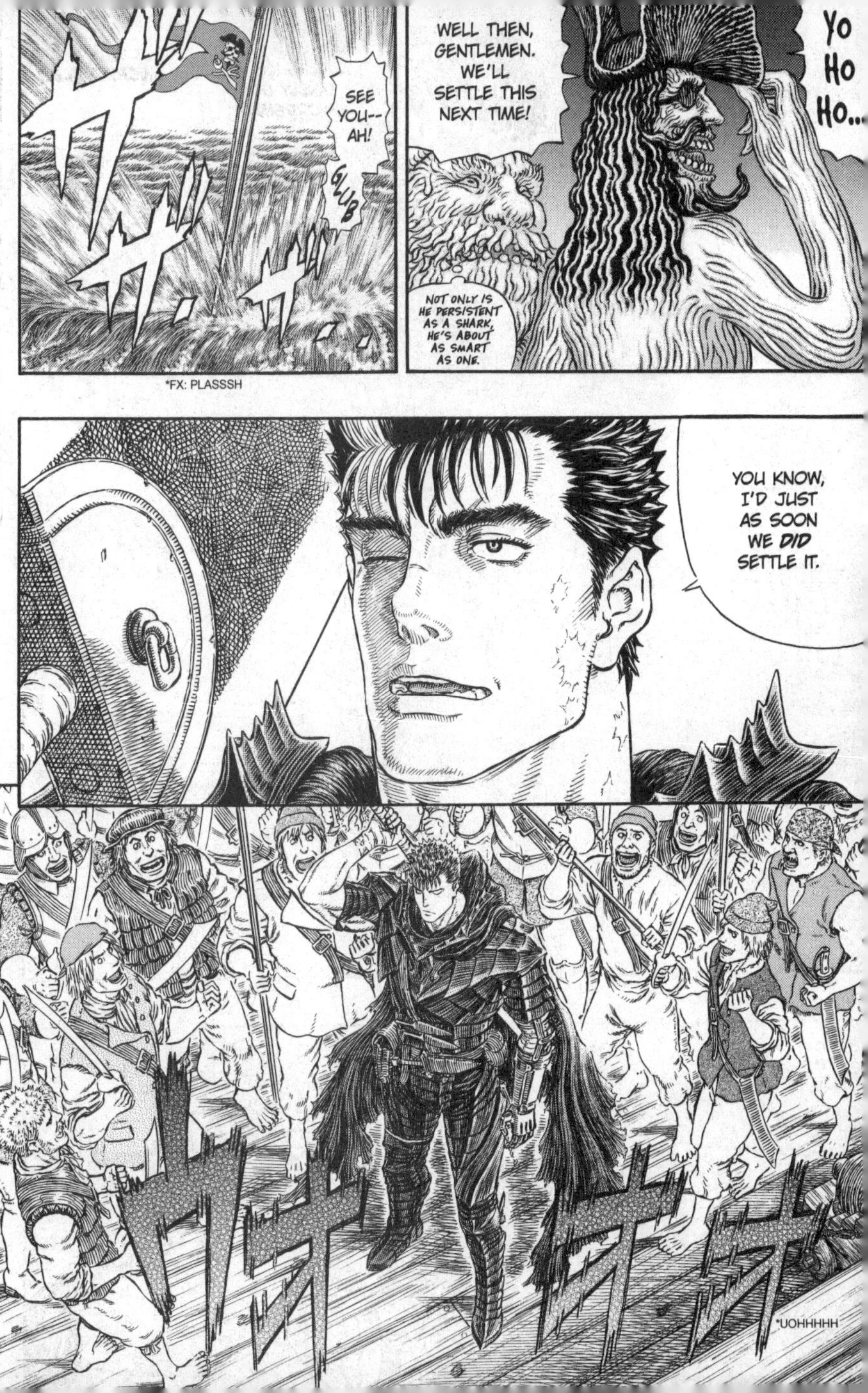
WELL THEN, GENTLEMEN. WE'LL SETTLE THIS NEXT TIME!
YO HO HO...
NOT ONLY IS HE PERSISTENT AS A SHARK, HE'S ABOUT AS SMART AS ONE.
SEE YOU-- AH!
GLUB
*FX: PLASSSH
YOU KNOW, I'D JUST AS SOON WE *DID* SETTLE IT.
*UOHHHH

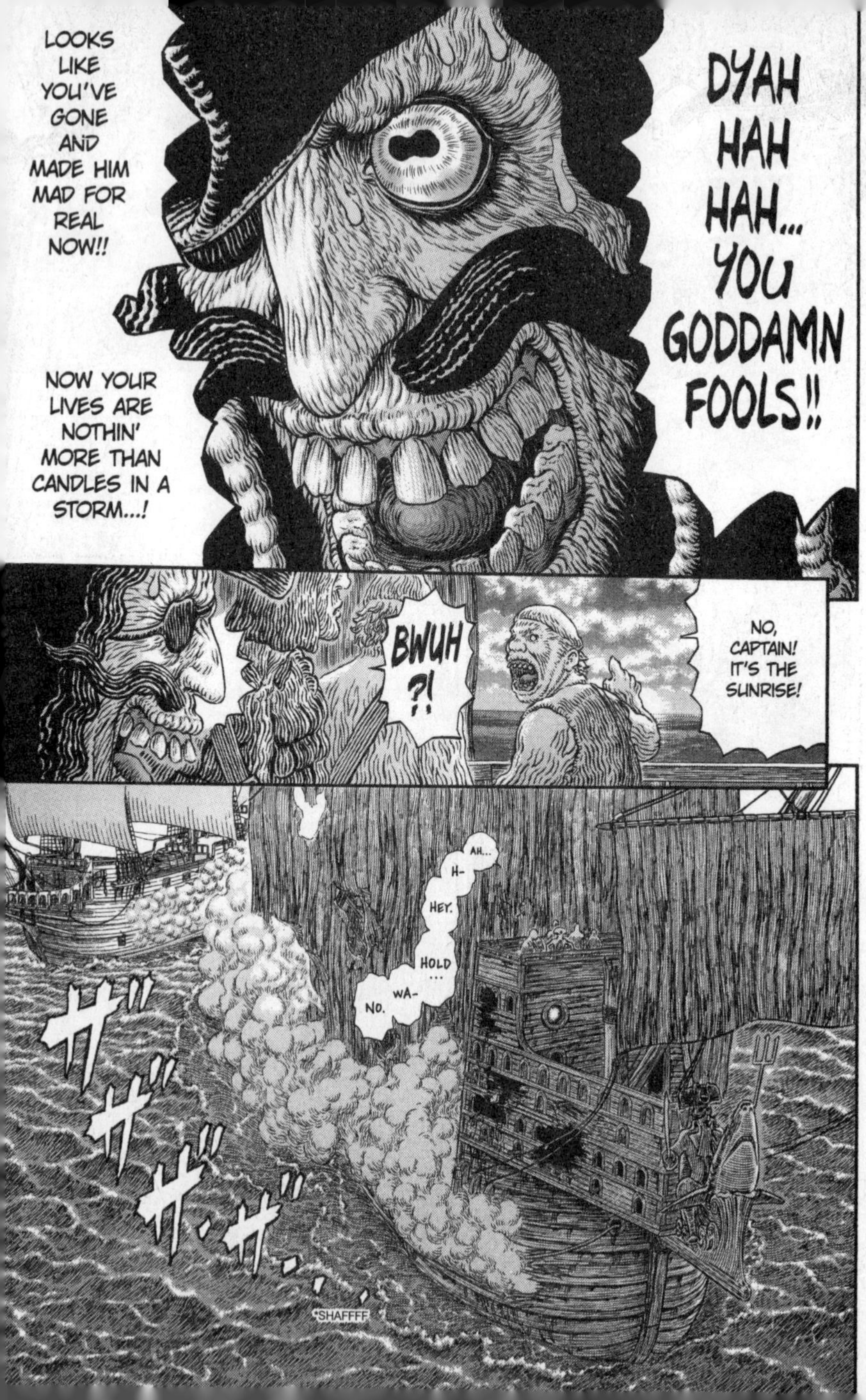
DYAH HAH HAH... YOU GODDAMN FOOLS!!
LOOKS LIKE YOU'VE GONE AND MADE HIM MAD FOR REAL NOW!!
NOW YOUR LIVES ARE NOTHIN' MORE THAN CANDLES IN A STORM...!
NO, CAPTAIN! IT'S THE SUNRISE!
BWUH ?!
AH...
H-
HEY.
HOLD...
WA-
NO.
ザ ザ ザ ザ ザ
*SHAFFFF

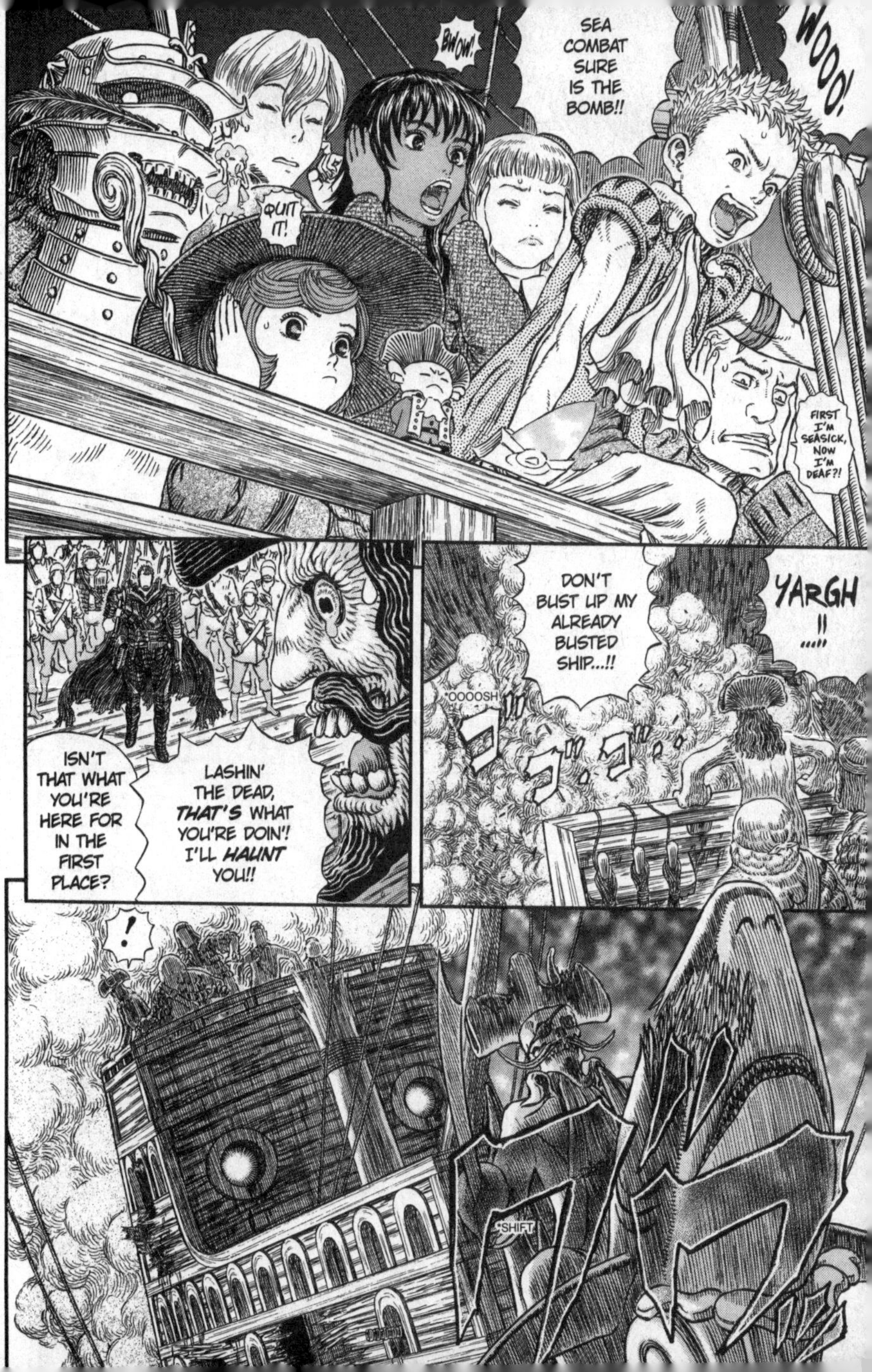
WOOO!
SEA COMBAT SURE IS THE BOMB!!
BWOW!
FIRST I'M SEASICK, NOW I'M DEAF?!
QUIT IT!
YARGH !! ....!!
DON'T BUST UP MY ALREADY BUSTED SHIP...!!
*OOOOSH
LASHIN' THE DEAD, *THAT'S* WHAT YOU'RE DOIN'! I'LL *HAUNT* YOU!!
ISN'T THAT WHAT YOU'RE HERE FOR IN THE FIRST PLACE?
!
*SHIFT

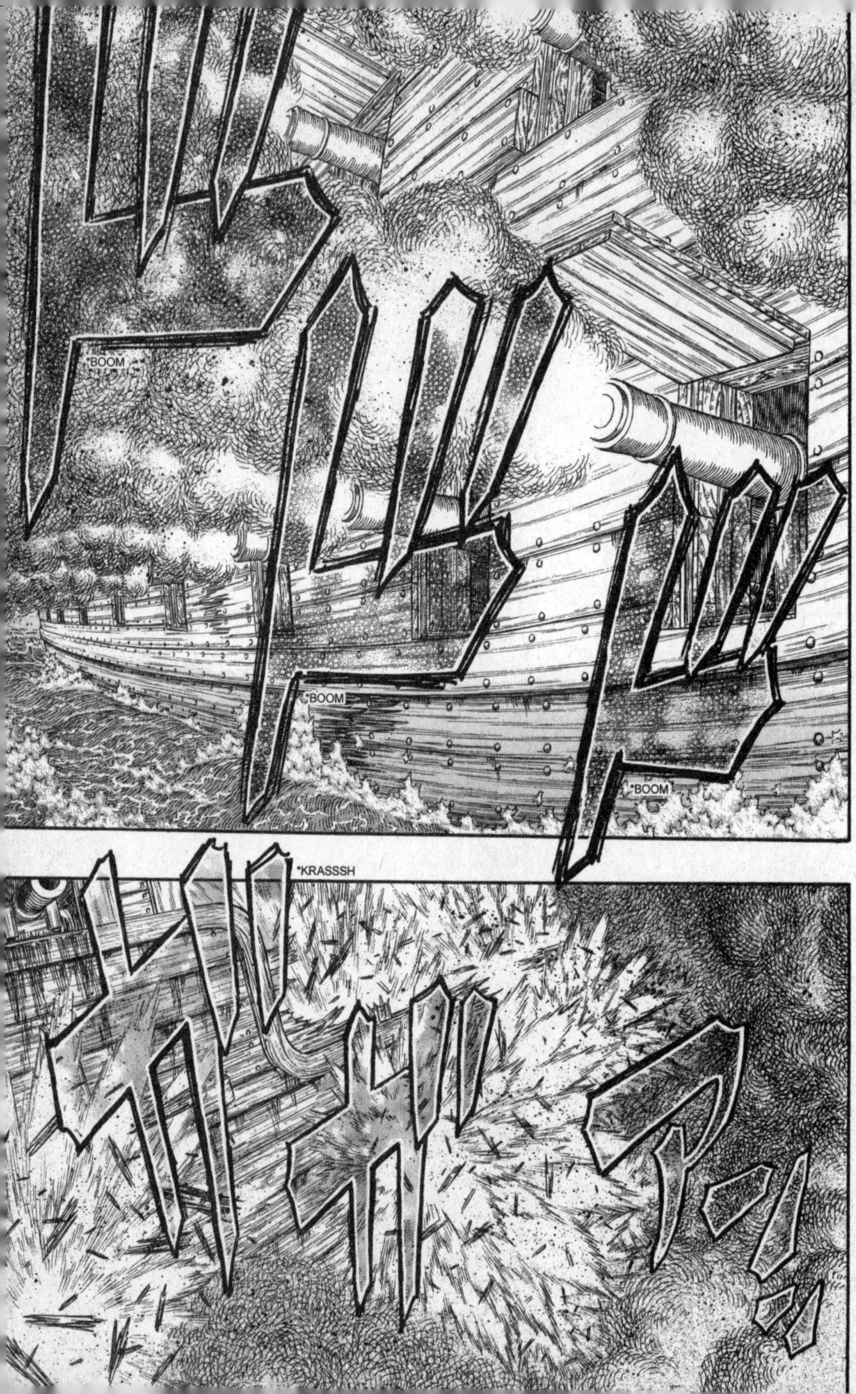
*BOOM
*BOOM
*BOOM
*KRASSSH

幻造世界（ファンタジア）篇／妖精島の章

孤島

SOLITARY ISLAND

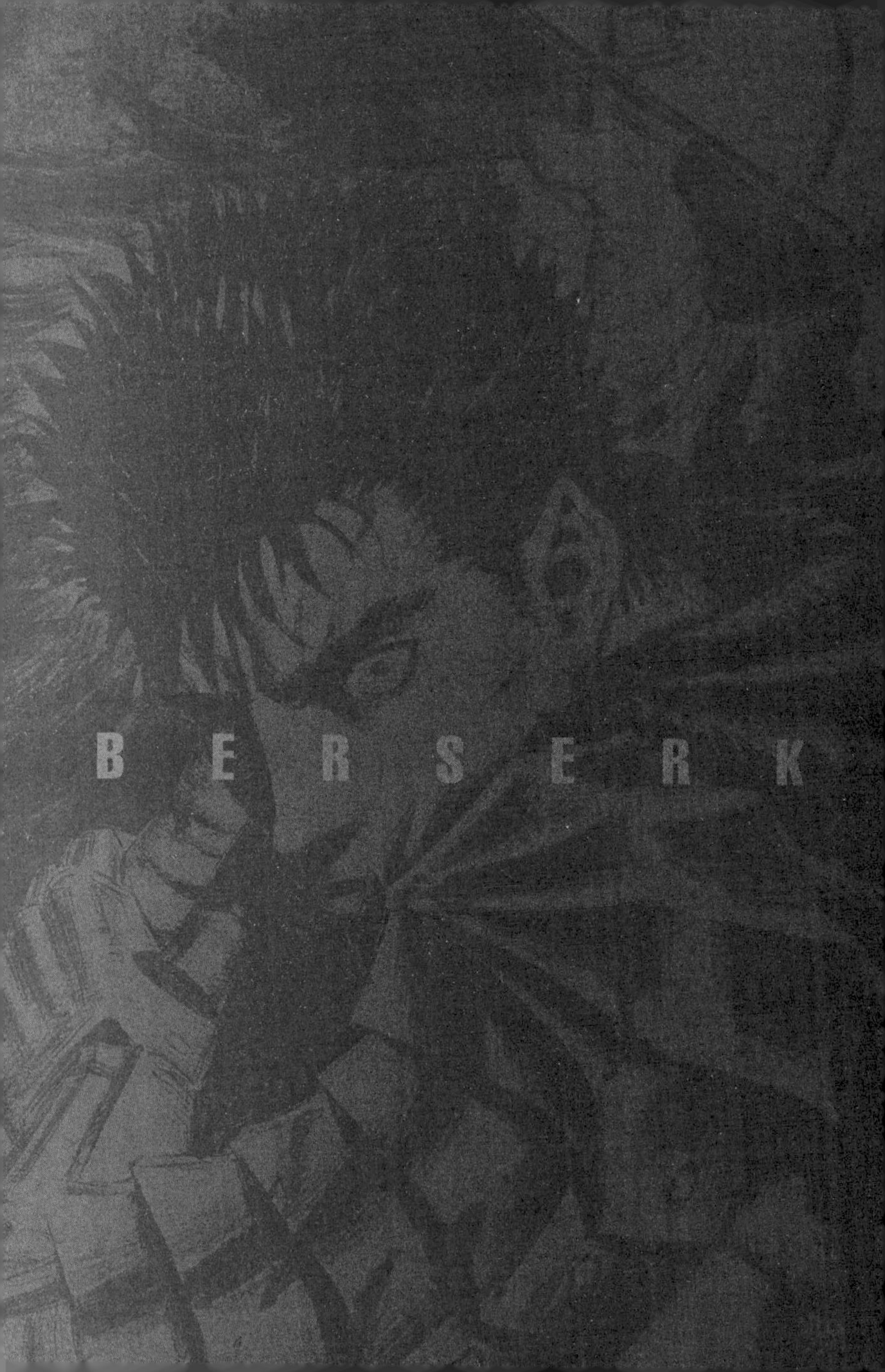
BERSERK

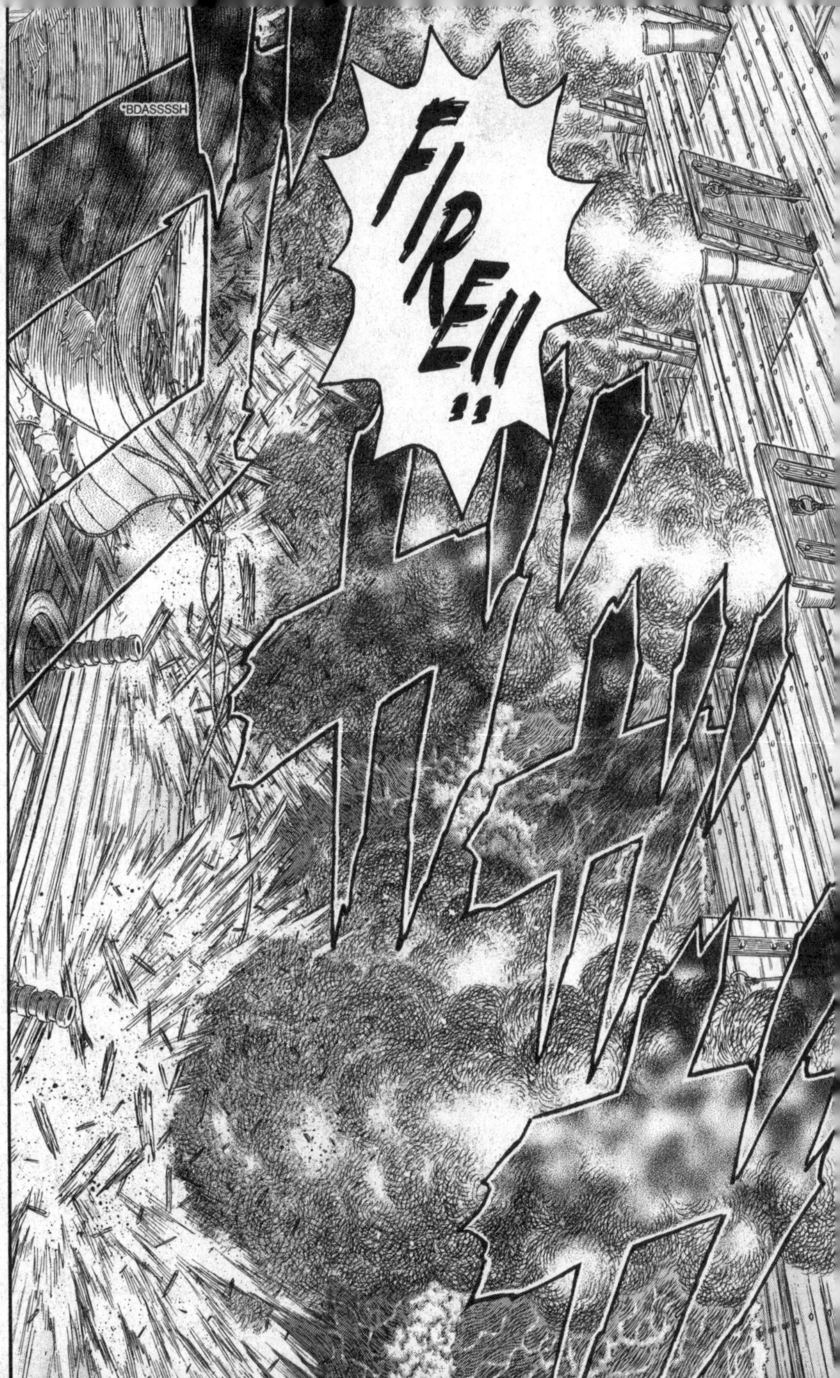

FIRE!!
*BDASSSSH

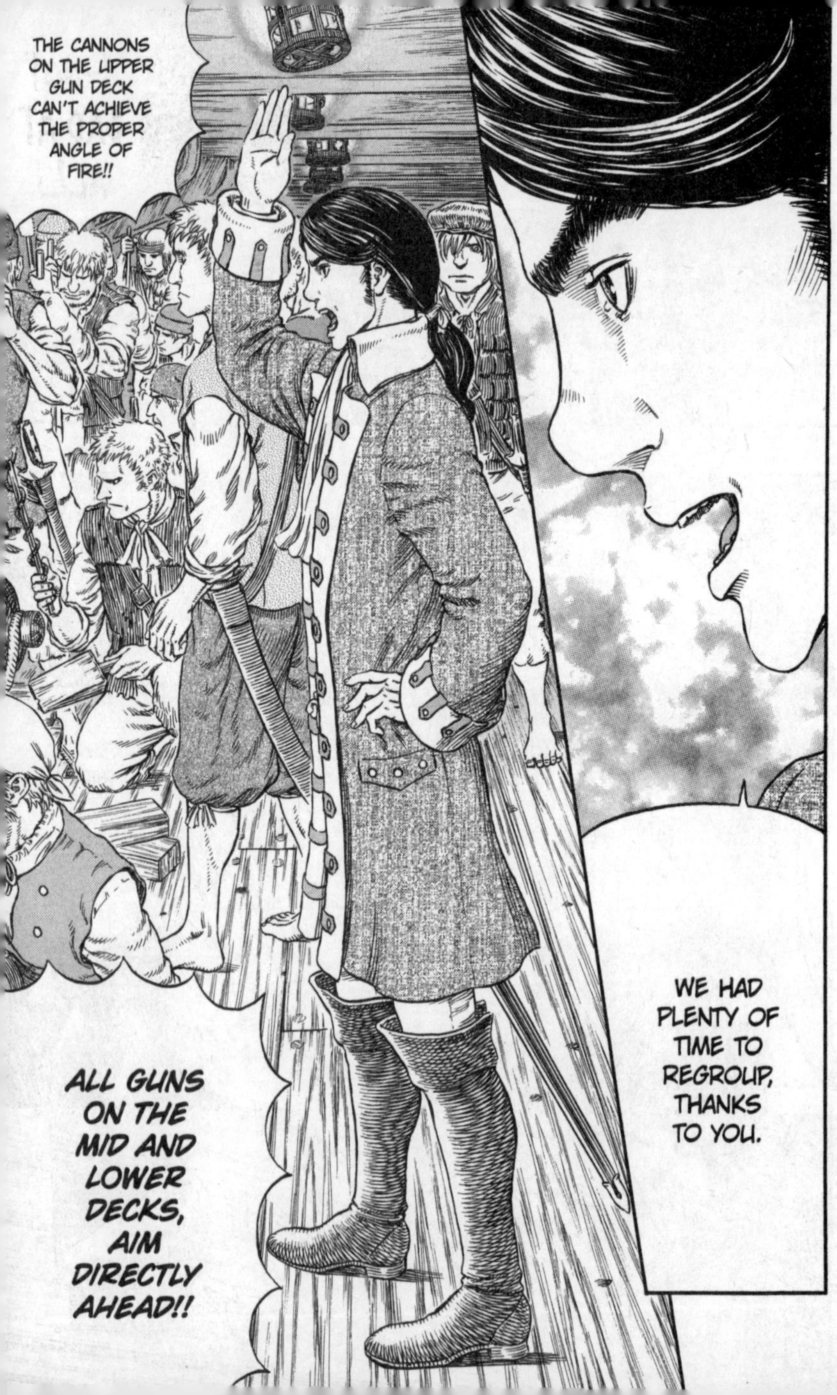
WE HAD PLENTY OF TIME TO REGROUP, THANKS TO YOU.
THE CANNONS ON THE UPPER GUN DECK CAN'T ACHIEVE THE PROPER ANGLE OF FIRE!!
ALL GUNS ON THE MID AND LOWER DECKS, AIM DIRECTLY AHEAD!!

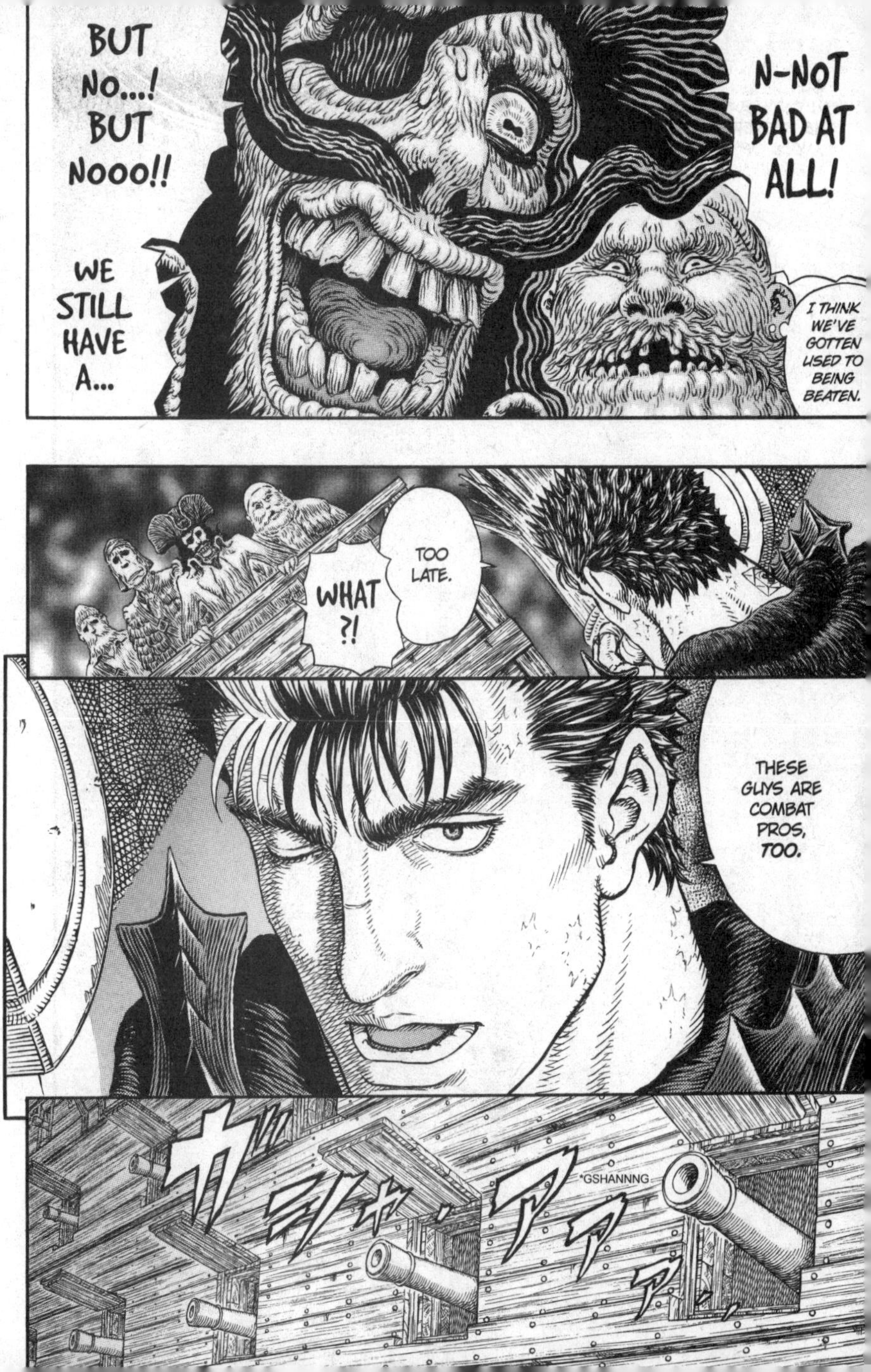
N-NOT BAD AT ALL!
I THINK WE'VE GOTTEN USED TO BEING BEATEN.
BUT NO...! BUT NOOO!!
WE STILL HAVE A...
TOO LATE.
WHAT ?!
THESE GUYS ARE COMBAT PROS, TOO.
*GSHANNNG

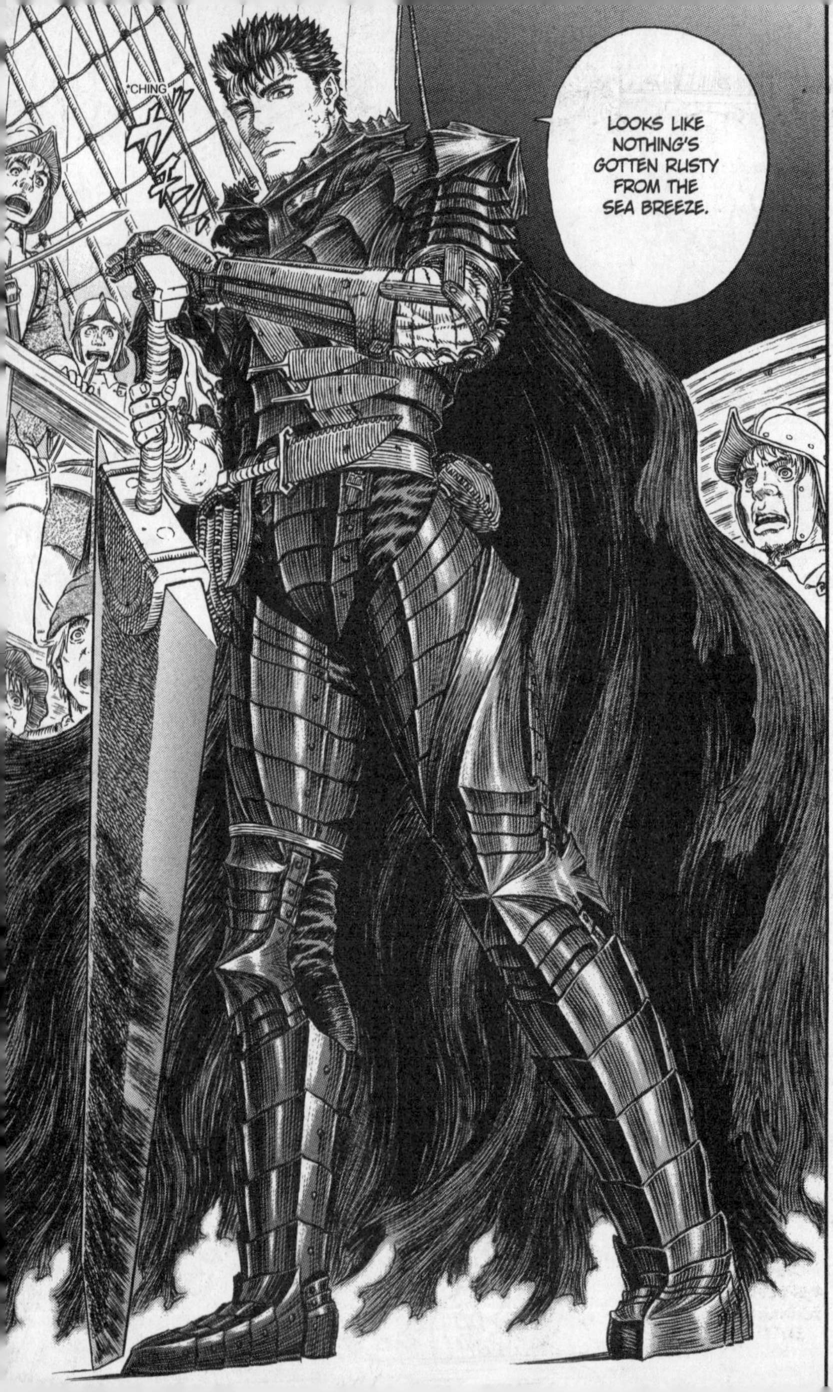
LOOKS LIKE NOTHING'S GOTTEN RUSTY FROM THE SEA BREEZE.
*CHING

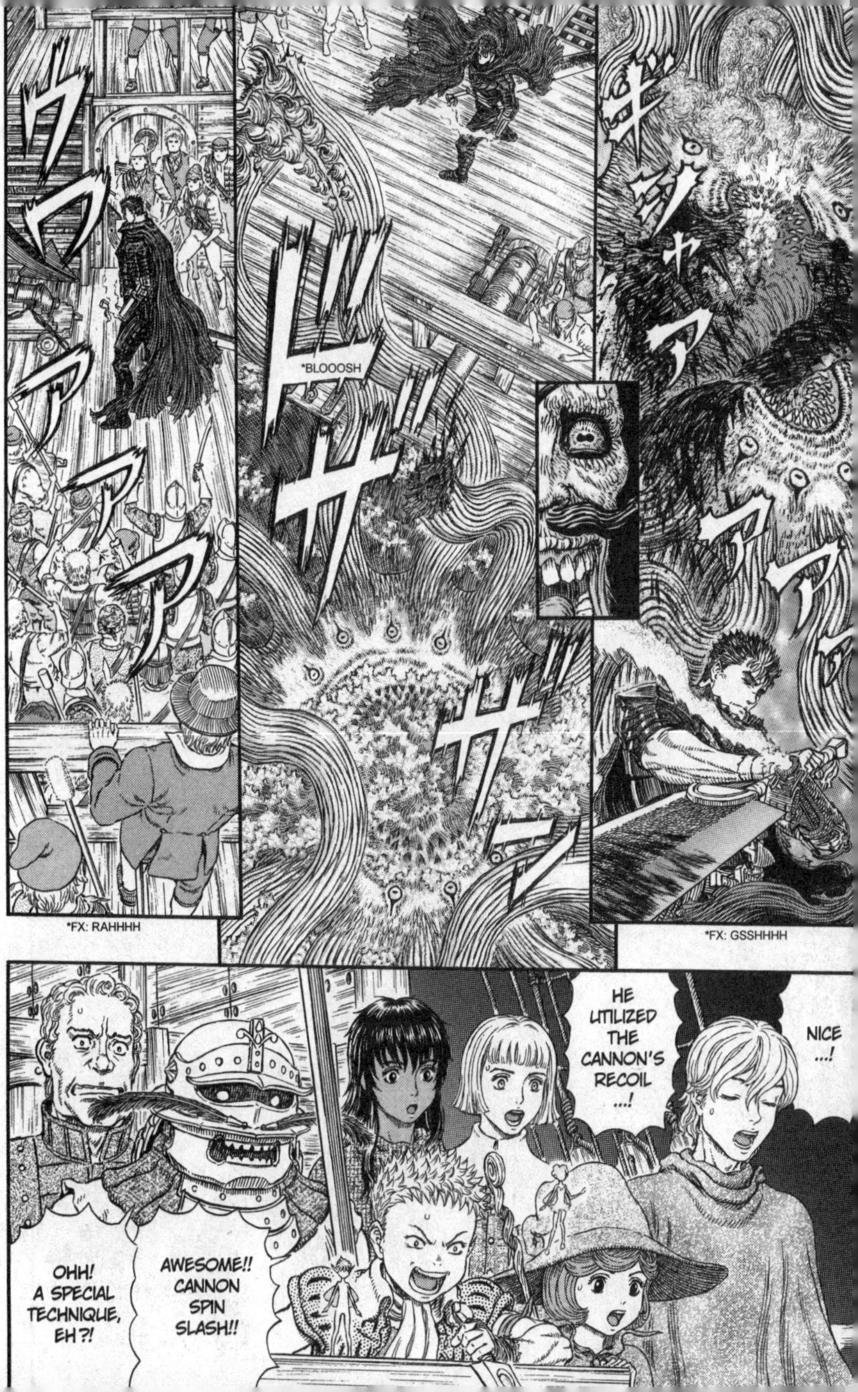
*FX: GSSHHHH
*BLOOOSH
*FX: RAHHHH
NICE ...!
HE UTILIZED THE CANNON'S RECOIL ...!
AWESOME!! CANNON SPIN SLASH!!
OHH! A SPECIAL TECHNIQUE, EH?!

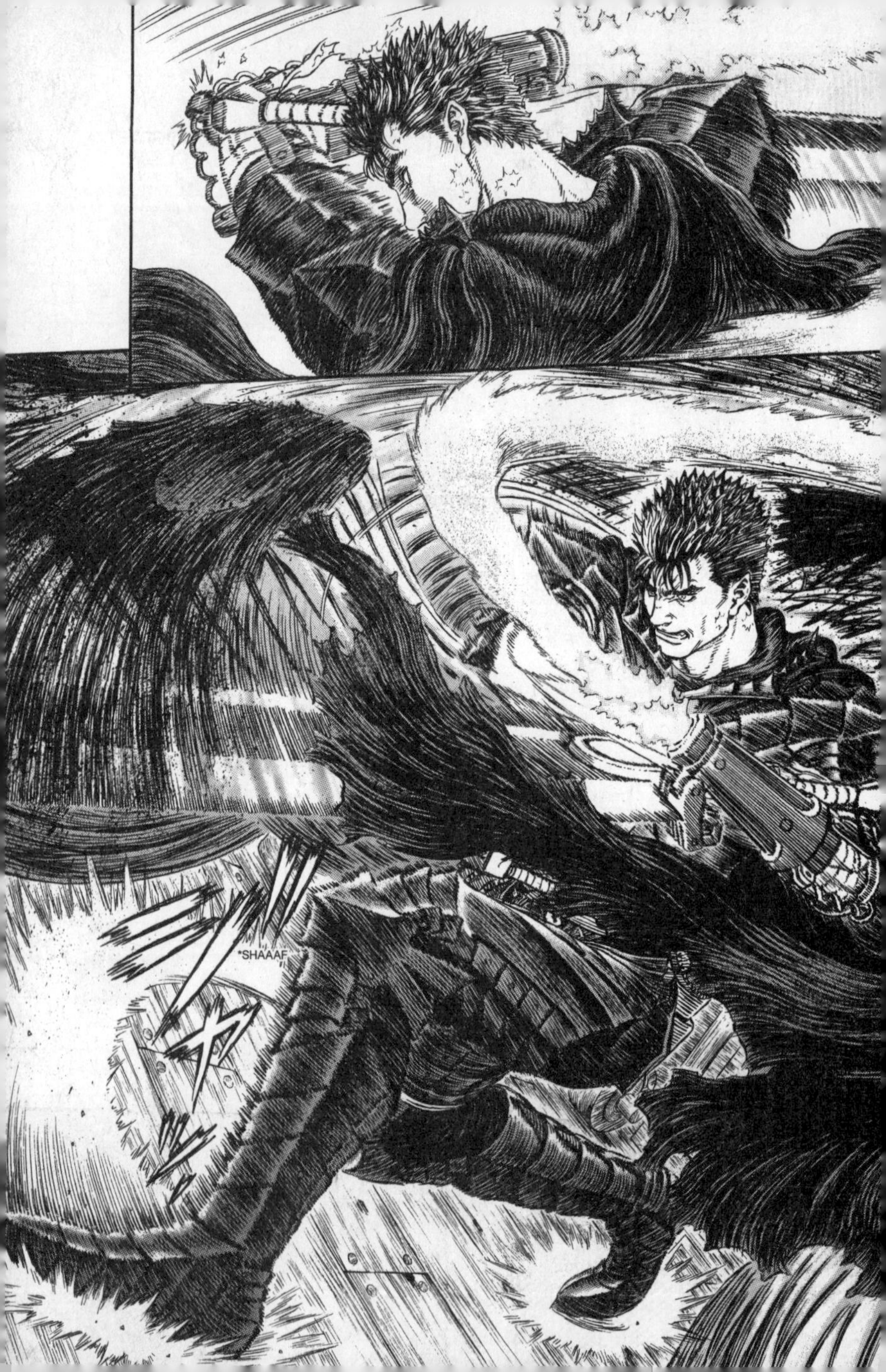
*SHAAAF

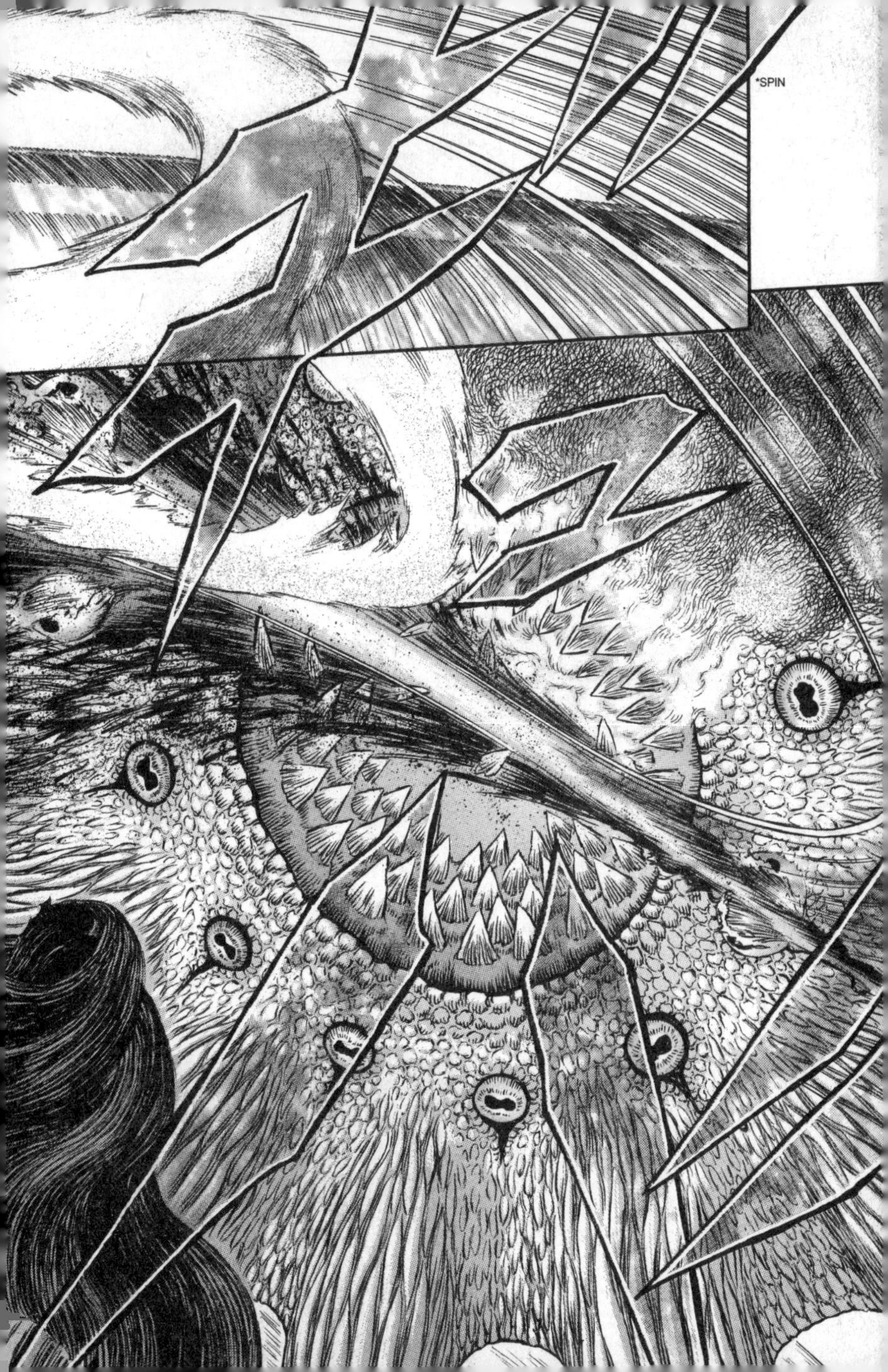
*SPIN

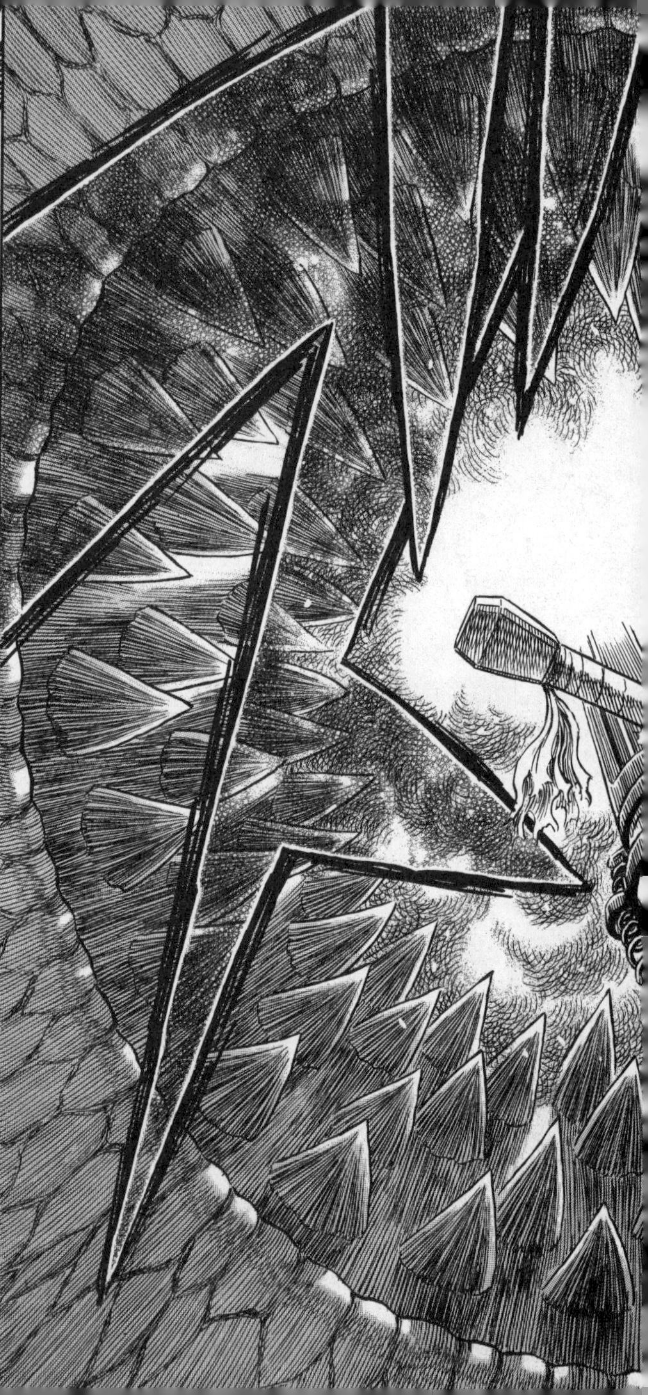

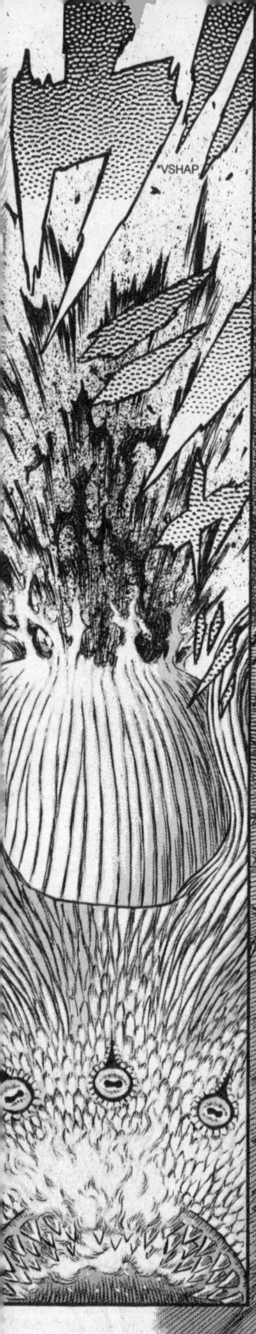
VSHAP

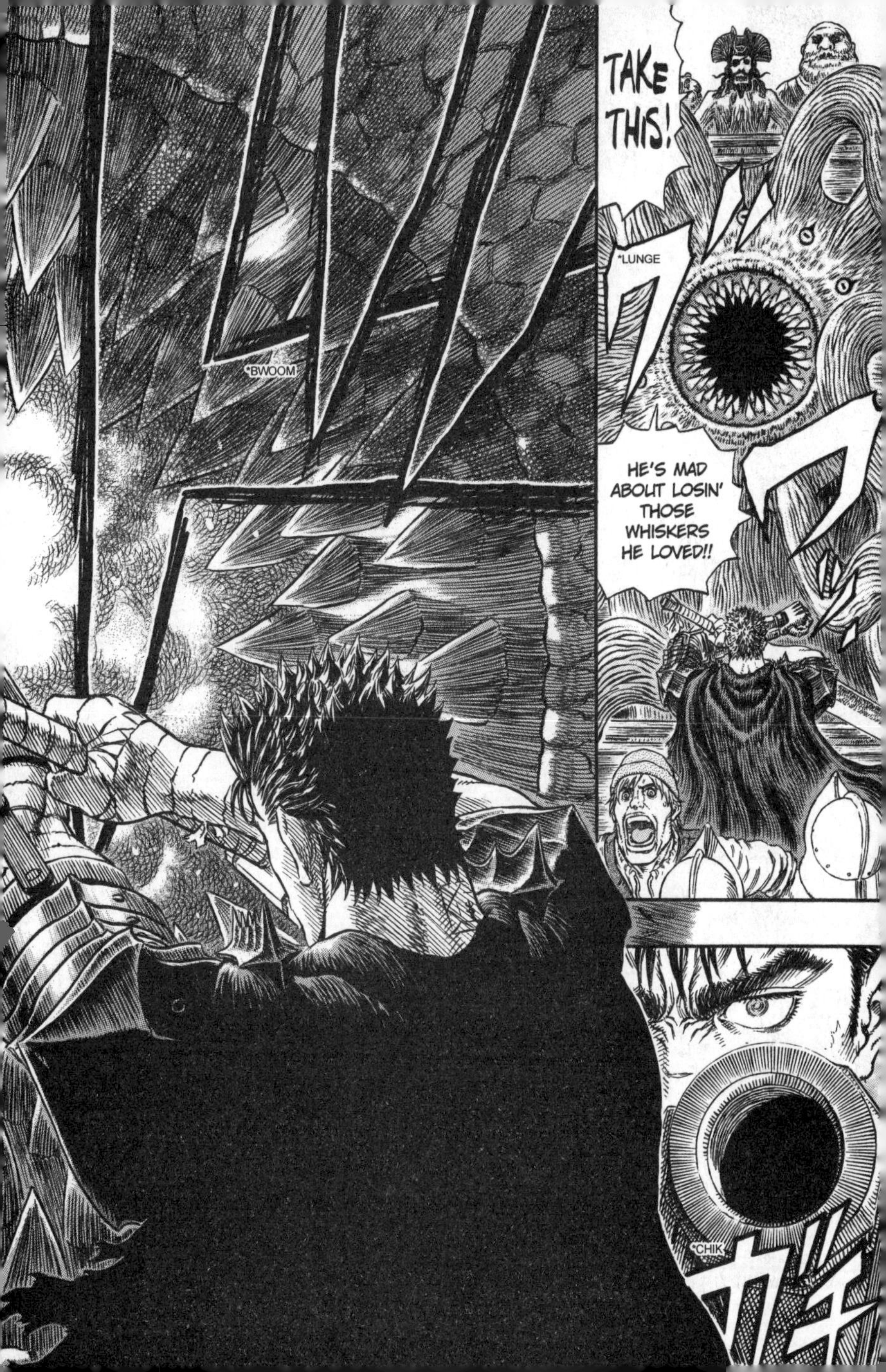
TAKE THIS!
*LUNGE
HE'S MAD ABOUT LOSIN' THOSE WHISKERS HE LOVED!!
*CHIK
*BWOOM

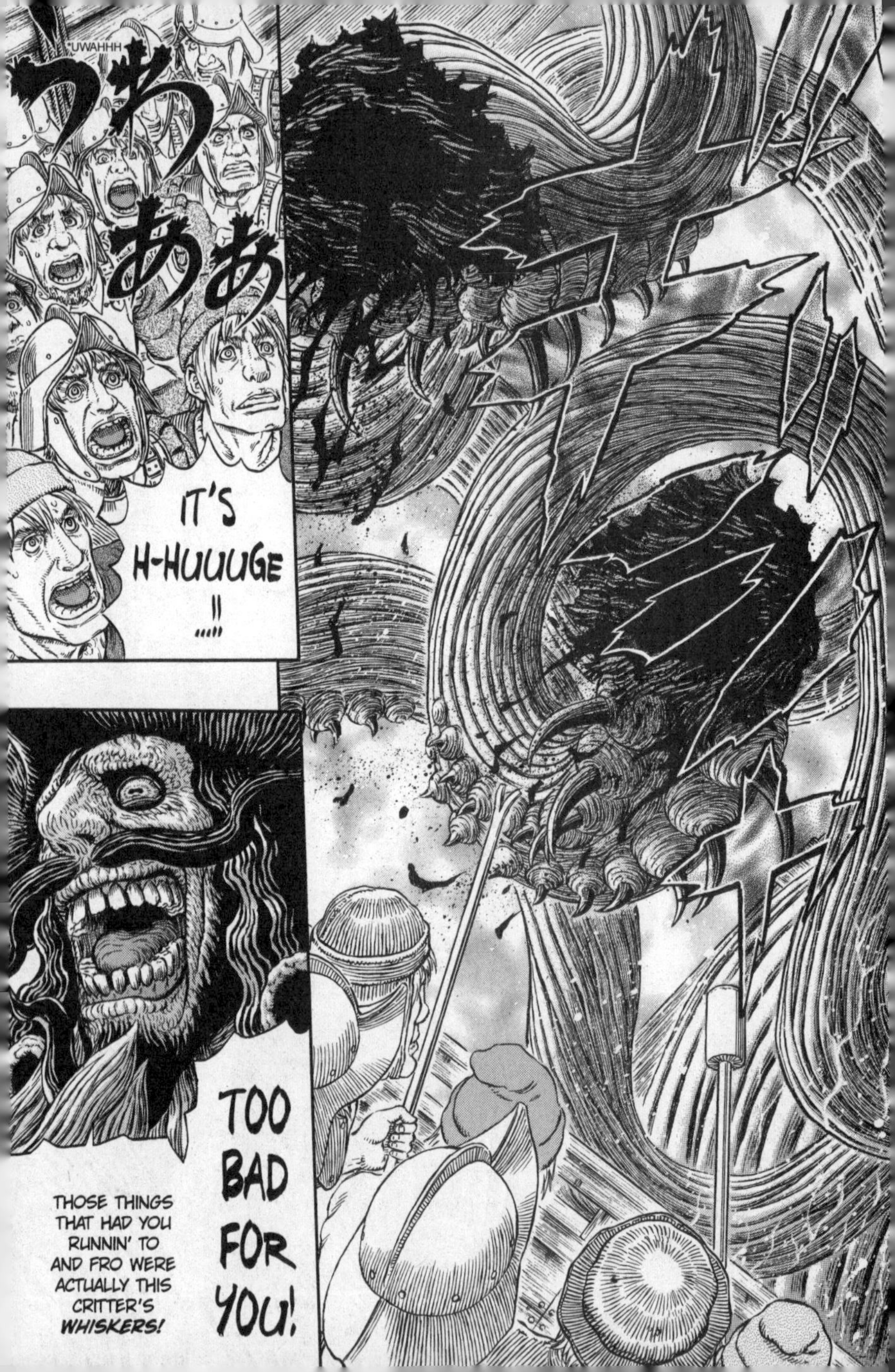
うわああ
*UWAHHH
IT'S H-HUUUGE ...!!
TOO BAD FOR YOU!
THOSE THINGS THAT HAD YOU RUNNIN' TO AND FRO WERE ACTUALLY THIS CRITTER'S *WHISKERS!*

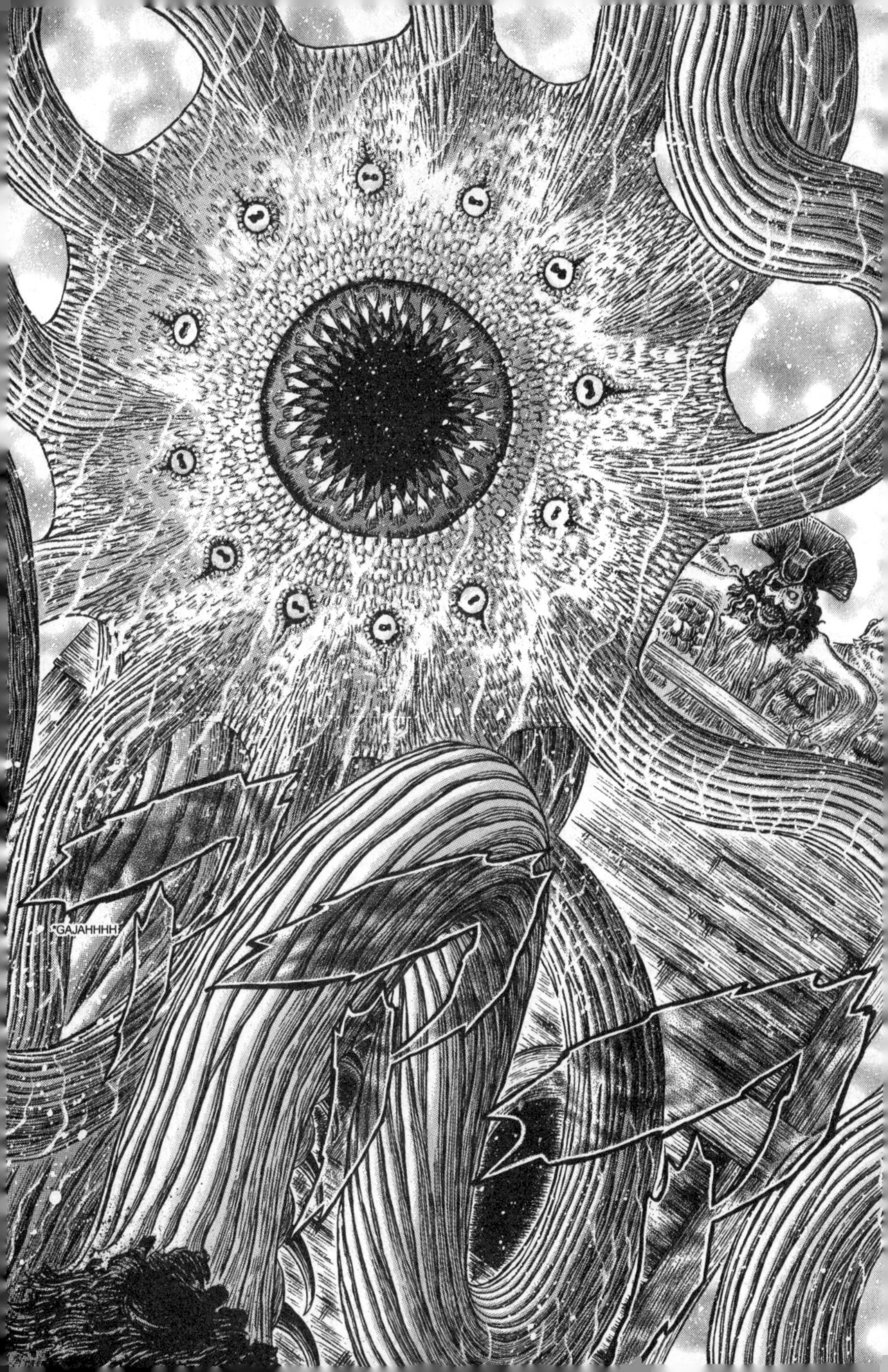
*GAJAHHHH

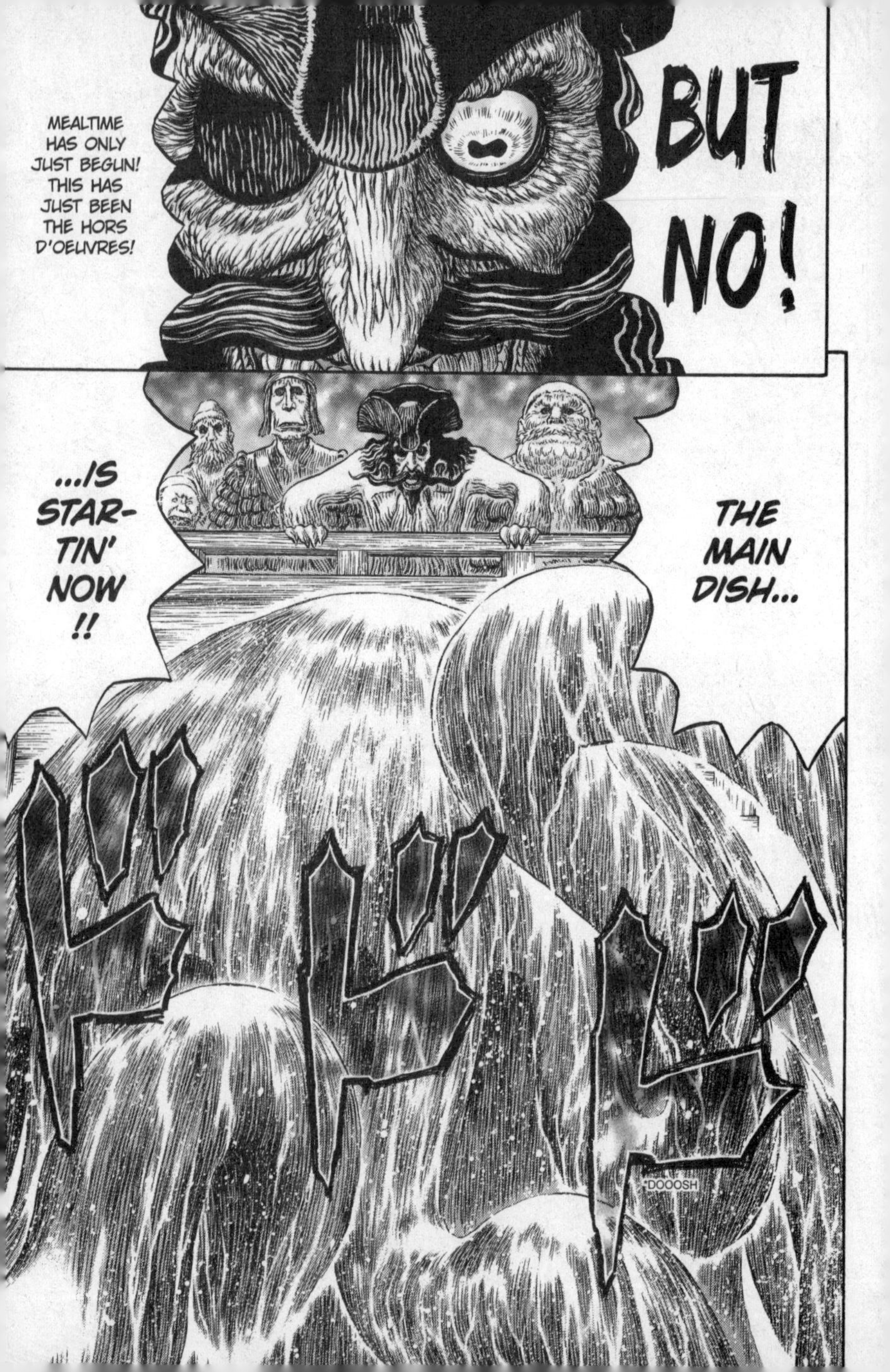
BUT NO!
MEALTIME HAS ONLY JUST BEGUN! THIS HAS JUST BEEN THE HORS D'OEUVRES!
THE MAIN DISH...
...IS STARTIN' NOW!!
*DOOOSH

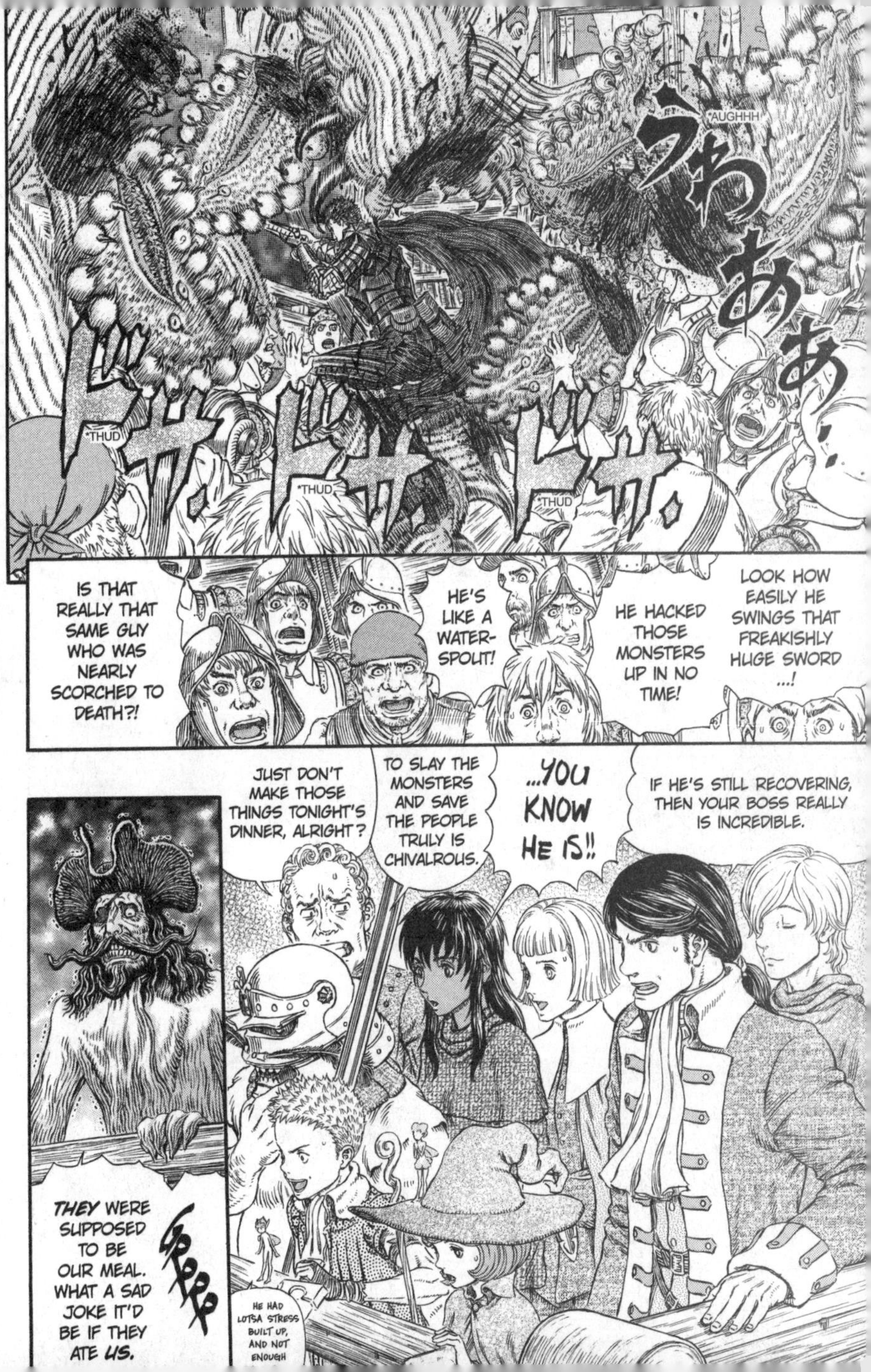
うわあああ
*AUGHHH
ドザッ
*THUD
ドザッ
*THUD
ドザッ
*THUD
LOOK HOW EASILY HE SWINGS THAT FREAKISHLY HUGE SWORD ...!
HE HACKED THOSE MONSTERS UP IN NO TIME!
HE'S LIKE A WATER-SPOUT!
IS THAT REALLY THAT SAME GUY WHO WAS NEARLY SCORCHED TO DEATH?!
IF HE'S STILL RECOVERING, THEN YOUR BOSS REALLY IS INCREDIBLE.
...YOU KNOW HE IS!!
TO SLAY THE MONSTERS AND SAVE THE PEOPLE TRULY IS CHIVALROUS.
JUST DON'T MAKE THOSE THINGS TONIGHT'S DINNER, ALRIGHT?
HE HAD LOTSA STRESS BUILT UP, AND NOT ENOUGH
THEY WERE SUPPOSED TO BE OUR MEAL. WHAT A SAD JOKE IT'D BE IF THEY ATE US.

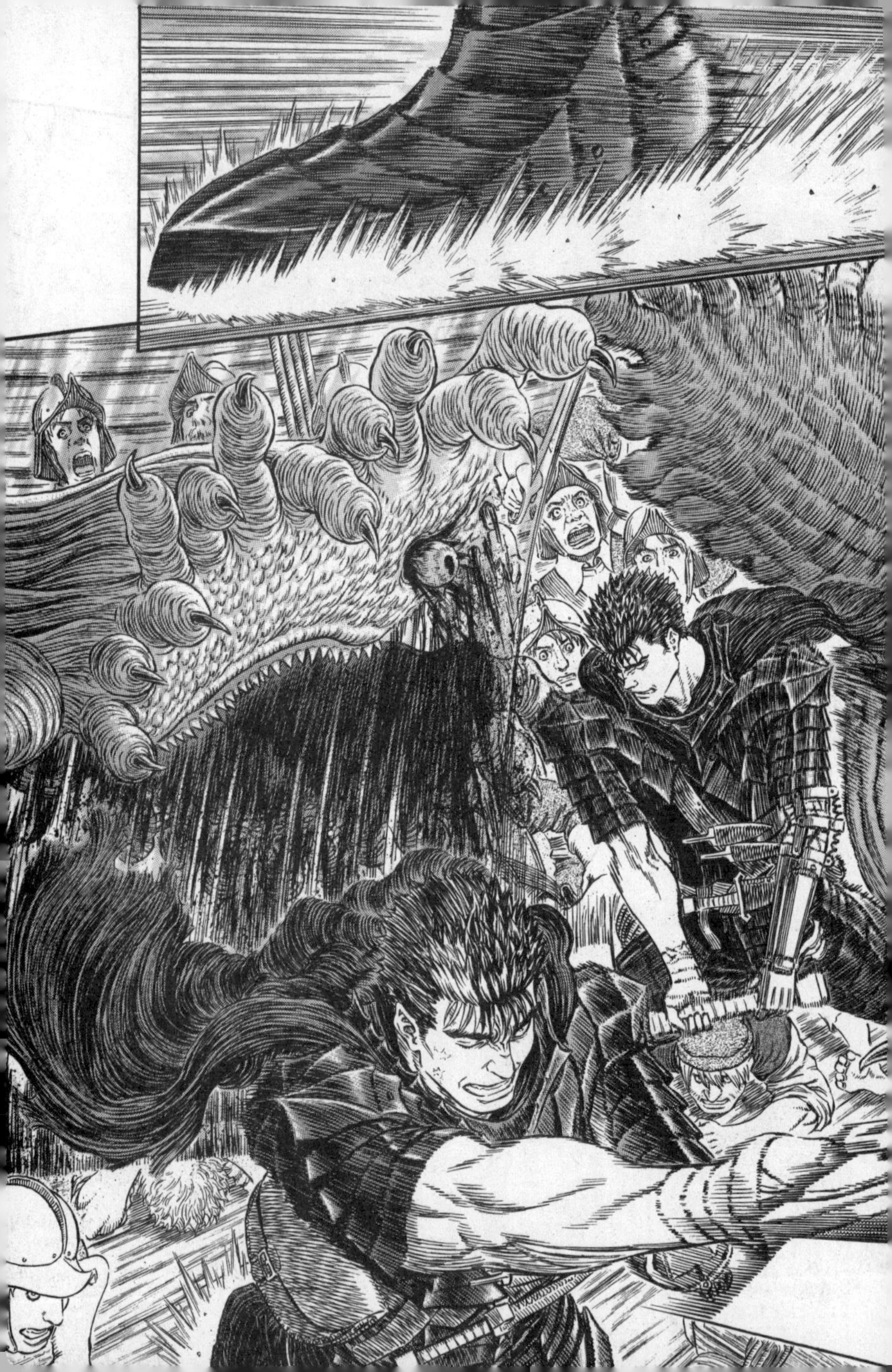

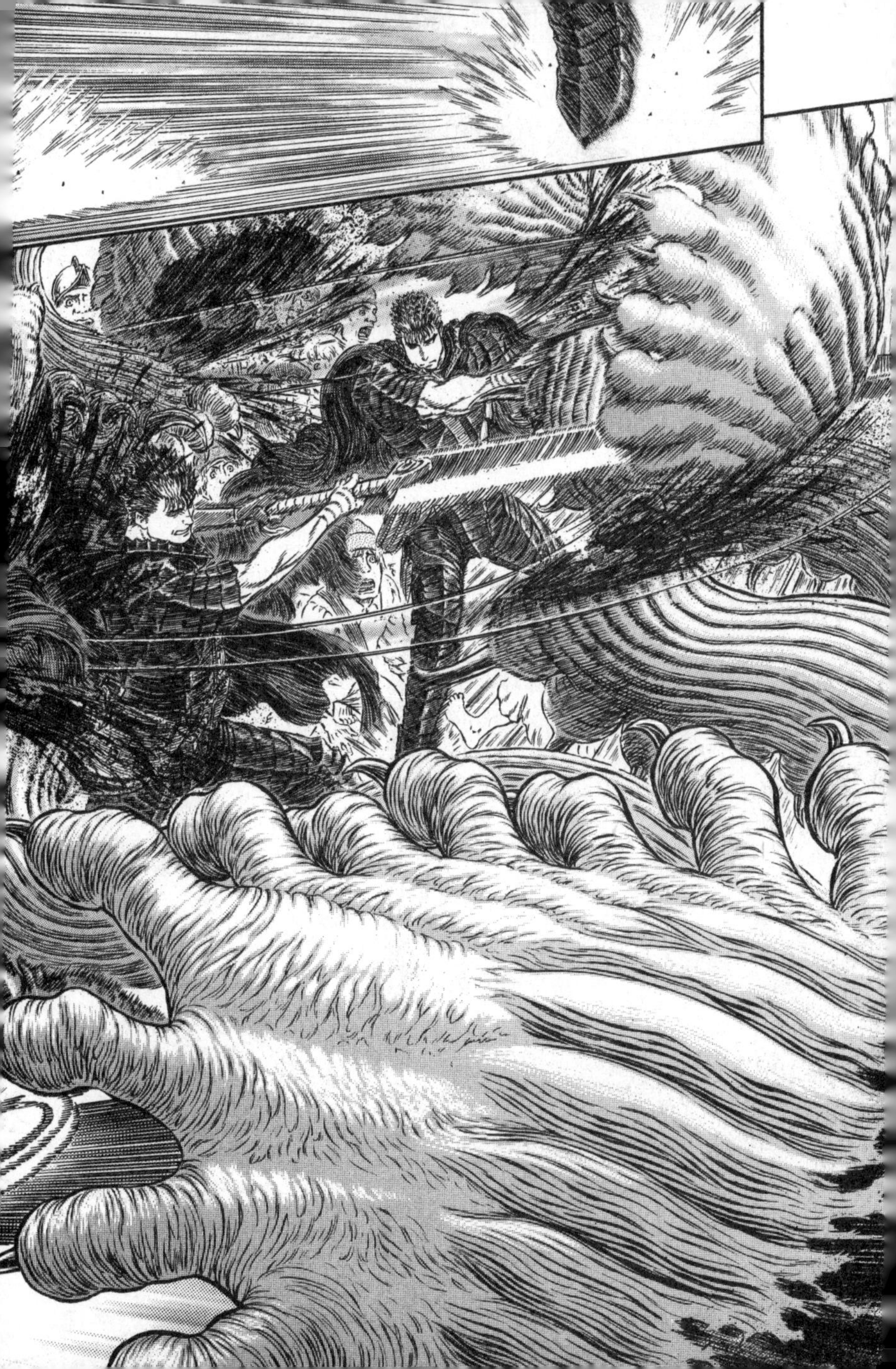

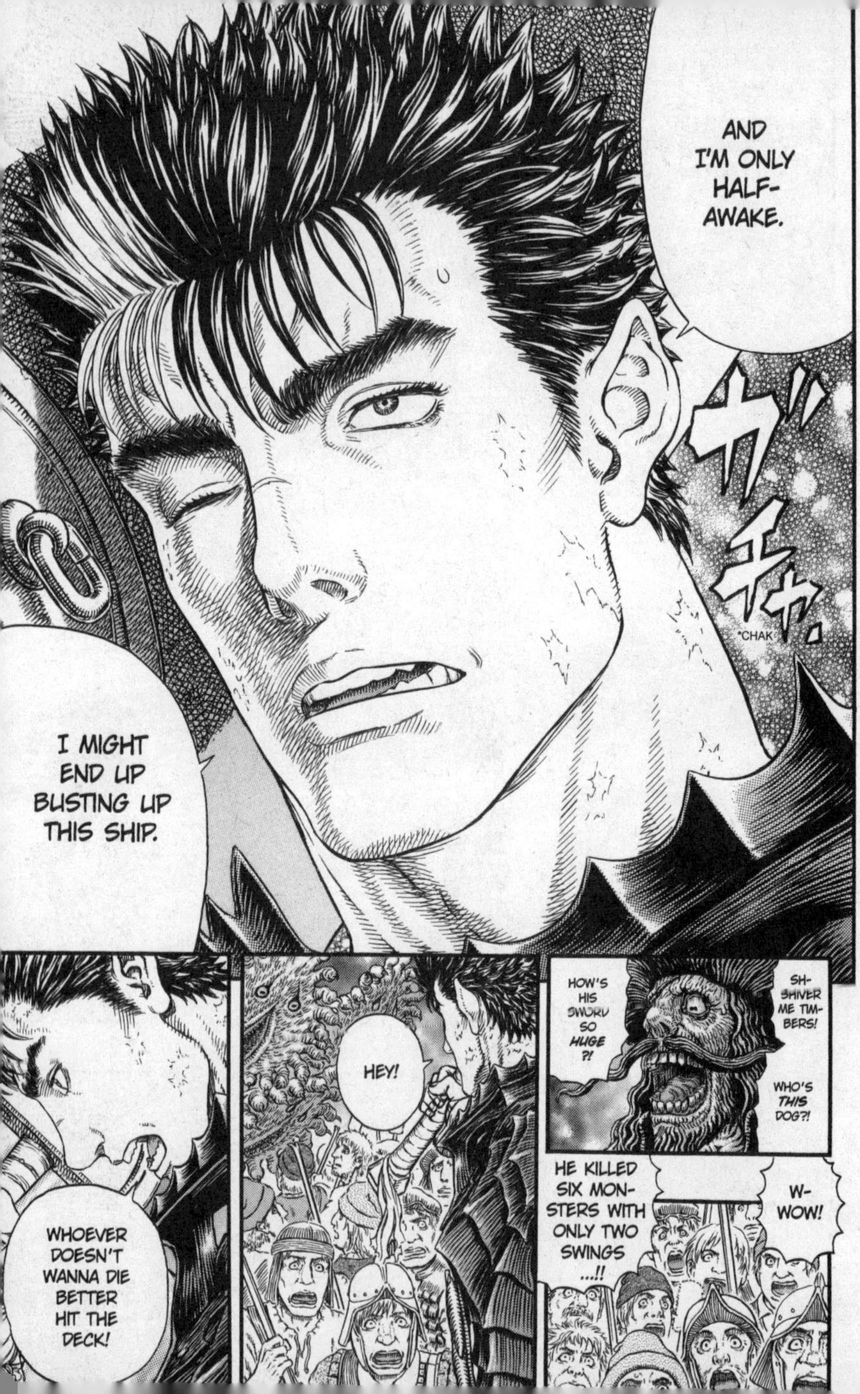
AND I'M ONLY HALF-AWAKE.
*CHAK
I MIGHT END UP BUSTING UP THIS SHIP.
SH-SHIVER ME TIMBERS!
HOW'S HIS SWORD SO HUGE?!
WHO'S THIS DOG?!
W-WOW!
HE KILLED SIX MONSTERS WITH ONLY TWO SWINGS ...!!
HEY!
WHOEVER DOESN'T WANNA DIE BETTER HIT THE DECK!

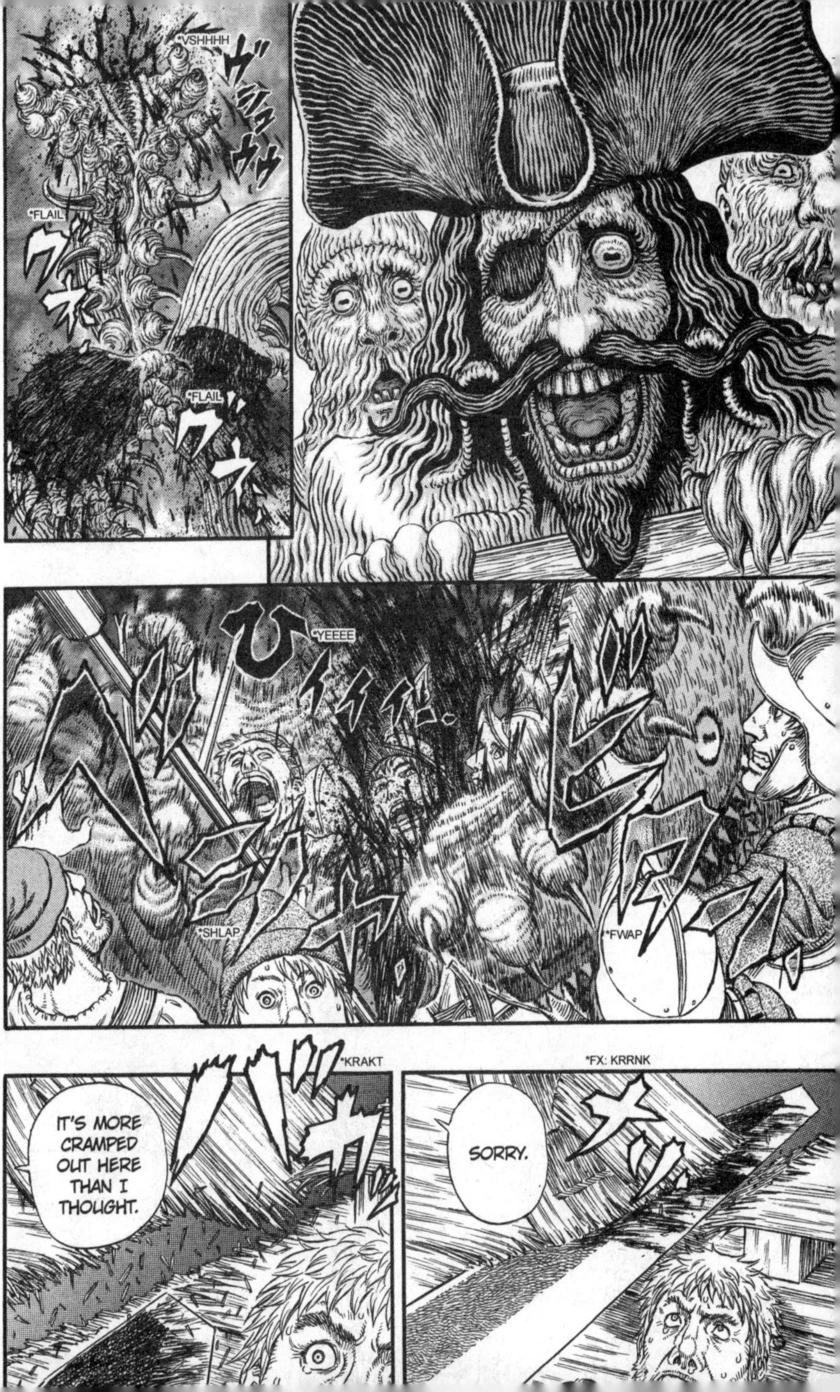
*VSHHHH
*FLAIL
*FLAIL
*YEEEE
*FWAP
*SHLAP
*FX: KRRNK
SORRY.
*KRAKT
IT'S MORE CRAMPED OUT HERE THAN I THOUGHT.

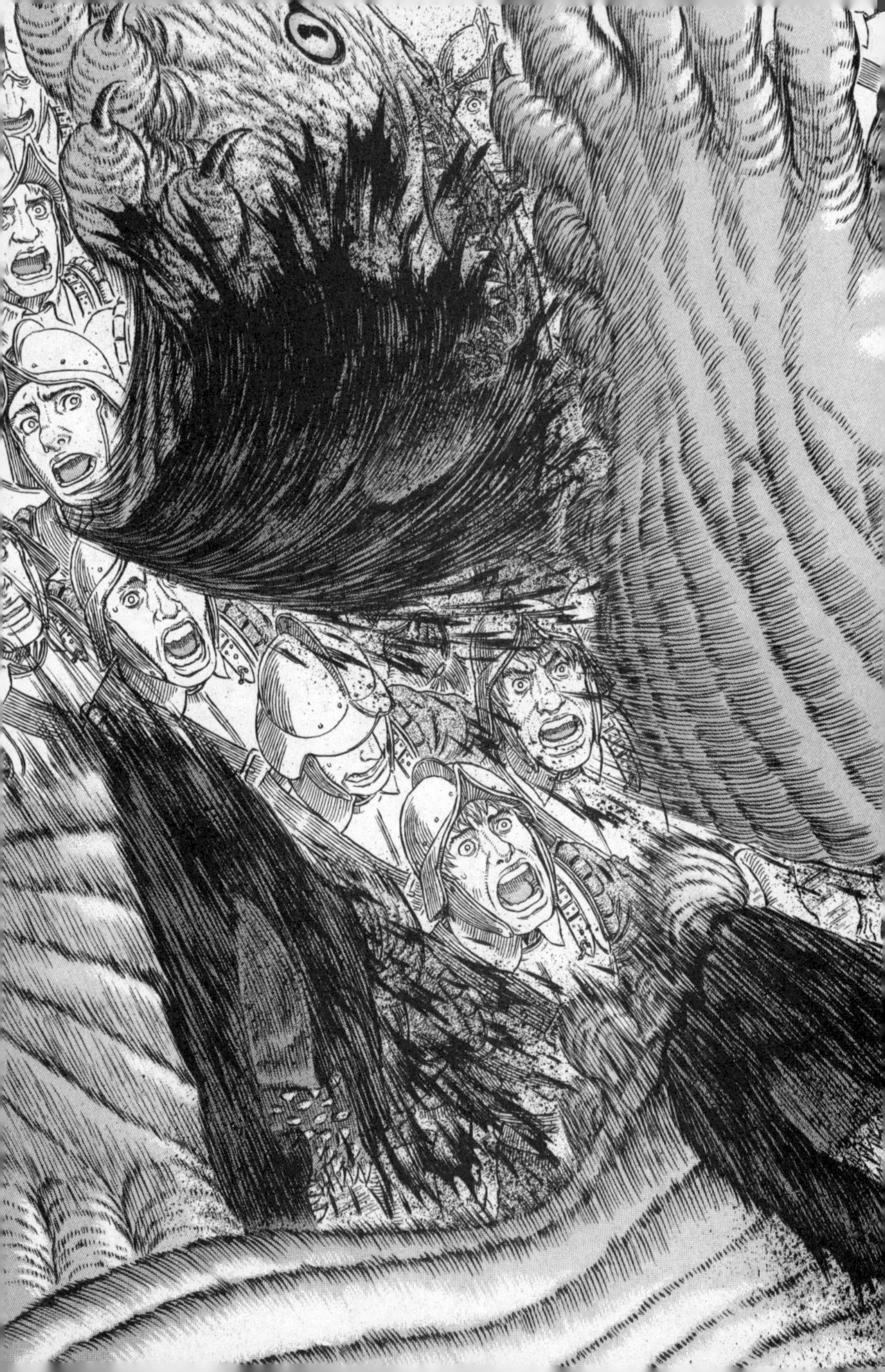

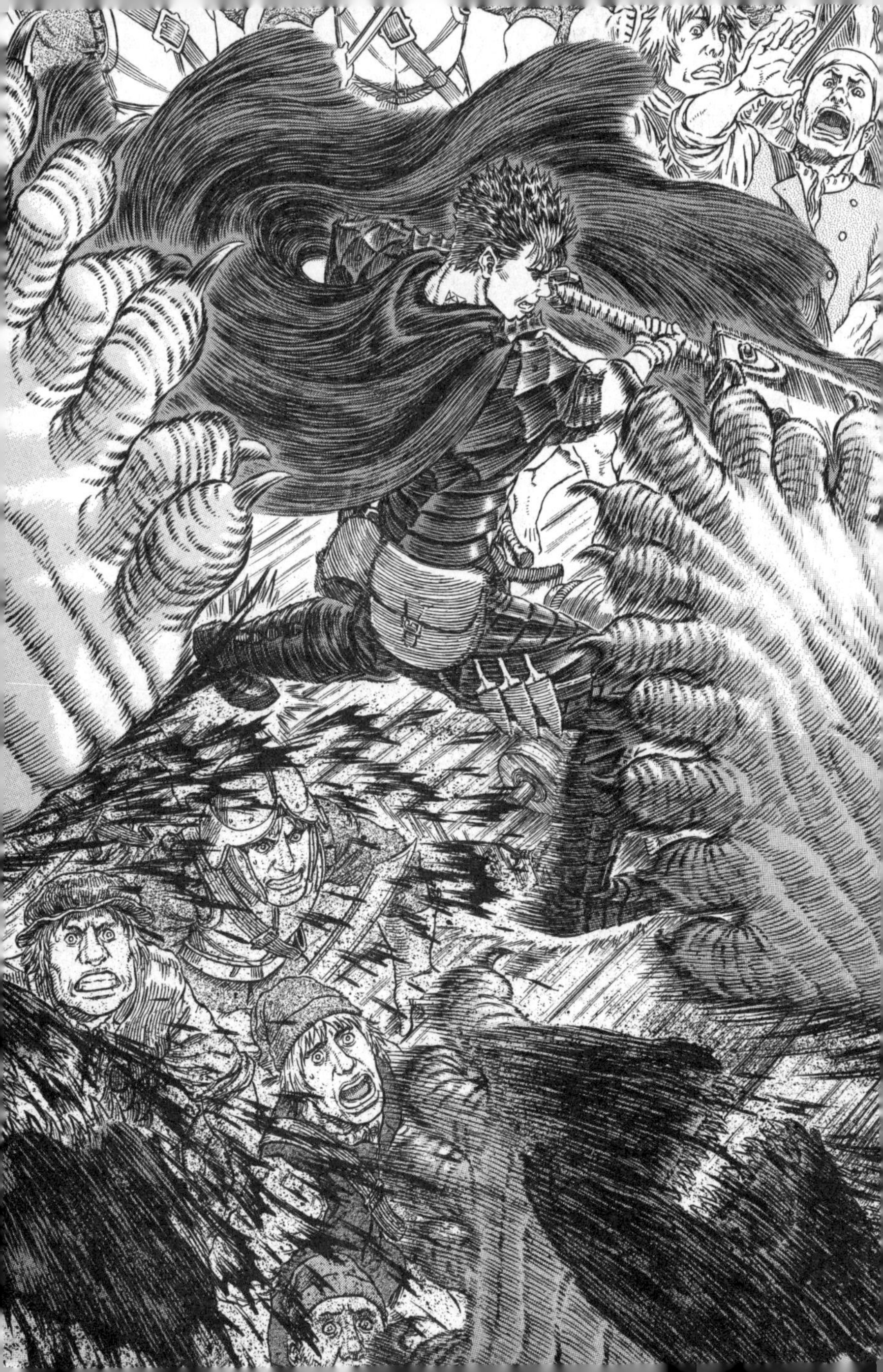

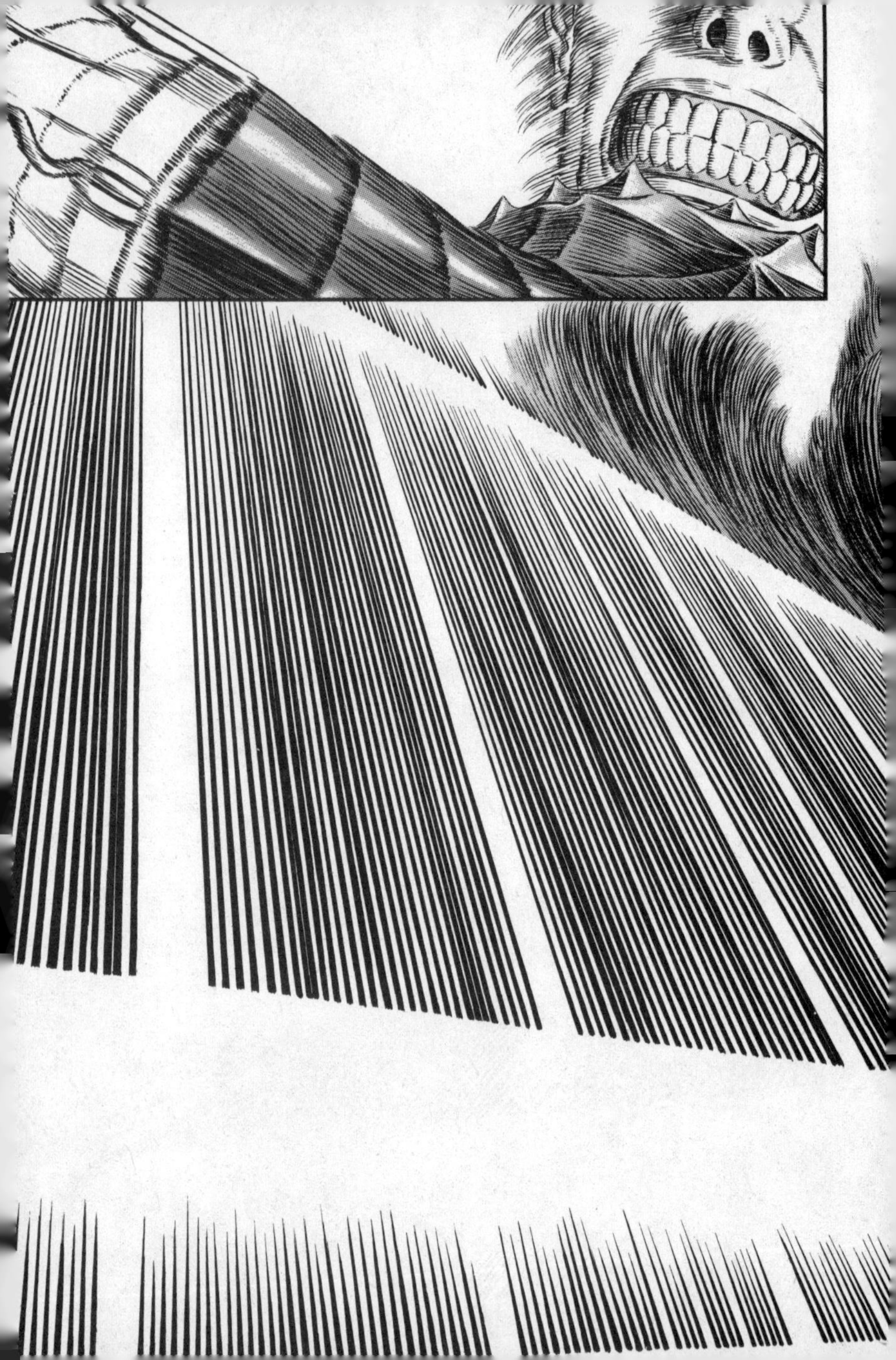

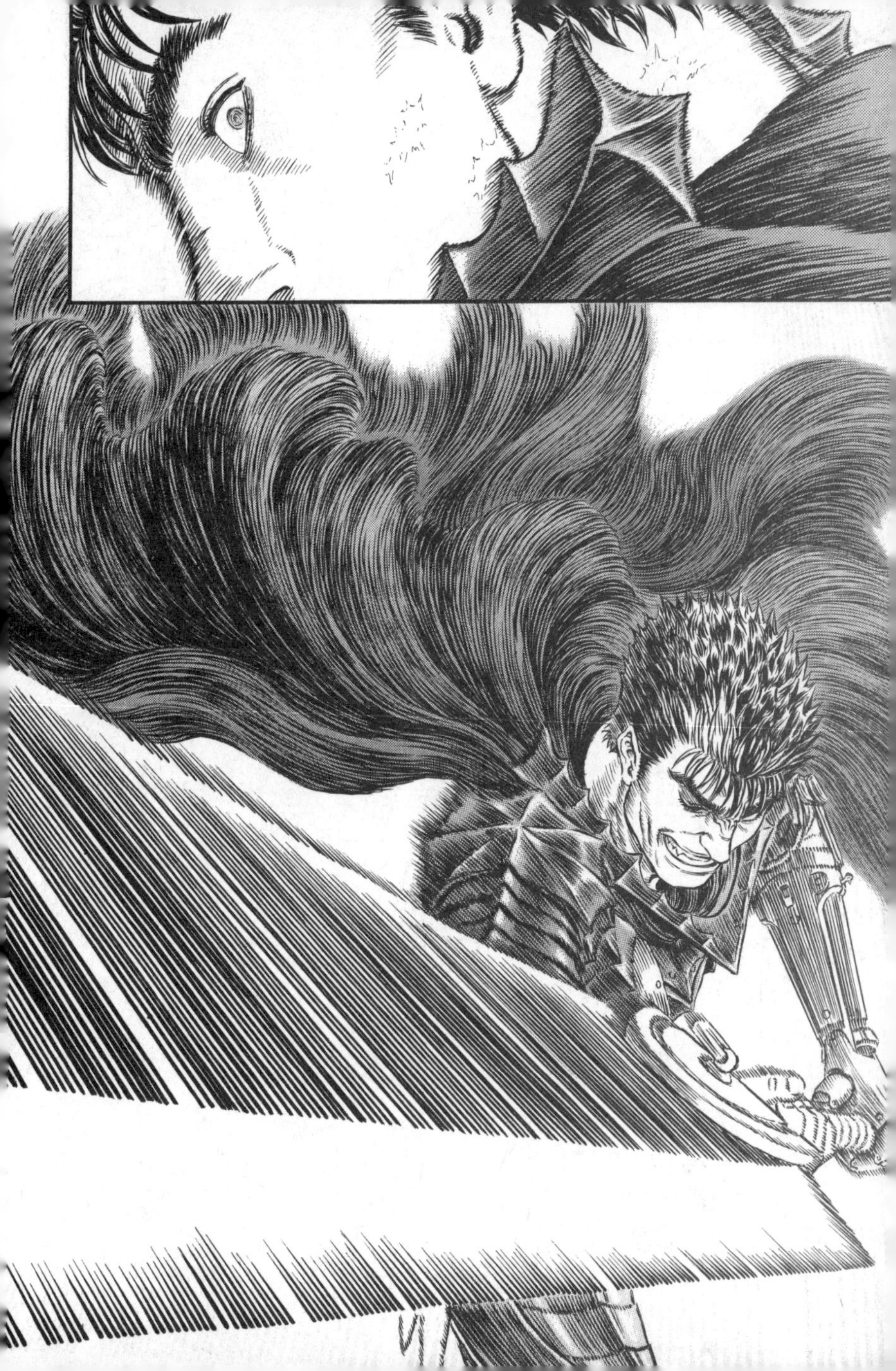

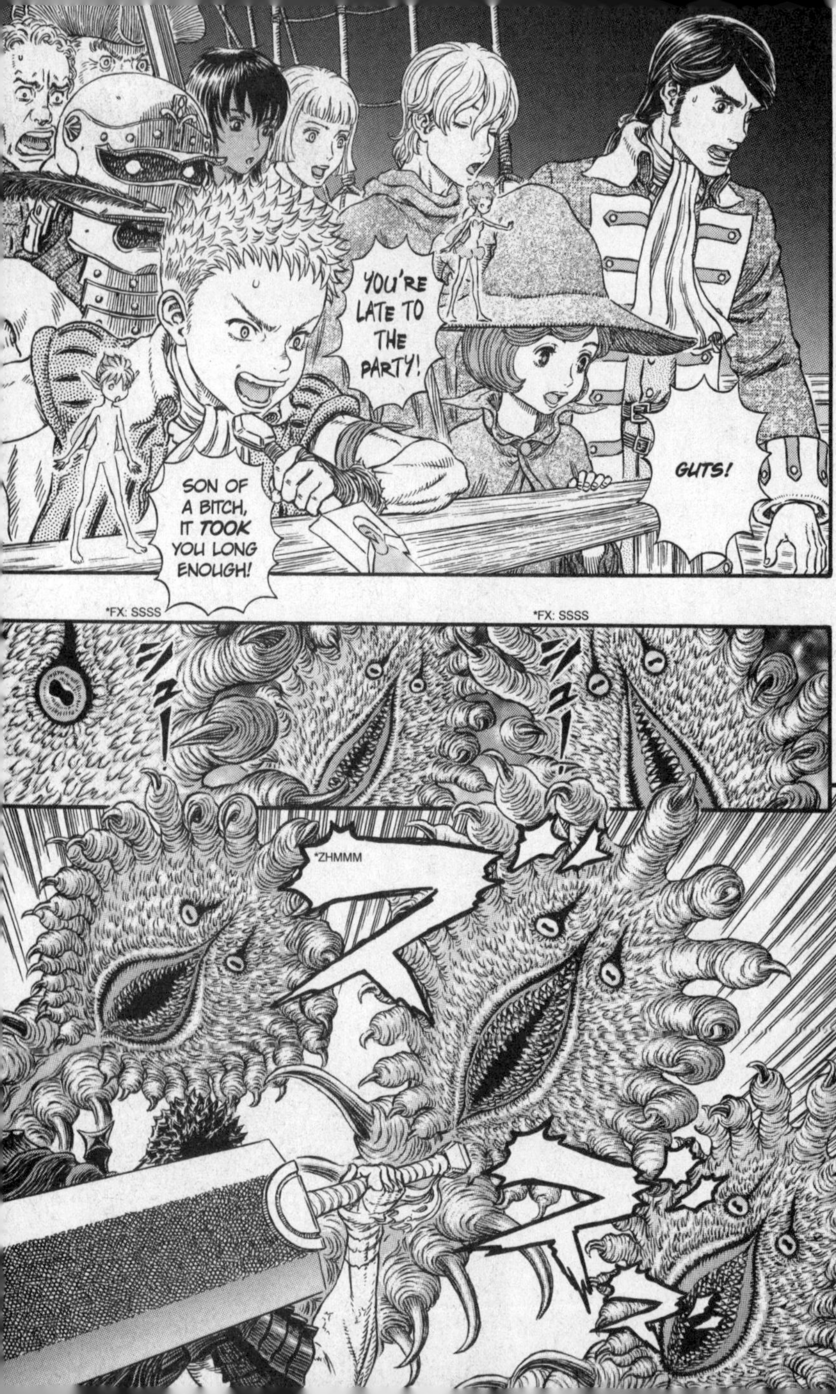
GUTS!
YOU'RE LATE TO THE PARTY!
SON OF A BITCH, IT TOOK YOU LONG ENOUGH!
*FX: SSSS
*FX: SSSS
*ZHMMM

幻造世界〈ファンタジア〉篇／妖精島の章

幽霊船③

GHOST SHIP, PART 3

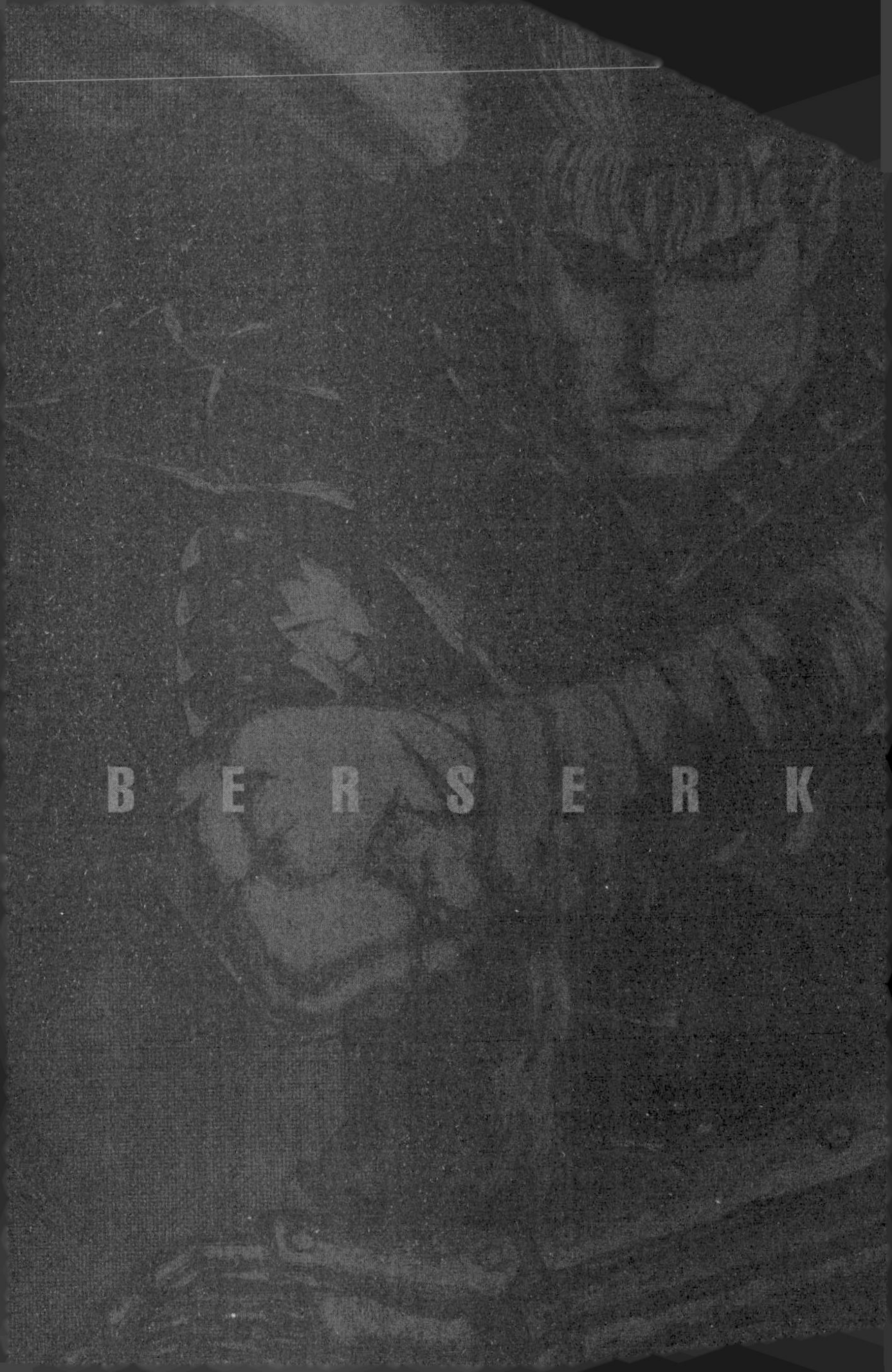
BERSERK

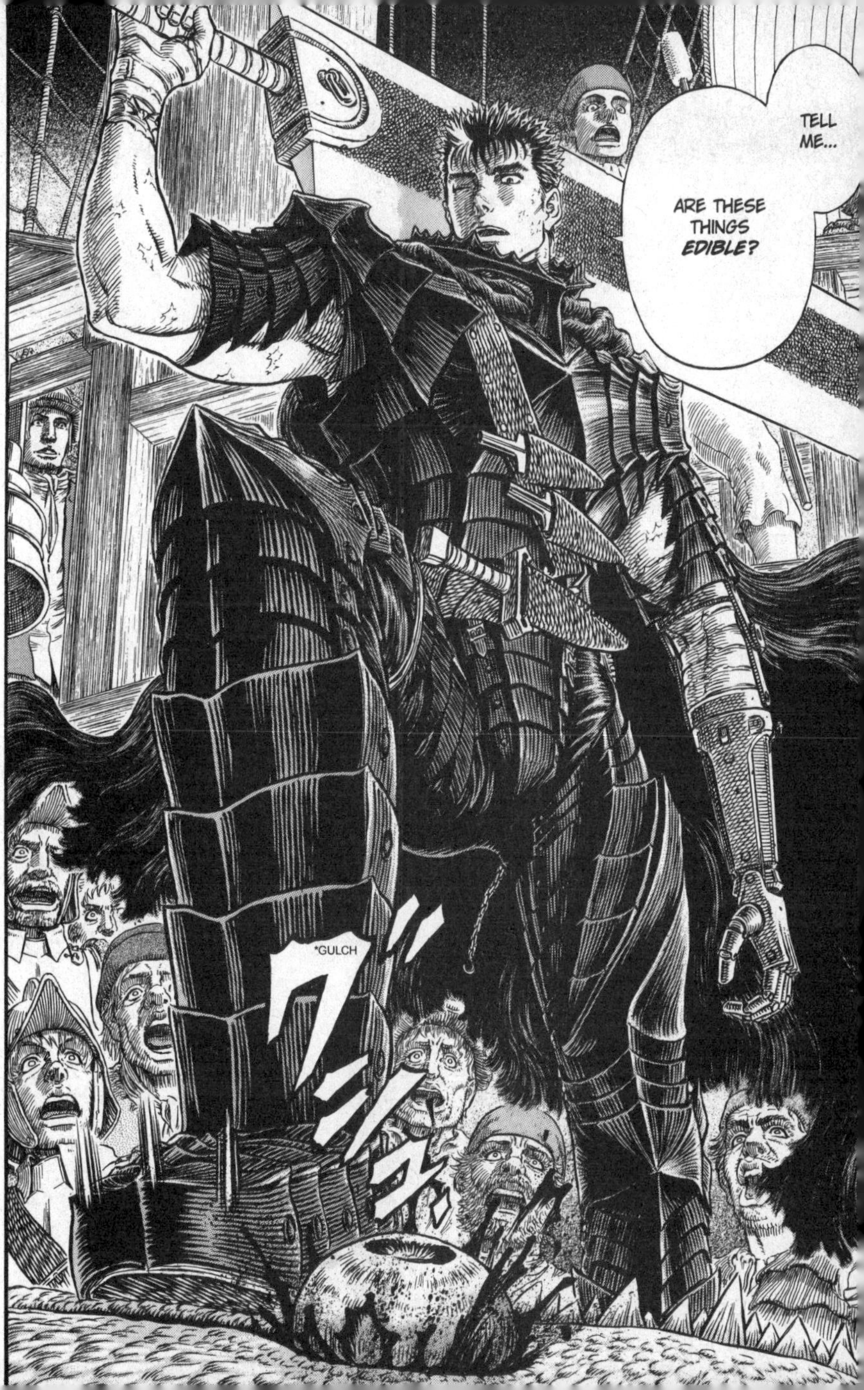
TELL ME...
ARE THESE THINGS EDIBLE?
*GULCH
ゴクン

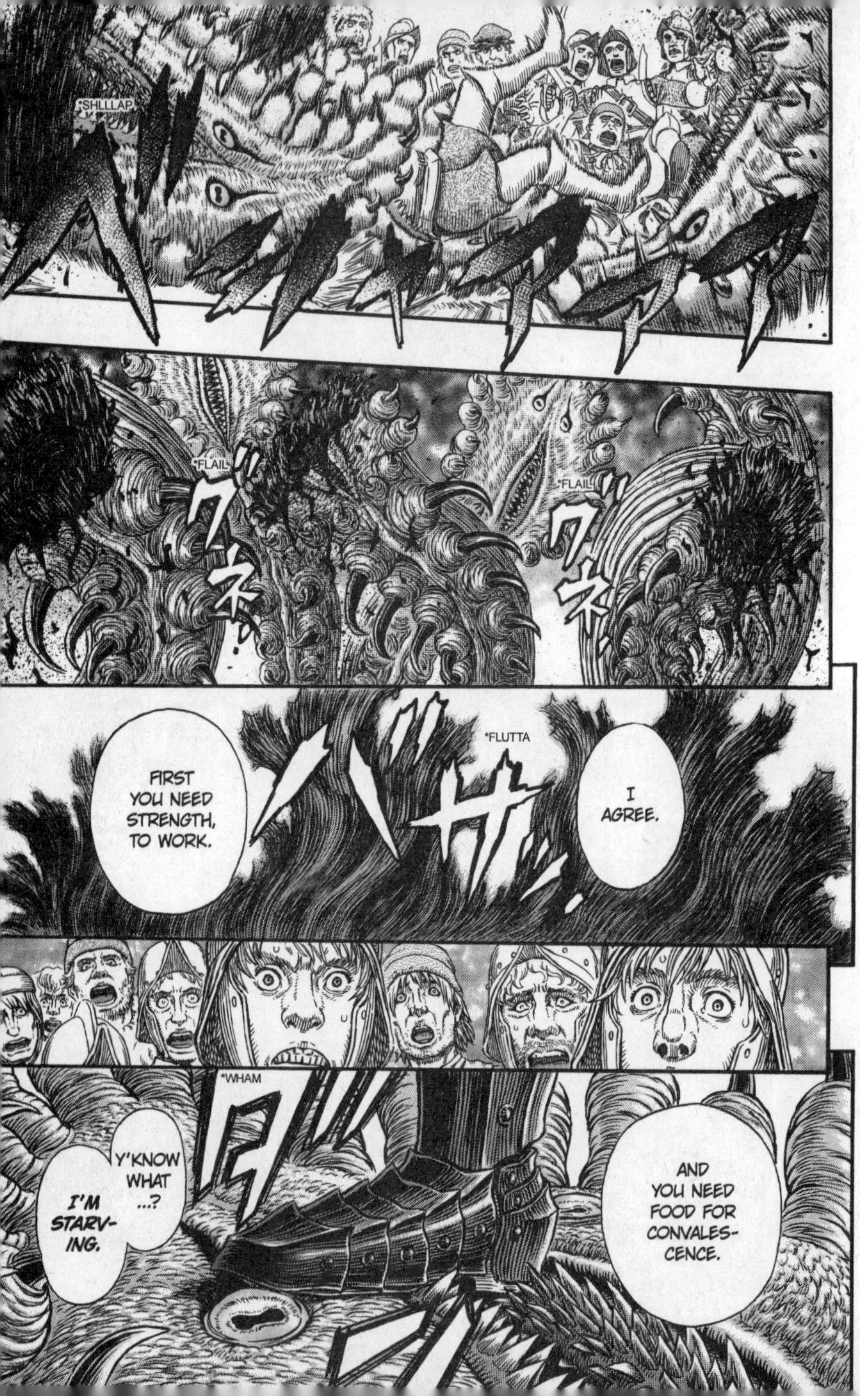
*SHLLLAP
*FLAIL
*FLAIL
I AGREE.
*FLUTTA
FIRST YOU NEED STRENGTH, TO WORK.
AND YOU NEED FOOD FOR CONVALES-CENCE.
*WHAM
Y'KNOW WHAT ...?
I'M STARV-ING.

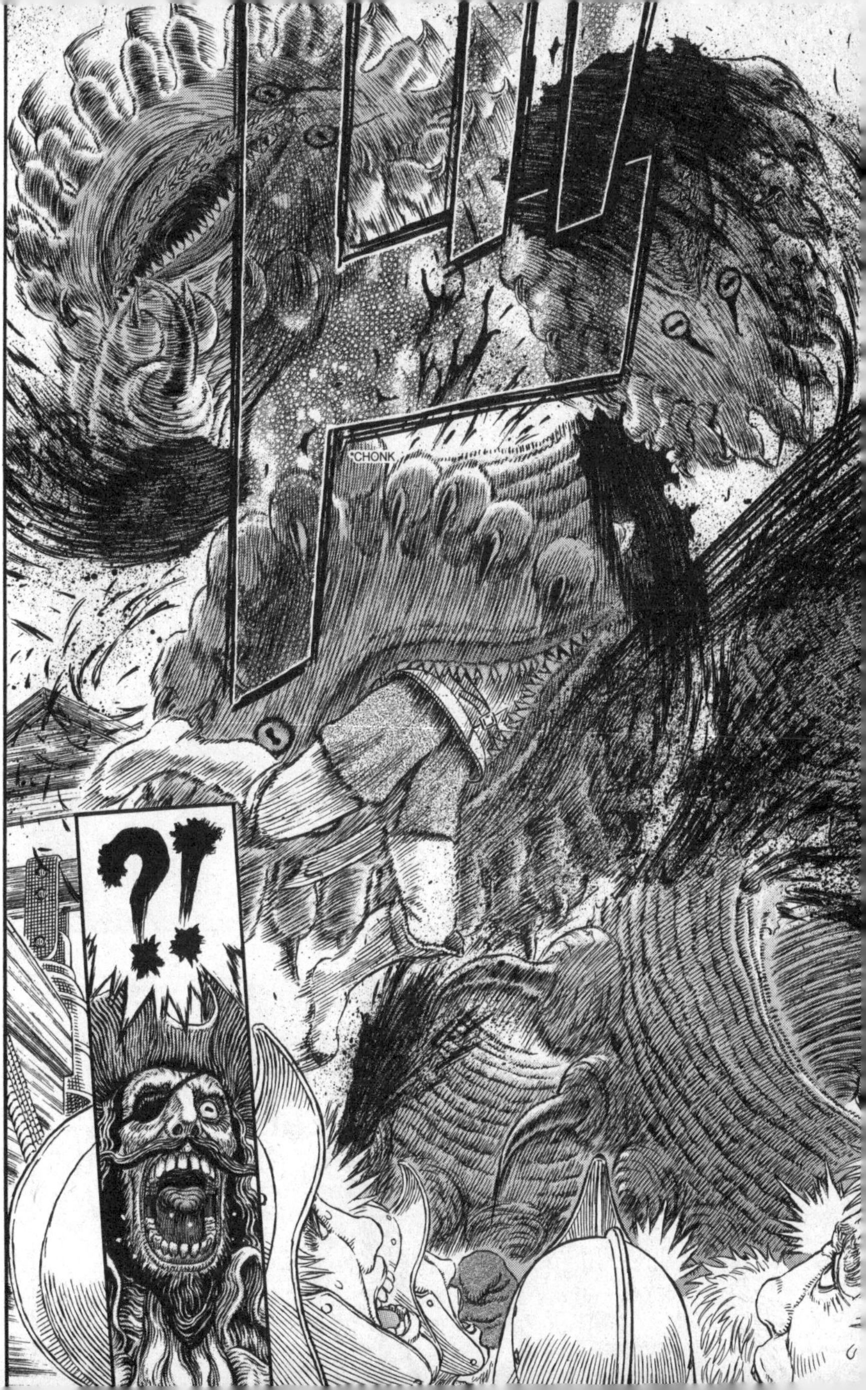
CHONK
?!

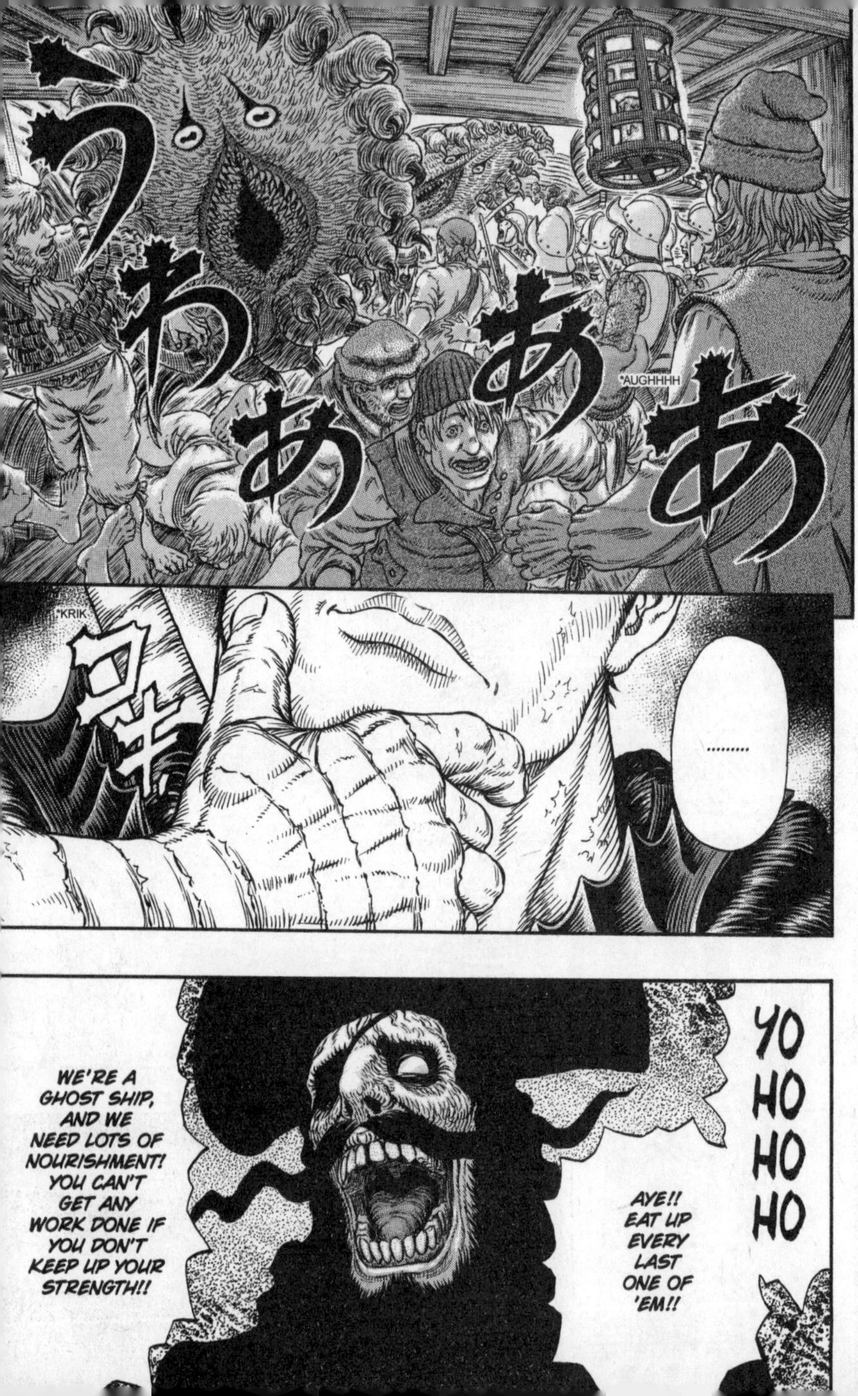
うわあああ
*AUGHHHH
ロキ
*KRIK
....
YO HO HO HO HO
AYE!! EAT UP EVERY LAST ONE OF 'EM!!
WE'RE A GHOST SHIP, AND WE NEED LOTS OF NOURISHMENT! YOU CAN'T GET ANY WORK DONE IF YOU DON'T KEEP UP YOUR STRENGTH!!

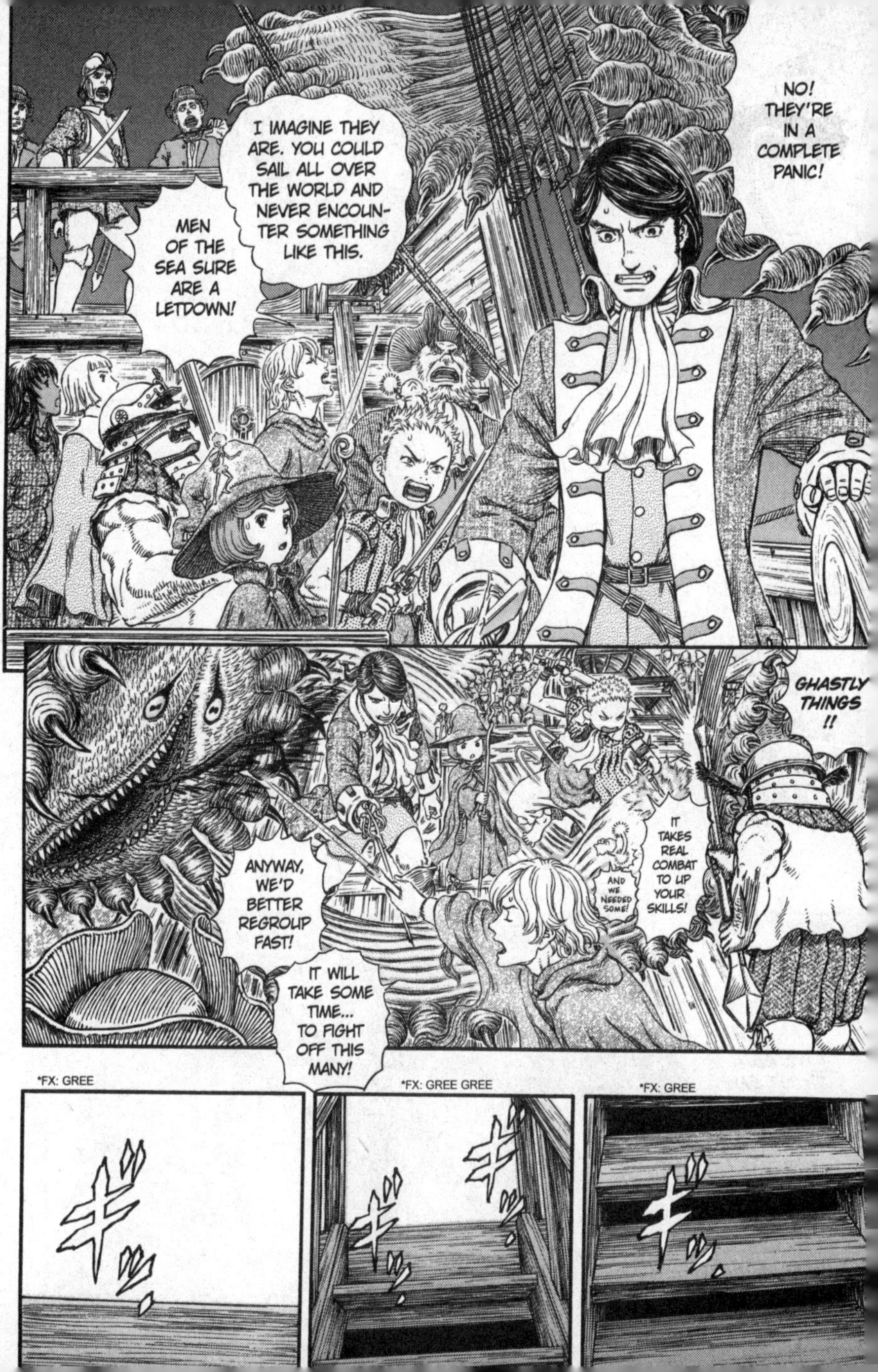
NO! THEY'RE IN A COMPLETE PANIC!
MEN OF THE SEA SURE ARE A LETDOWN!
I IMAGINE THEY ARE. YOU COULD SAIL ALL OVER THE WORLD AND NEVER ENCOUNTER SOMETHING LIKE THIS.
GHASTLY THINGS !!
IT TAKES REAL COMBAT TO UP YOUR SKILLS!
AND WE NEEDED SOME!
ANYWAY, WE'D BETTER REGROUP FAST!
IT WILL TAKE SOME TIME... TO FIGHT OFF THIS MANY!
*FX: GREE
*FX: GREE GREE
*FX: GREE

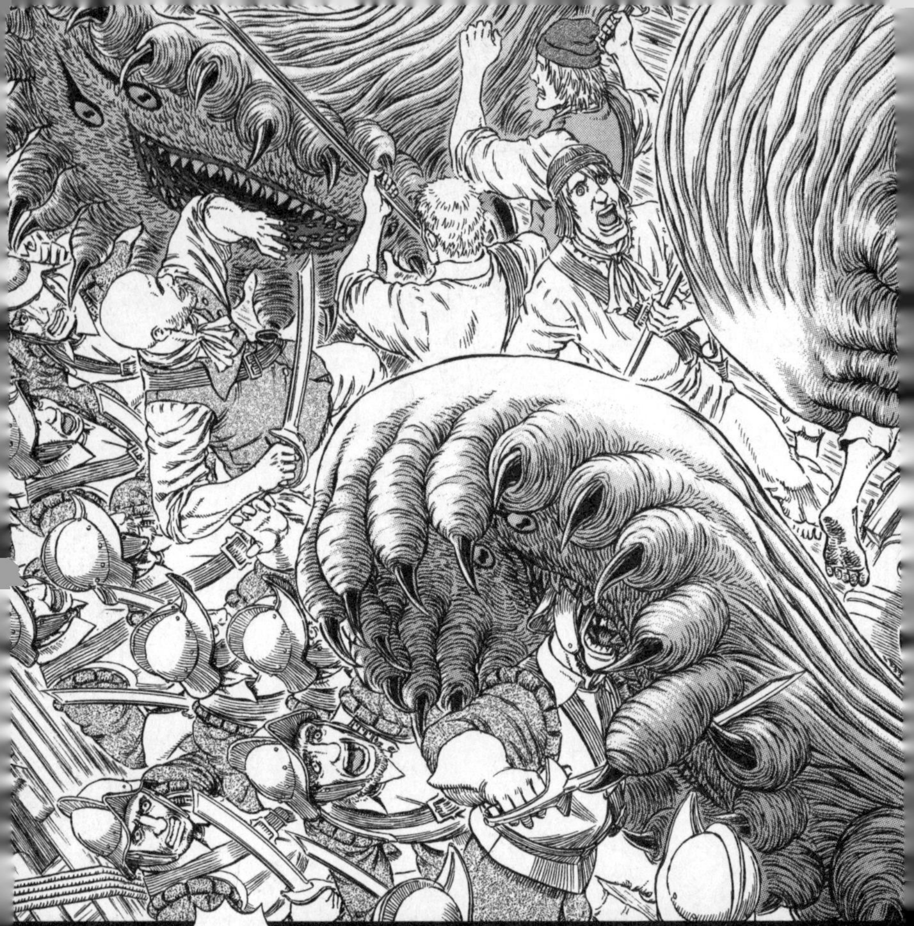

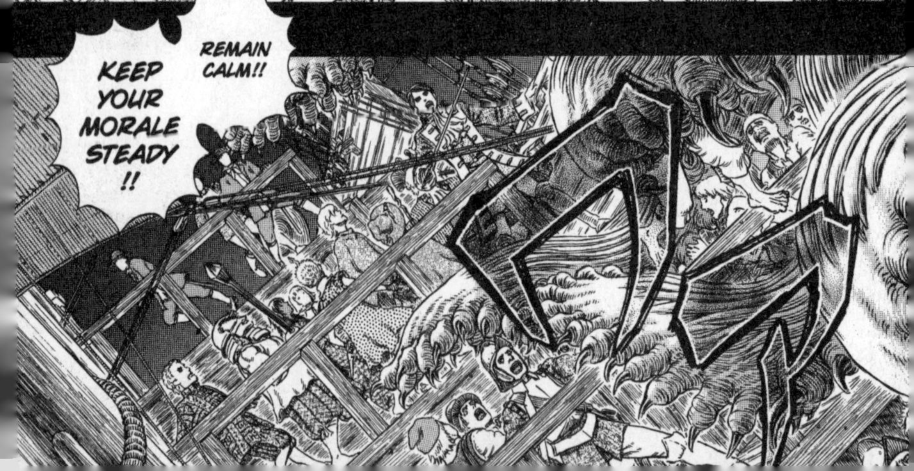
REMAIN CALM!!
KEEP YOUR MORALE STEADY !!

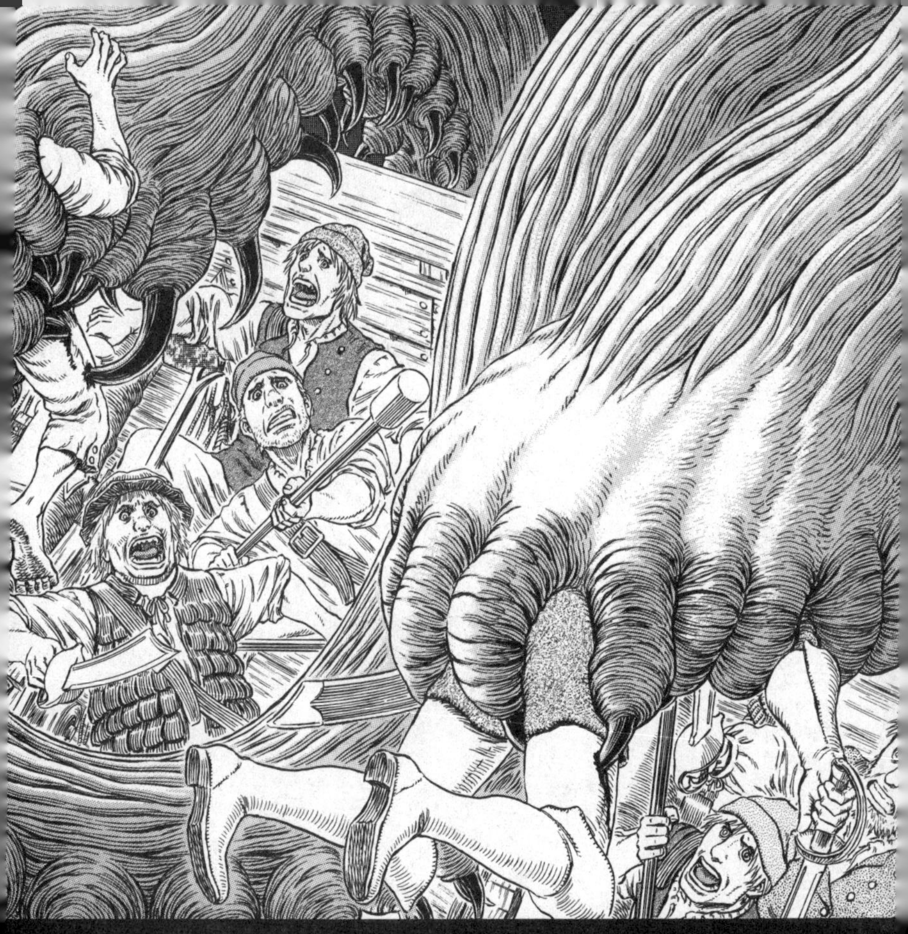

*FX: AUGHHHH

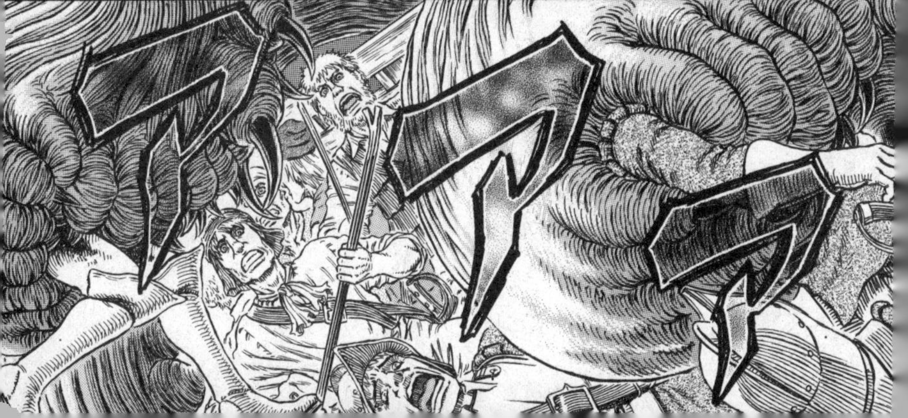
ワァァ

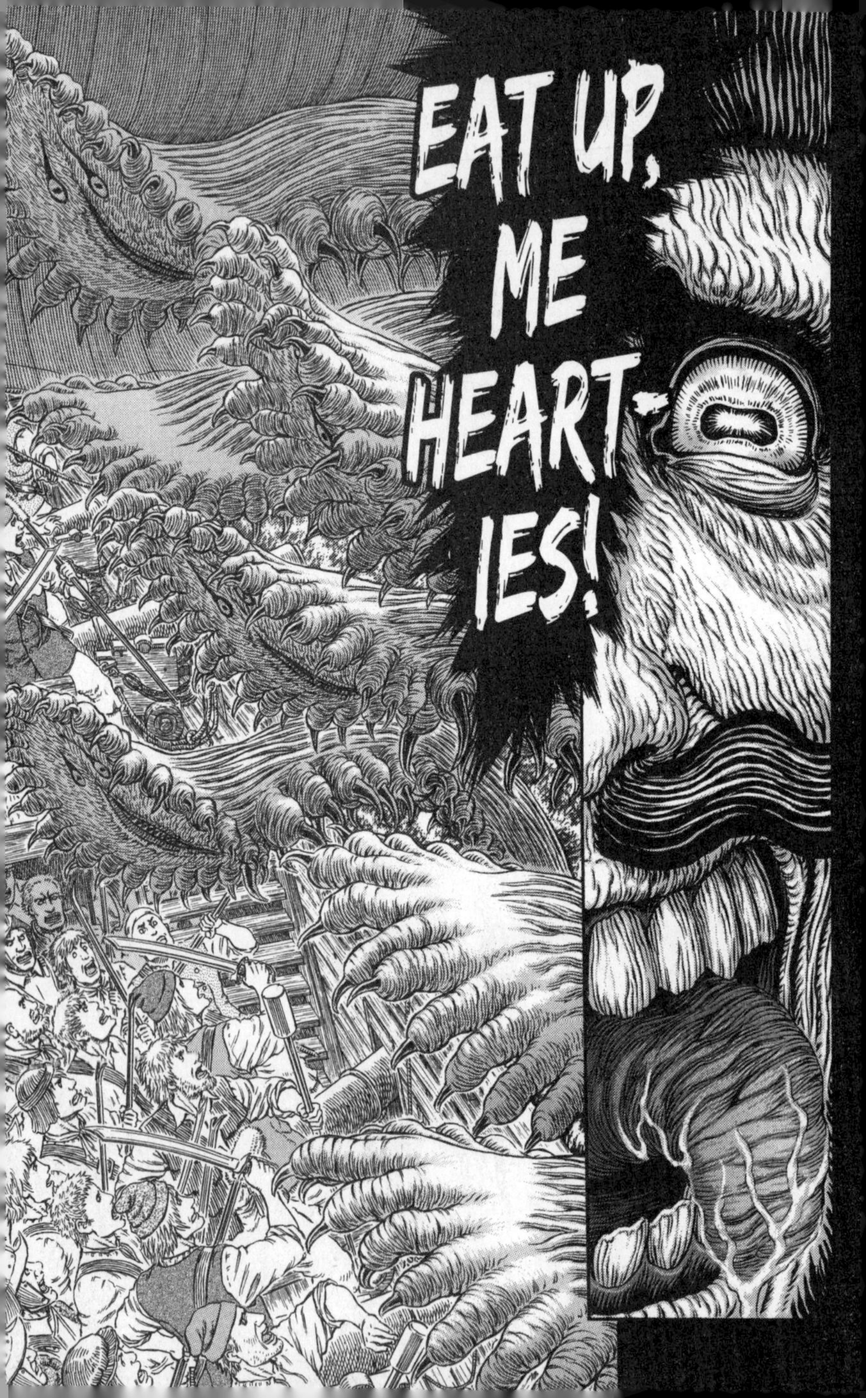
EAT UP, ME HEART-IES!

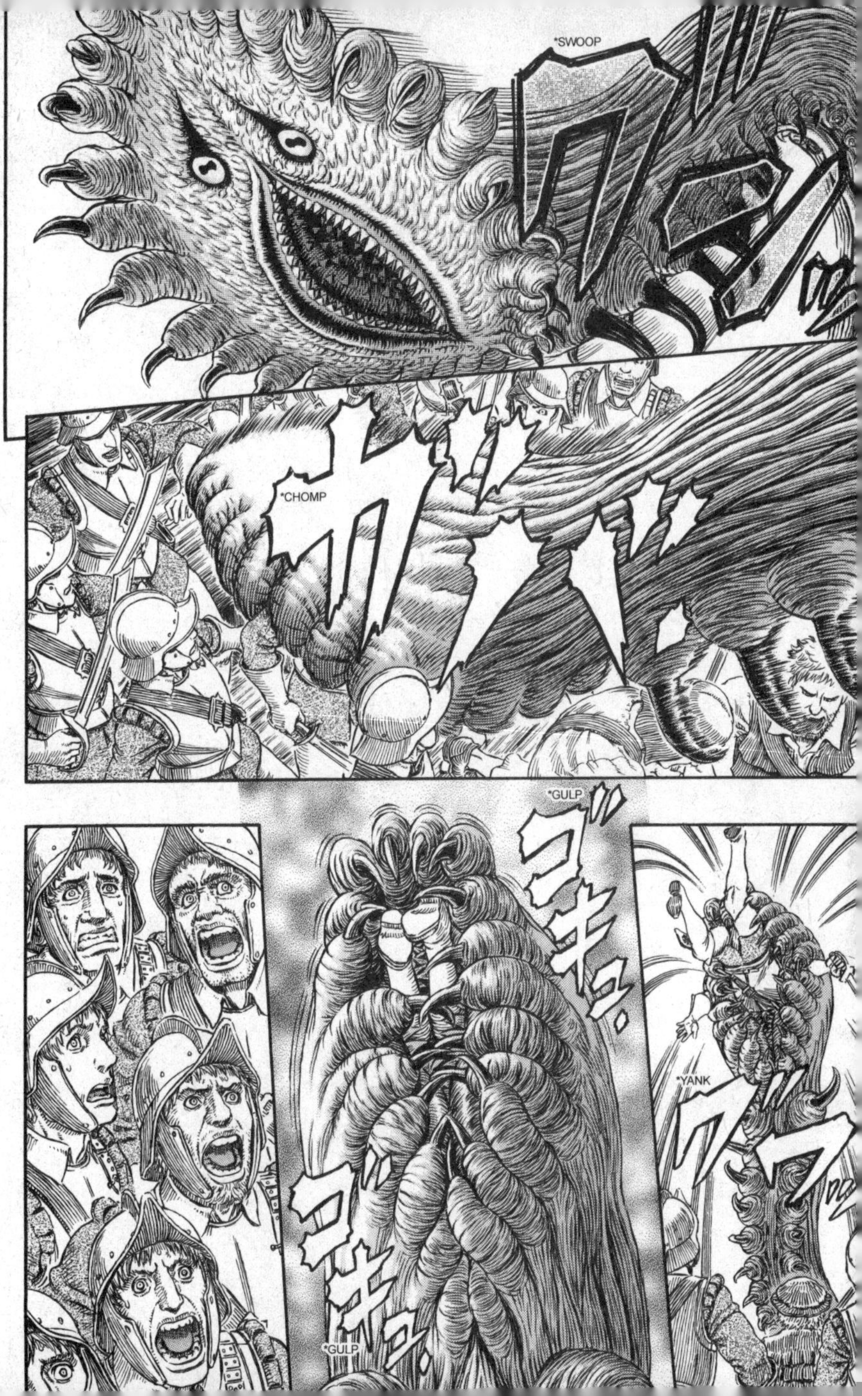
*SWOOP
*CHOMP
*YANK
*GULP
*GULP

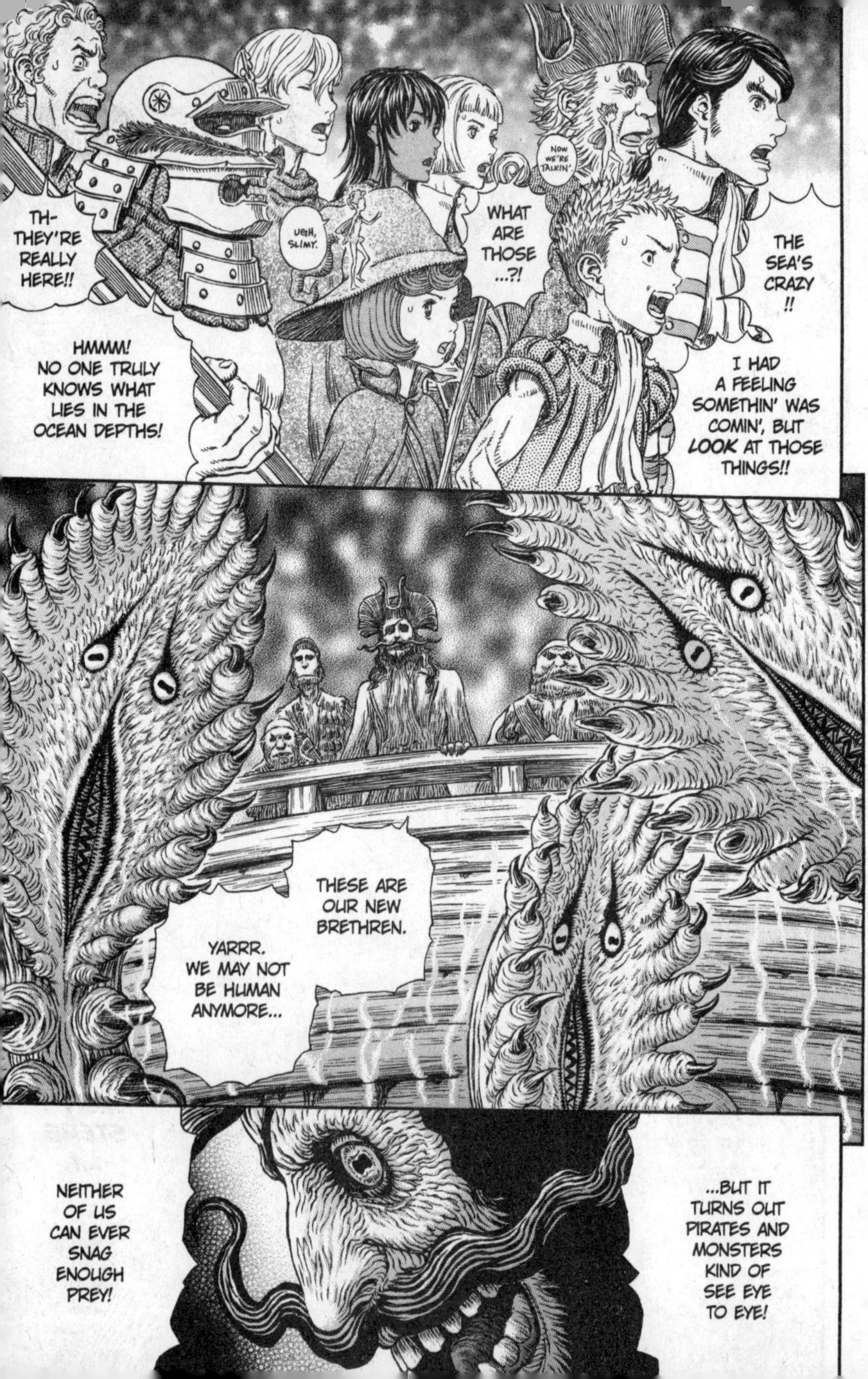

NOW WE'RE TALKIN'.
THE SEA'S CRAZY!!
WHAT ARE THOSE ...?!
UGH, SLIMY.
TH- THEY'RE REALLY HERE!!
I HAD A FEELING SOMETHIN' WAS COMIN', BUT LOOK AT THOSE THINGS!!
HMMM! NO ONE TRULY KNOWS WHAT LIES IN THE OCEAN DEPTHS!
THESE ARE OUR NEW BRETHREN.
YARRR. WE MAY NOT BE HUMAN ANYMORE...
...BUT IT TURNS OUT PIRATES AND MONSTERS KIND OF SEE EYE TO EYE!
NEITHER OF US CAN EVER SNAG ENOUGH PREY!

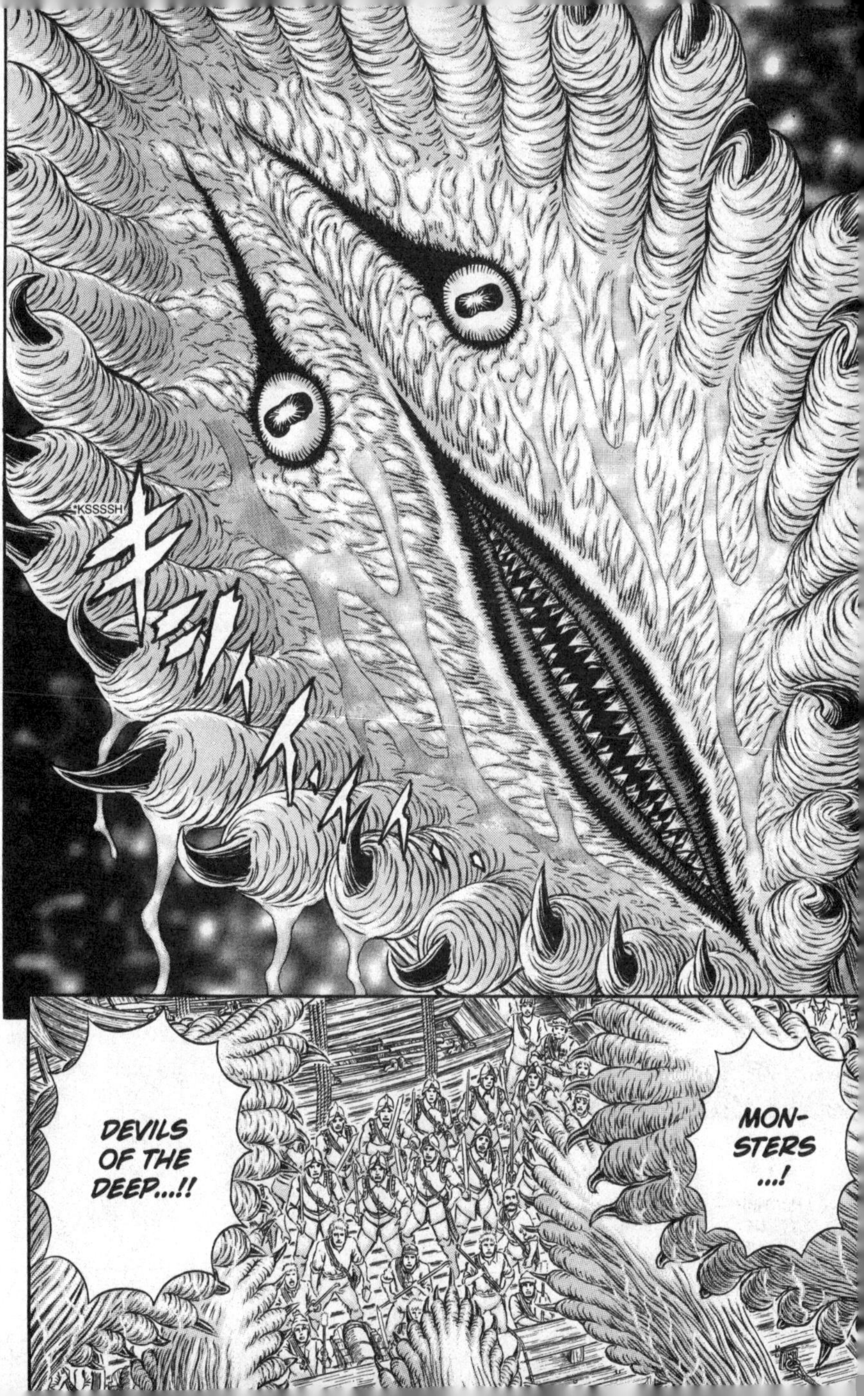
*KSSSSH
MON-STERS ...!
DEVILS OF THE DEEP...!!

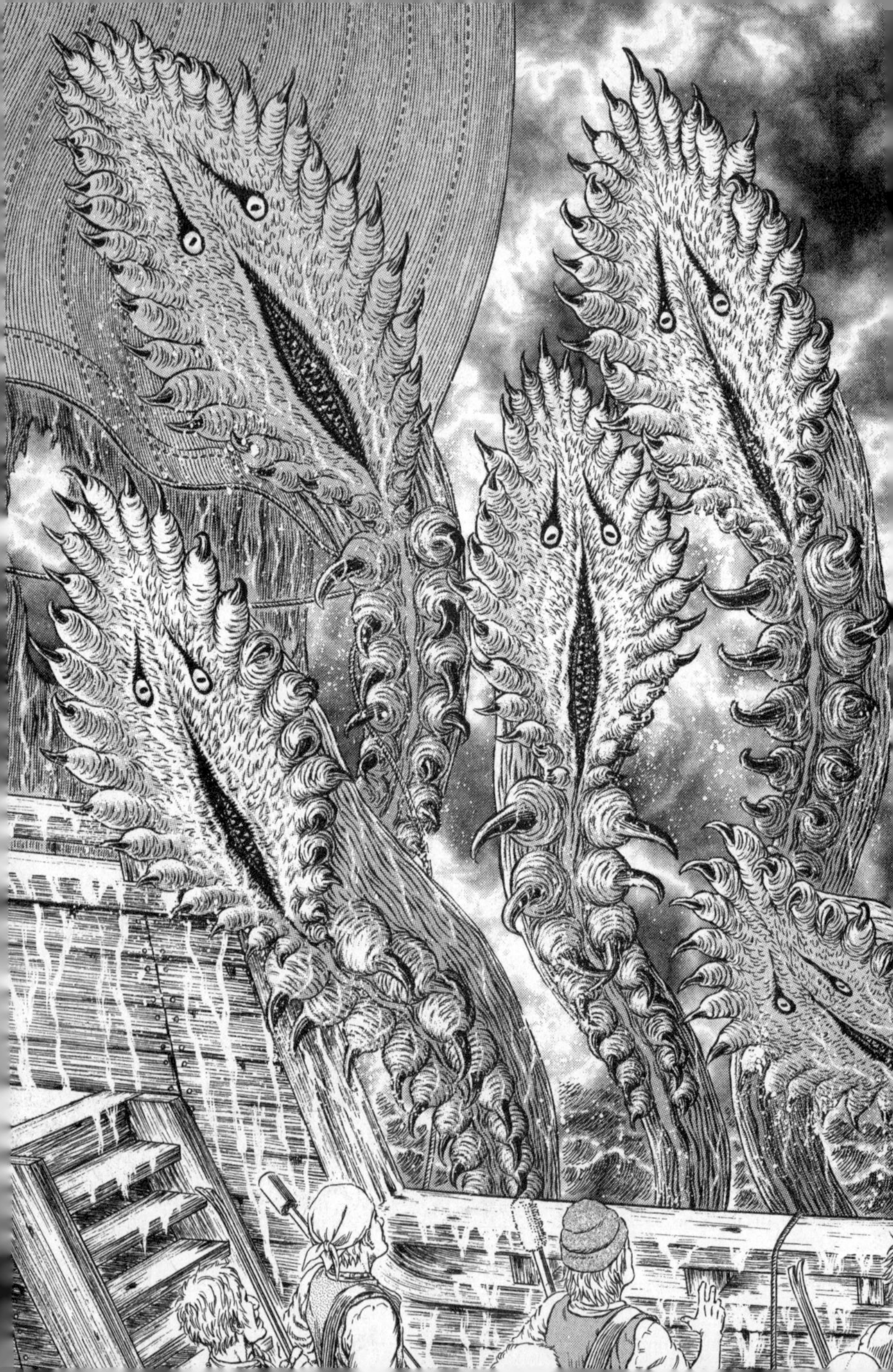

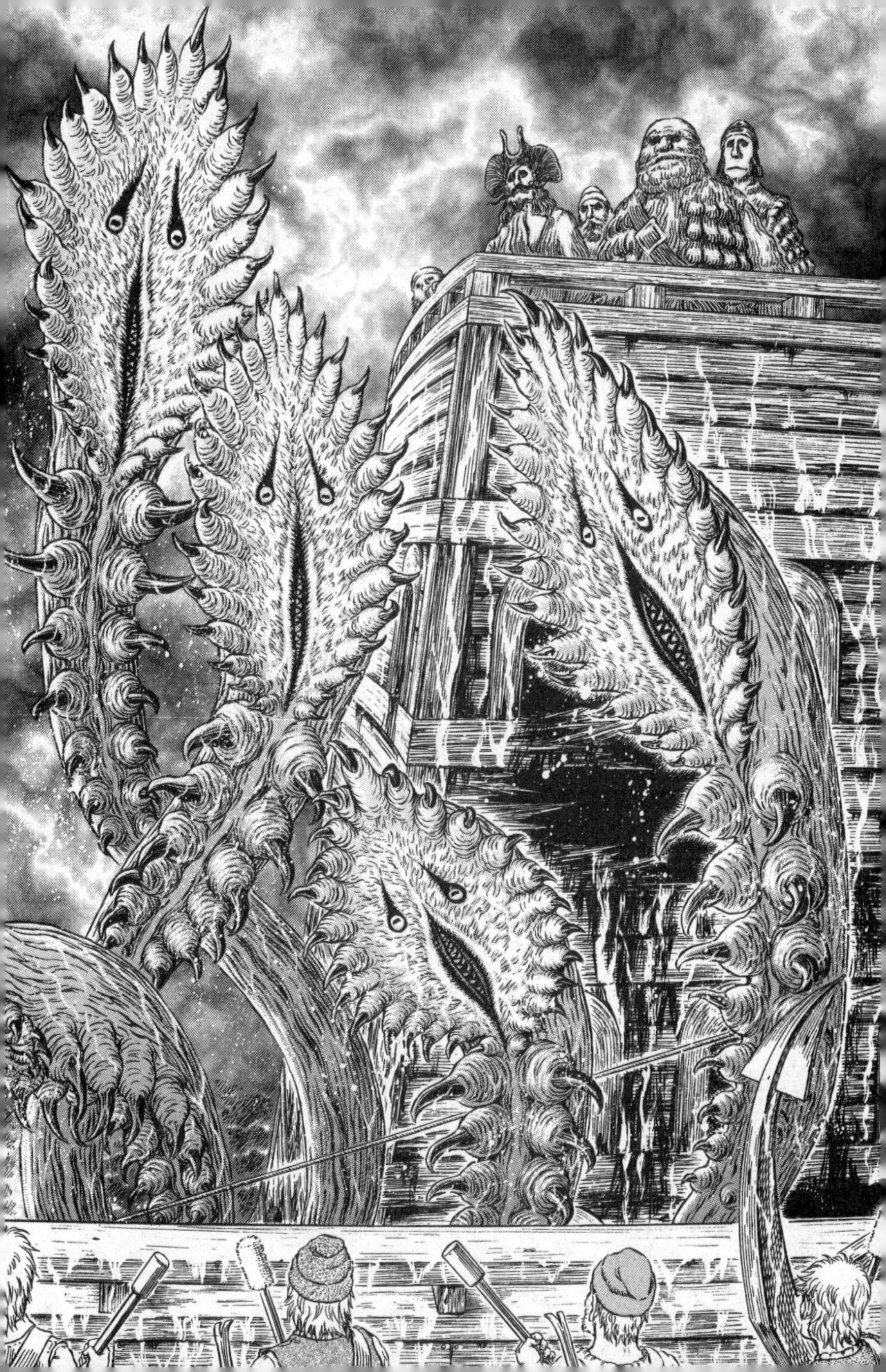

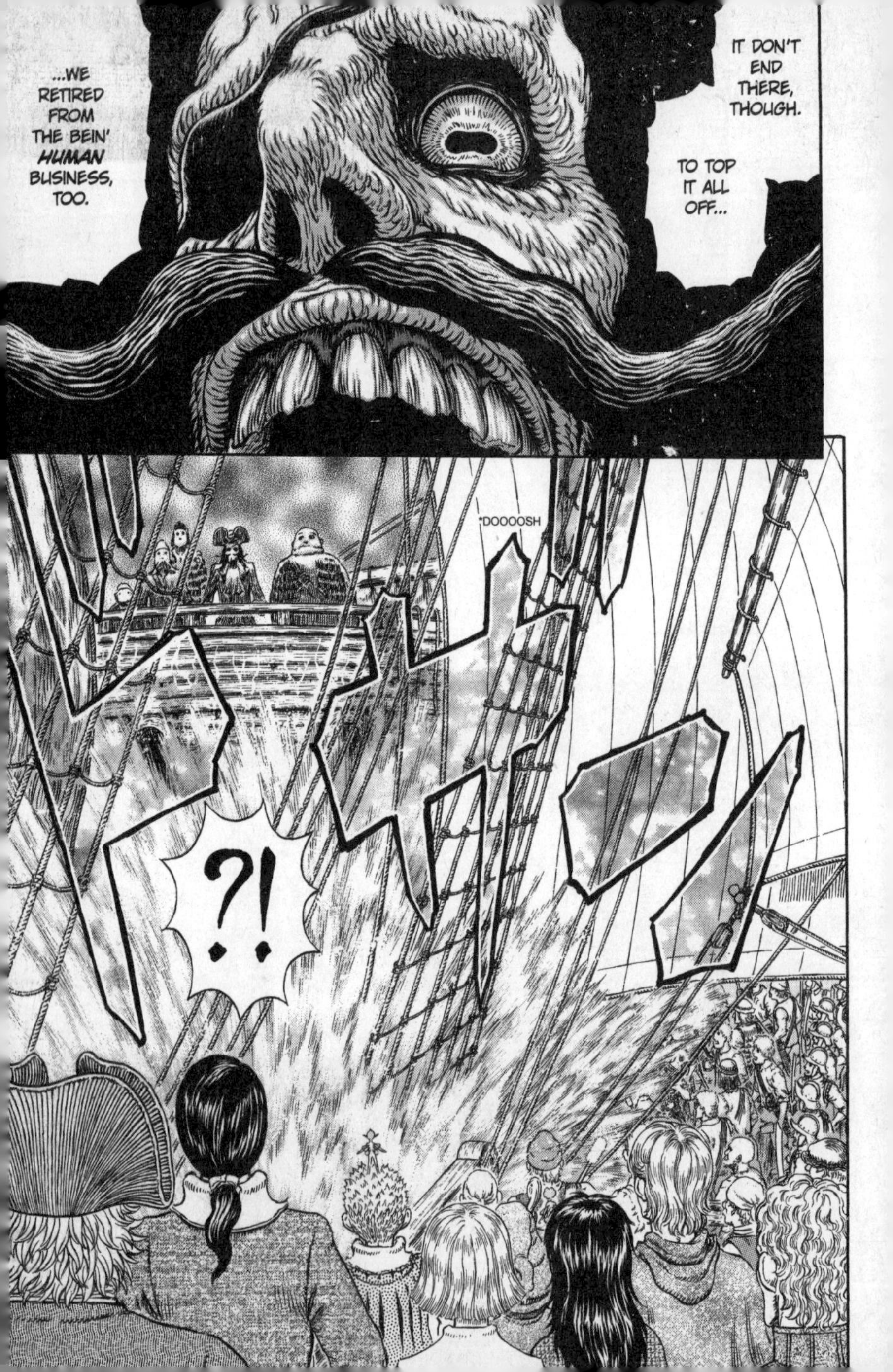
...WE RETIRED FROM THE BEIN' HUMAN BUSINESS, TOO.
IT DON'T END THERE, THOUGH.
TO TOP IT ALL OFF...
*DOOOOSH
?!

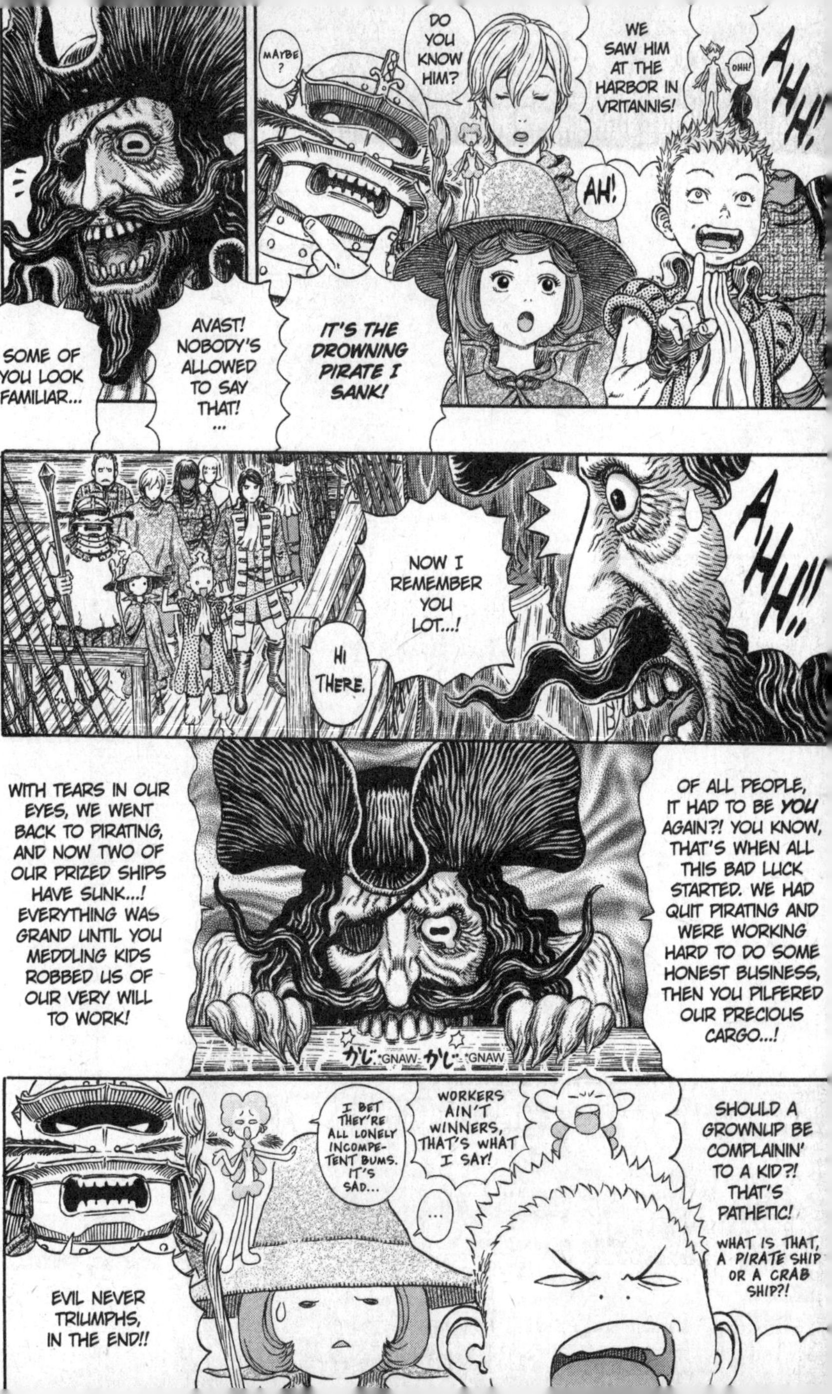
AHHH!
OHH!
WE SAW HIM AT THE HARBOR IN VRITANNIS!
DO YOU KNOW HIM?
MAYBE ?
AH!
IT'S THE DROWNING PIRATE I SANK!
AVAST! NOBODY'S ALLOWED TO SAY THAT! ...
SOME OF YOU LOOK FAMILIAR...
AHHH!!
NOW I REMEMBER YOU LOT...!
HI THERE.
OF ALL PEOPLE, IT HAD TO BE *YOU* AGAIN?! YOU KNOW, THAT'S WHEN ALL THIS BAD LUCK STARTED. WE HAD QUIT PIRATING AND WERE WORKING HARD TO DO SOME HONEST BUSINESS, THEN YOU PILFERED OUR PRECIOUS CARGO...!
WITH TEARS IN OUR EYES, WE WENT BACK TO PIRATING, AND NOW TWO OF OUR PRIZED SHIPS HAVE SUNK...! EVERYTHING WAS GRAND UNTIL YOU MEDDLING KIDS ROBBED US OF OUR VERY WILL TO WORK!
かじ GNAW かじ GNAW
SHOULD A GROWNUP BE COMPLAININ' TO A KID?! THAT'S PATHETIC!
WHAT IS THAT, A *PIRATE SHIP* OR A *CRAB SHIP*?!
WORKERS AIN'T WINNERS, THAT'S WHAT I SAY!
I BET THEY'RE ALL LONELY INCOMPETENT BUMS. IT'S SAD...
...
EVIL NEVER TRIUMPHS, IN THE END!!

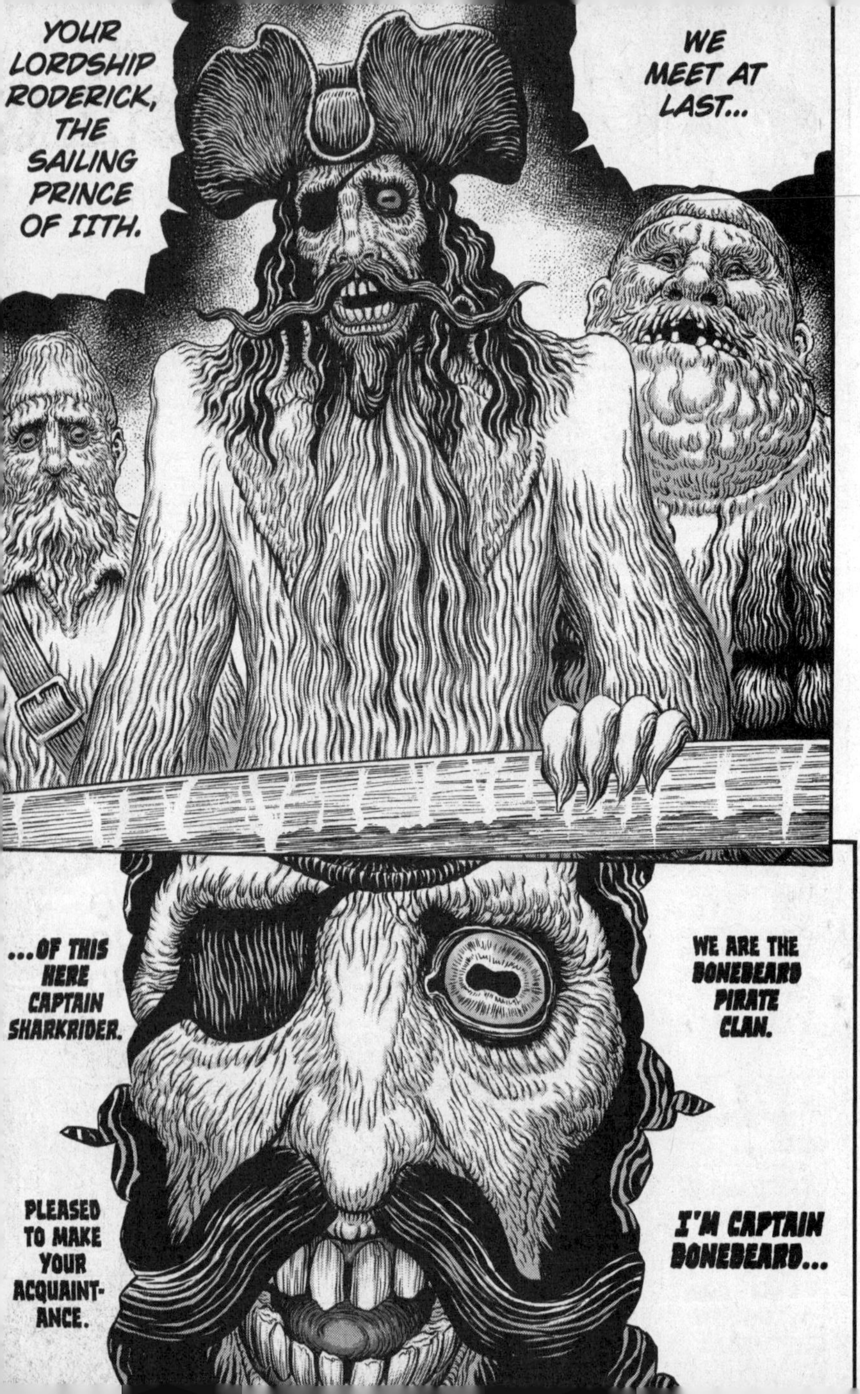
WE MEET AT LAST...
YOUR LORDSHIP RODERICK, THE SAILING PRINCE OF IITH.
WE ARE THE BONEBEARD PIRATE CLAN.
...OF THIS HERE CAPTAIN SHARKRIDER.
I'M CAPTAIN BONEBEARD...
PLEASED TO MAKE YOUR ACQUAINT-ANCE.

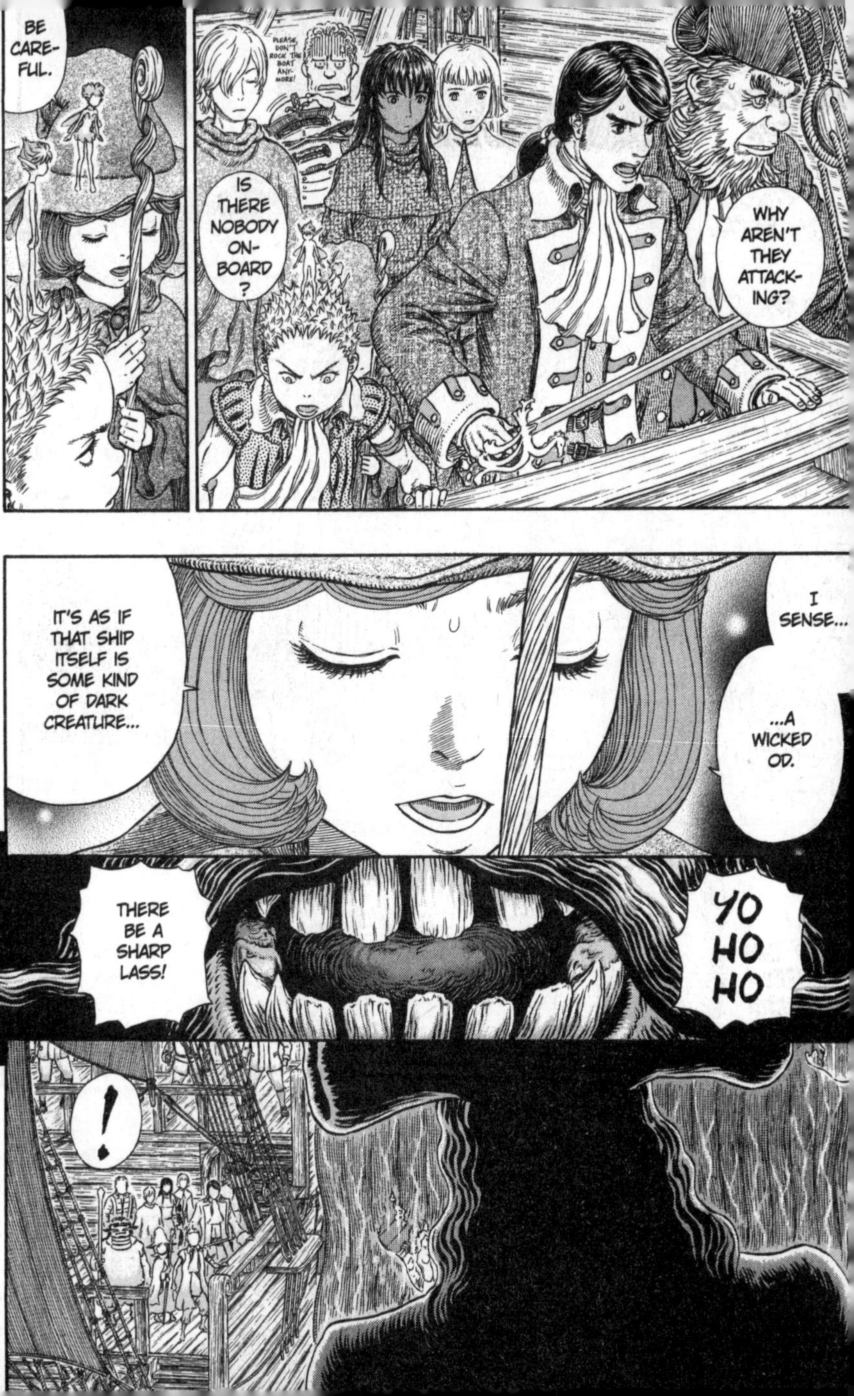
WHY AREN'T THEY ATTACKING?
PLEASE DON'T ROCK THE BOAT ANY-MORE!
IS THERE NOBODY ON-BOARD?
BE CARE-FUL.
I SENSE...
...A WICKED OD.
IT'S AS IF THAT SHIP ITSELF IS SOME KIND OF DARK CREATURE...
YO HO HO
THERE BE A SHARP LASS!
!

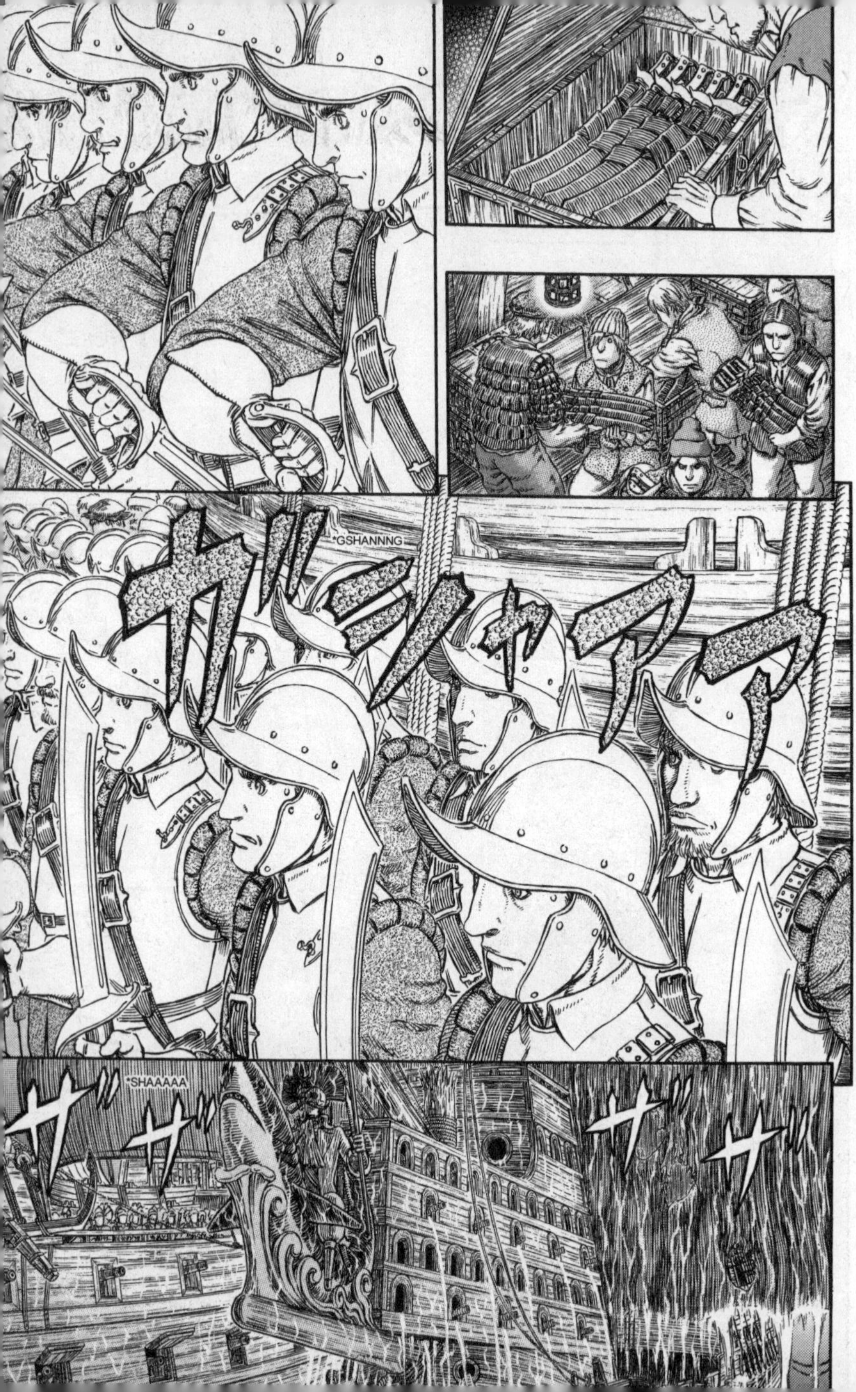
*GSHANNNG
ザシャアア
*SHAAAAA
ザッ ザッ
ザッ ザッ

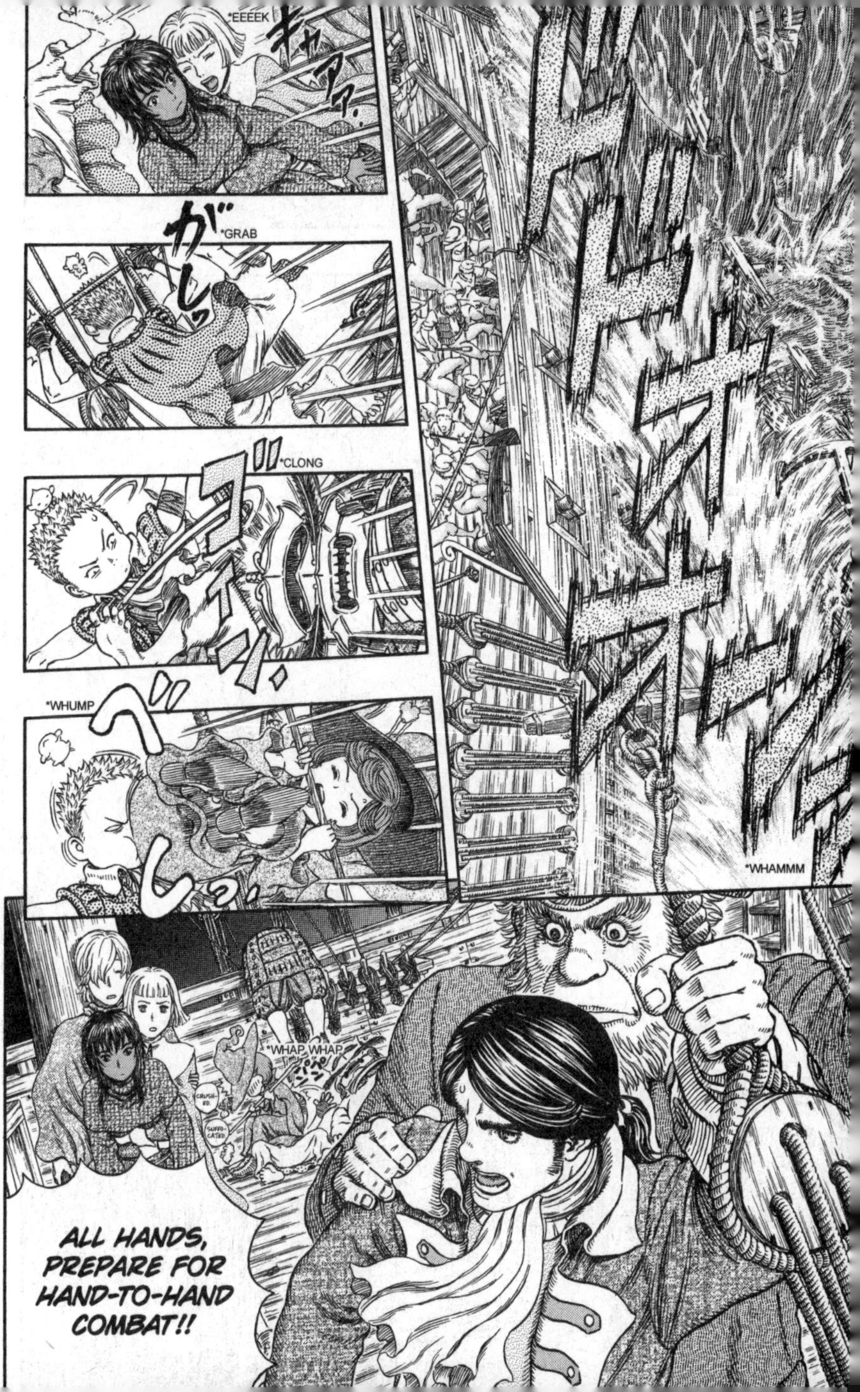
*WHAMMM
*EEEEK
*GRAB
*CLONG
*WHUMP
*WHAP WHAP
CRUSH-ED.
SUFFO-CATED.
ALL HANDS, PREPARE FOR HAND-TO-HAND COMBAT!!

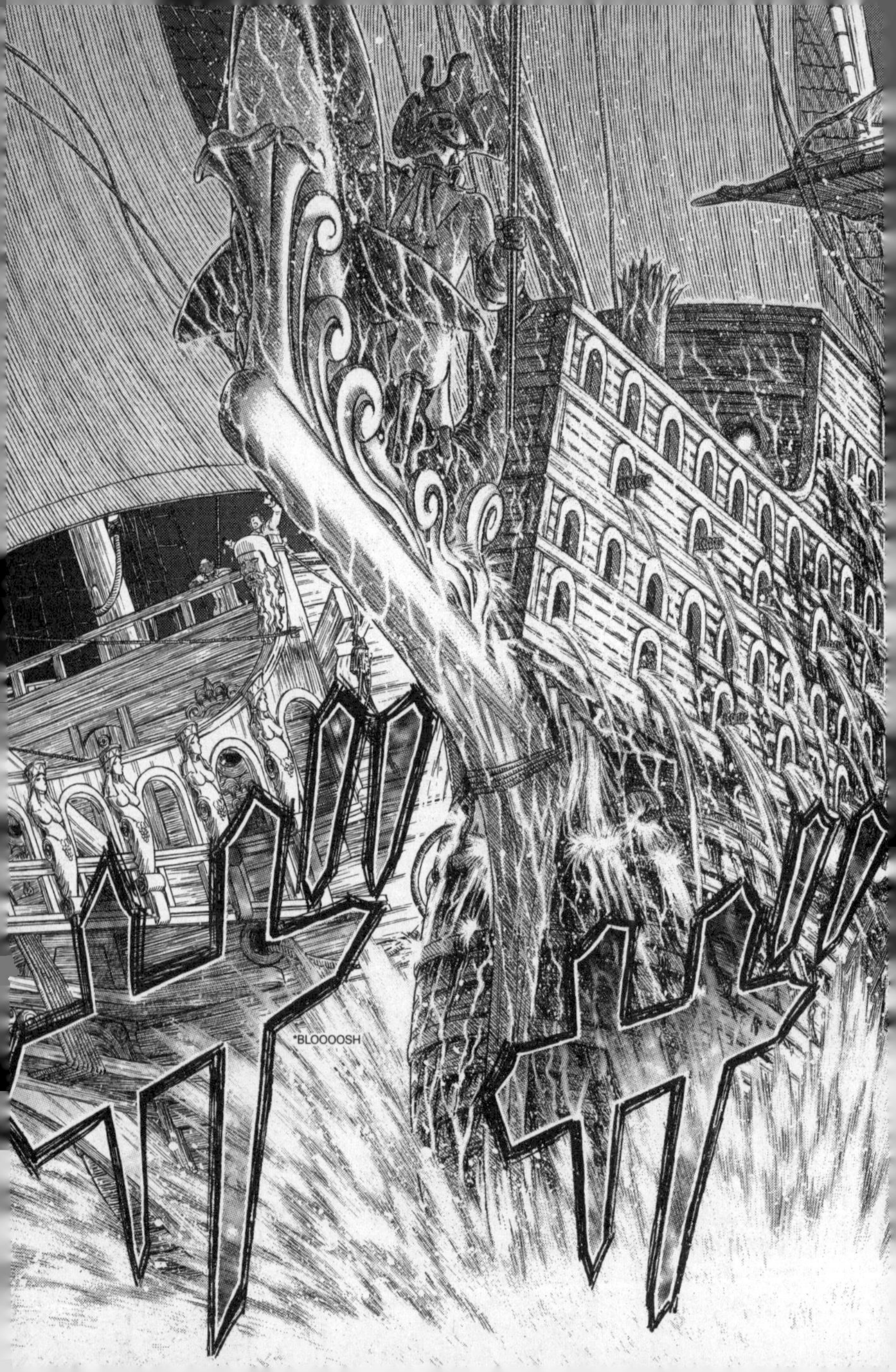
*BLOOOOSH

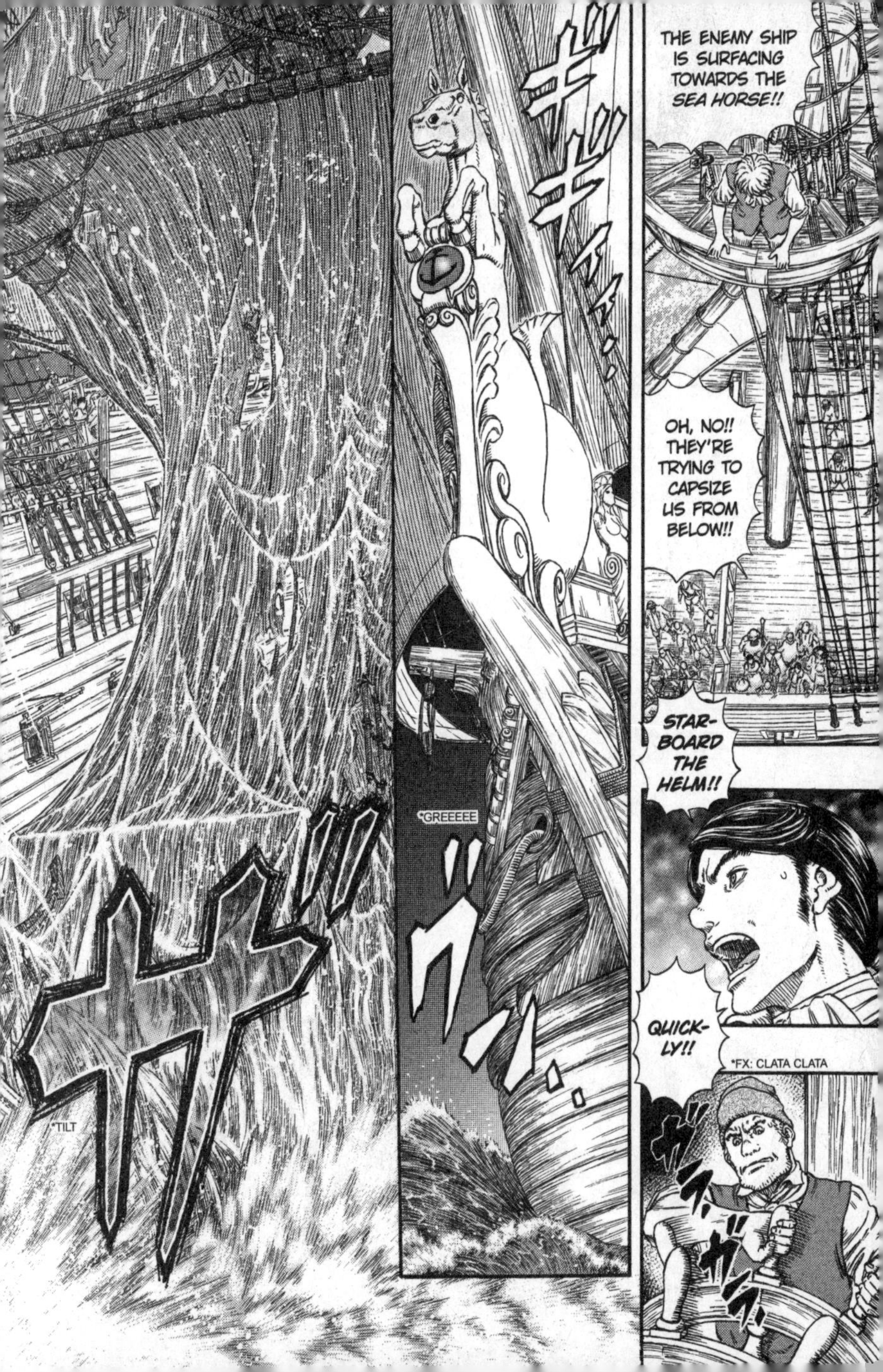
THE ENEMY SHIP IS SURFACING TOWARDS THE SEA HORSE!!
OH, NO!! THEY'RE TRYING TO CAPSIZE US FROM BELOW!!
STAR-BOARD THE HELM!!
QUICK-LY!!
*FX: CLATA CLATA
*GREEEEE
*TILT

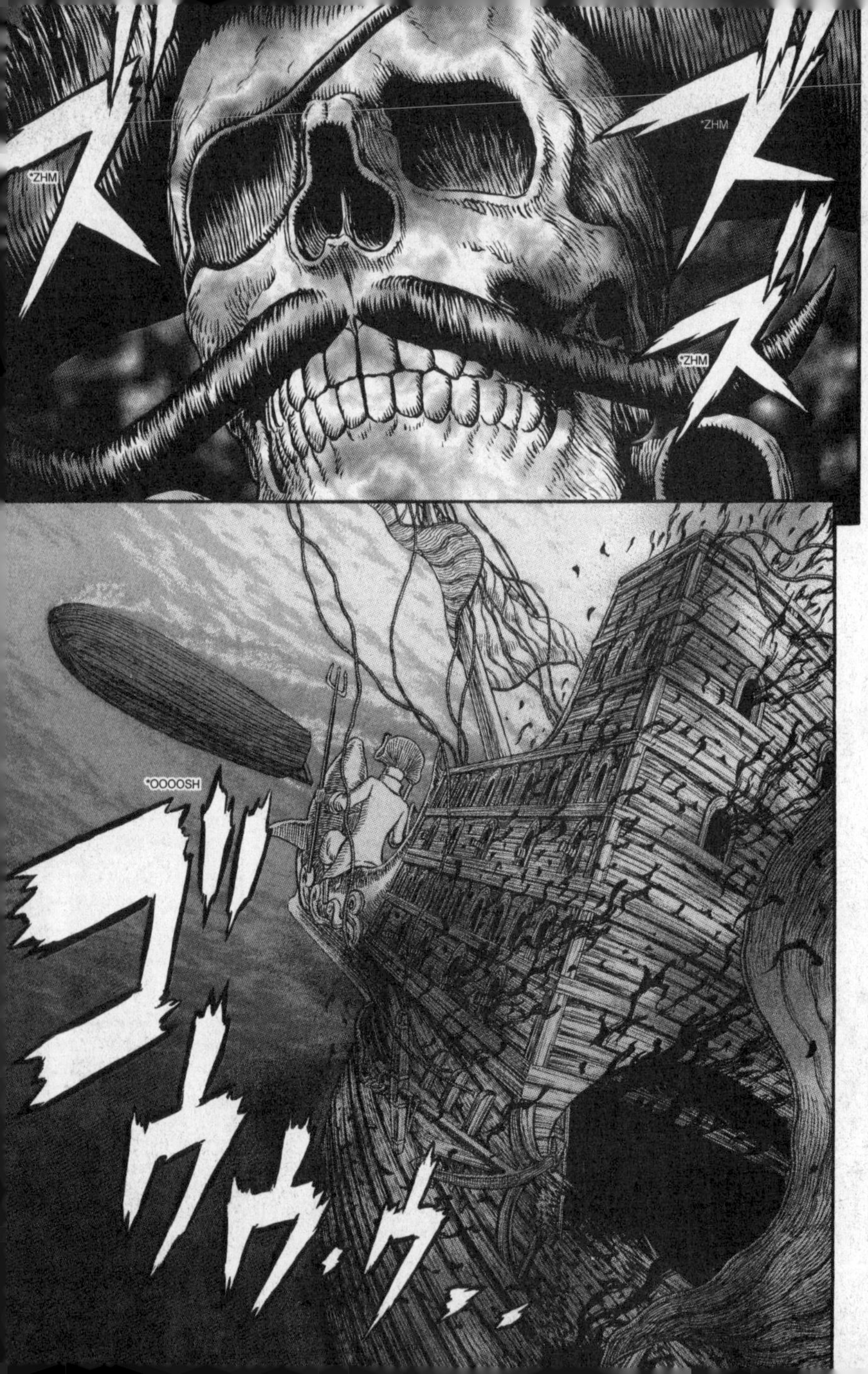
*ZHM
*ZHM
*ZHM
*OOOOSH

幻造世界ファンタジア篇／妖精島の章

幽霊船 ②

GHOST SHIP, PART 2

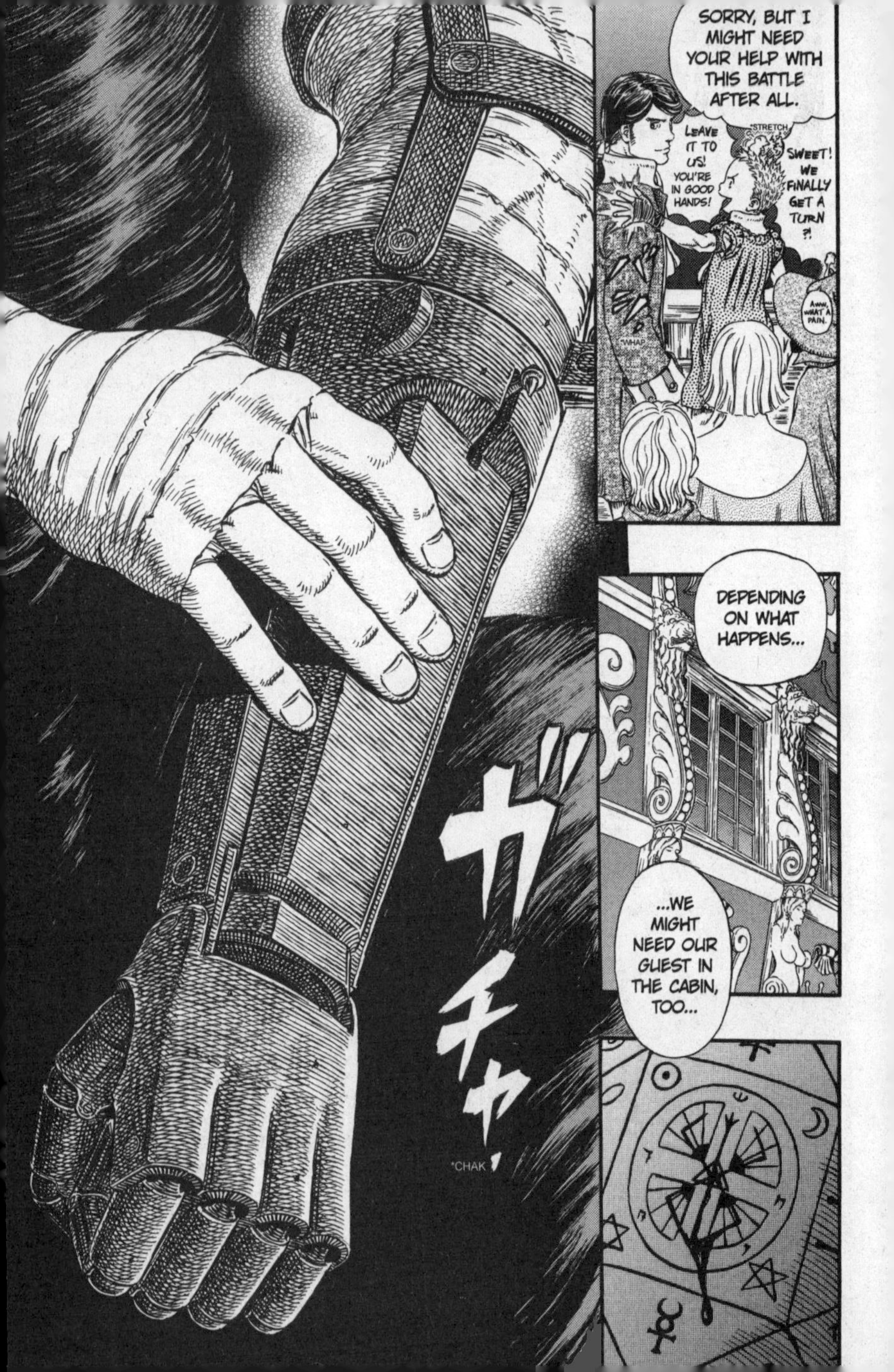
SORRY, BUT I MIGHT NEED YOUR HELP WITH THIS BATTLE AFTER ALL.
*STRETCH
SWEET! WE FINALLY GET A TURN ?!
LEAVE IT TO US! YOU'RE IN GOOD HANDS!
*WHAP
AWW, WHAT A PAIN.
DEPENDING ON WHAT HAPPENS...
...WE MIGHT NEED OUR GUEST IN THE CABIN, TOO...
ガチャ
*CHAK

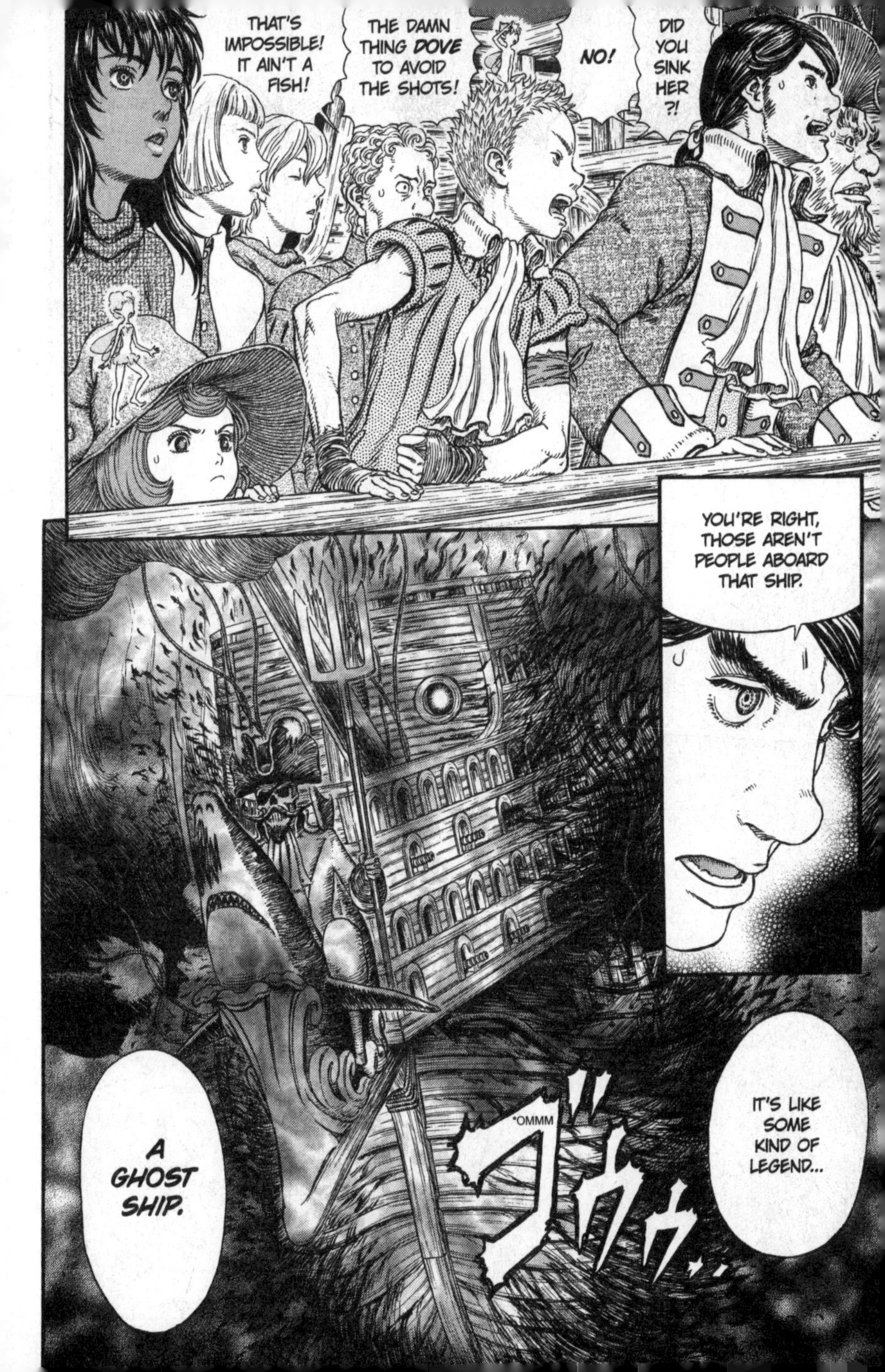
DID YOU SINK HER?!
NO!
THE DAMN THING DOVE TO AVOID THE SHOTS!
THAT'S IMPOSSIBLE! IT AIN'T A FISH!
YOU'RE RIGHT, THOSE AREN'T PEOPLE ABOARD THAT SHIP.
IT'S LIKE SOME KIND OF LEGEND...
*OMMM
A GHOST SHIP.

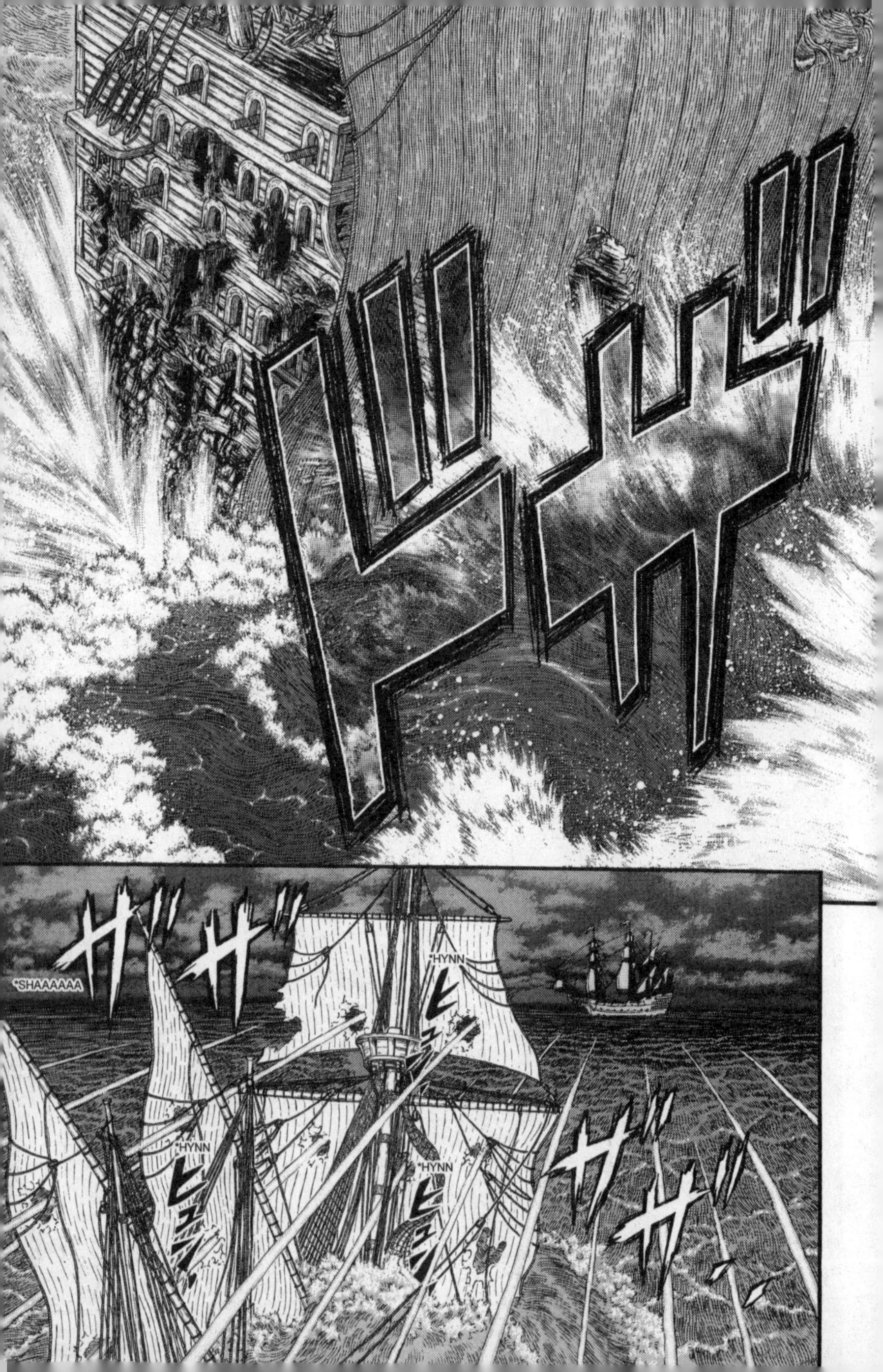
*HYNN
*SHAAAAA
*HYNN
*HYNN

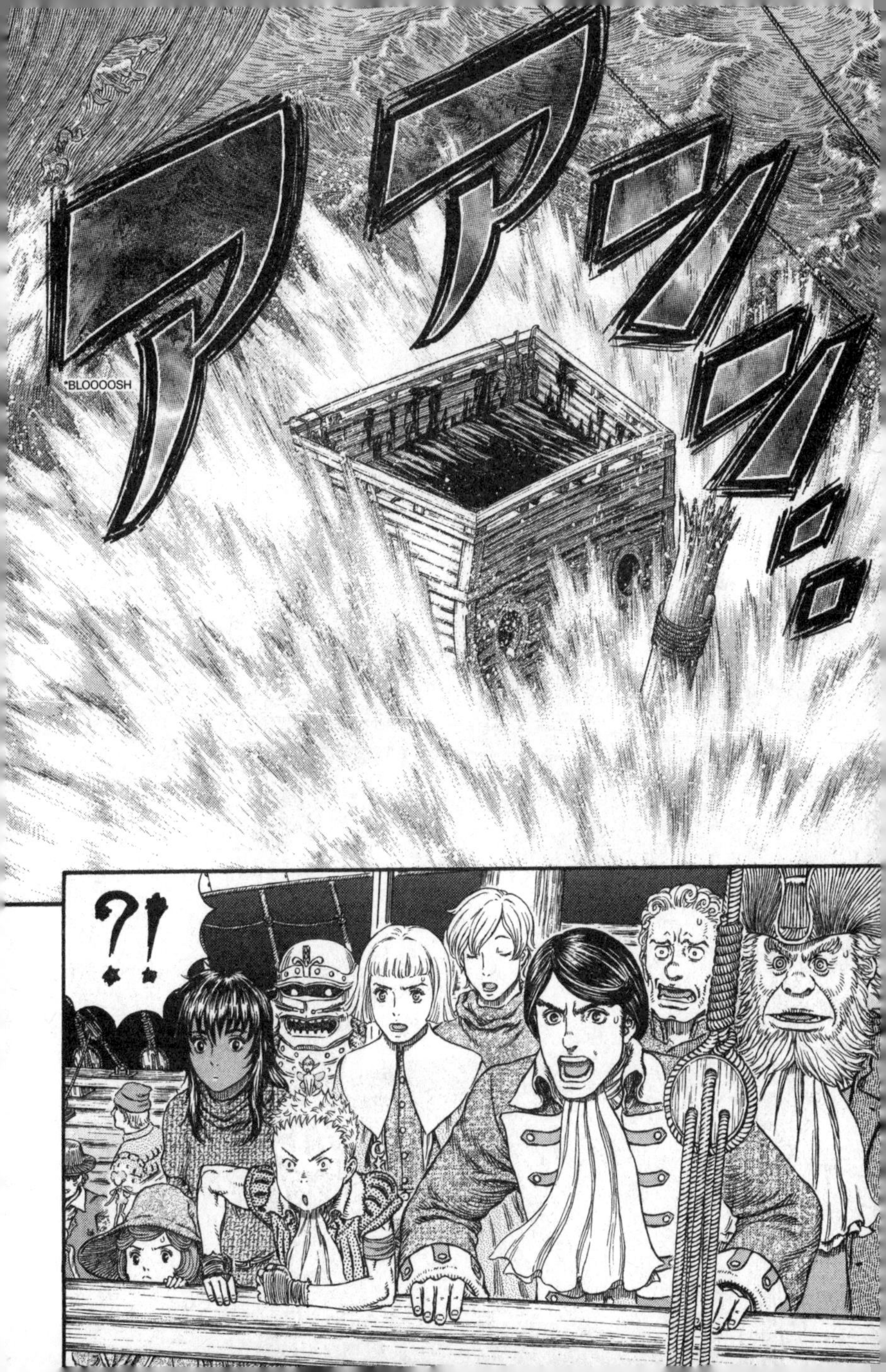
*BLOOOOSH
?!

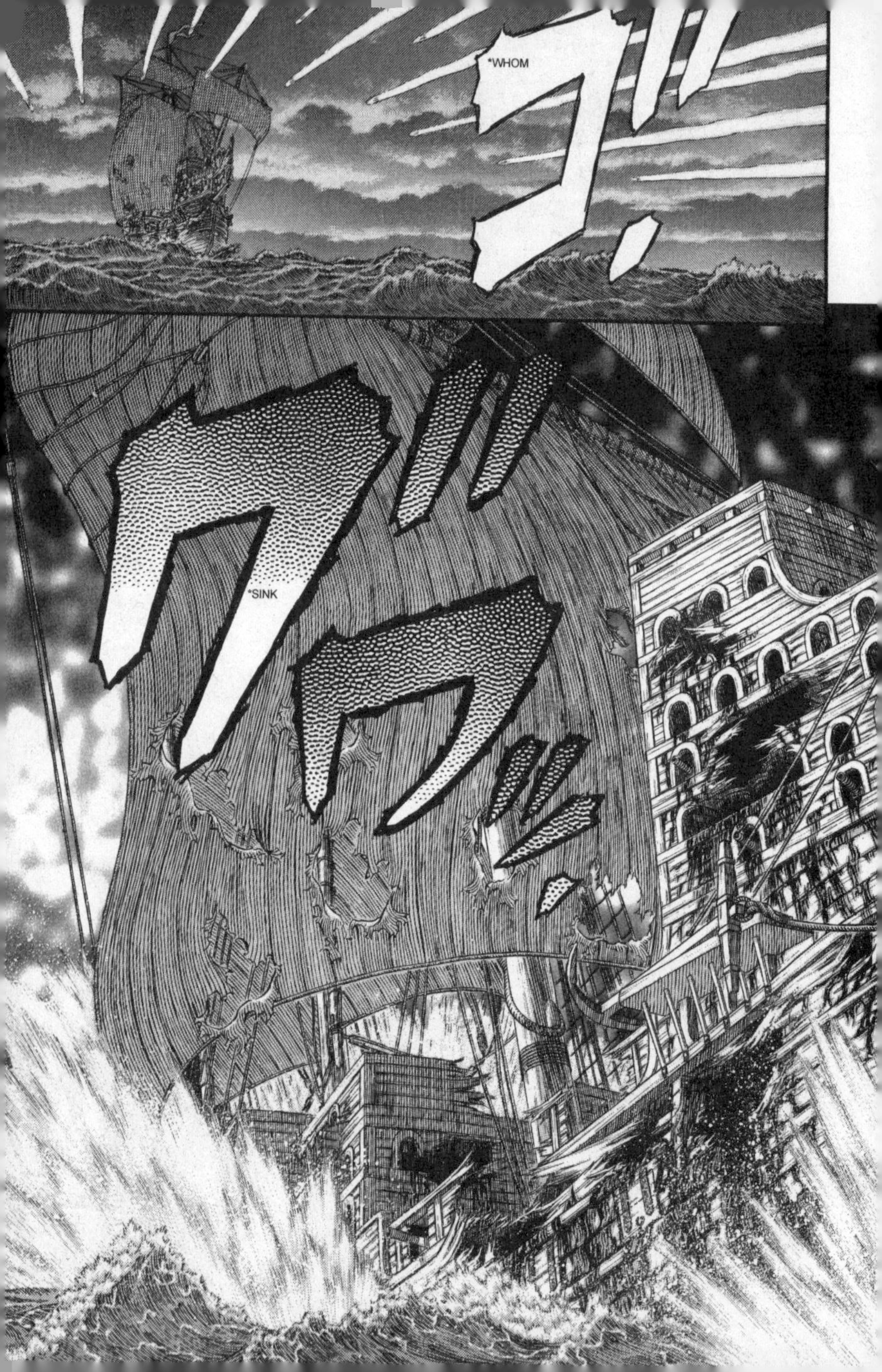
*WHOM
*SINK

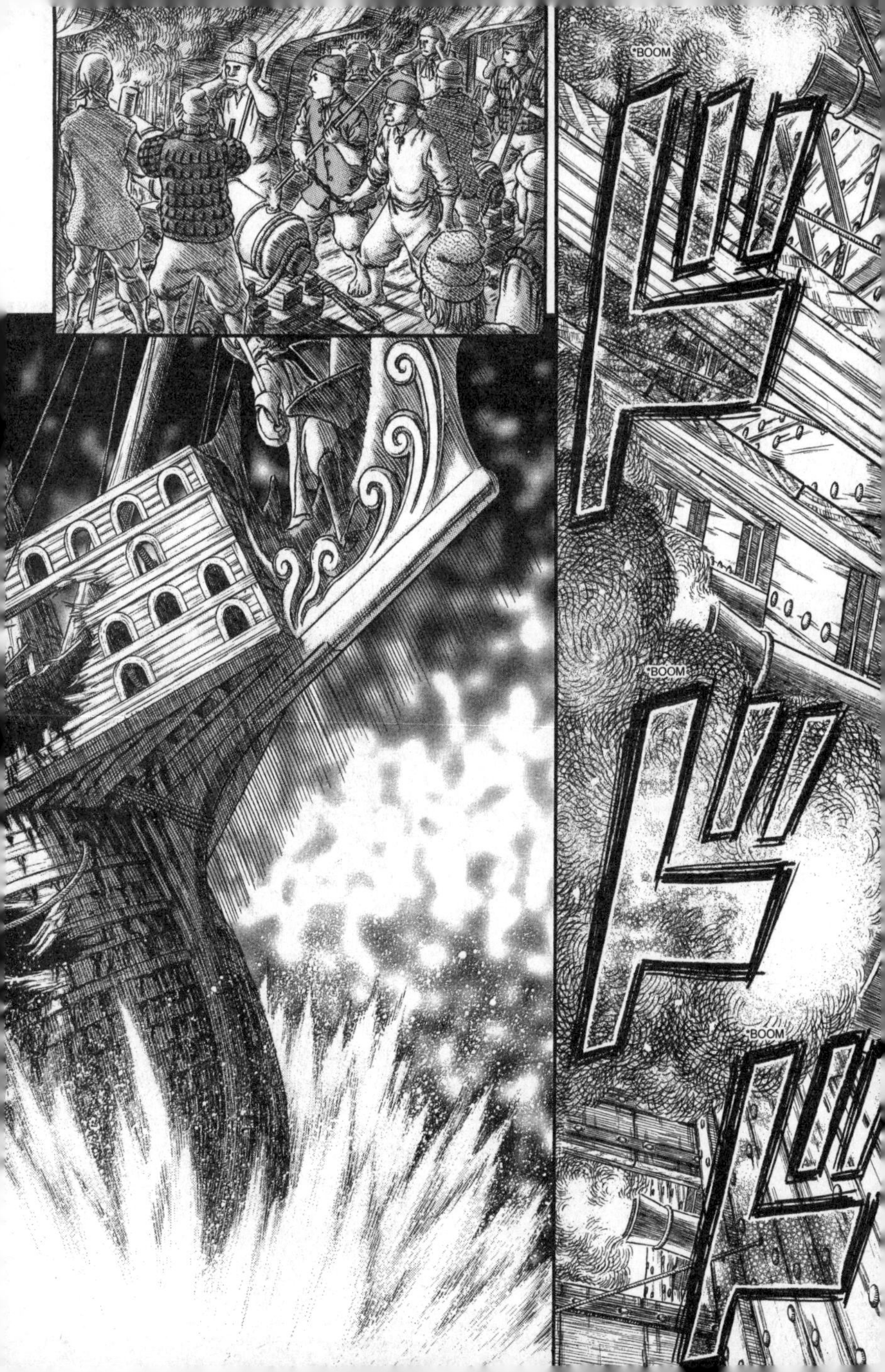
BOOM
BOOM
BOOM

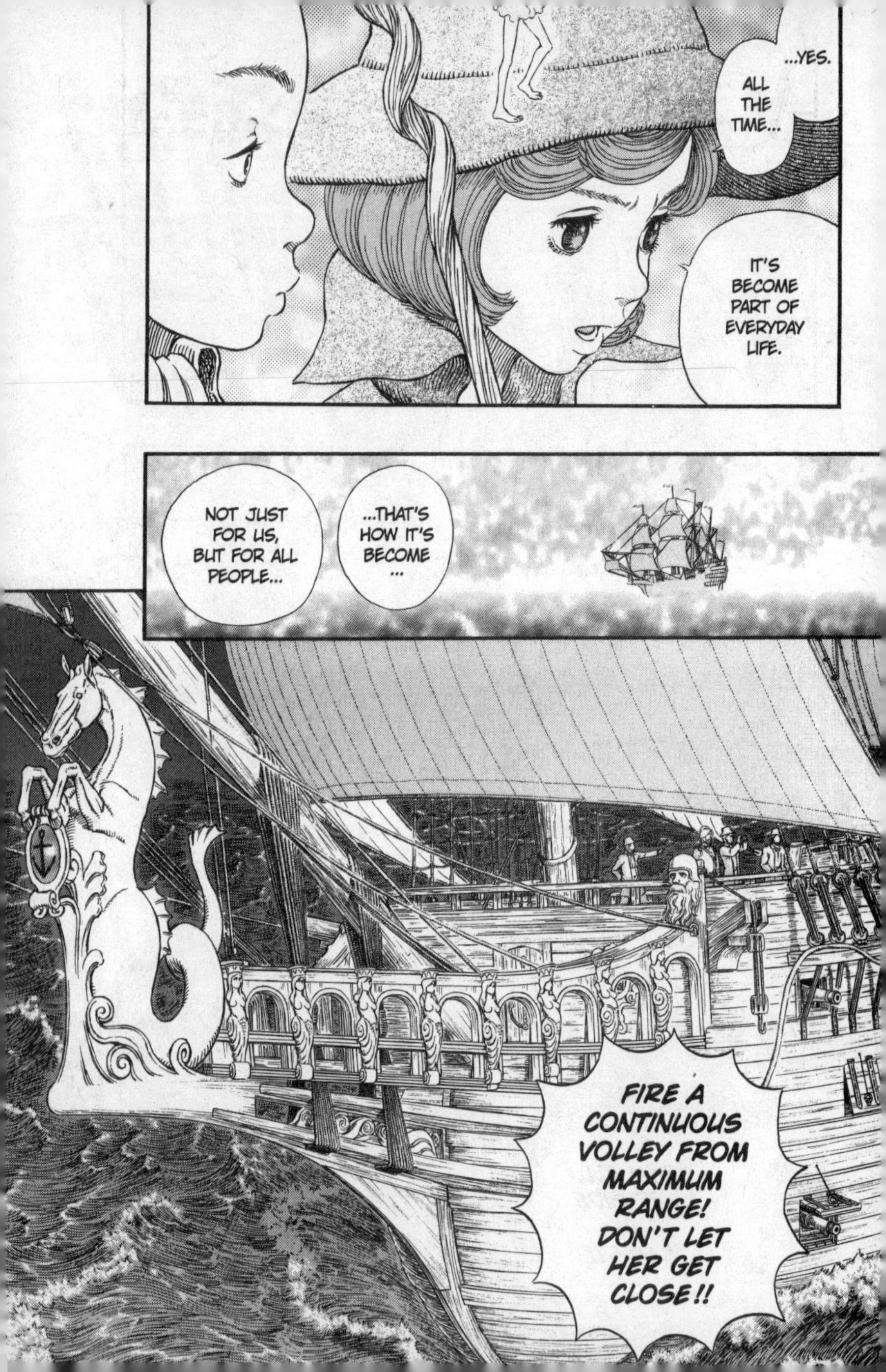
...YES.
ALL THE TIME...
IT'S BECOME PART OF EVERYDAY LIFE.
...THAT'S HOW IT'S BECOME ...
NOT JUST FOR US, BUT FOR ALL PEOPLE...
FIRE A CONTINUOUS VOLLEY FROM MAXIMUM RANGE! DON'T LET HER GET CLOSE!!

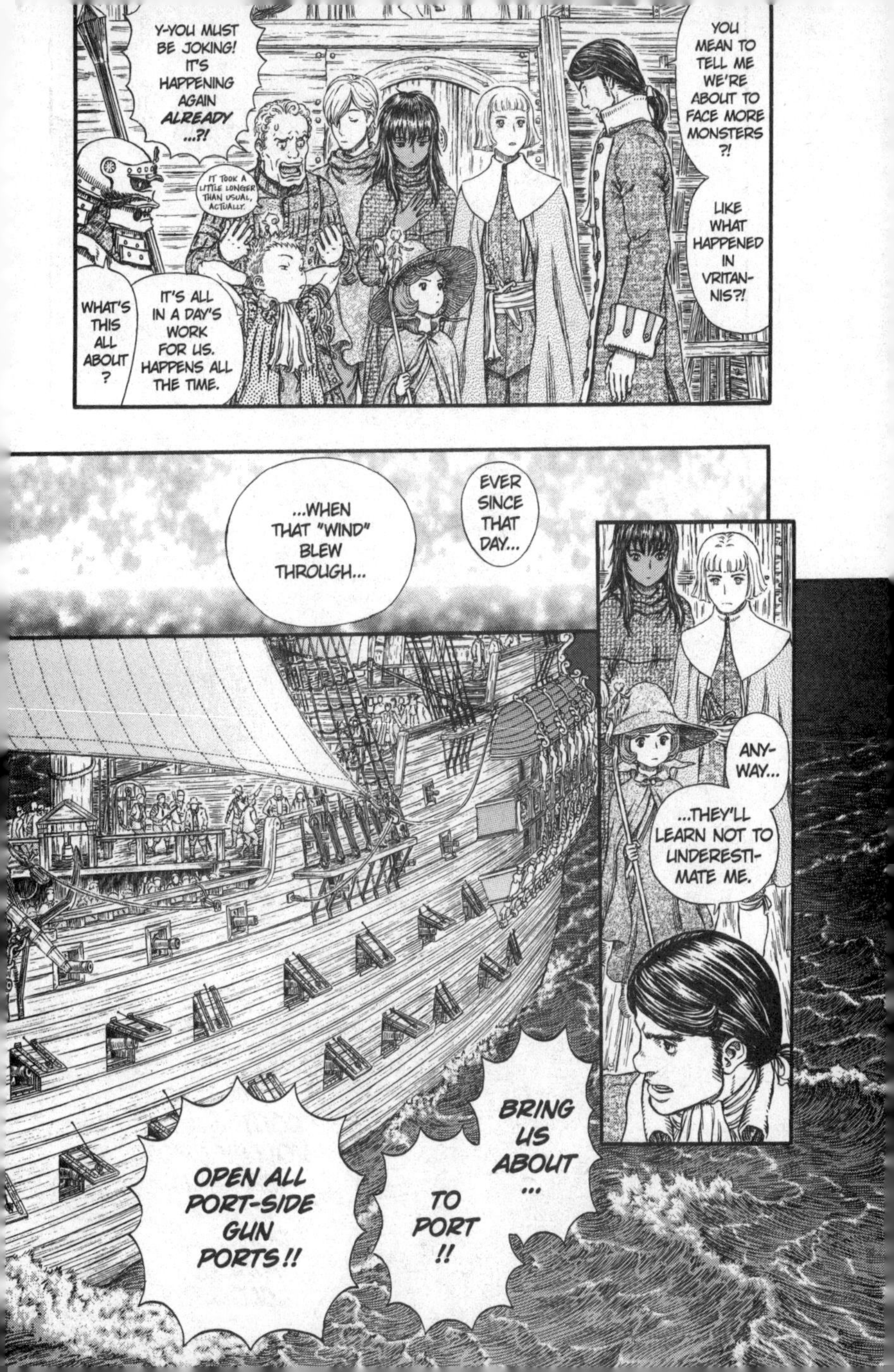
YOU MEAN TO TELL ME WE'RE ABOUT TO FACE MORE MONSTERS ?!
LIKE WHAT HAPPENED IN VRITAN-NIS?!
Y-YOU MUST BE JOKING! IT'S HAPPENING AGAIN ALREADY ...?!
IT TOOK A LITTLE LONGER THAN USUAL, ACTUALLY.
IT'S ALL IN A DAY'S WORK FOR US. HAPPENS ALL THE TIME.
WHAT'S THIS ALL ABOUT ?
EVER SINCE THAT DAY...
...WHEN THAT "WIND" BLEW THROUGH...
ANY-WAY...
...THEY'LL LEARN NOT TO UNDERESTI-MATE ME.
BRING US ABOUT ...
TO PORT !!
OPEN ALL PORT-SIDE GUN PORTS !!

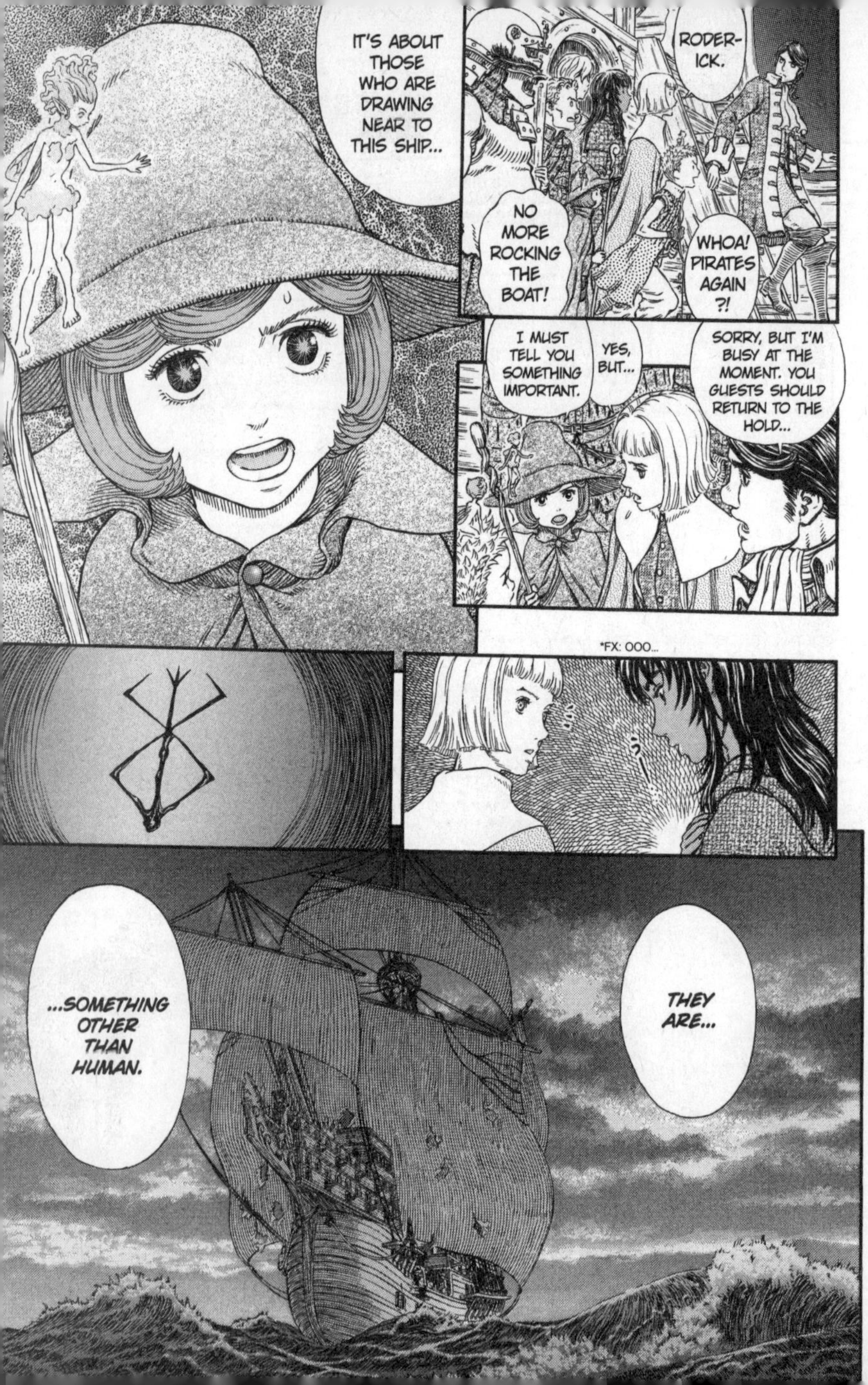
RODER-ICK.
WHOA! PIRATES AGAIN?!
NO MORE ROCKING THE BOAT!
SORRY, BUT I'M BUSY AT THE MOMENT. YOU GUESTS SHOULD RETURN TO THE HOLD...
YES, BUT...
I MUST TELL YOU SOMETHING IMPORTANT.
IT'S ABOUT THOSE WHO ARE DRAWING NEAR TO THIS SHIP...
*FX: OOO...
THEY ARE...
...SOMETHING OTHER THAN HUMAN.

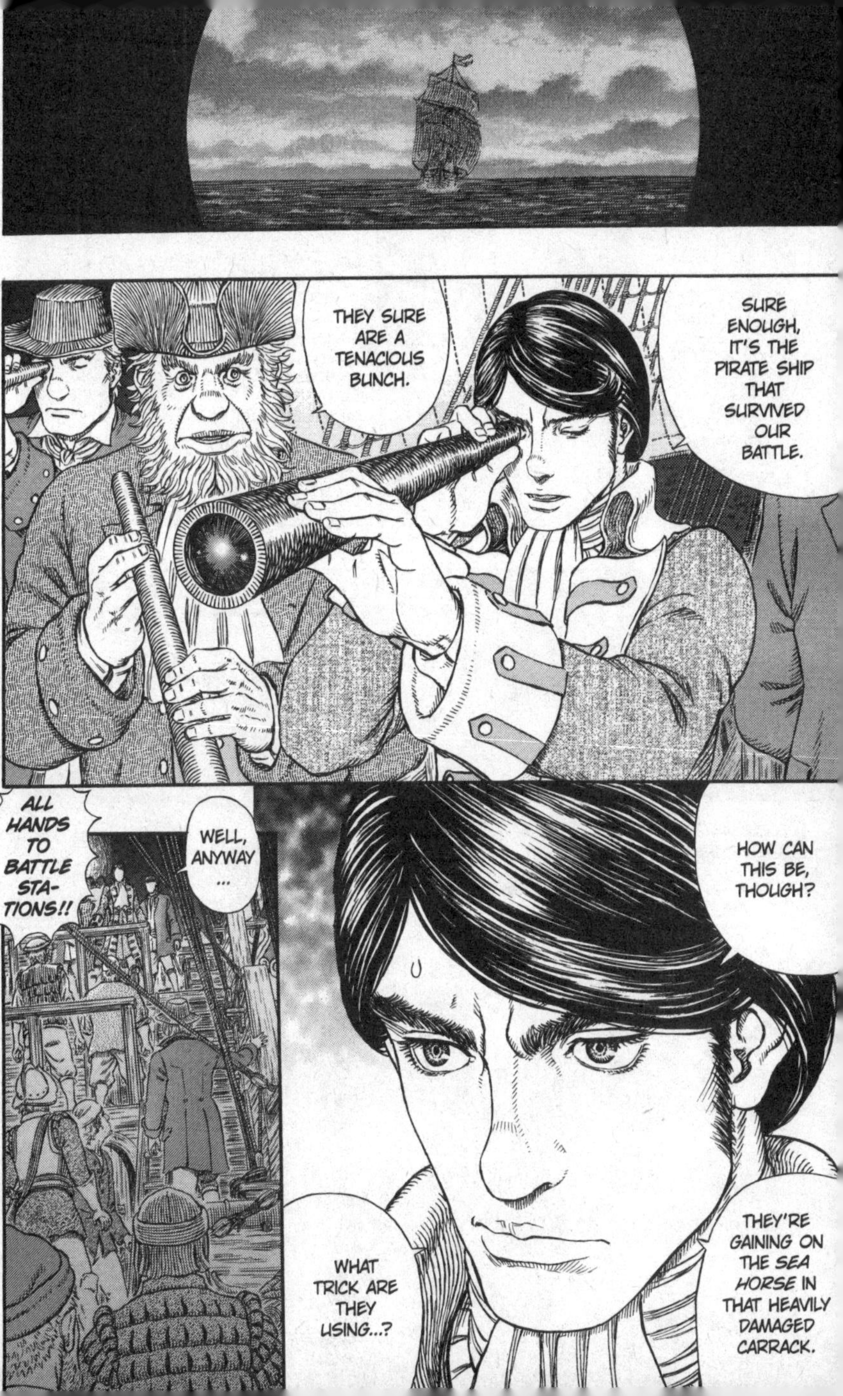
SURE ENOUGH, IT'S THE PIRATE SHIP THAT SURVIVED OUR BATTLE.
THEY SURE ARE A TENACIOUS BUNCH.
HOW CAN THIS BE, THOUGH?
THEY'RE GAINING ON THE *SEA HORSE* IN THAT HEAVILY DAMAGED CARRACK.
WHAT TRICK ARE THEY USING...?
WELL, ANYWAY ...
ALL HANDS TO BATTLE STA-TIONS!!

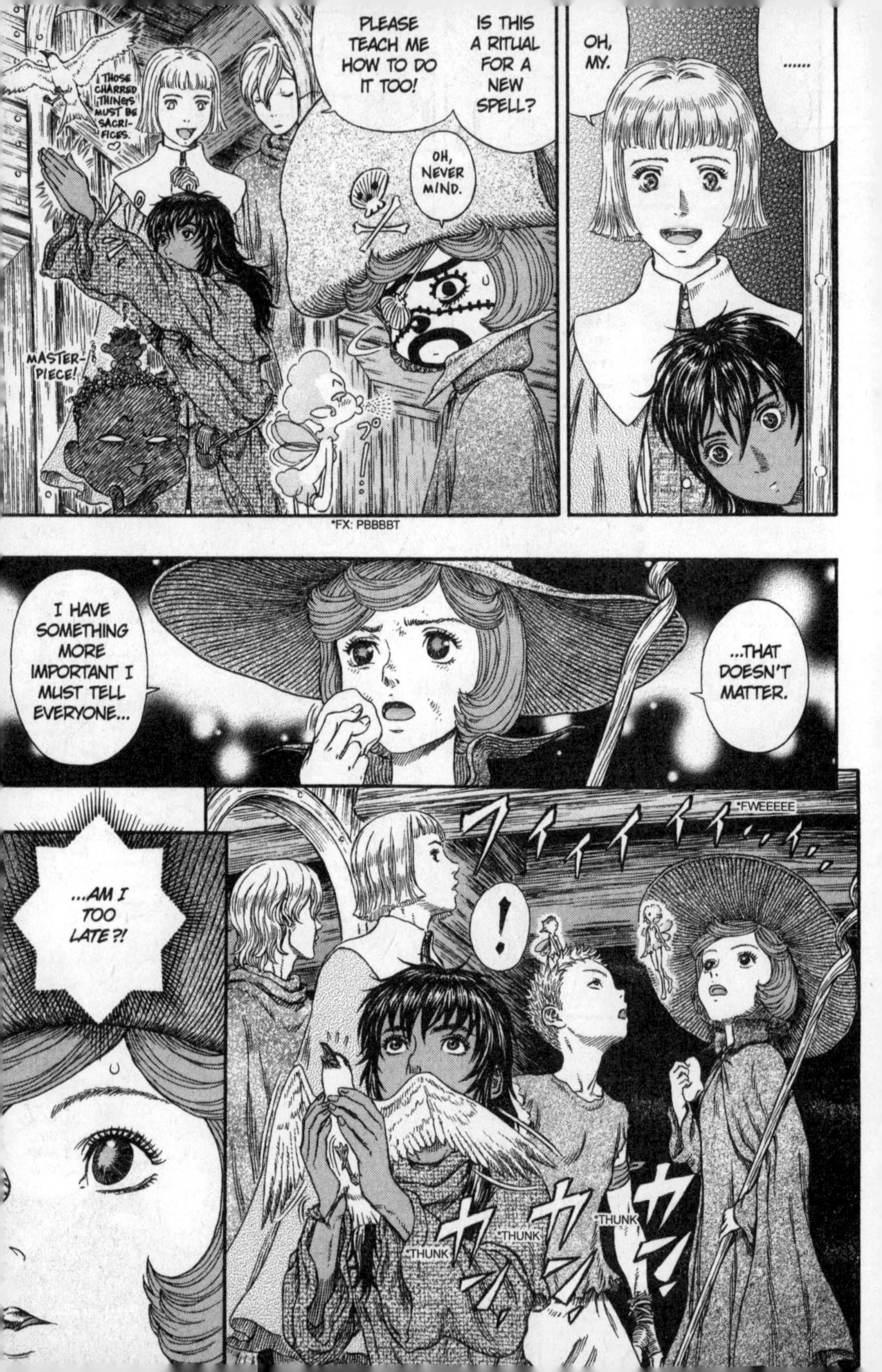
......
OH, MY.
IS THIS A RITUAL FOR A NEW SPELL?
PLEASE TEACH ME HOW TO DO IT TOO!
OH, NEVER MIND.
THOSE CHARRED THINGS MUST BE SACRIFICES.
MASTER-PIECE!
プ!!
*FX: PBBBBT
...THAT DOESN'T MATTER.
I HAVE SOMETHING MORE IMPORTANT I MUST TELL EVERYONE...
フィイイイイ...ィ
*FWEEEEE
!
カン
*THUNK
カン
*THUNK
カン
*THUNK
...AM I TOO LATE?!

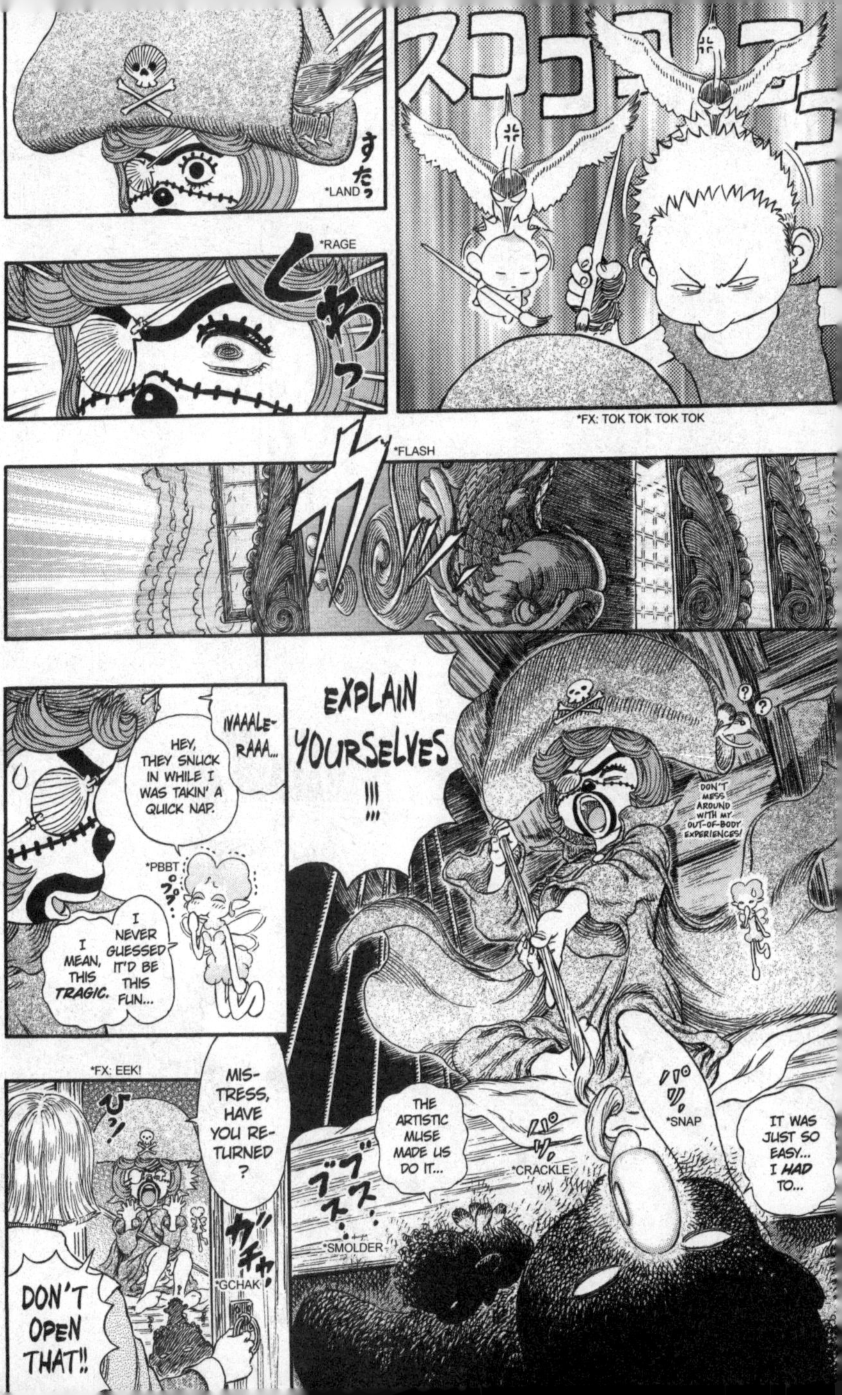

*FX: TOK TOK TOK TOK
すたっ
*LAND
くわっ
*RAGE
*FLASH
EXPLAIN YOURSELVES !!!
DON'T MESS AROUND WITH MY OUT-OF-BODY EXPERIENCES!
IT WAS JUST SO EASY... I *HAD* TO...
*SNAP
*CRACKLE
THE ARTISTIC MUSE MADE US DO IT...
*SMOLDER
IVAAALE-RAAA...
HEY, THEY SNUCK IN WHILE I WAS TAKIN' A QUICK NAP.
*PBBT
I NEVER GUESSED IT'D BE THIS FUN...
I MEAN, THIS *TRAGIC.*
MIS-TRESS, HAVE YOU RE-TURNED ?
*GCHAK
*FX: EEK!
DON'T OPEN THAT!!

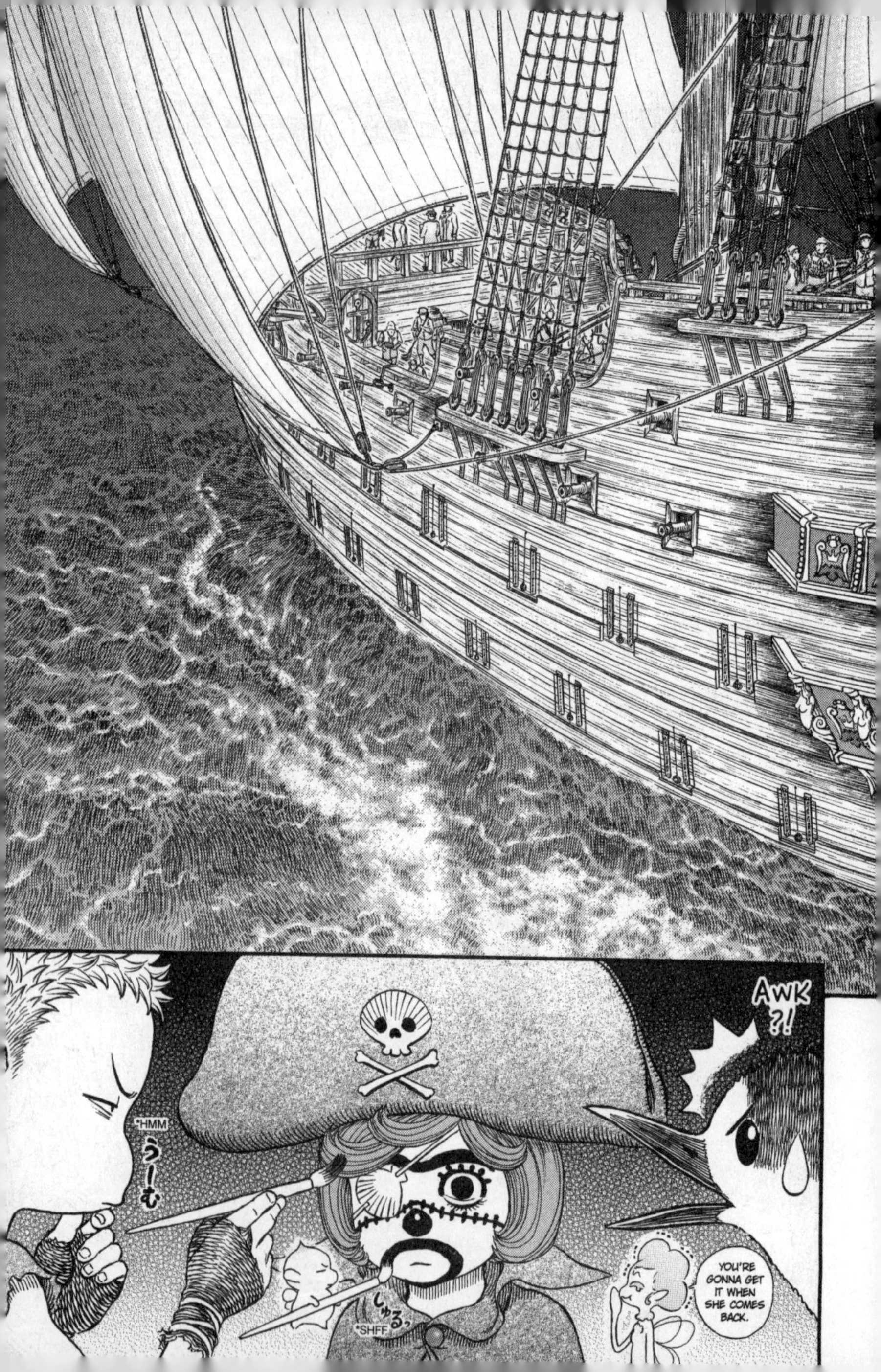
AWK ?!
YOU'RE GONNA GET IT WHEN SHE COMES BACK.
うーむ
*HMM
しゅるっ
*SHFF

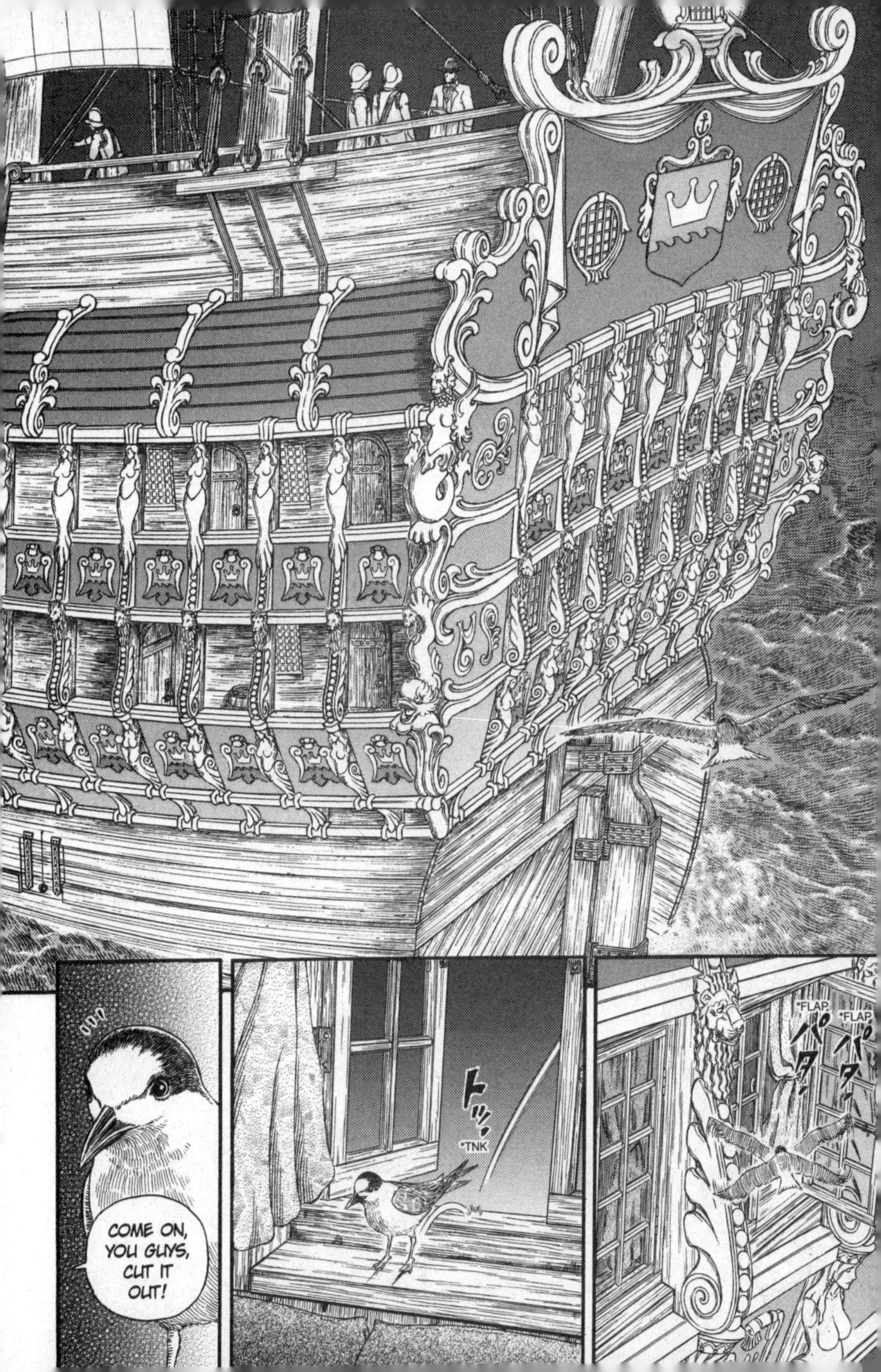
*FLAP
*FLAP
*TNK
COME ON, YOU GUYS, CUT IT OUT!

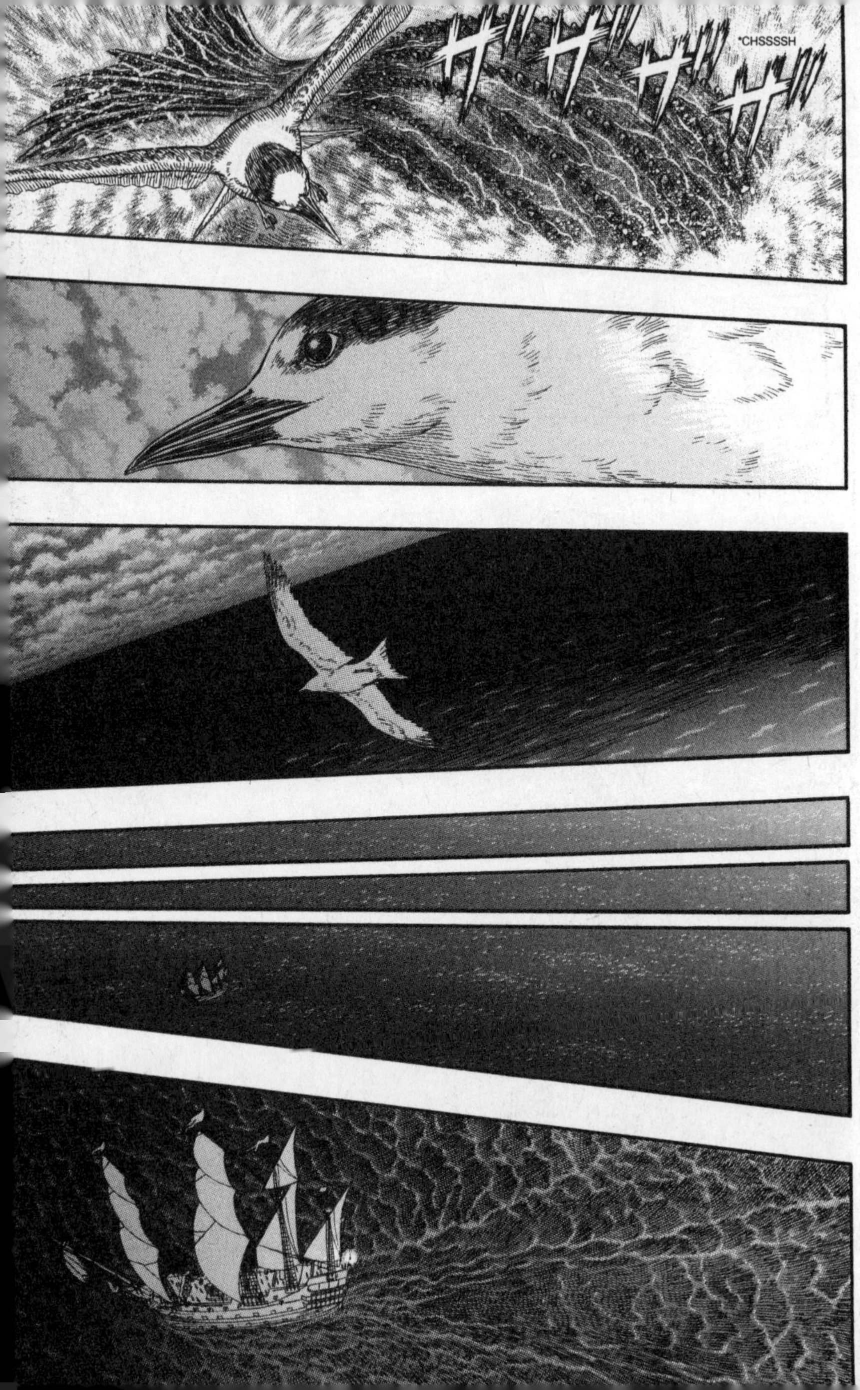
*CHSSSSH

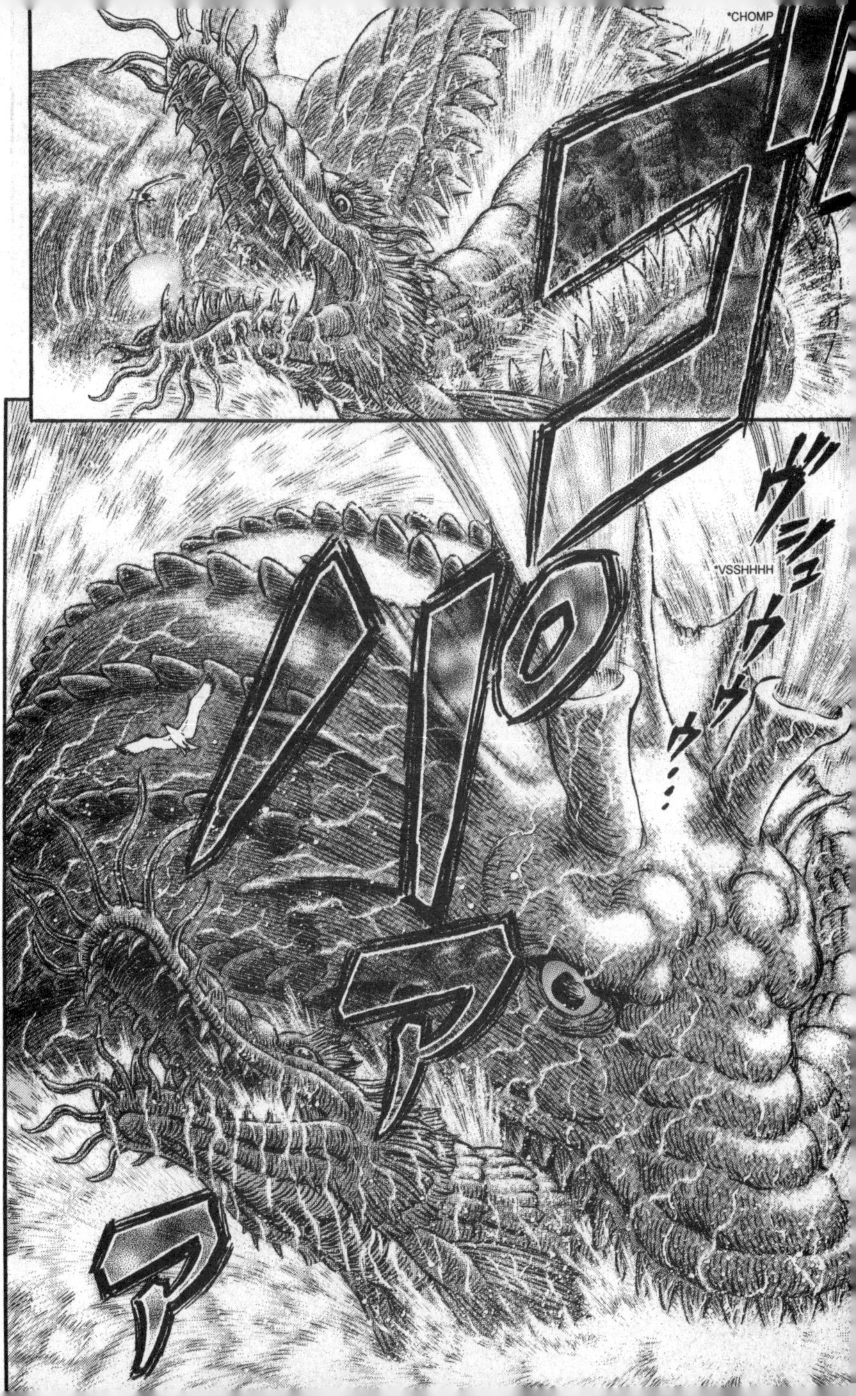
*CHOMP
ヴシュウウウウ…
*VSSHHHH

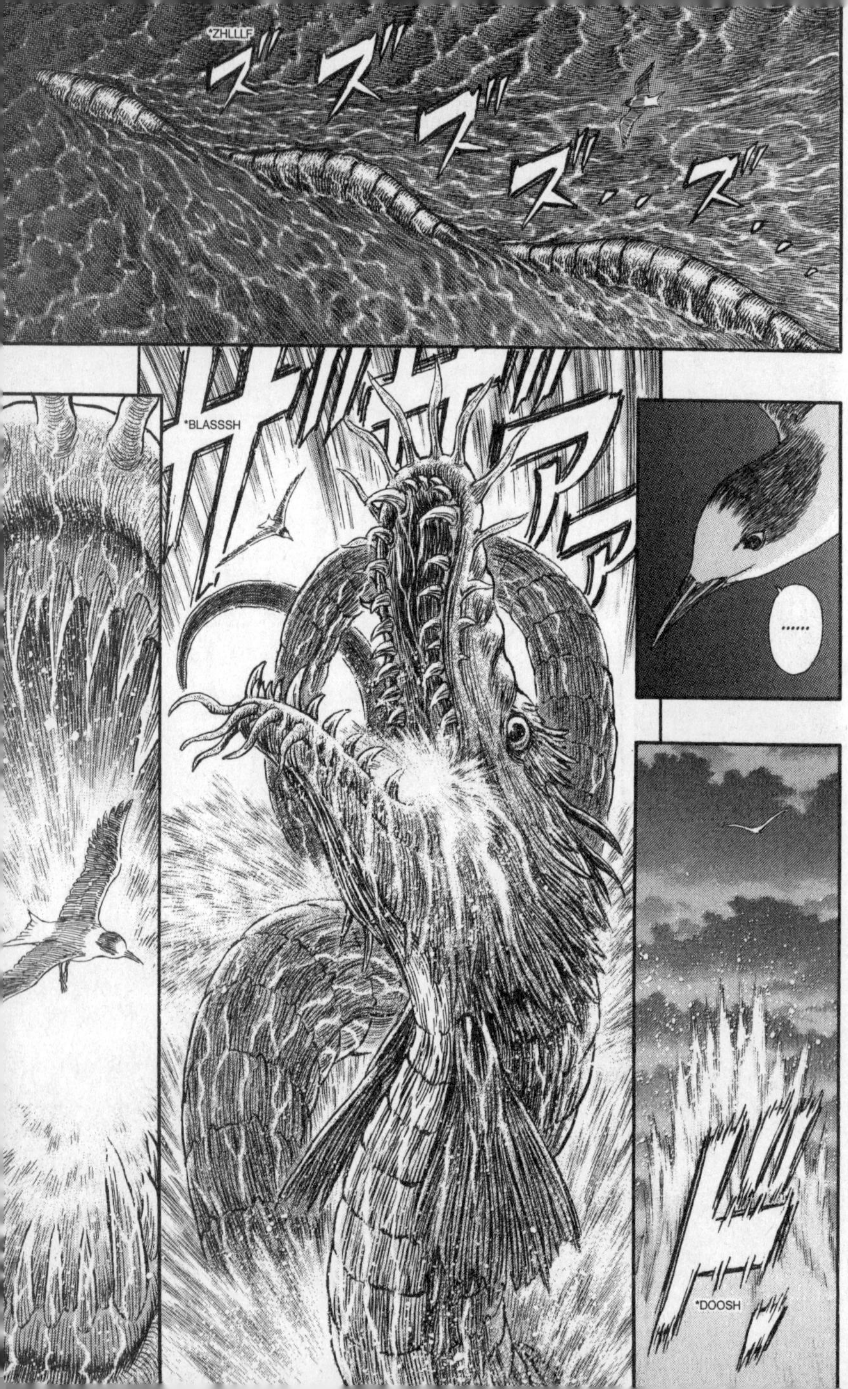
*ZHLLLF
......
*DOOSH
*BLASSSH

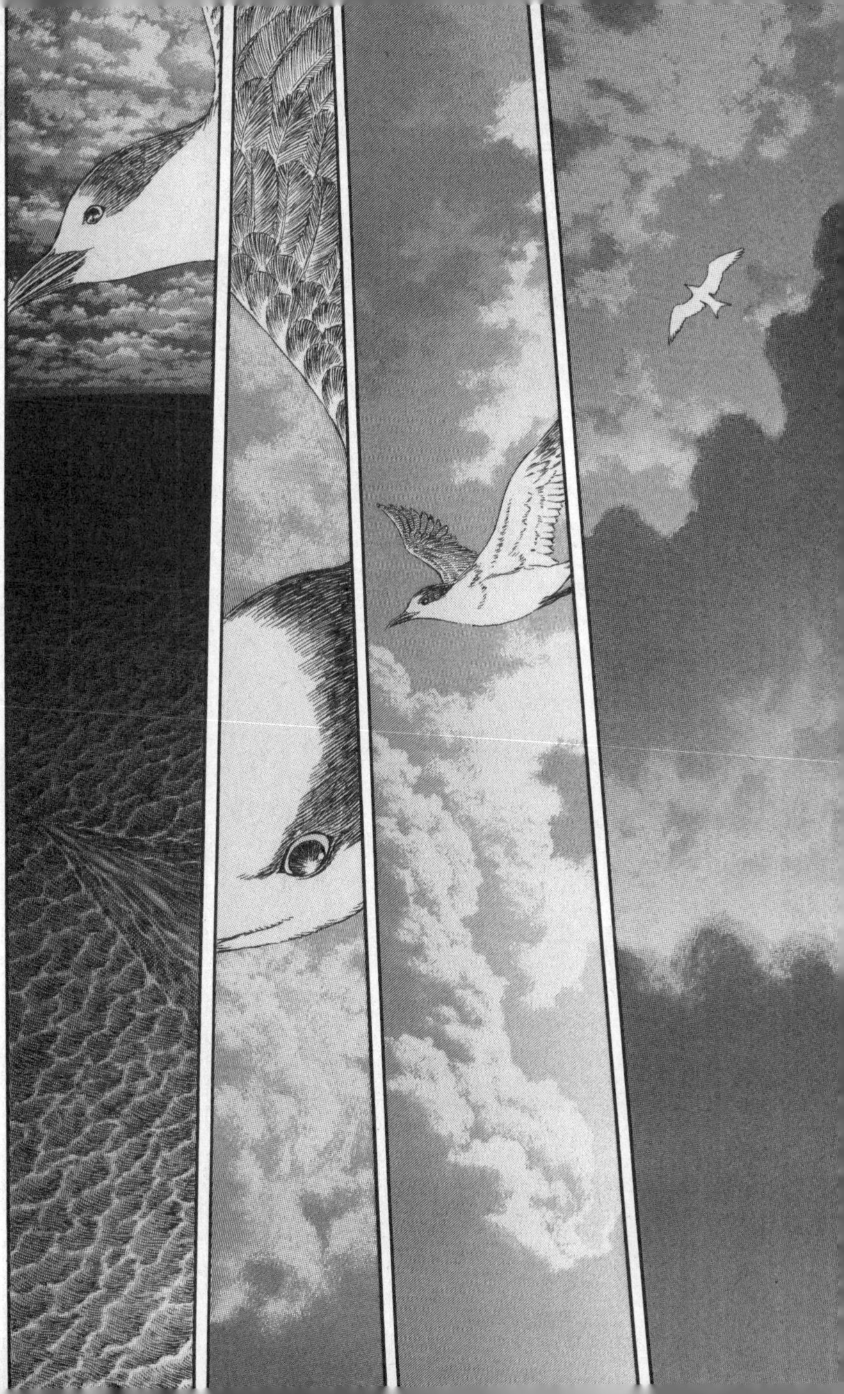

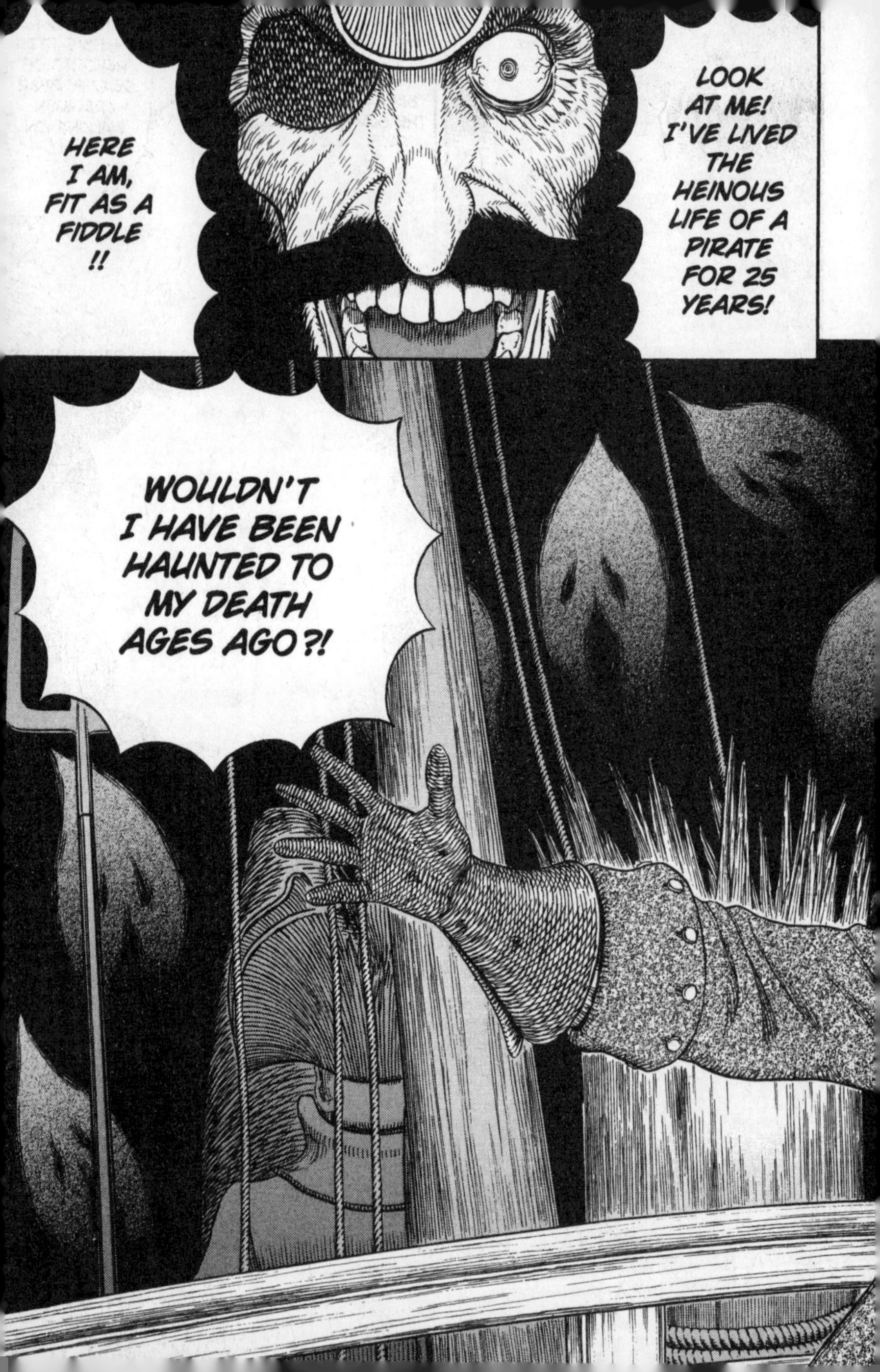
LOOK AT ME! I'VE LIVED THE HEINOUS LIFE OF A PIRATE FOR 25 YEARS!
HERE I AM, FIT AS A FIDDLE !!
WOULDN'T I HAVE BEEN HAUNTED TO MY DEATH AGES AGO?!

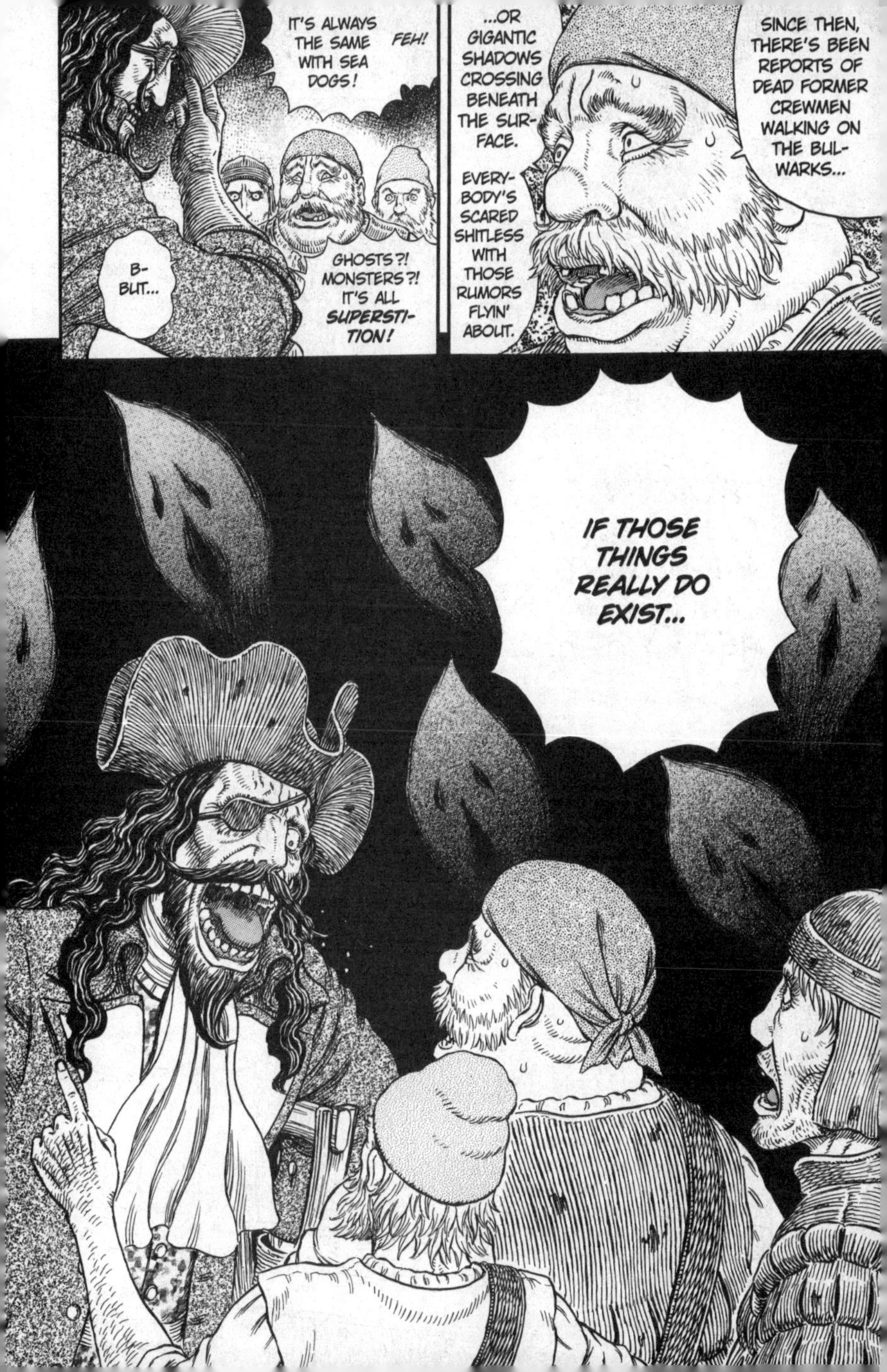
SINCE THEN, THERE'S BEEN REPORTS OF DEAD FORMER CREWMEN WALKING ON THE BUL-WARKS...
...OR GIGANTIC SHADOWS CROSSING BENEATH THE SUR-FACE.
EVERY-BODY'S SCARED SHITLESS WITH THOSE RUMORS FLYIN' ABOUT.
FEH!
IT'S ALWAYS THE SAME WITH SEA DOGS!
GHOSTS?! MONSTERS?! IT'S ALL SUPERSTI-TION!
B-BUT...
IF THOSE THINGS REALLY DO EXIST...

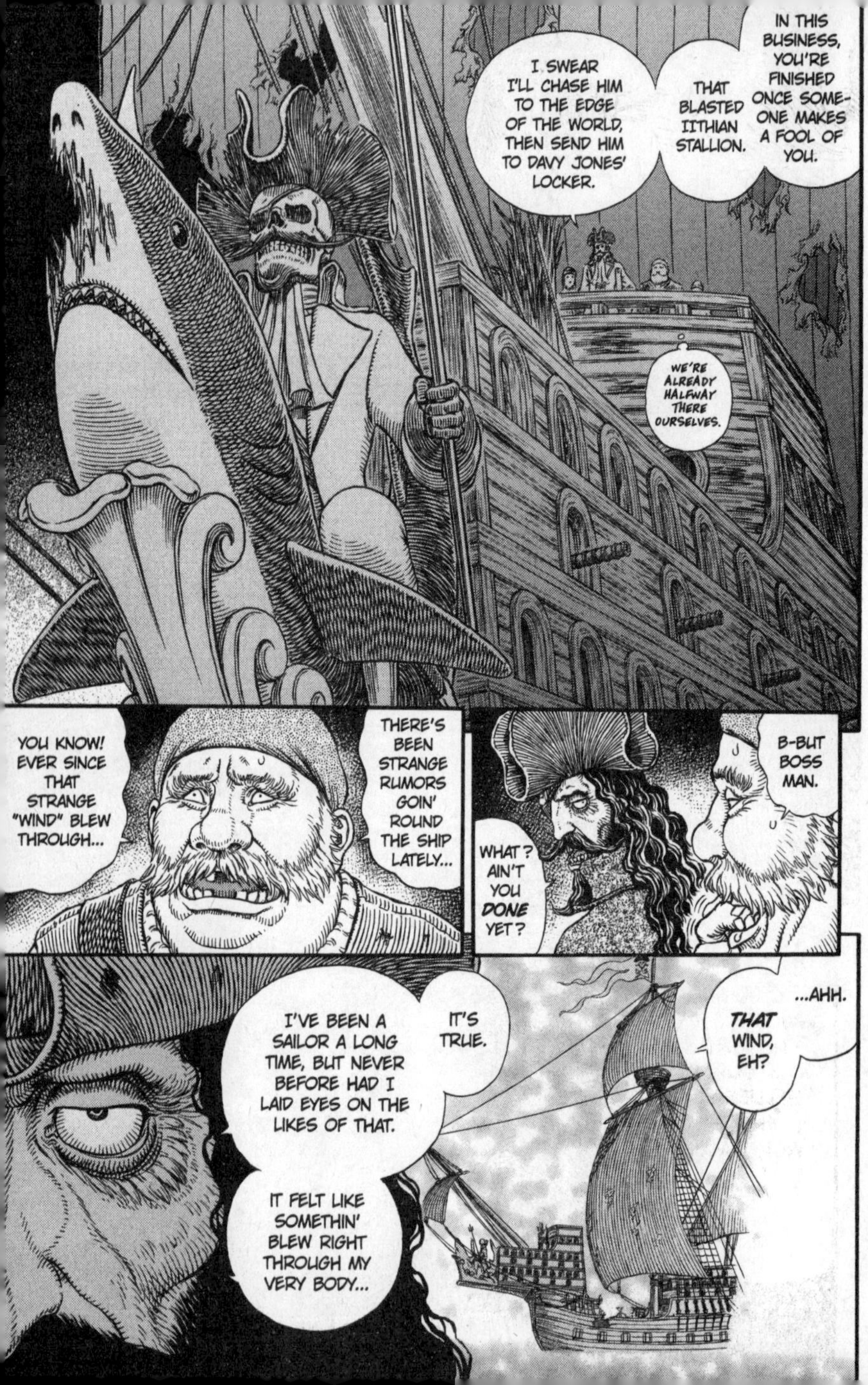
IN THIS BUSINESS, YOU'RE FINISHED ONCE SOME-ONE MAKES A FOOL OF YOU.
THAT BLASTED IITHIAN STALLION.
I SWEAR I'LL CHASE HIM TO THE EDGE OF THE WORLD, THEN SEND HIM TO DAVY JONES' LOCKER.
WE'RE ALREADY HALFWAY THERE OURSELVES.
B-BUT BOSS MAN.
WHAT? AIN'T YOU *DONE* YET?
THERE'S BEEN STRANGE RUMORS GOIN' ROUND THE SHIP LATELY...
YOU KNOW! EVER SINCE THAT STRANGE "WIND" BLEW THROUGH...
...AHH.
THAT WIND, EH?
IT'S TRUE.
I'VE BEEN A SAILOR A LONG TIME, BUT NEVER BEFORE HAD I LAID EYES ON THE LIKES OF THAT.
IT FELT LIKE SOMETHIN' BLEW RIGHT THROUGH MY VERY BODY...

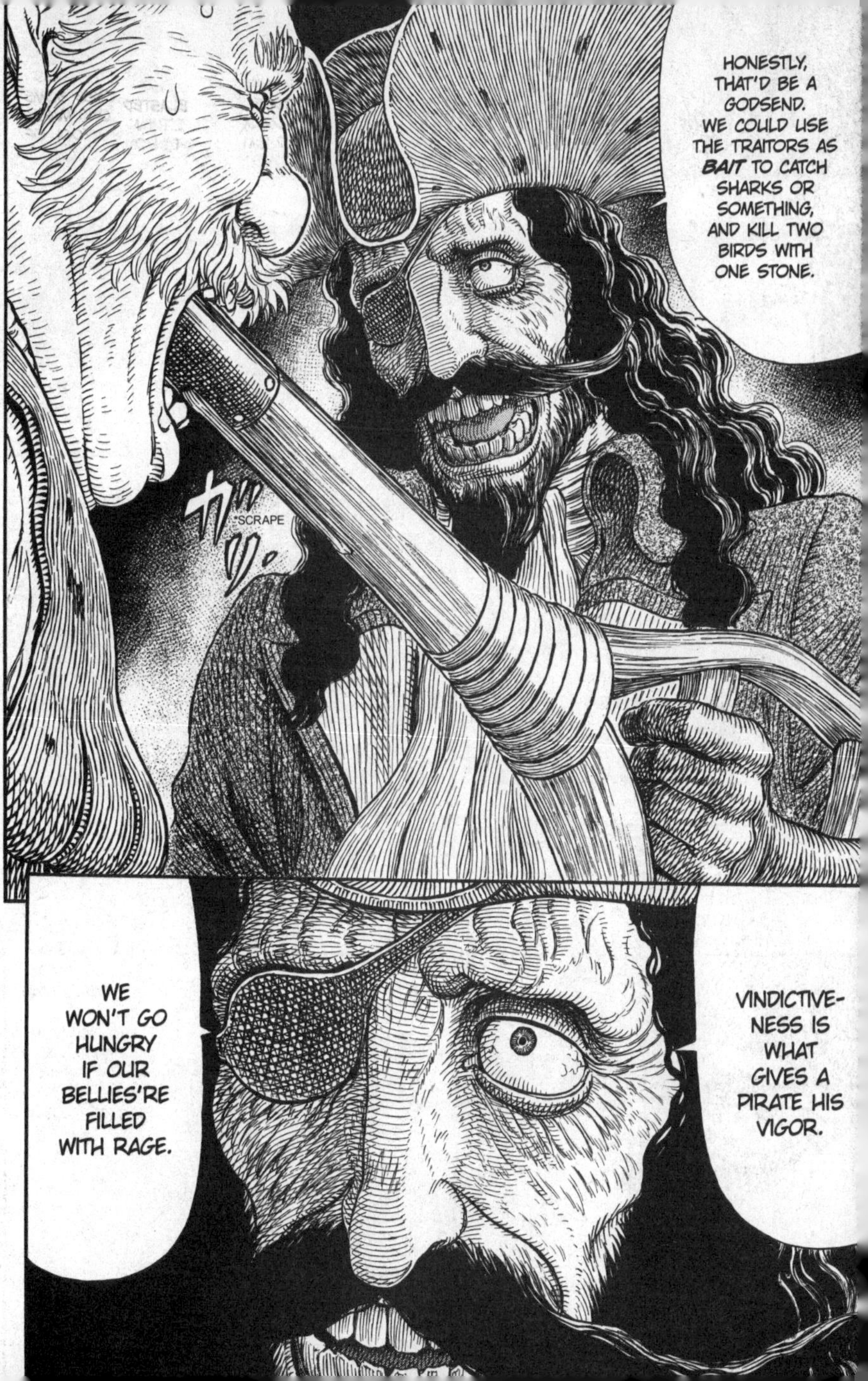
HONESTLY, THAT'D BE A GODSEND. WE COULD USE THE TRAITORS AS ***BAIT*** TO CATCH SHARKS OR SOMETHING, AND KILL TWO BIRDS WITH ONE STONE.
SCRAPE
VINDICTIVE-NESS IS WHAT GIVES A PIRATE HIS VIGOR.
WE WON'T GO HUNGRY IF OUR BELLIES'RE FILLED WITH RAGE.

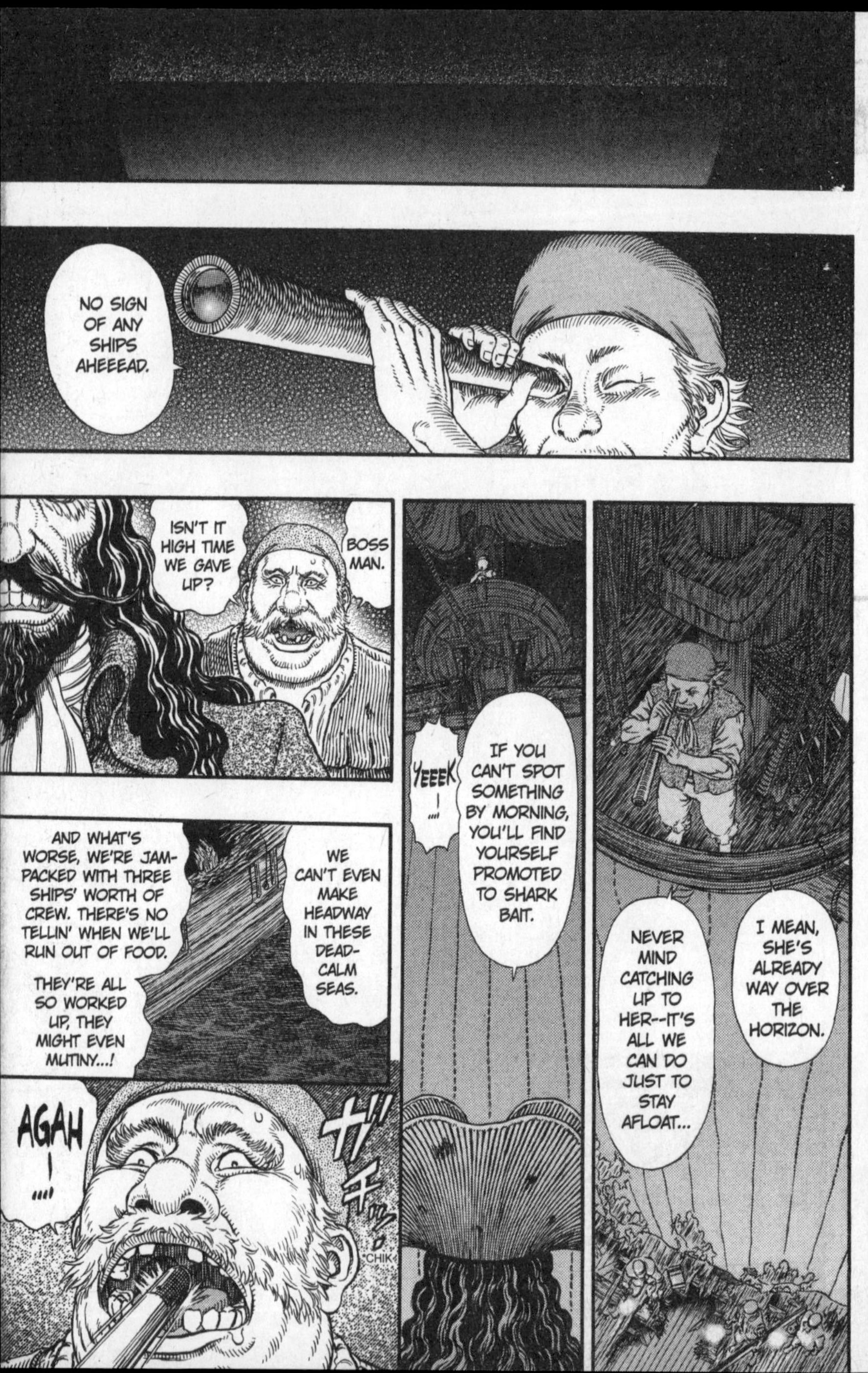
NO SIGN OF ANY SHIPS AHEEEAD.
I MEAN, SHE'S ALREADY WAY OVER THE HORIZON.
NEVER MIND CATCHING UP TO HER--IT'S ALL WE CAN DO JUST TO STAY AFLOAT...
IF YOU CAN'T SPOT SOMETHING BY MORNING, YOU'LL FIND YOURSELF PROMOTED TO SHARK BAIT.
YEEEK...!
BOSS MAN.
ISN'T IT HIGH TIME WE GAVE UP?
WE CAN'T EVEN MAKE HEADWAY IN THESE DEAD-CALM SEAS.
AND WHAT'S WORSE, WE'RE JAM-PACKED WITH THREE SHIPS' WORTH OF CREW. THERE'S NO TELLIN' WHEN WE'LL RUN OUT OF FOOD.
THEY'RE ALL SO WORKED UP, THEY MIGHT EVEN MUTINY...!
AGAH...!
*CHIK

幻造世界「ファンタジア」篇　妖精島の章

幽霊船①

GHOST SHIP, PART 1

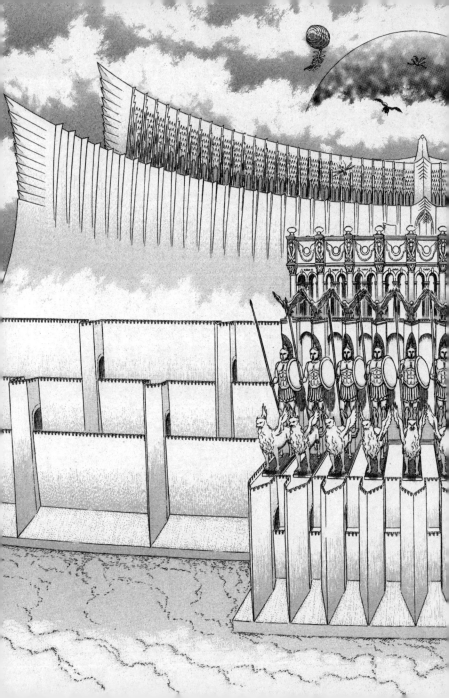

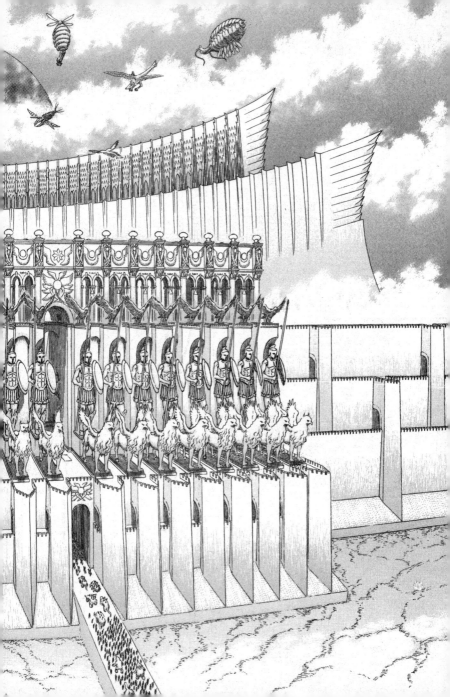

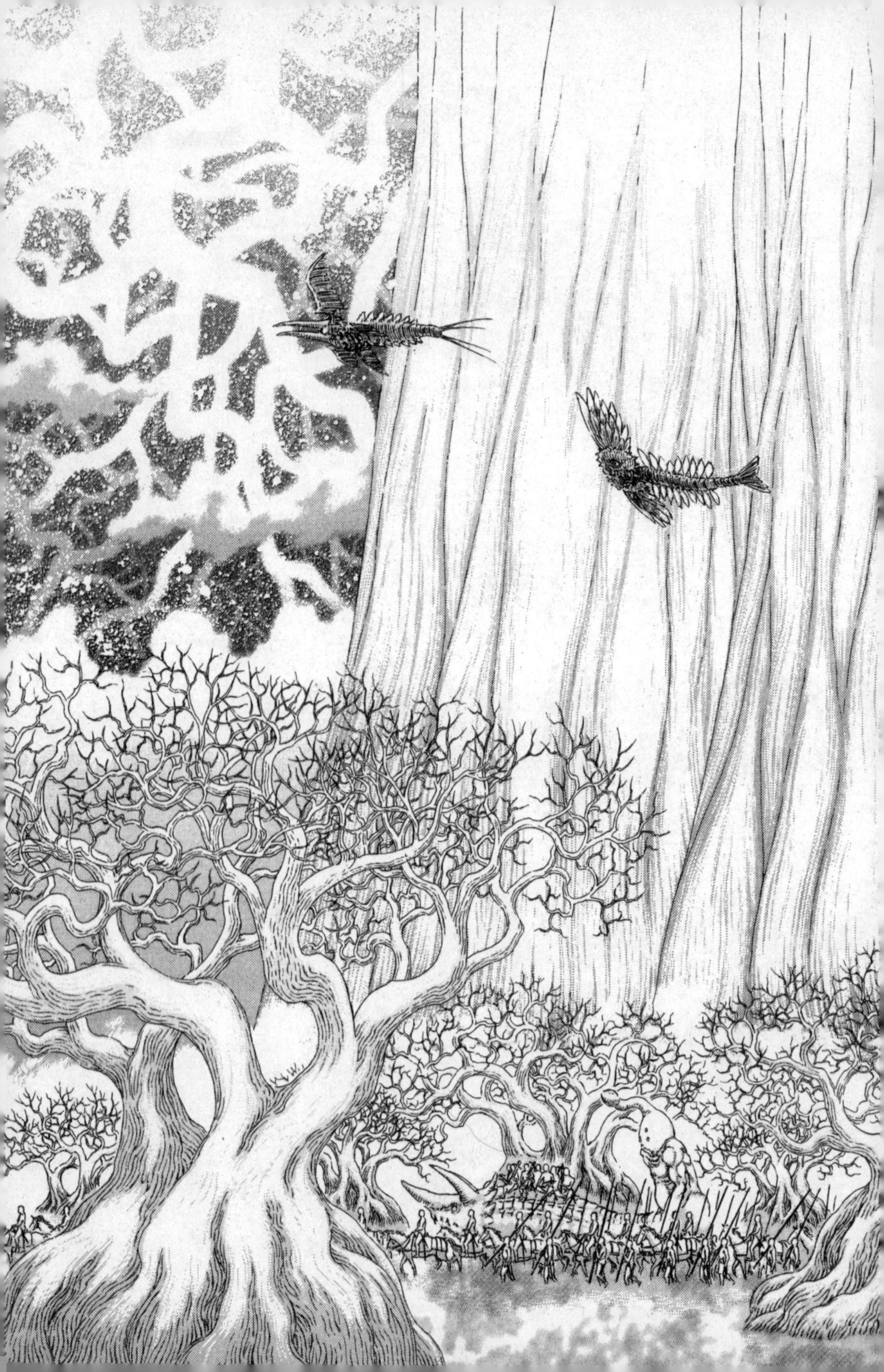

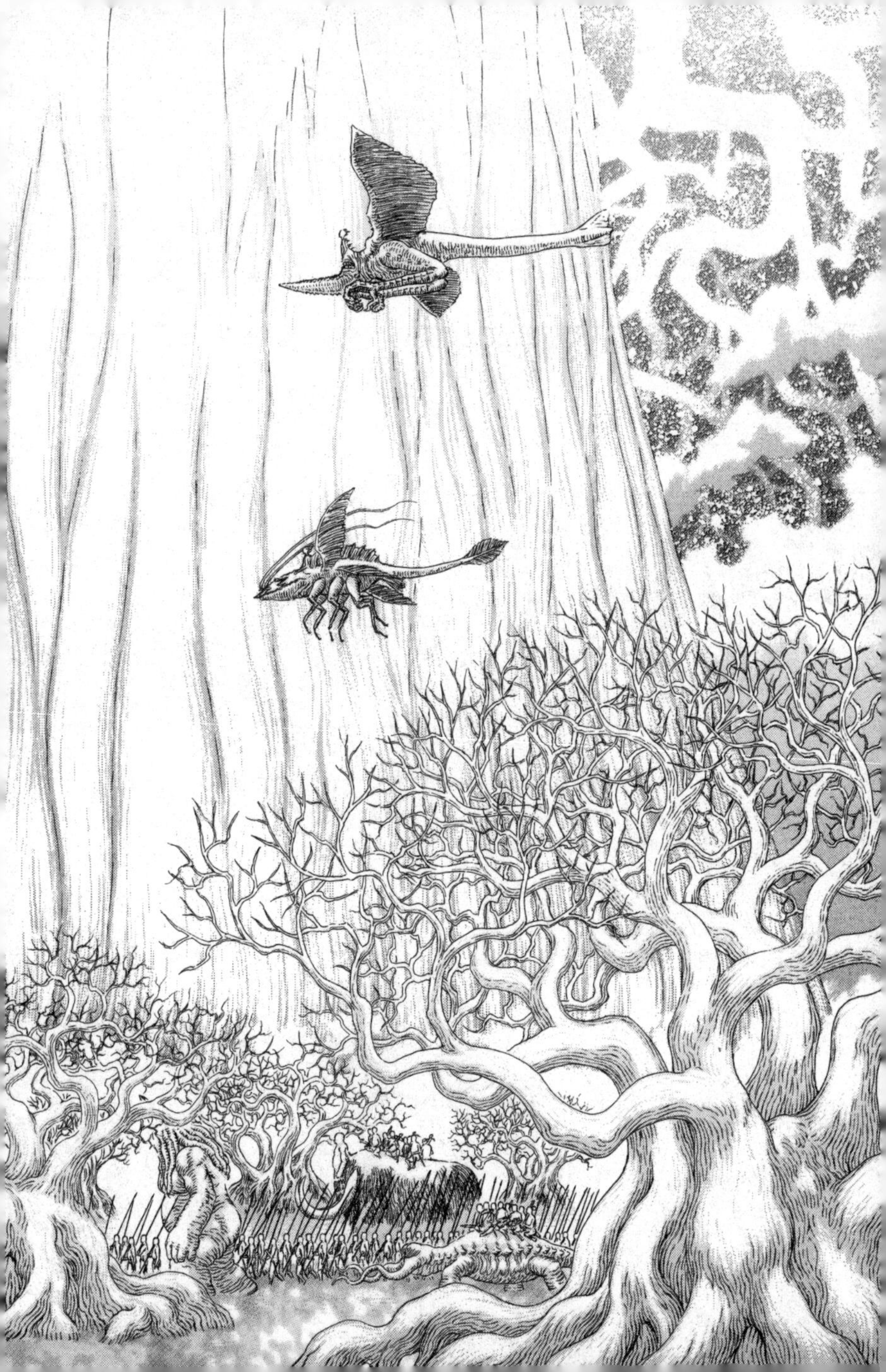

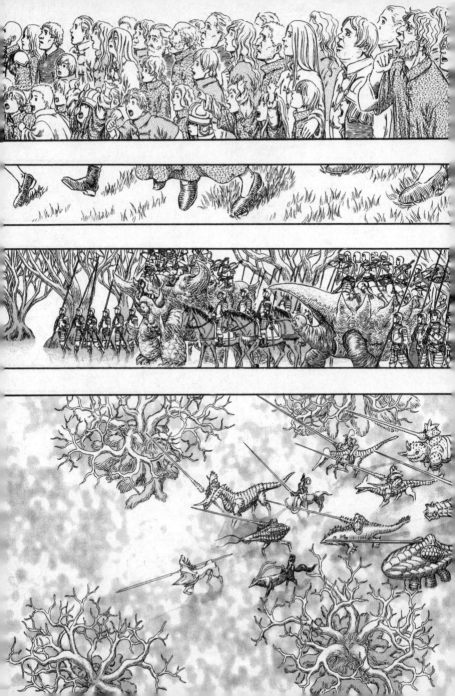

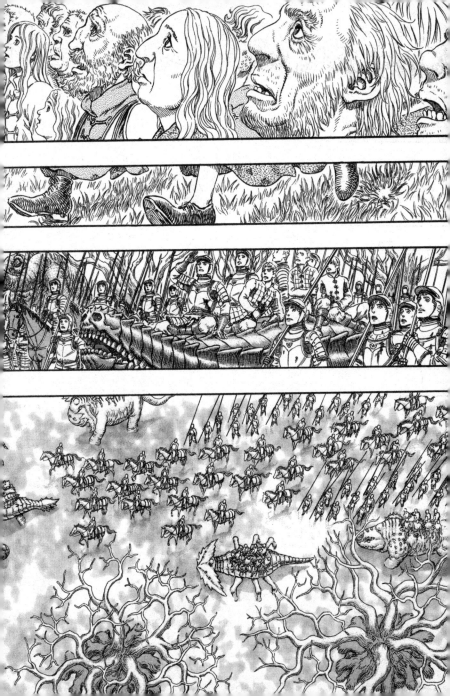

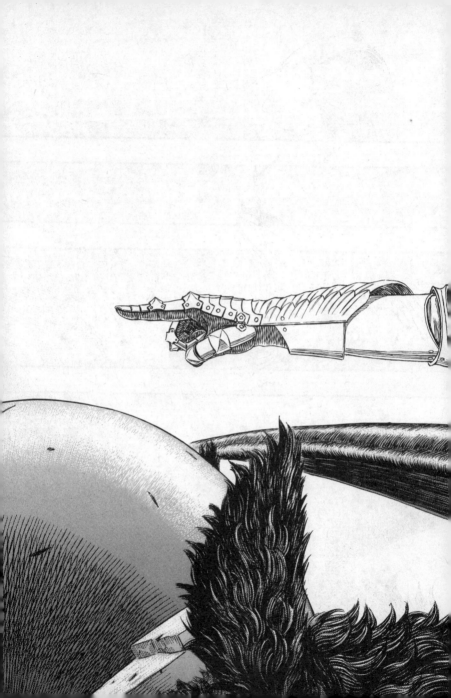

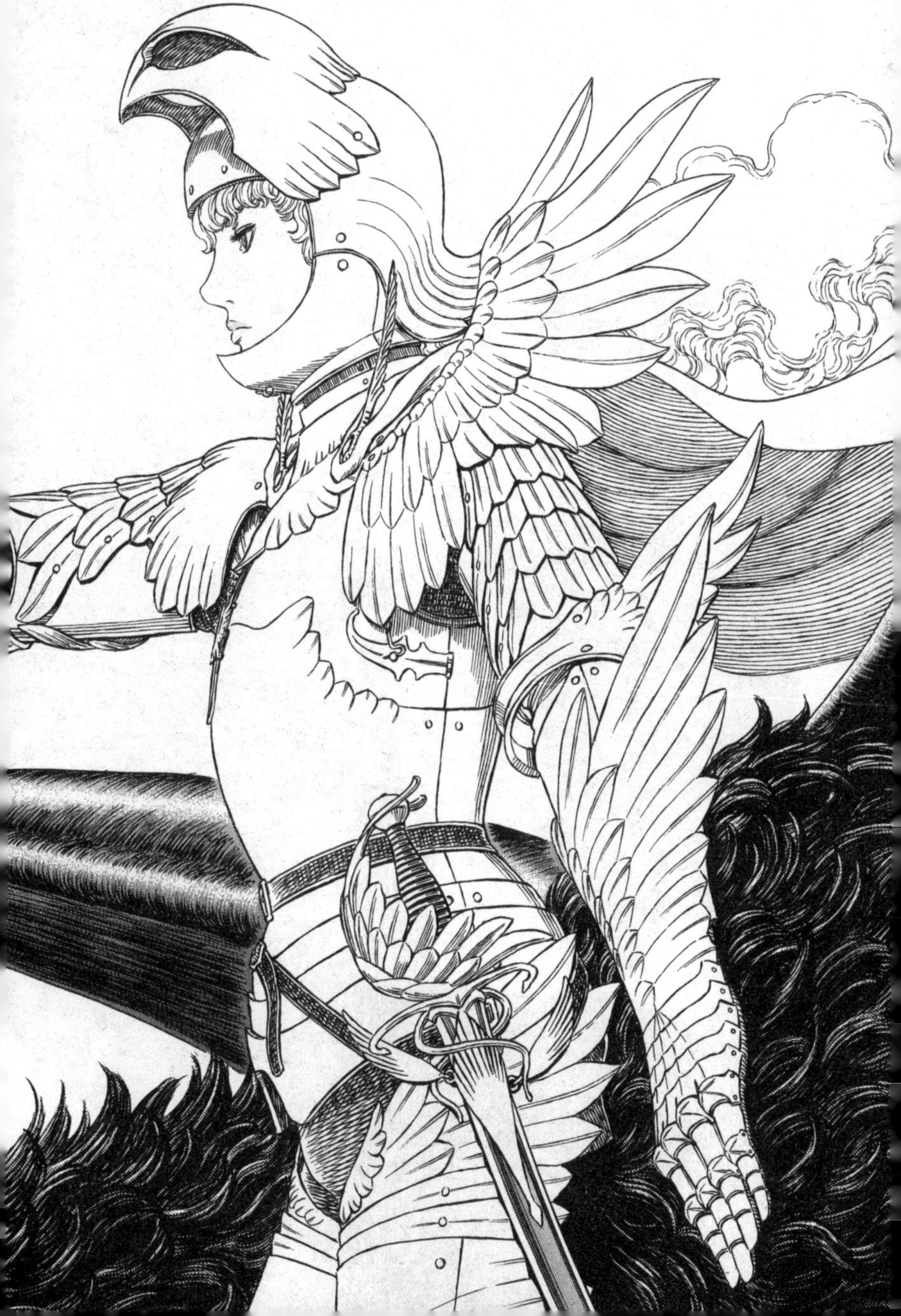

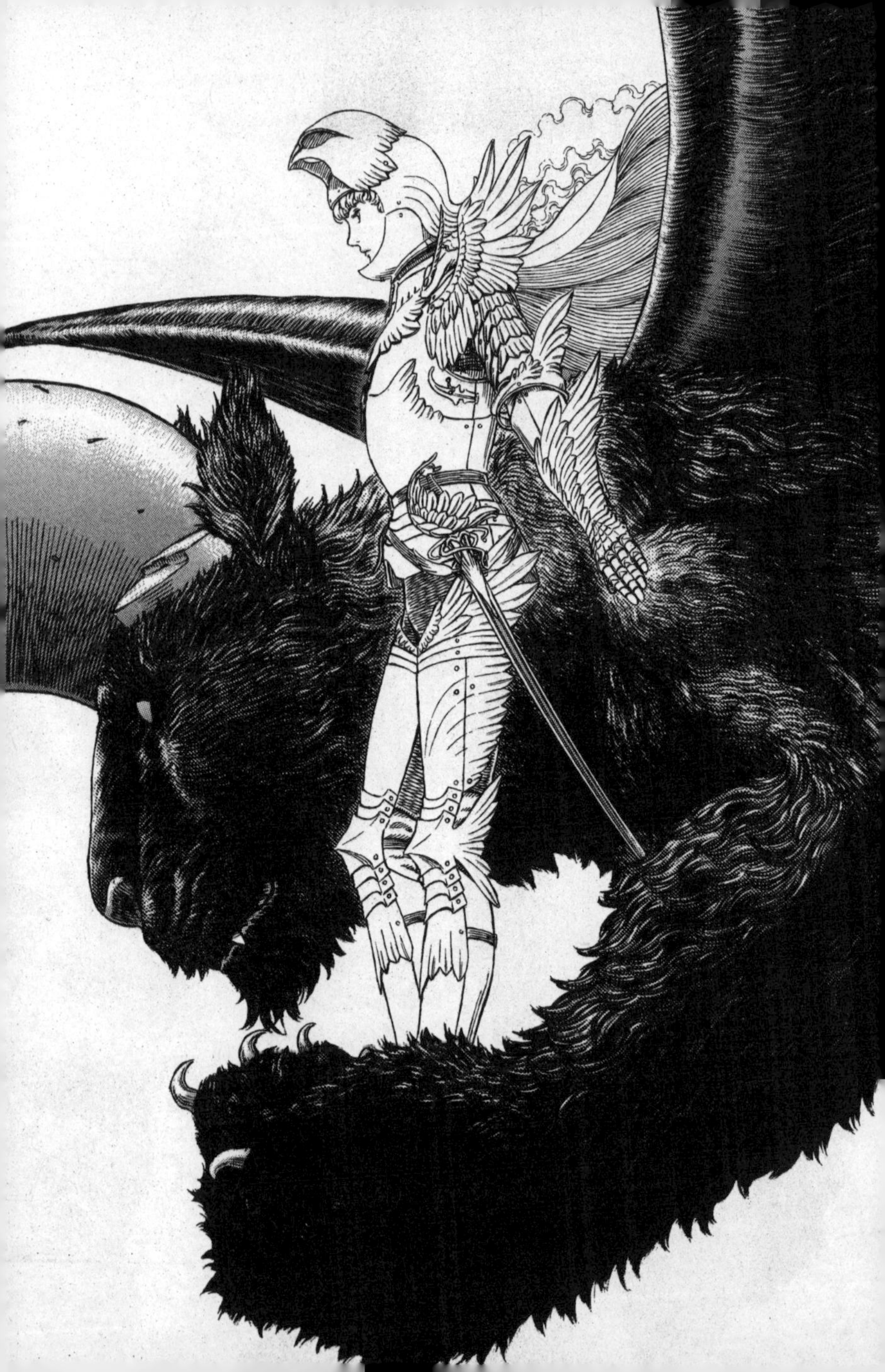

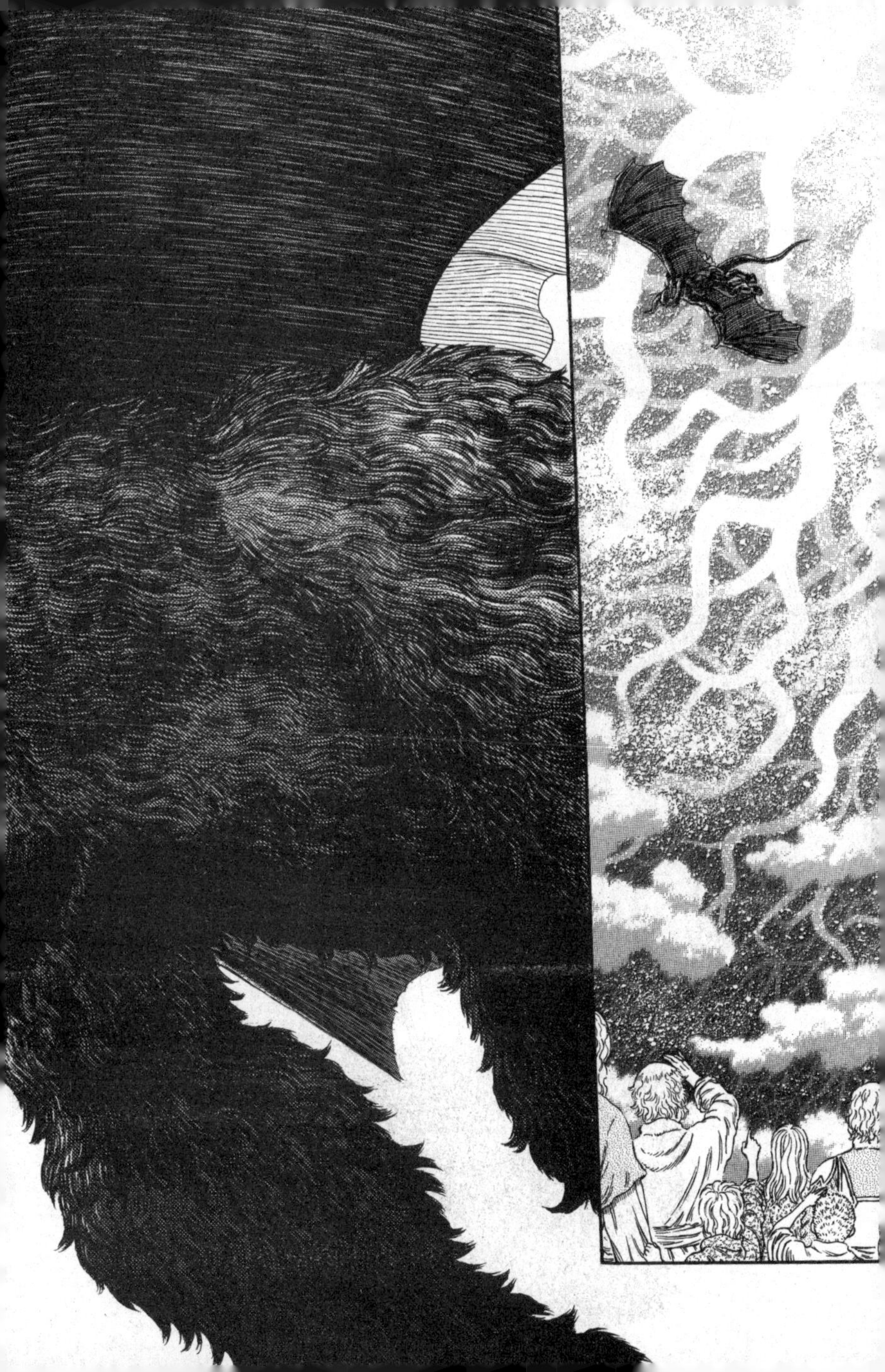

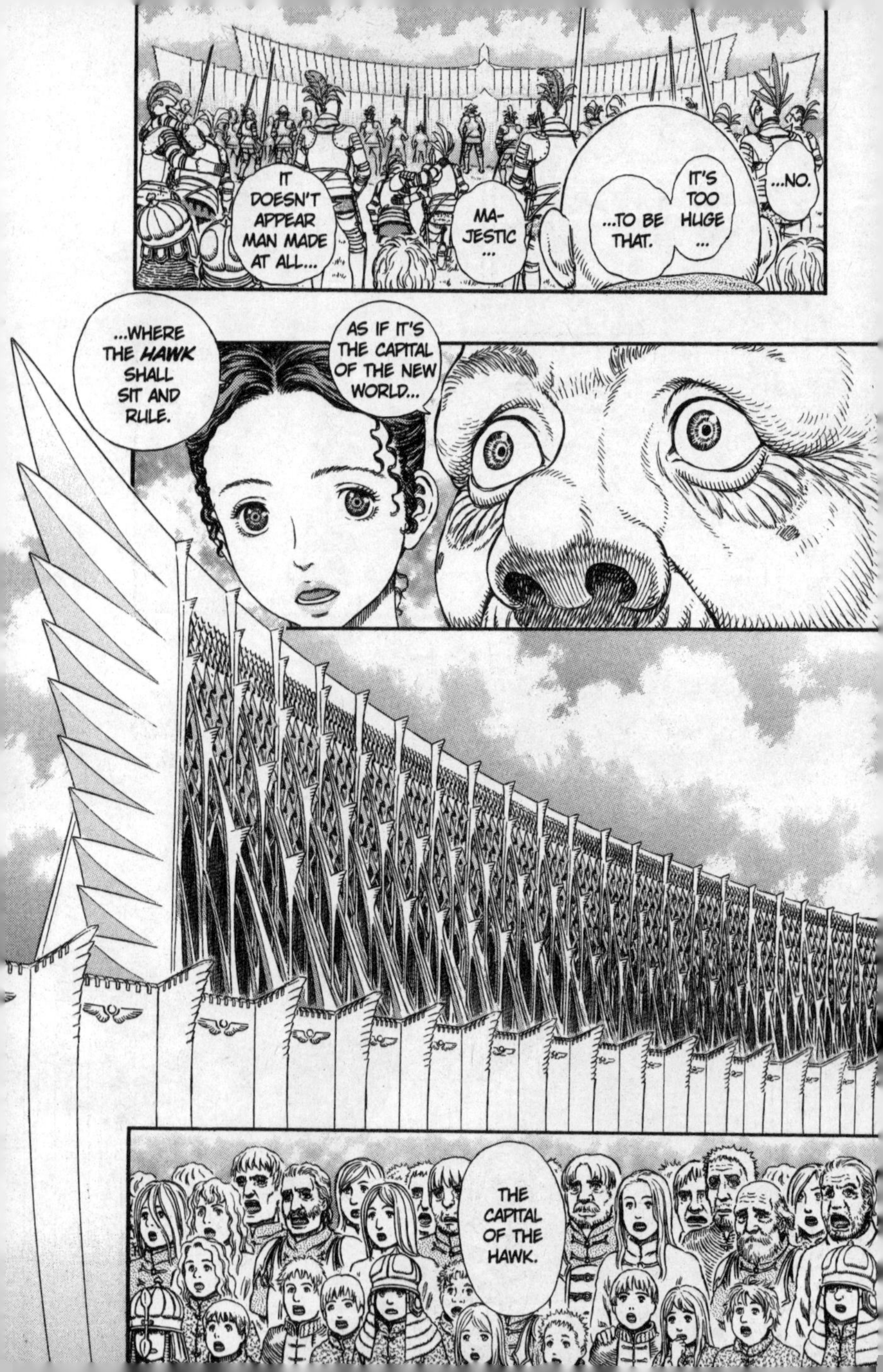

...NO.
IT'S TOO HUGE ...
...TO BE THAT.
MA-JESTIC ...
IT DOESN'T APPEAR MAN MADE AT ALL...
AS IF IT'S THE CAPITAL OF THE NEW WORLD...
...WHERE THE *HAWK* SHALL SIT AND RULE.
THE CAPITAL OF THE HAWK.

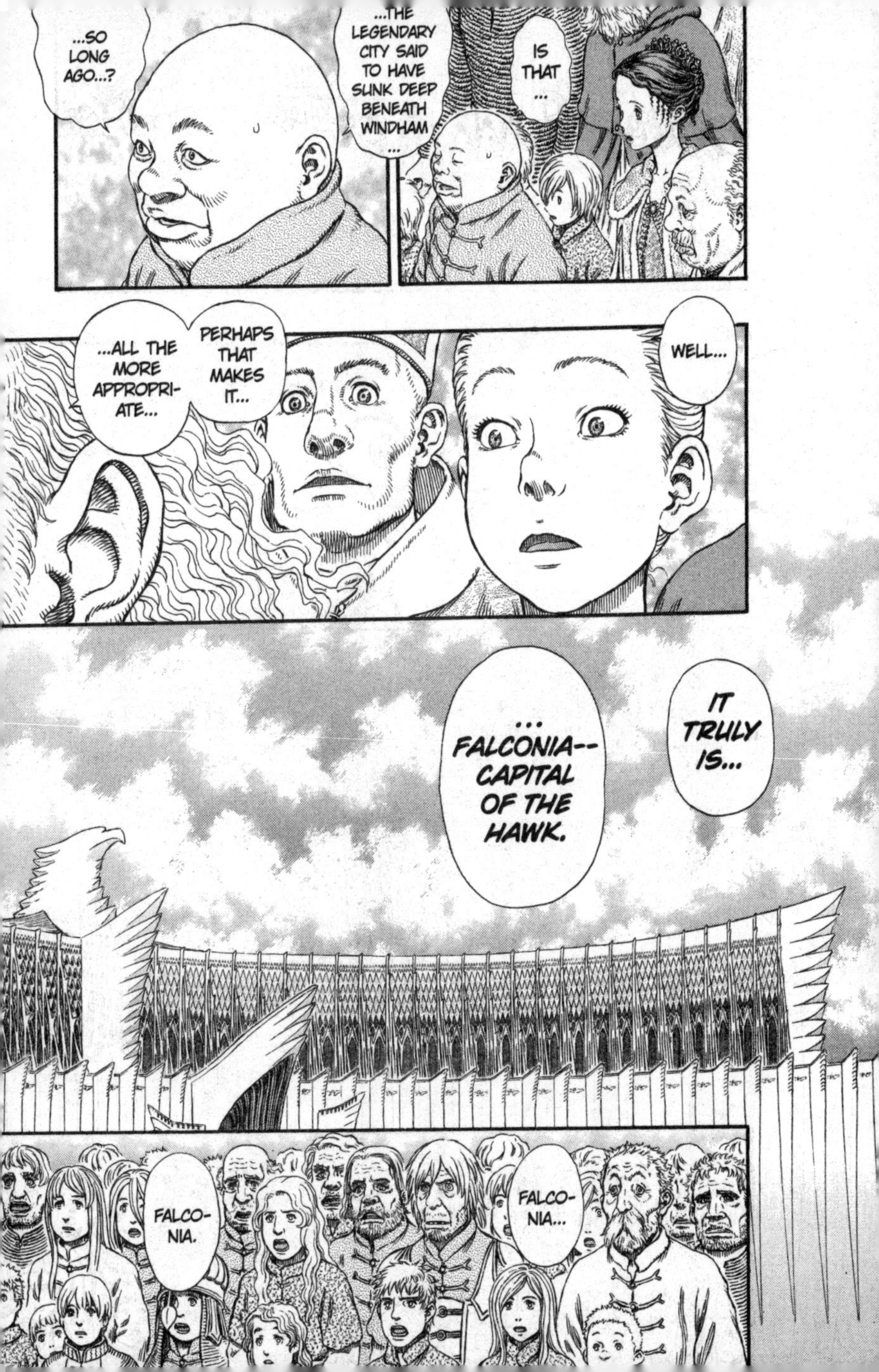
IS THAT ...
...THE LEGENDARY CITY SAID TO HAVE SUNK DEEP BENEATH WINDHAM ...
...SO LONG AGO...?
WELL...
PERHAPS THAT MAKES IT...
...ALL THE MORE APPROPRIATE...
IT TRULY IS...
... FALCONIA--CAPITAL OF THE HAWK.
FALCONIA...
FALCONIA.

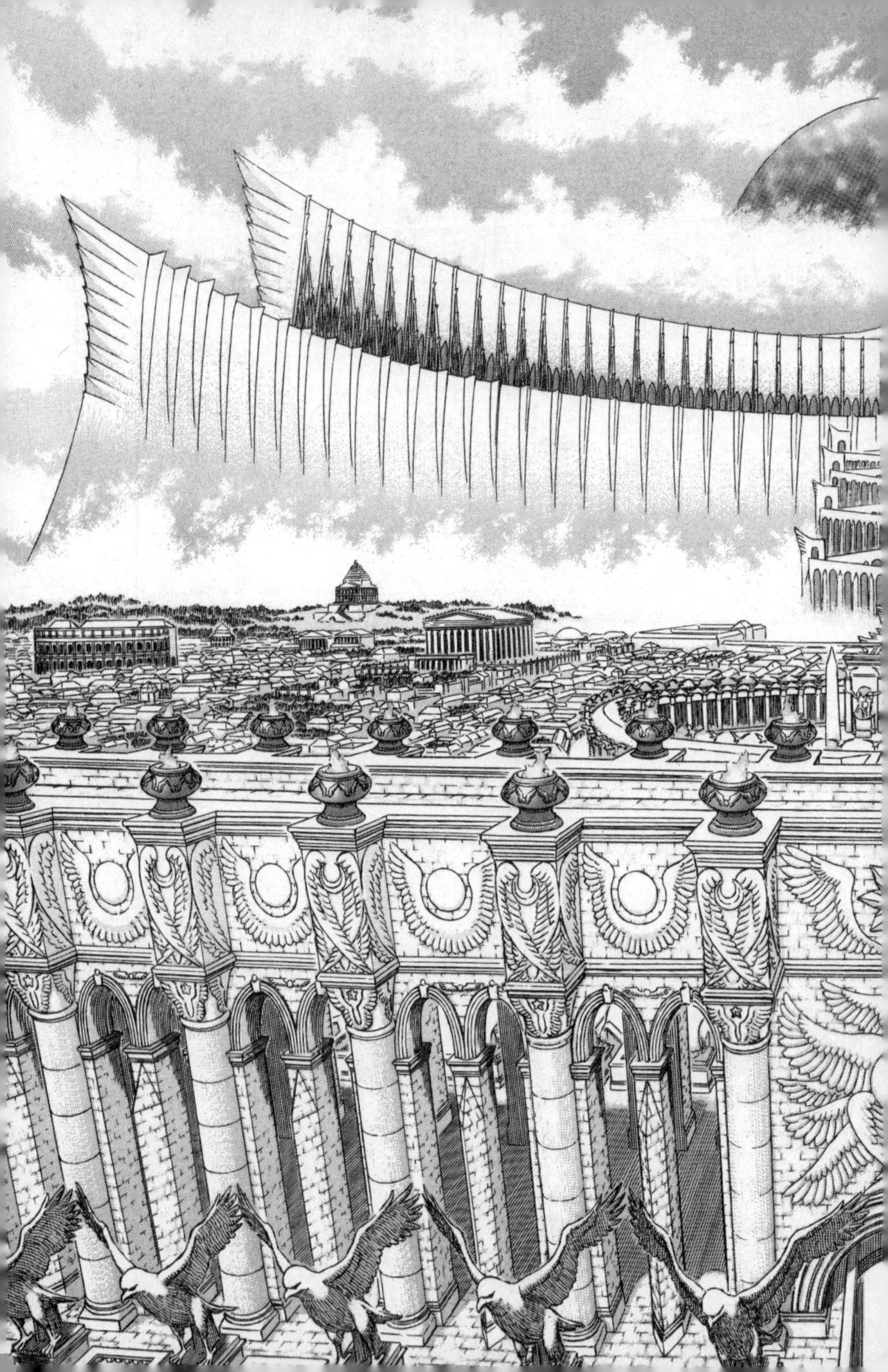

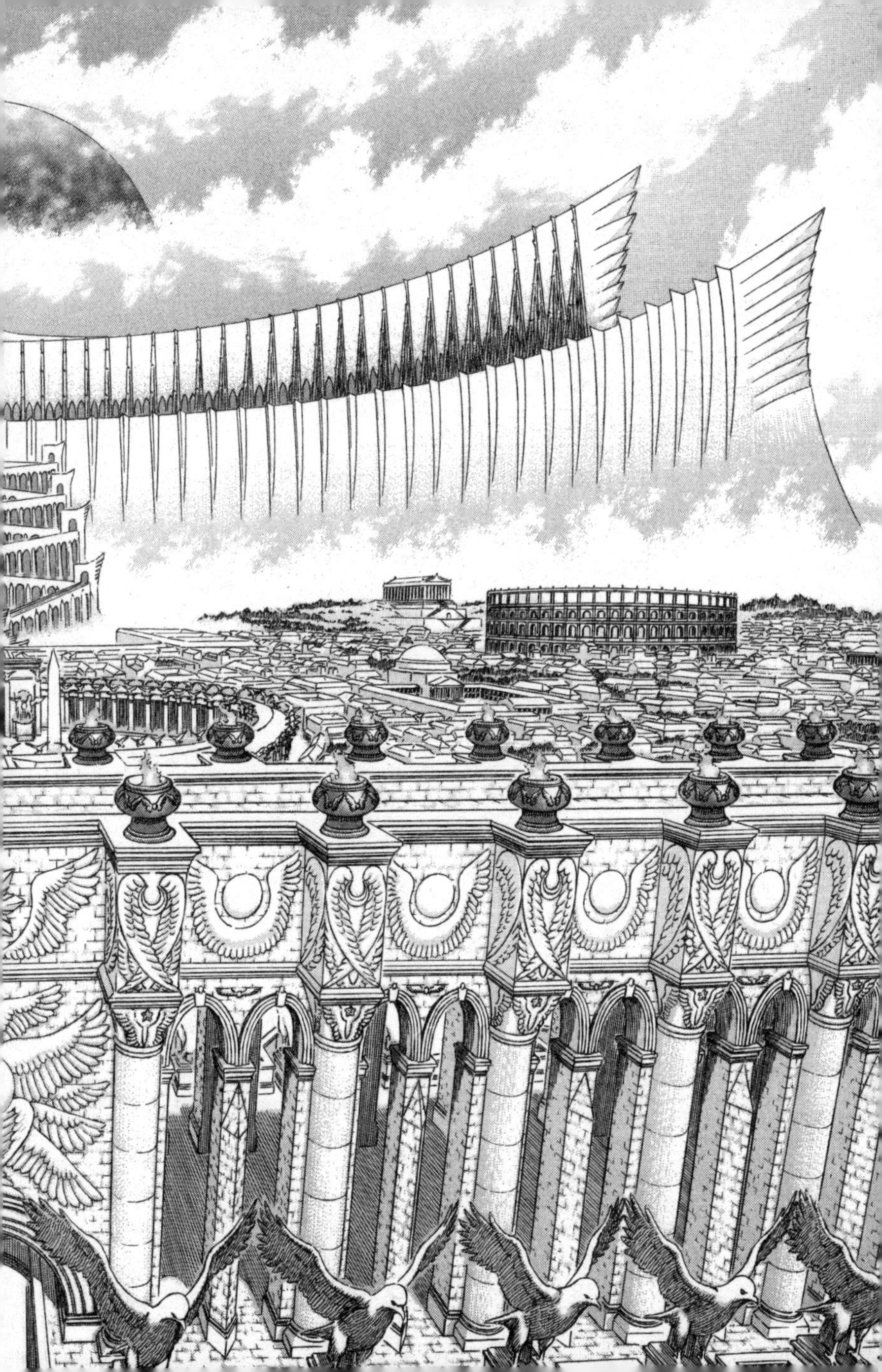

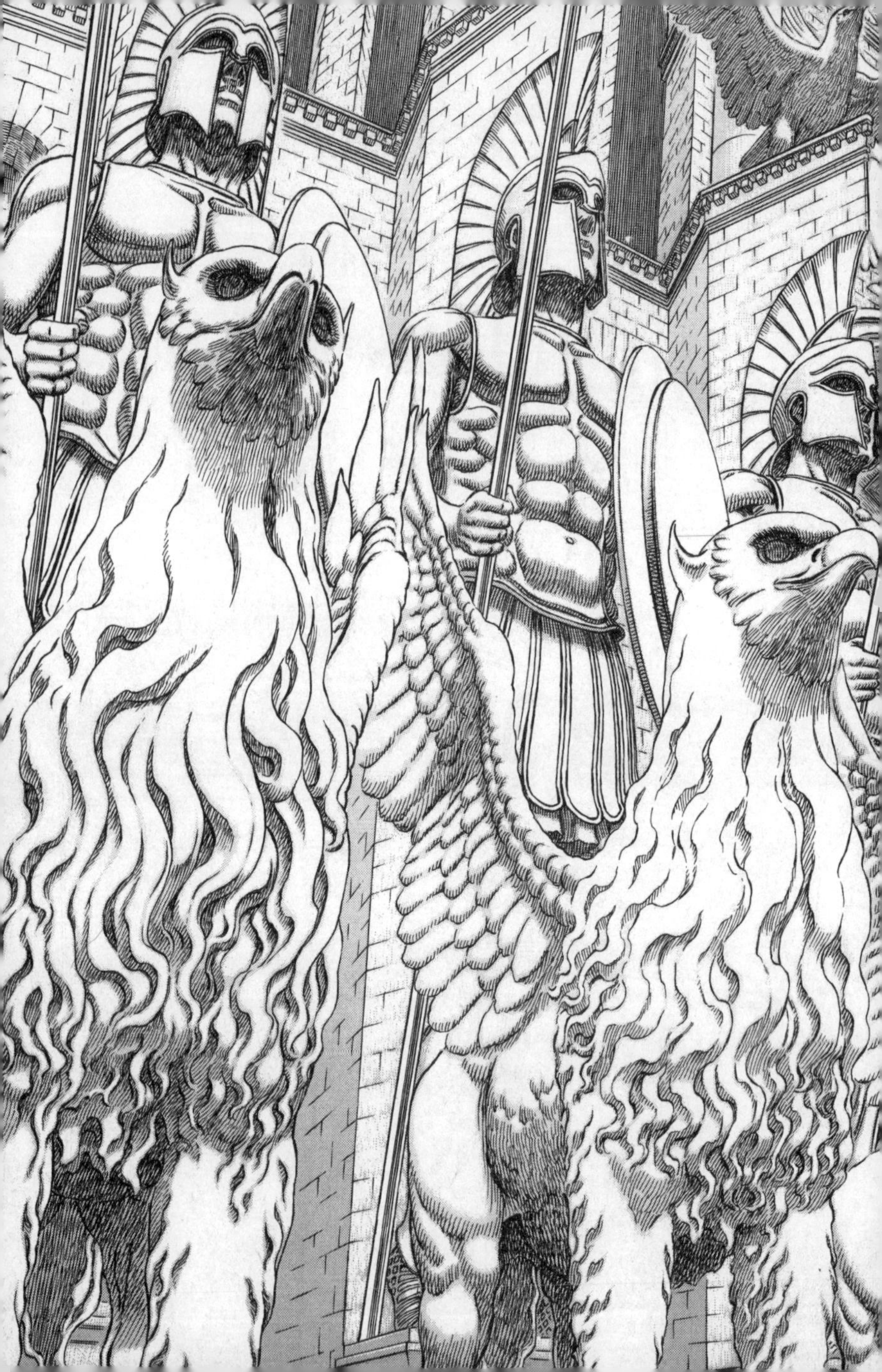

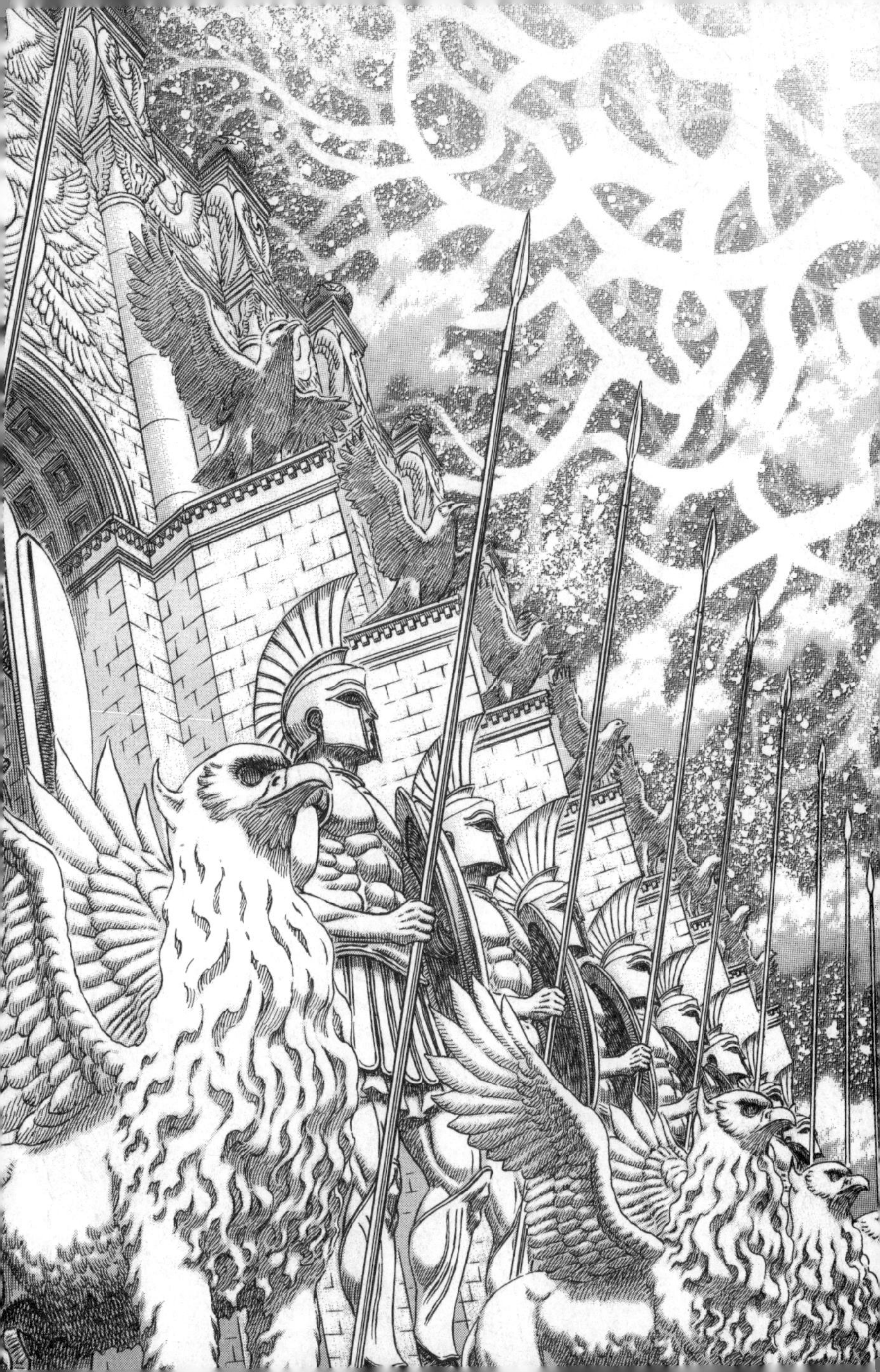

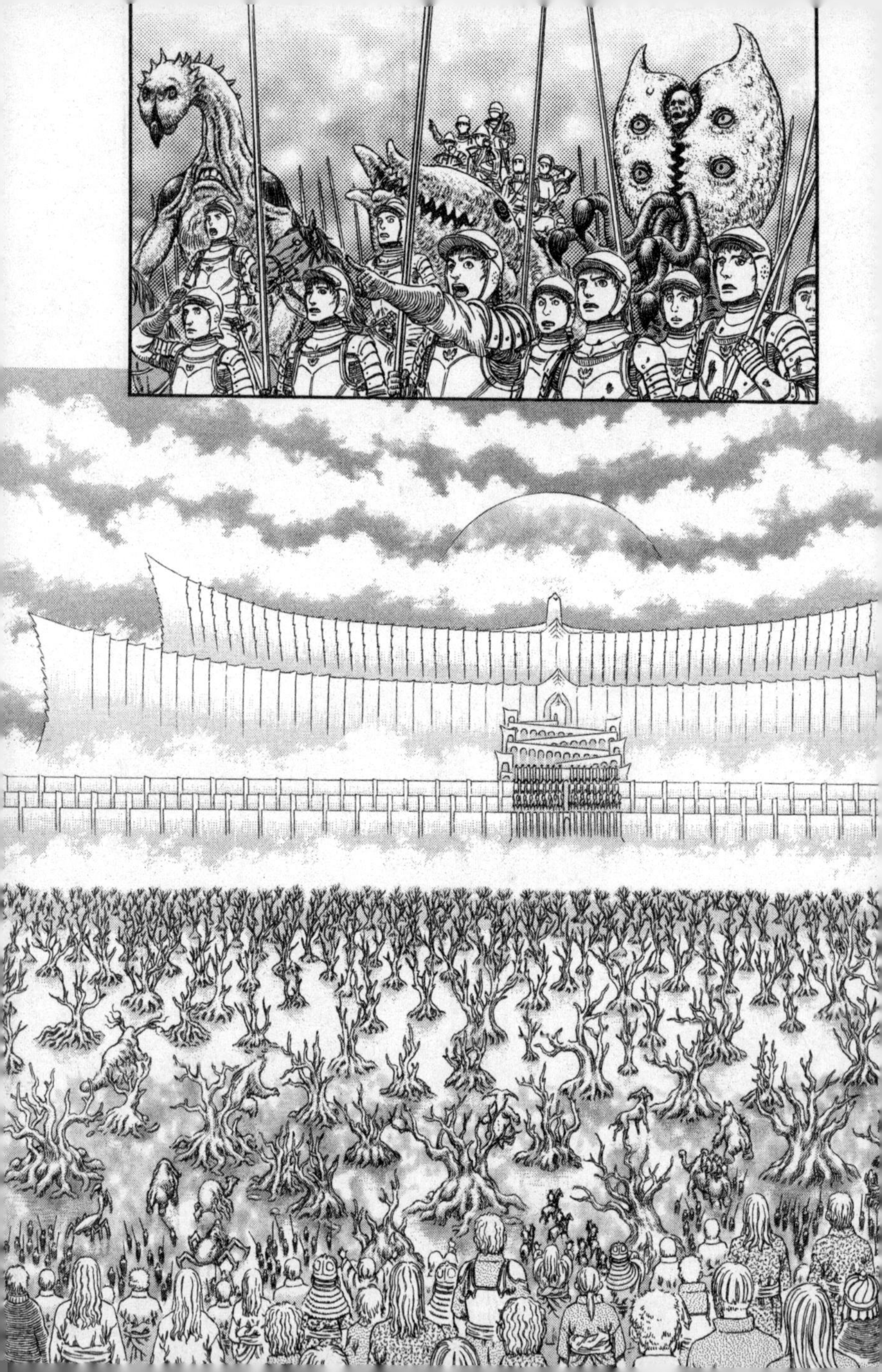

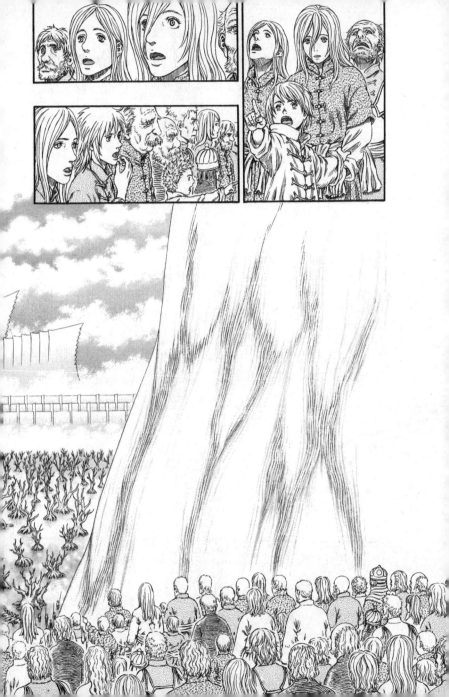

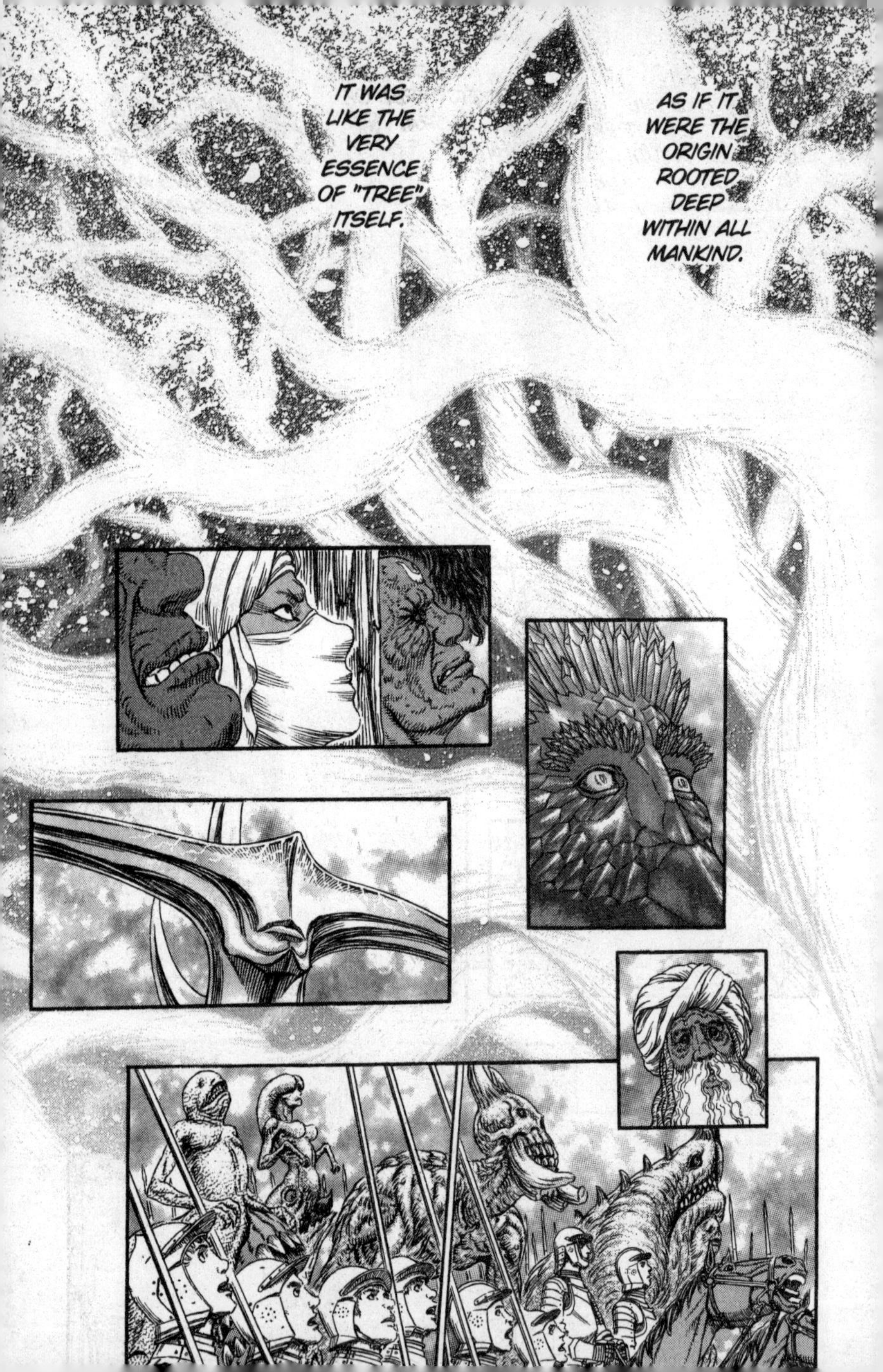
AS IF IT WERE THE ORIGIN ROOTED DEEP WITHIN ALL MANKIND.
IT WAS LIKE THE VERY ESSENCE OF "TREE" ITSELF.

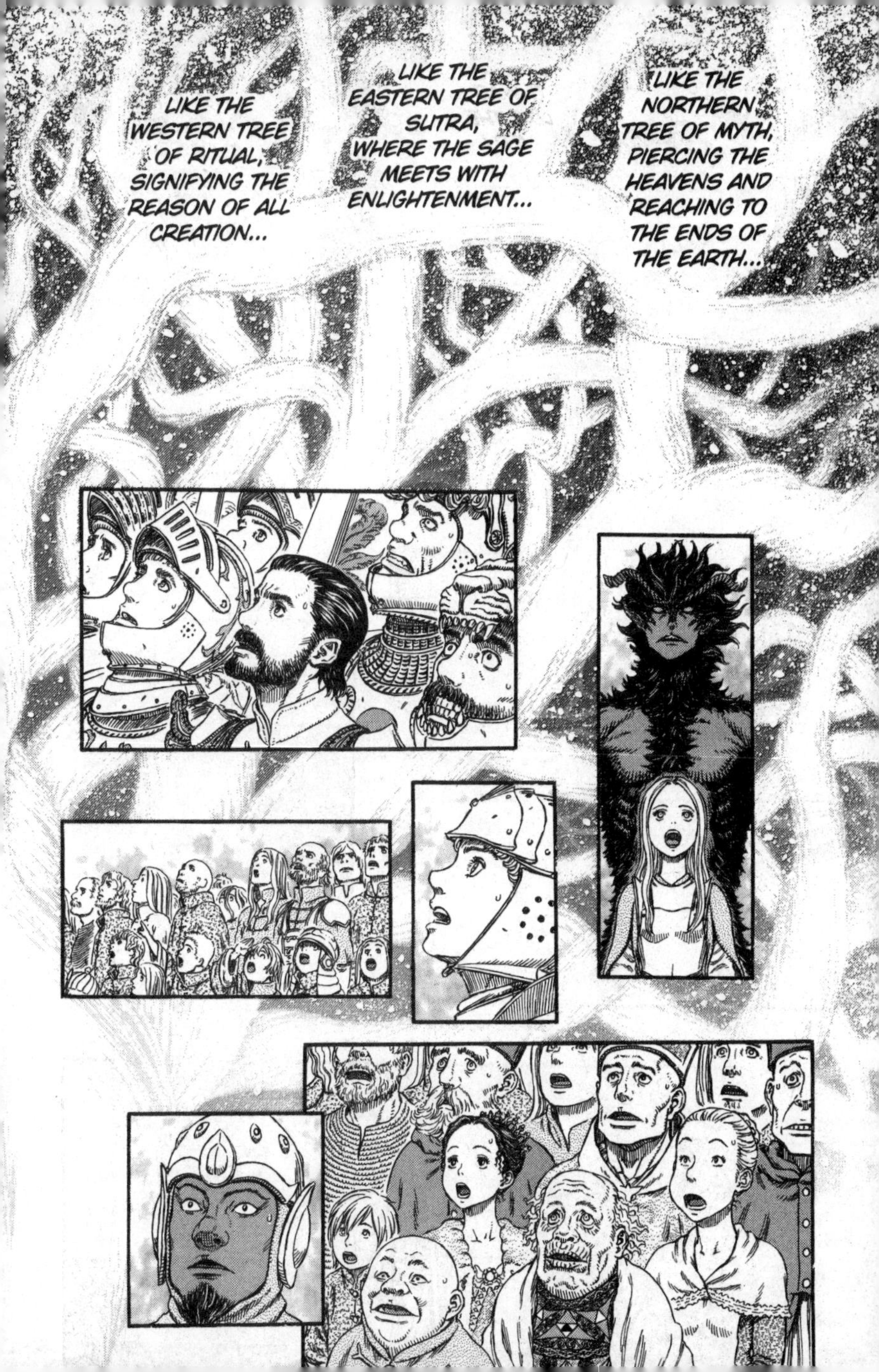
LIKE THE NORTHERN TREE OF MYTH, PIERCING THE HEAVENS AND REACHING TO THE ENDS OF THE EARTH...
LIKE THE EASTERN TREE OF SUTRA, WHERE THE SAGE MEETS WITH ENLIGHTENMENT...
LIKE THE WESTERN TREE OF RITUAL, SIGNIFYING THE REASON OF ALL CREATION...

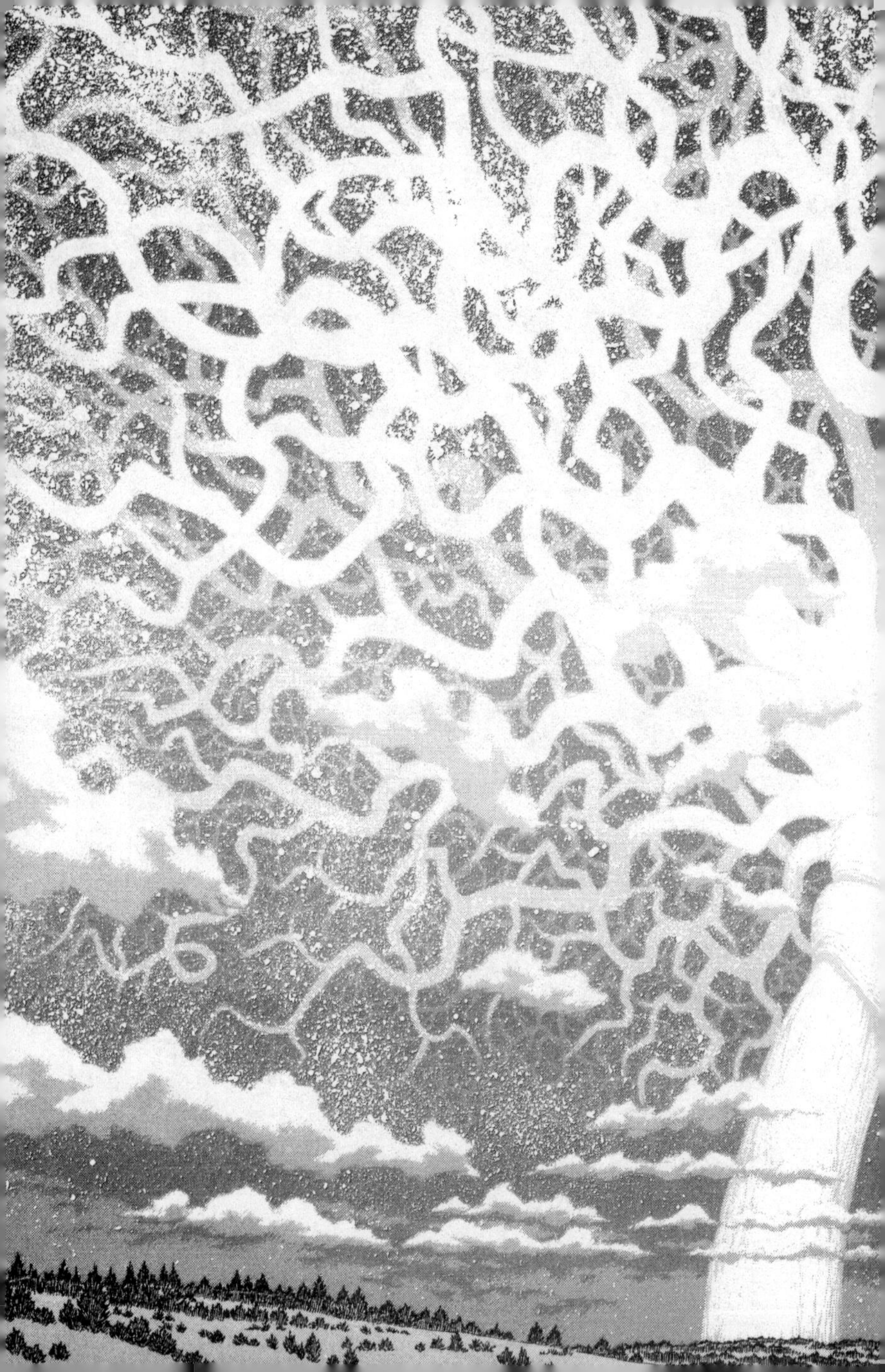

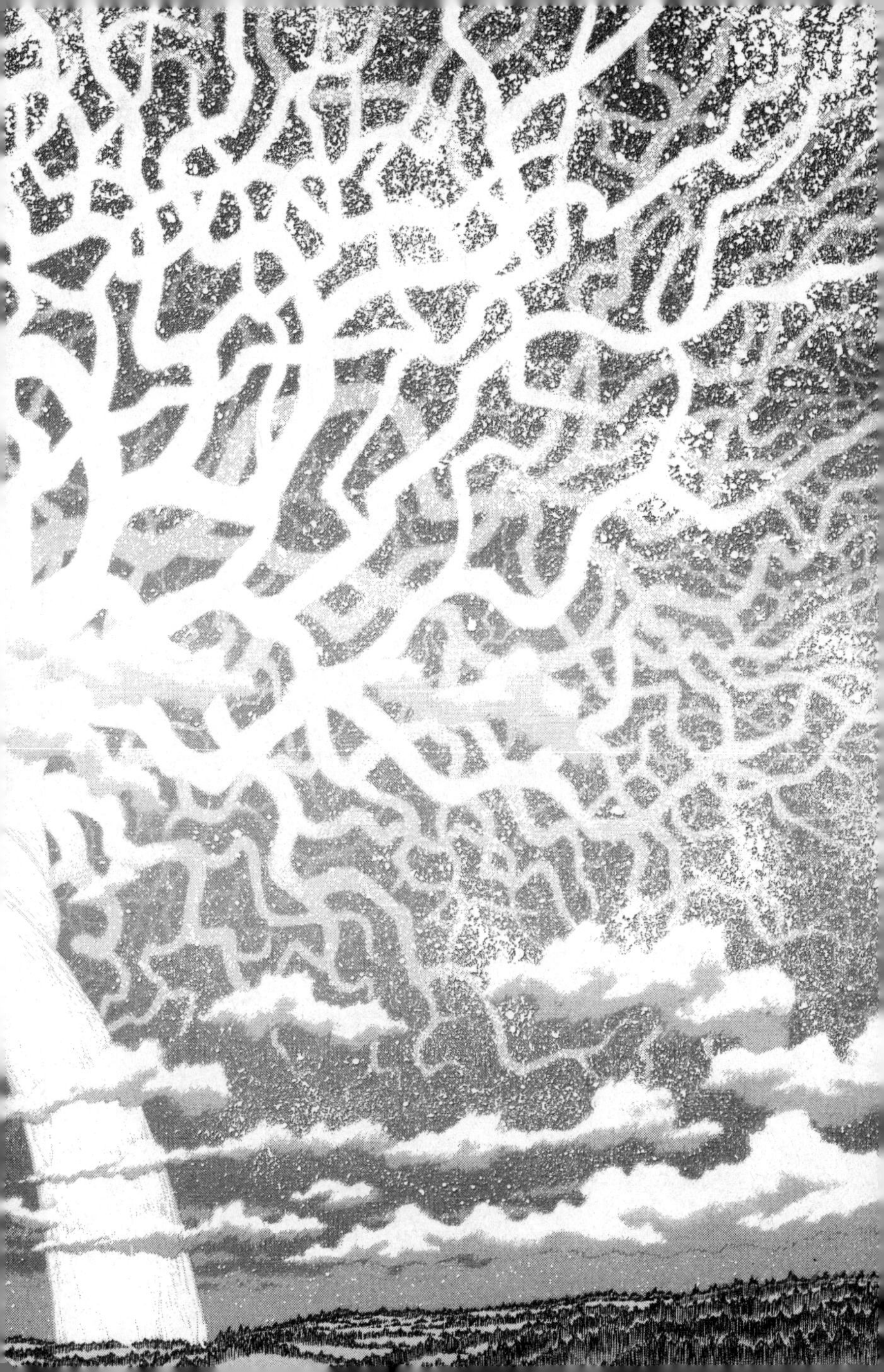

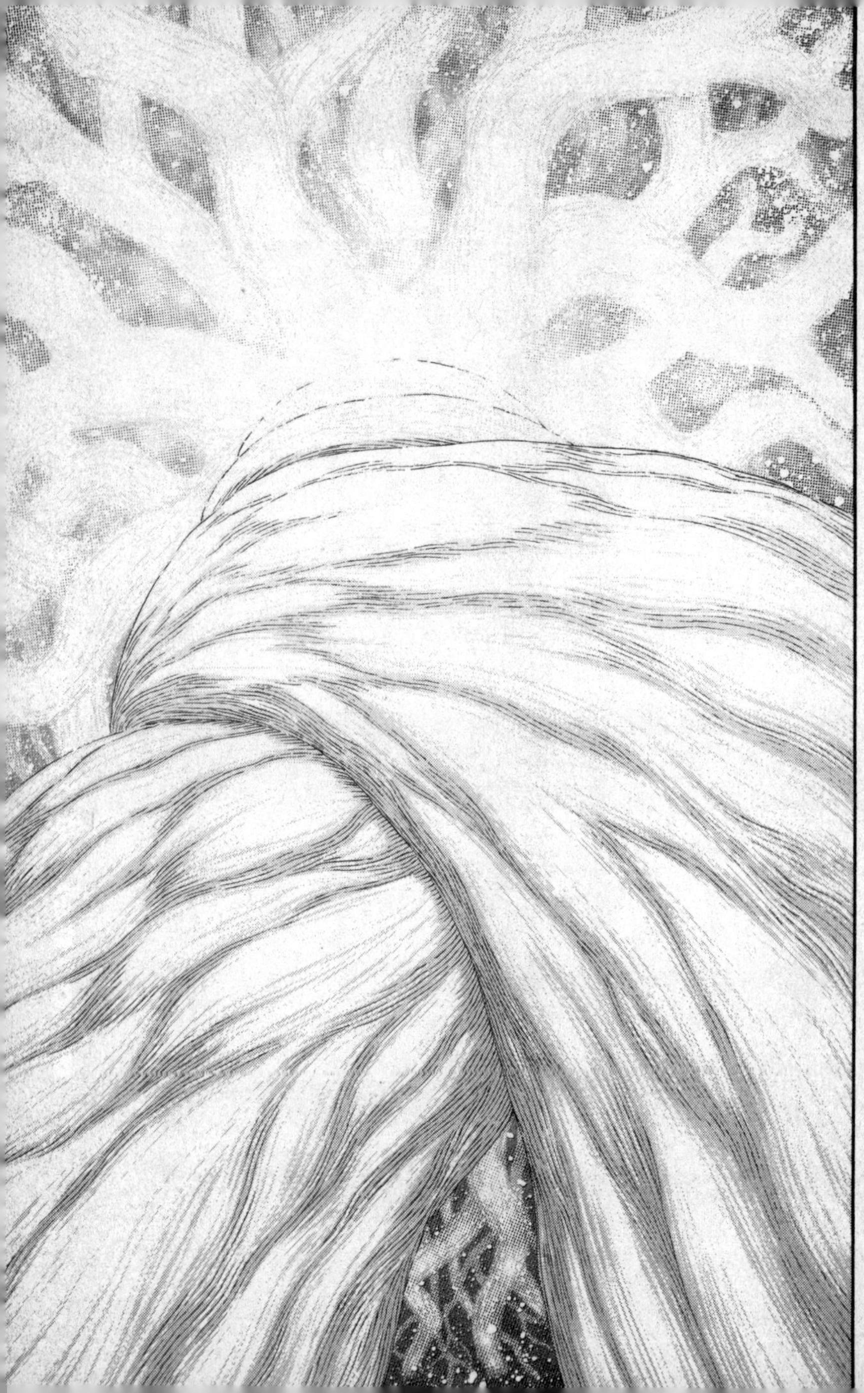

千年帝国の鷹〈ミレニアム・ファルコン〉篇／鷹都〈ファルコニア〉の章

ファルコニア

FALCONIA

ベルセルク 35

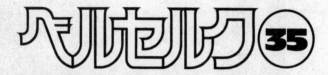

CONTENTS

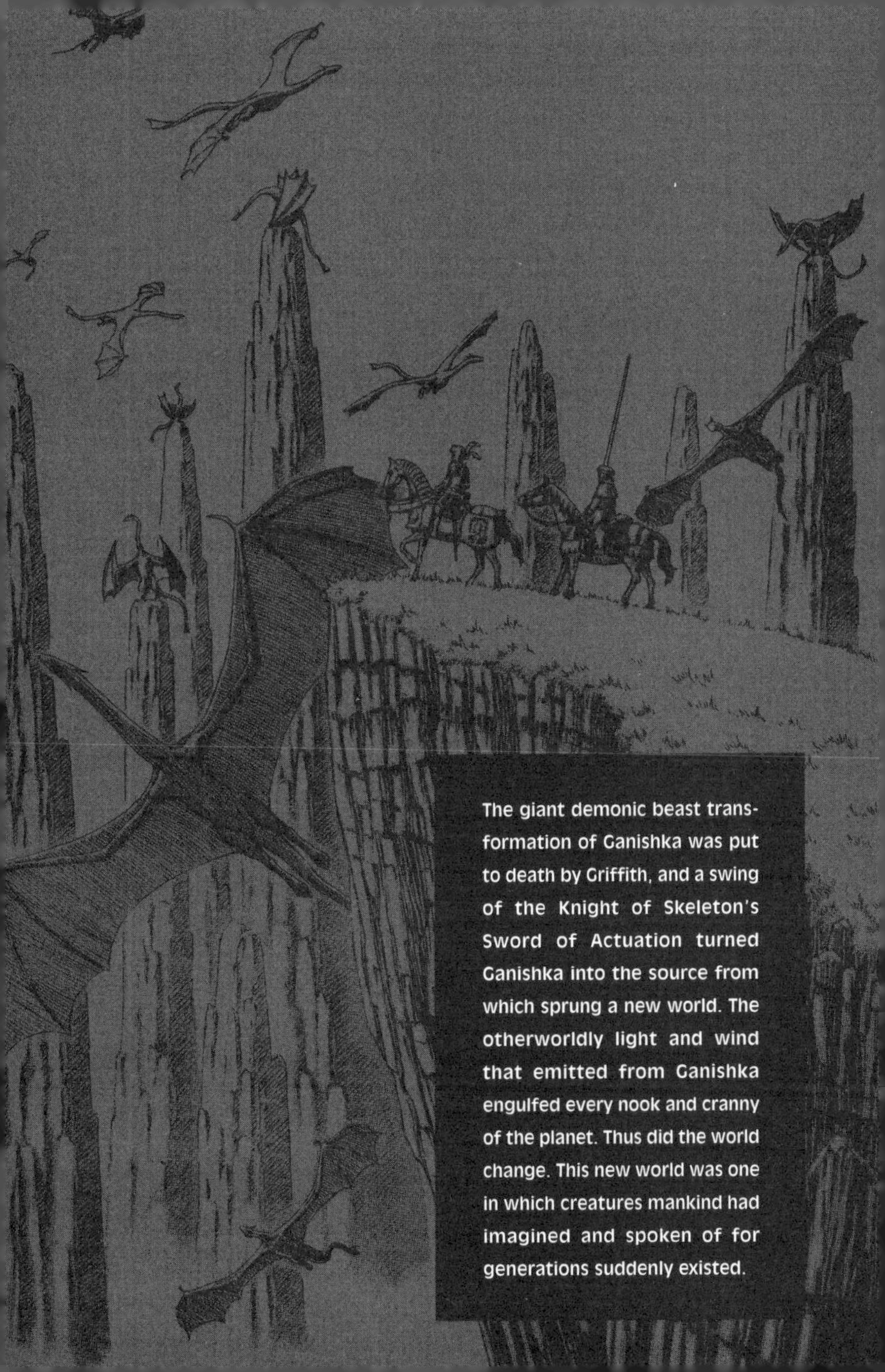

The giant demonic beast transformation of Ganishka was put to death by Griffith, and a swing of the Knight of Skeleton's Sword of Actuation turned Ganishka into the source from which sprung a new world. The otherworldly light and wind that emitted from Ganishka engulfed every nook and cranny of the planet. Thus did the world change. This new world was one in which creatures mankind had imagined and spoken of for generations suddenly existed.

グリフィス *Griffith*

Through the eclipse of the Crimson Behelit, he was reborn as Femto of the Godhand. Later he was incarnated in the imitation eclipse catalyzed by the egg-shaped apostle, thus returning to the physical world, in which he became the "absolute," without equal. He leads the reborn Band of the Hawk.

ファルネーゼ *Farnese*

Former commander of the Holy See's Holy Iron Chain Knights, and daughter of the Vandimion family, one of influential status and wealth in the religious sphere. She seeks to learn from Guts her own means of survival, and about the reality of the world.

セルピコ *Serpico*

Attendant of Farnese, and actually her brother. However, Farnese is not aware of the blood relationship. He is skilled in fighting, and currently clad in a fetish granted the protection of wind elementals.

ロデリック *Roderick*

Captain of the naval vessel *Seahorse* and third in line to the royal throne of lith, a maritime power within the domain of the Holy See. He is a friend of Farnese's brother and has become her fiancé. He is currently taking Guts and the others to Skellig Island, where the Elfhelm is located.

マニフィコ *Magnifico*

Third son of the Vandimion family, and Farnese's legitimate brother. He is also a friend of Roderick's. Though he's an ordinary person, the course of events has led him to accompany Guts' group.

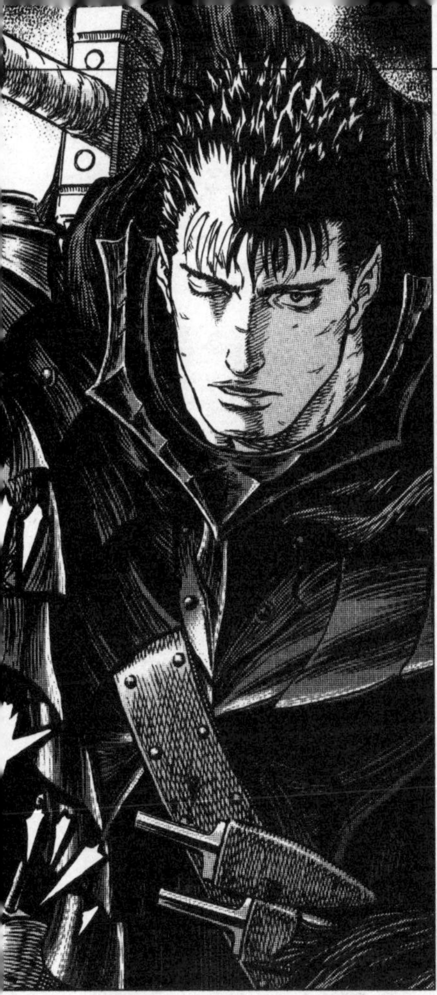

ガッツ *Guts*

The main character of the story, the Black Swordsman. He exists in the interstice, wears the Berserker armor, and his soul is constantly torn between protecting Casca and challenging Griffith. That struggle is nothing short of sublime.

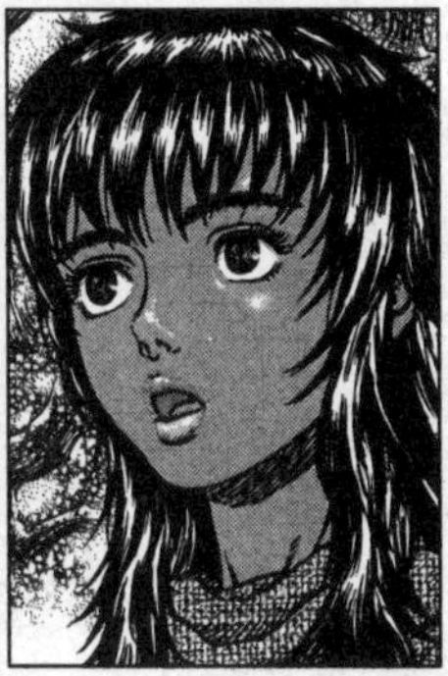

キャスカ *Casca*

Former unit commander of the Band of the Hawk; mentally regressed from her experience in the eclipse. She now neither speaks nor conveys any feelings. Her brand, which reacts to evil, is narrowly shielded by Flora's talisman.

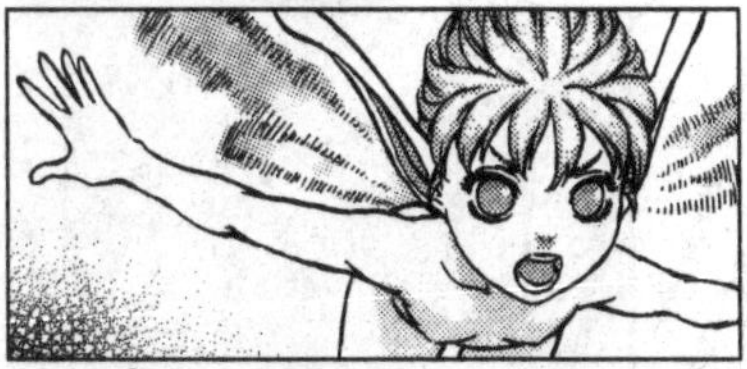

パック *Puck*

An elf who's long been with Guts on his journeys. His dust has the power to heal wounds. He confirmed that he's a wind spirit, and he also changes into Chestnut Puck.

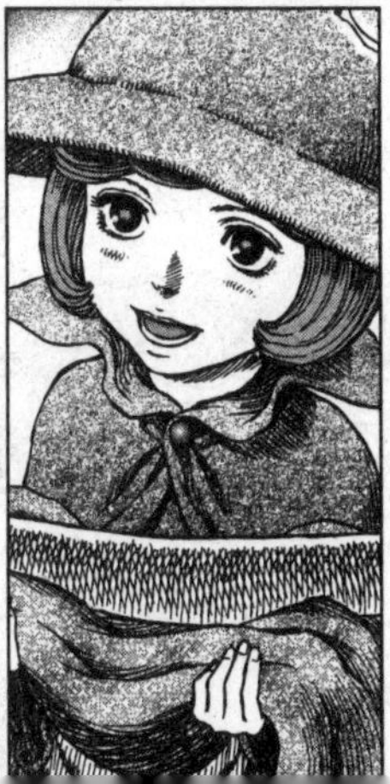

シールケ *Schierke*

Disciple of Flora, witch of the spirit tree mansion. She supports Guts and the others through her use of magic; however, among her spells are some beyond her mastery, which occasionally place her in great peril as she tries to aid her allies. She has a stilted side to her personality.

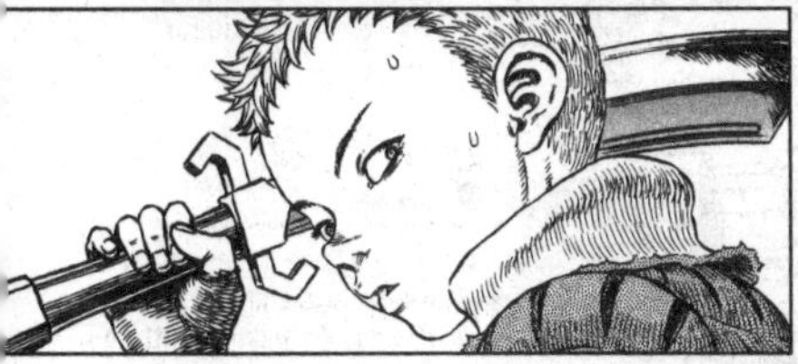

イシドロ *Isidro*

Dreams of being the "ultimate swordsman," but his actual talent, not up to snuff, repeatedly endangers him. Nevertheless, the boy endeavors toward his dream. He is currently equipped with a fetish granted the protection of fire elementals.

BERSERK

ベルセルク 35

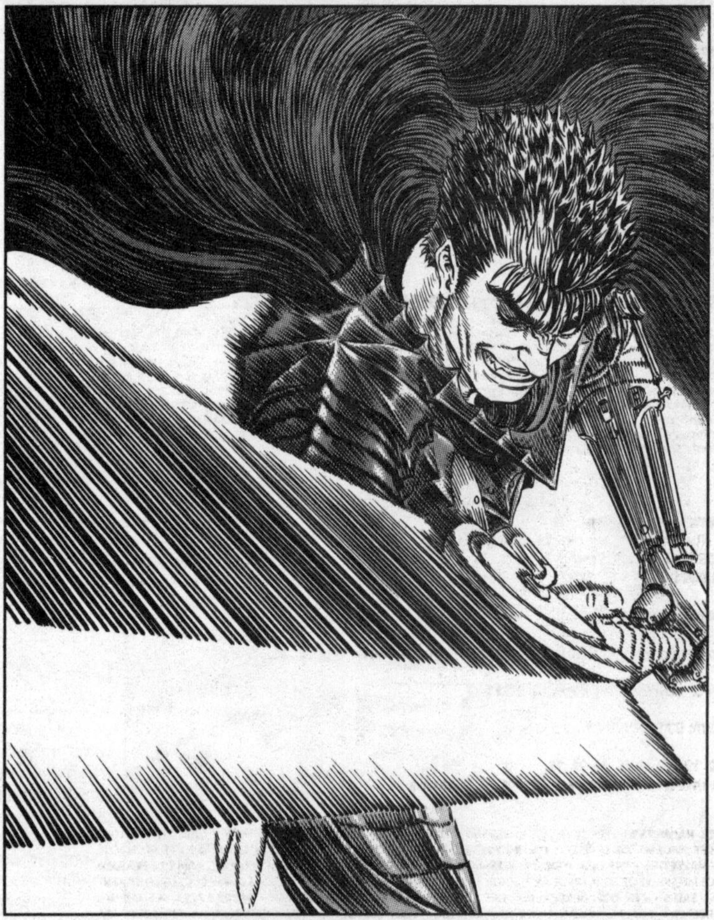

三浦建太郎

PRESIDENT AND PUBLISHER
MIKE RICHARDSON

US EDITORS
CHRIS WARNER
FRED LUI

COLLECTION DESIGNER
DAVID NESTELLE

BERSERK vol. 35 by KENTARO MIURA

Dark Horse Manga
A division of Dark Horse Comics LLC
10956 SE Main Street
Milwaukie OR 97222

DarkHorse.com

To find a comics shop in your area, go to comicshoplocator.com

First edition: September 2011

ISBN 978-1-59582-695-4

20 19 18 17 16 15 14 13
Printed in the United States of America

NEIL HANKERSON EXECUTIVE VICE PRESIDENT • TOM WEDDLE CHIEF FINANCIAL OFFICER • DALE LAFOUNTAIN
CHIEF INFORMATION OFFICER • TIM WIESCH VICE PRESIDENT OF LICENSING • MATT PARKINSON VICE PRESIDENT
OF MARKETING • VANESSA TODD-HOLMES VICE PRESIDENT OF PRODUCTION AND SCHEDULING • MARK BERNARDI
VICE PRESIDENT OF BOOK TRADE AND DIGITAL SALES • RANDY LAHRMAN VICE PRESIDENT OF PRODUCT DEVELOPMENT
AND SALES • KEN LIZZI GENERAL COUNSEL • DAVE MARSHALL EDITOR IN CHIEF • DAVEY ESTRADA EDITORIAL
DIRECTOR • CHRIS WARNER SENIOR BOOKS EDITOR • CARY GRAZZINI DIRECTOR OF SPECIALTY PROJECTS • LIA
RIBACCHI ART DIRECTOR • MATT DRYER DIRECTOR OF DIGITAL ART AND PREPRESS • MICHAEL GOMBOS SENIOR
DIRECTOR OF LICENSED PUBLICATIONS • KARI YADRO DIRECTOR OF CUSTOM PROGRAMS • KARI TORSON DIRECTOR
OF INTERNATIONAL LICENSING

ベルセルク

BERSERK ㉟

BY
KENTARO
MIURA
三浦建太郎

TRANSLATION
DUANE JOHNSON
LETTERING AND RETOUCH
REPLIBOOKS

DARK
HORSE
MANGA